HARDEN'S

London
Restaurants
2002

© Harden's Limited 2001

ISBN 1-873721-42-0 (paperback)
ISBN 1-873721-43-9 (bonded leather)

British Library Cataloguing-in-Publication data:
a catalogue record for this book is available from the British Library.

Printed and bound in Finland by
WS Bookwell Ltd

Research Manager: Antonia Russell
Production Manager: Elizabeth Warman

Harden's Limited
14 Buckingham Street
London WC2N 6DF

CONTENTS

Ratings & prices

RATINGS & PRICES

Ratings

How ratings are calculated – see 'Whose views?' on page 19.

Our rating system is unlike those found in other guides (most of which tell you nothing more helpful than that expensive restaurants are, as a general rule, better than cheap ones).

What we do is to compare each restaurant's performance – as judged by the average of the grades awarded by reporters in the survey – with other restaurants in the same price-bracket.

This approach has the advantage that it helps you find – whatever your budget for any particular meal – where you will get the best "bang for your buck".

The following qualities are assessed:

> **F** — Food
> **S** — Service
> **A** — Ambience

The rating indicates that, **in comparison with other restaurants in the same price-bracket**, performance is …

> **❶** — Exceptional
> **❷** — Very good
> **❸** — Good
> ④ — Mediocre
> ⑤ — Disappointing

Prices

The price shown for each restaurant is the cost for one (1) person of an average three-course *dinner* with half a bottle of house wine and coffee, any cover charge, service and VAT. Lunch is often cheaper. With BYO restaurants, we have assumed that two people share a £5 bottle of off-licence wine.

Telephone number – all numbers should be prefixed with '020' if dialling from outside the London area.

Map reference – shown immediately after the telephone number. (Major coffee shop chains are not shown on the maps.)

Rated on Editors' assessment – entries including this text have been rated by the editors, rather than being statistically derived from the survey.

Website – the first entry in the small print after any note re: Editors' assessment.

Last orders time – the first entry in the small print, after the website (if applicable); Sunday may be up to 90 minutes earlier.

Opening hours – unless otherwise stated, restaurants are open for lunch and dinner seven days a week.

Credit and debit cards – unless otherwise stated, Mastercard, Visa, Amex and Switch are accepted.

Dress – where appropriate, the management's preferences concerning patrons' dress are given.

Smoking – cigarette smoking restrictions are noted. Pipe or cigar smokers should always check ahead.

Special menus – if we know of a particularly good value set menu we note this (eg "set weekday L"), together with its formula price (FP) calculated exactly as in 'Prices' above. Details change, so always check ahead.

SURVEY – MOST MENTIONED

These are the restaurants which were most frequently mentioned by reporters. (Last year's position is given in brackets.) An asterisk* indicates the first appearance in the list of a recently-opened restaurant.

1	The Ivy (1)
2	Oxo Tower (2)
3	Mirabelle (3)
4	Nobu (4)
5	Le Caprice (6)
6	J Sheekey (16)
7	Chez Bruce (13)
8	Gordon Ramsay (11)
9	Blue Elephant (7)
10	Pétrus (23)
11	Bank (12)
12	Zafferano (14)
13	Zaika (31)
14	The Square (9)
15	Club Gascon (21)
16	La Poule au Pot (17=)
17=	The River Café (10)
17=	Andrew Edmunds (27)
19	The Sugar Club (24)
20	Le Gavroche (19)
21=	Bluebird (5)
21=	The Criterion (17=)
23=	Moro (38)
23=	Coq d'Argent (25)
25	City Rhodes (22)
26	Smiths of Smithfield*
27	Bleeding Heart (-)
28	Bibendum (20)
29	Quaglino's (16)
30	Chutney Mary (29)
31	Mezzo (28)
32=	Le Palais du Jardin (30)
32=	Incognico (-)
34	Rules (39)
35	Joe Allen (40)
36	Tas*
37=	Vong (26)
37=	Asia de Cuba (-)
39=	1 Lombard Street (33)
39=	The Eagle (32)

SURVEY – NOMINATIONS

Ranked by the number of reporters' votes for:

Top gastronomic experience

1 Gordon Ramsay (1)
2 The Ivy (2)
3 Nobu (4)
4 Chez Bruce (5)
5 Pétrus (8)
6 Mirabelle (3)
7 Club Gascon (9)
8 The Square (6)
9 Le Gavroche (7)
10 Zafferano (-)

Favourite

1 The Ivy (1)
2 Le Caprice (3)
3 Chez Bruce (2)
4 Nobu (5)
5 Mirabelle (4)
6 Gordon Ramsay (6)
7 Moro (-)
8 Zafferano (8)
9 Andrew Edmunds (-)
10 Oxo Tower (9)

Best for business

1 City Rhodes (1)
2 Bank (4)
3 1 Lombard Street (2)
4 Coq d'Argent (7)
5 Oxo Tower (9)
6 The Square (3)
7 Savoy Grill (8)
8 The Ivy (5)
9 Prism (10)
10 Bleeding Heart (-)

Best for romance

1 La Poule au Pot (1)
2 Andrew Edmunds (2)
3 The Ivy (3)
4 Julie's (6)
5 Oxo Tower (4)
6 Odette's (5)
7 Le Caprice (8)
8 Blue Elephant (7)
9 Bleeding Heart (-)
10 Launceston Place (9)

regular updates at www.hardens.com

Best breakfast/brunch

1 Bank (1)
2 Pâtisserie Valerie (-)
3 Simpsons-in-the-Strand (3)
4 Giraffe (-)
5 Smiths of Smithfield (-)
6 Balans (-)
7 Boiled Egg & Soldiers (9)
8 Dakota (-)
9 Fox & Anchor (4)
10 Tootsies (-)

Best bar/pub food

1 The Eagle (1)
2 The Engineer (3)
3 Churchill Arms (2)
4 Admiral Codrington (6)
5 The Anglesea Arms (4)
6 The Havelock Tavern (5)
7 The Cow (8)
8 The Duke of Cambridge N1 (-)
9 The Ladbroke Arms (9)
10 The Builder's Arms (-)

Most disappointing cooking

1 Oxo Tower (2)
2 Bluebird (1)
3 Mezzo (3)
4 Quaglino's (4)
5 Titanic (5)
6 The Ivy (9)
7 Mirabelle (7)
8 The Criterion (8)
9 The River Café (6)
10 Coq d'Argent (10)

Most overpriced restaurant

1 Oxo Tower (1)
2 Nobu (6)
3 The River Café (5)
4 Mezzo (7)
5 Bluebird (2)
6 Quaglino's (10)
7 Mirabelle (9)
8 Spoon + (-)
9 The Ivy (-)
10 Coq d'Argent (-)

SURVEY – HIGHEST RATINGS

FOOD	SERVICE

£60+

FOOD	SERVICE
1 Gordon Ramsay	1 Gordon Ramsay
2 Tatsuso	2 Le Gavroche
3 Pétrus	3 Le Soufflé
4 Le Gavroche	4 Connaught
5 Capital Hotel	5 Dorchester Grill

£50-£59

FOOD	SERVICE
1 Nobu	1 Clarke's
2 Monsieur Max	2 Restaurant One-O-One
3 Restaurant One-O-One	3 Goring Hotel
4 Clarke's	4 Monsieur Max
5 Shogun	5 Indigo

£35-£49

FOOD	SERVICE
1 Chez Bruce	1 Oslo Court
2 Chinon	2 Le Caprice
3 Assaggi	3 Chez Bruce
4 Zafferano	4 The Ivy
5 Club Gascon	5 Zafferano

£25-£34

FOOD	SERVICE
1 Pizza Metro	1 Abeno
2 Rasa W1, N16	2 Potemkin
3 The Gate W6, NW3	3 Hunan
4 Basilico	4 The Parsee
5 Thailand	5 Soulard

£24 or less

FOOD	SERVICE
1 Kastoori	1 Patio
2 K10	2 Kastoori
3 Lahore Kebab House	3 Paul
4 Talad Thai	4 Pizzeria Castello
5 Ranoush	5 Lomo

AMBIENCE

1	Blakes Hotel
2	The Ritz
3	Windows on the World
4	Dorchester Grill
5	Gordon Ramsay

1	Lanesborough
2	Belvedere
3	The Criterion
4	Twentyfour
5	Goring Hotel

1	Les Trois Garçons
2	Pasha
3	Momo
4	Blue Elephant
5	La Poule au Pot

1	Sarastro
2	Souk
3	Andrew Edmunds
4	Windsor Castle
5	Café Bagatelle

1	Gordon's Wine Bar
2	Iznik
3	Il Pagliaccio
4	The Wine Library
5	Bar Italia

OVERALL

1	Gordon Ramsay
2	Le Gavroche
3	Blakes Hotel
4	The Ritz
5	Capital Hotel

1	Monsieur Max
2	Restaurant One-O-One
3	Clarke's
4	L'Oranger
5	Nobu

1	Chez Bruce
2	The Ivy
3	Assaggi
4	La Trompette
5	L'Aventure

1	Pizza Metro
2	Soulard
3	Rasa W1, N16
4	Andrew Edmunds
5	Mesclun

1	Paul
2	K10
3	Kastoori
4	Iznik
5	Patio

SURVEY – BEST BY CUISINE

These are the restaurants which received the best average food ratings.

Where the most common types of cuisine are concerned, we present the results in two price-brackets. For less common cuisines, we list the top three, regardless of price.

For further information about restaurants which are particularly notable for their food, see the lists starting on page 214. These indicate, using an asterisk (*), restaurants which offer exceptional or very good food.

Modern British

£40 and over
1 Chez Bruce
2 Clarke's
3 City Rhodes
4 Lindsay House
5 The Ivy

Under £40
1 The Glasshouse
2 Mesclun
3 The Stepping Stone
4 Parade
5 The Havelock Tavern

French

£40 and over
1 Gordon Ramsay
2 Pétrus
3 Le Gavroche
4 Monsieur Max
5 Capital Hotel

Under £40
1 Chinon
2 Les Associés
3 La Trompette
4 Soulard
5 Café du Marché

Italian/Mediterranean

£40 and over
1 Assaggi
2 Zafferano
3 Toto's
4 Passione
5 Teca

Under £40
1 Riva
2 Enoteca Turi
3 Alba
4 Il Bordello
5 Il Convivio

Indian

£40 and over
1 Zaika
2 Salloos
3 The Cinnamon Club
4 Tamarind
5 La Porte des Indes

Under £40
1 Kastoori
2 Rasa
3 Lahore Kebab House
4 Sarkhel's
5 Vama

Chinese

£40 and over
1 Kai
2 Ken Lo's Memories
3 Dorchester, Oriental
4 Mr Wing
5 Mr Chow

Under £40
1 Royal China
2 Hunan
3 Mandarin Kitchen
4 Mr Kong
5 Fung Shing

Japanese

£40 and over
1 Tatsuso
2 City Miyama
3 Shogun
4 Matsuri
5 Suntory

Under £40
1 K10
2 Café Japan
3 Sushi Say
4 Inaho
5 Abeno

British, Traditional
1 Connaught
2 Dorchester Grill
3 Odin's

Vegetarian
1 The Gate W6, NW3
2 Blah! Blah! Blah!
3 Food for Thought

Burgers, etc
1 Gourmet Burger K'n
2 Hard Rock Café
3 Sticky Fingers

Pizza
1 Pizza Metro
2 Basilico
3 Pizzeria Castello

East/West
1 Nobu
2 Ubon
3 The Sugar Club

Thai
1 Thailand
2 Talad Thai
3 Chiang Mai

Fish & Chips
1 Faulkner's
2 Nautilus
3 Seashell

Fish & Seafood
1 Chez Liline
2 J Sheekey
3 Poissonnerie de l'Ave

Greek
1 The Real Greek
2 Vrisaki
3 Daphne

Spanish
1 Cambio de Tercio
2 Lomo
3 Gaudi

Turkish
1 Pasha
2 Ozer
3 Iznik

Lebanese
1 Ranoush
2 Phoenicia
3 Fairuz

TOP SPECIAL DEALS

The following menus allow you to eat in the restaurants concerned at a significant discount when compared to their evening à la carte prices.

The prices used are calculated in accordance with our usual formula (ie three courses with house wine, coffee and tip).

Special menus are by their nature susceptible to change – please check that they are still available.

Weekday lunch

£50+ Gordon Ramsay

£45+ Connaught
John Burton-Race

£40+ Aubergine
Capital Hotel
Conrad Gallagher
Le Gavroche
Lindsay House
Pied à Terre
Le Pont de la Tour
Savoy River Restaurant
Le Soufflé
The Square

£35+ Dorchester, Oriental
Floriana
Foliage
The Guinea
Ikeda
Rhodes in the Square
Suntory

£30+ Belvedere
Bice
Che
The Criterion
Defune
Drones
The Fifth Floor
L'Incontro
Mju
Putney Bridge
Restaurant One-O-One
Santini
Simpsons-in-the-Strand
Six-13
Smiths of Smithfield
The Tenth

£25+ Artigiano
L'Aventure
Bank
Boisdale
Circus
Dover Street
Incognico
Kaya Korean
The Lanesborough
Maison Novelli
Manzi's
Mezzo
Mon Plaisir

Montpeliano
Noura
Orsino
Orso
La Poule au Pot
Quaglino's
Roussillon
Salloos
Le Suquet
Tamarind
Teatro
Turner's
Villa Bianca
Zaika

£20+ Ayoush
Big Easy
Blue Elephant
Bradley's
La Brasserie Townhouse
Buchan's
Butlers Wharf
Chop-house
Café des Amis du Vin
Café du Jardin
Café Lazeez
Café Med
Cantina del Ponte
Chez Moi
Cucina
Da Mario
Del Buongustaio
Frederick's
Frocks
Getti
Italian Kitchen
La Mancha
Mediterraneo
Mitsukoshi
Odette's
Organic Café
Ost. Antica Bologna
Ozer
Parisienne Chophouse
Pellicano
Rain
Royal Opera House Café
S&P
The Salisbury Tavern
San Frediano
Sri Siam City
Stratford's

Stream
Tandoori of Chelsea
Thai on the River
Vama
Wódka

£15+ Bangkok Brasserie
Bengal Clipper
Blakes
Boudin Blanc
Busabong Too
Cantinetta Venegazzú
Cuba Libre
Ditto
Exhibition
Il Falconiere
Garbo's
Goya
Inaho
Khan's of Kensington
Lemonia
Lou Pescadou
Mandarin Kitchen
Newton's
Noto
The Papaya Tree
The Polish Club
Sabai Sabai
Le Shop
Singapore Garden
Sofra
Tartuf
Thailand
Toff's
Vegia Zena
Yoshino

£10+ Anglo Asian Tandoori
Café Japan
Daquise
Fish in a Tie
Galicia
Mandalay
Le Mercury
Ragam
Le Sacré-Coeur
Troika
Yum Yum

Pre/post theatre
(and early evening)

£45+ Savoy Grill

£40+ Conrad Gallagher
Savoy River Restaurant

£35+ Connaught

£30+ Belvedere
Christopher's
The Criterion
Le Pont de la Tour
Six-13

£25+ Bank
Bank Westminster

Chutney Mary
Circus
Incognico
Luigi's
Maison Novelli
Mezzo
Orsino
Orso
Quaglino's
Teatro

£20+ Ayoush
Butlers Wharf
   Chop-house
Café des Amis du Vin
Café du Jardin
L'Estaminet
Frederick's
Manzi's
Mitsukoshi
Ozer
Parisienne Chophouse
Stratford's
Toast

£15+ Bengal Clipper
Blues
Boudin Blanc
Goya
Hujo's
Mon Plaisir

£10+ The Little Bay

Sunday lunch

£40+ Putney Bridge
Savoy River Restaurant

£35+ Belvedere
Wiltons

£30+ Drones

£25+ The Ivy
Lou Pescadou
Mezzo
Orsino
Quaglino's
Rowley's
J Sheekey
Tamarind
Vama

£20+ Ayoush
Goolies
Ozer
Pellicano
Thai on the River

£15+ Battersea Rickshaw
Bengal Clipper
Café Spice Namaste
Mims
prospectGrill
Tartuf

END OF THE CHAIN GANG?

It is a fact universally acknowledged that in the late-1990s commercial restaurant groups suddenly came to dominate the top end of the London restaurant scene (which had traditionally been regarded as largely the preserve of the independent operator).

How could one measure this objectively? What is a top-end place? A good yardstick is to see which are the restaurants which are generating the greatest number of reports (good or bad) in our annual survey – these are the restaurants people are most interested in, and each year we publish a 'league table' on this basis (see page 9).

The following table shows the number of independently run restaurants among the Top 20 in that league table each year since 1995:

Edition	'95	'96	'97	'98	'99	'00	'01	'02
'Indies'	13	13	11	8	6	3	6	11

As you can see, by 2000, only three indies were left. Remarkably, though, in the two short years since, the indies have fought right back to their 1997 level!

Conran Restaurants, London's biggest 'quality' operator, accounts for much of this sea change. Since 1994, there has always been a Conran restaurant in the Top 20, and by 2000 the group occupied five Top 20 slots. And this year... none! As much as any shift in restaurant fashion can deserve the term 'seismic', this is it. For years, reporters have been telling us – loudly – of the disappointments of dining chez Conran. This year's they have voted even more eloquently – with their feet.

Two years ago, there were four other major groups with a presence in the Top 20 – Belgo (three restaurants), Marco Pierre White (two), Harvey Nichols (one) and Groupe Chez Gérard (one). MPW and GCG have each lost a representative. Harvey Nics hangs on to its Top 20 position thanks only to the Oxo Tower restaurant, with its unbeatable 'location, location and location'.

The surprise is Belgo. It still has three representatives – the eponymous moules halls having been replaced by J Sheekey, which has stormed into the Top 20 at no 6, to join the Ivy (1) and Le Caprice (5). We understand that the three restaurants are run as a sub-group within Belgo. This is a scale of operations broadly similar to London's leading independent restaurateur – Nigel Platts-Martin, who has four establishments (including nos 7 and 14 in the Top 20) – and not much greater than that of leading chef, Gordon Ramsay, whose three establishments (one of them in Glasgow) include numbers 8 and 10 in the Top 20.

So it seems there's nothing *inherently* impossible about groups maintaining (or even building) a top-end presence. But it does seem that quality restaurants will only prosper if their management can bring themselves to 'think small'.

FROM THE EDITORS

This annual guide is designed to help you find the right London restaurant for any particular occasion and then, as briefly as possible, to tell you everything you need to know about it.

The Survey

Once again, the guide has been compiled with the benefit of survey contributions from an expanded consumer base. This year over 5,300 people sent us their views. We are very grateful to everyone who took part, and also to those who have helped expand the range of the survey by introducing friends and colleagues.

Reporters eat out, on average, 3.2 times a week. Thus the survey reflects the experiences of over 900,000 meals eaten in the preceding 12 months.

Whose views?

We have ourselves visited every restaurant or chain listed in this book – always anonymously and at our own expense. But we do not seek to impose our personal views. Rather, we seek – from our informed starting-point – to analyse the comments and ratings from our 'reporters'. In the rare cases where we feel that we can add something by noting our dissent from the general view, we do so in the text. The numerical ratings reflect the survey results.

We believe that this pragmatic combination of the views of thousands of people with our own impressions enables the production of an up-to-date guide of unequalled reliability.

The survey, which closed in June 2001, could not provide useful information on the new summer openings. In these cases, the review and the numerical ratings reflect our personal assessment. To emphasise the more limited basis of the review, we have this year included a note in the small print – "Rated on Editors' assessment".

Please help us to make the next edition even more accurate. If you register for free updates, you will be invited, in the spring of 2002, to take part in our next survey. **If you take part in the survey, you will, on publication, receive a complimentary copy of *Harden's London Restaurants 2003*.**

Richard Harden   **Peter Harden**

THE RESTAURANT SCENE

Record activity continues
This year we record 131 newcomers (listed opposite), exceeding last year's former high watermark figure of 120. There were 65 closings (listed on page 22) – slightly up on last year's former record figure of 59.

The year started slowly, but in more recent months there has been a spate of interesting openings. In contrast to recent years, when much of the activity was in the middle price brackets, this year saw an unusually high number of pricier openings, usually with culinary ambitions to match.

Each year, we select what we see as the ten most *notable* openings of the past 12 months, and they are as follows:

Babylon	Mju
Champor-Champor	Nahm
The Cinnamon Club	Les Trois Garçons
Conrad Gallagher	La Trompette
Hakkasan	Wapping Food

Prices rises still beating inflation
Prices have on average risen by slightly over 3 per cent this year, fractionally ahead of inflation. In the £40+ bracket, prices are some 5 per cent higher.

Trends
As we noted last year, in the more mature post-millennial restaurant scene, trends are more diffuse than was the case in the '90s (and often a reaction against the trends which became apparent in the latter half of the decade).

Among the themes discernible in new openings this year are the following:

• in European restaurants, a preference for a clear Italian or French style over British ('modern' or otherwise)

• the acceptance of Indian as a 'natural' cuisine for fashionable restaurants

• continuing interesting developments in the 'fusion' of European and Eastern styles

• a greater willingness in the higher price brackets to try innovative concepts, rather than to accept 'haute cuisine' as the obvious choice

• comfort, and a 'human' scale of operations.

• good 'gastropubs' are now so common they seem almost ten-a-penny.

Geographically, some traditionally unfashionable areas are doing well, with notable levels of activity to the north, south and east of the City. At last, there is a range of places in Canary Wharf (if not many of great originality). Covent Garden – once home to some notable restaurants, but in recent years regarded mainly as a tourist playground – is enjoying a modest renaissance.

OPENINGS AND CLOSINGS

OPENINGS

Aix
Aperitivo
Archipelago
Attica
Auberge
Babylon
Baltic
Banana Leaf Canteen
Bankside
Baraonda
Bellamys
Bibo Cibo
Bistro I WC2
Blandford Street
Bonds
Café Nikolaj
I Cardi
Cecconi's
Chada W1
Chamberlain's
Champor-Champor
Chula
Cigala
The Cinnamon Club
Conrad Gallagher
Coromandel
Cottons
The Court Restaurant
La Deuxième
DK's
The Don
Drones
Elephant Royale
Exhibit
Eyre Brothers
Fat Boy's TW1
The Fire Stables
Flâneur
The Fox
Fuego EC2
Furnace
Fusion
George II
Ginger
Goose
Gordon Ramsay at
    Claridges
Gourmet Burger Kitchen
Grand Central
Gravy
Haandi

Hakkasan
Heartstone
Ichizen Noodle Bar
Itsu W1
Jago
Just Oriental
Kandoo
LMNT
Loch Fyne SW6, N8
Lots Road
Maggiore's
Manor
Mao Tai SW3
Maquis
Masala Zone
Mash Mayfair
Mju
The Montrose
Mosaica
Nahm
Neat
Niksons
No 6
Noodle Noodle
Opium
Organic Café SW7
Otto
Pan-Asian Canteen
Parisienne Chophouse
The Parsee
Passion
Paul
Pellicano
Perc%nto
The Perseverance
Phoenix Palace
Le Potiron Sauvage
The Providores
Quod
Raccolto
Randall & Aubin SW10
Rasa Travancore
Red Cube
RIBA Cafe
Saints
Sakoni's SW17
Salon
San Frediano (again)
Scuzi E14
Serafino
Shish

OPENINGS (cont'd)

Six-13
Soshomatch
La Spiga SW3
Sway
Tabla
Tas (Borough High St)
Tasca E14
The Thai
Touzai
Les Trois Garçons
La Trompette
La Trouvaille
Truc Vert
Tuscan Steak
Twelfth House

Ubon
Vertigo
The Vestry
Viet-Anh
Wapping Food
The Wardroom
The Well
West Street Restaurant
The White House
Yas on the Park
Yelo
Zaika Bazaar
Zilli Fish Too
Zuccato EC4
Zucchina

CLOSINGS

Al Bustan
L' Anis*
Anna's Place
The Apprentice
Babe Ruth's NW3
Barra
The Birdcage
Brompton Bay
Busabong Tree
Caviar House
Cheng Du
City Brasserie
Claridges
Coast
Duemila
Emile's SW6
Euphorium
French House
Grano
Gresslin's
Halcyon Hotel
Halkin
Heather's
High Holborn*
The Honest Goose*
Justin de Blank*
Kavanagh's
Lawn
Little Havana
Luigi Malones
Lunch
Magno's Brasserie
Mandeer

The Mission
Moxon's
The New End*
Nine Golden Square
19:20 (now a bar)*
Nosh Brothers
Offshore
Olio & Farina
Osteria d'Isola*
Palais du Jardin Chelsea*
The Park
Pimlico Tandoori
Red River*
El Rincón*
Saigon Times
SaintM*
San Martino
Schnecke* N1, W1
Seven*
Shiraz*
6 Clarendon Road
Sixty Two
Soho Soho
Stephen Bull
Time
Tuba
Upper Street Fish Shop
Viceroy
Whittington's
Wilson's
Woody's (now a bar)*
Zen Garden

* was a newcomer last year

DIRECTORY

Comments in "double quotation-marks" were made by reporters.

Establishments which we judge to be particularly notable have their NAME IN CAPITALS.

a.k.a. WCl £ 36 ④④❸
18 West Central St   7836 0110   4–1C
"Go for the music or a party" – this north Covent Garden
nightclub seems to have abandoned its earlier aspirations to
offer quality dining, though the "decent bar snacks" still win
praise. / www.akalondon.com; 11 pm; closed Mon, Sat L & Sun L.

Abbaye £ 30 ④⑤④
102 Old Brompton Rd, SW7   7373 2403   5–2B
55 Charterhouse St, EC1   7253 1612   9–2A
Sometimes "terrible" service is a bugbear at these Smithfield
and South Kensington mussel parlours, which are otherwise
"OK for what they are". / EC1 10.30 pm – SW7 10.45 pm; EC1 closed
Sun; no smoking areas.

Abeno WCl £ 28 ❷❶❸
47 Museum St   7405 3211   2–1C
For "a different experience" and one that's "fun" and "very
reasonably priced", try the okonomi-yaki – a "delicious and
filling novelty", akin to an exotic omelette – served by notably
"friendly" and "attentive" staff at this simple Japanese café,
near the British Museum. / 10 pm; no smoking area.

The Abingdon W8 £ 35 ❸❸❸
54 Abingdon Rd   7937 3339   5–2A
"Atmospheric" booths are a top feature at this "amiable"
former Kensington boozer – now an "excellent bar/diner
combo", where the food delivers "no surprises", but "no shocks"
either. / www.nip.to\theabingdon.com; 11 pm.

L'Accento Italiano W2 £ 32 ❸④④
16 Garway Rd   7243 2201   6–1B
"Hearty", "vaguely Sicilian" cooking (with "good-value" set
menus) ensures this "local Italian" (just off Westbourne Park
Road) stays "buzzing"; the "harsh" setting is often "crowded".
/ 11.30 pm.

Adams Café W12 £ 24 ❸❷❸
77 Askew Rd   8743 0572   7–1B
This characterful Shepherd's Bush café has a split personality –
"daytime greasy spoon, night-time Tunisian couscous house";
fortunately, both Dr Jekyll and Mr Hyde deliver dishes that are
"great for what they are", and you can BYO. / 11 pm; D only, closed
Sun.

Admiral Codrington SW3 £ 37 ❸❸❸
17 Mossop St   7581 0005   5–2C
"Improved loads", since its days as Sloane Central, this elegantly
revamped boozer serves "surprisingly good" food at prices that
are "reasonable" for Brompton Cross; outside tables and
a retractable roof add to its appeal. / 11 pm.

The Admiralty
Somerset House WC2   £ 50   ④④④

Strand   7845 4646   2–2D

Even by Oliver Peyton's standards, this year-old Somerset House venture has "gone down the pan" remarkably quickly – its Gallic cooking is "nothing special", but "very expensive", and service can be "the worst"; perhaps new chef Morgan Meunier will improve things. / 10.45 pm; closed Sun D; no smoking area.

Afghan Kitchen N1   £ 16   ❷④④

35 Islington Grn   7359 8019   8–3D

For "interesting", "homely" food at "decent" prices, it's hard to beat this "tiny" Islington café, but it's "cramped" and "not a place to linger". / 11 pm; closed Mon & Sun; no credit cards.

Aglio e Olio SW10   £ 27   ❷❸❸

194 Fulham Rd   7351 0070   5–3B

"Shame it's cramped, as the pasta is superb" – and the other cooking "very fresh and flavourful" – at this "noisy" Chelsea "canteen". / 11.30 pm.

Aix
Halcyon Hotel W11   £ 45   ❸❷❸

81 Holland Park Ave   7727 5411   6–2B

It's had a "nice makeover", but it's hard to disagree with those who say the dining room of this Holland Park villa-hotel is "pleasant but dullish" – the Provençale cooking is similarly good but difficult to get too excited about. / www.thehalcyon.com; 10.15 pm; closed Sat L & Sun.

Al Duca SW1   £ 34   ❷❷❸

4-5 Duke Of York St   7839 3090   3–3D

It's no wonder that Claudio Pulze's "stylish" (if slightly "cold") St James's restaurant gets "overcrowded" – the "well presented and executed" Italian cooking is "always reliable", and "good value" too. / www.alduca-restaurant.co.uk; 10.15 pm, Fri & Sat 10.45 pm; closed Sun L.

Al Hamra W1   £ 39   ❸④④

31-33 Shepherd Mkt   7493 1954   3–4B

One of the best Lebaneses in town, this "spacious" Shepherd Market fixture provides quality cooking and splendid outside tables in summer; complaints about the (legendarily disagreeable) service were this year notable by their absence. / 11.30 pm.

Al San Vincenzo W2   £ 45   ❷❷❸

30 Connaught St   7262 9623   6–1D

"Real, seasonal Italian cooking" and "a genuine welcome" made something of a comeback this year for the Borgonzolo family's tiny, quirky Bayswater fixture; there were still one or two reports, however, of "variable" food and "erratic" service. / 9.30 pm; closed Sat L & Sun; no Amex or Switch.

Al Sultan W1　　　　　　£ 36　　❷❷④
51-52 Hertford St　7408 1155　3–4B
*This Shepherd Market Lebanese is rather overshadowed by the
longer-established Al Hamra, nearby, but its cooking – "refined",
"delicious" and "fresh" – is more than a match for the
competition. / www.alsultan.co.uk; 11.30 pm.*

Al's EC1　　　　　　£ 26　　④④❸
11-13 Exmouth Mkt　7837 4821　9–1A
*It's "looking a bit tacky now", but this boho Clerkenwell "caff"
still makes a "relaxed" hang-out, especially for a spot of brunch.
/ 10 pm.*

Al-Waha W2　　　　　　£ 28　　❷❷④
75 Westbourne Grove　7229 0806　6–1B
*Hailed in the press (and by one or two reporters) as "London's
best Lebanese by a long chalk", this slightly "odd" Bayswater
spot is certainly "good" and "consistent", but it doesn't merit
the rave reviews. / 11.30 pm; no Switch.*

Alastair Little W1　　　　　　£ 48　　❷❷④
49 Frith St　7734 5183　4–2A
*"Wasn't this famous once?" – indeed it was, and if this
"austere" but "relaxed" and "efficient" Soho café can maintain
the "excellent" standard of preparation of its "small" menu, this
could be a great comeback story. / 11 pm; closed Sat L & Sun.*

Alastair Little, Lancaster Rd W11　£ 38　　❷❷④
136a Lancaster Rd　7243 2220　6–1A
*"Innovative" and "sensibly-priced" cooking helps make this
Notting Hill establishment "the ultimate neighbourhood place"
for some reporters; sceptics, though, find the food "boring",
and the setting "like a corridor". / 11 pm; closed Sun.*

Alba EC1　　　　　　£ 35　　❷❸④
107 Whitecross St　7588 1798　9–1B
*The location is "unpromising" and the décor "dull", but this
low-key spot near the Barbican, is probably "the best Italian in
the City"; the "first-rate thin and crispy pizzas" have
a particular following. / 11 pm; closed Sat & Sun.*

Alfred WC2　　　　　　£ 36　　❸❸④
245 Shaftesbury Ave　7240 2566　4–1C
*An "interesting" array of "slightly quirky" British dishes has long
made this "sparse" Theatreland spot "better than it looks";
standards over the past year, though, have been a tad "wobbly".
/ 11 pm; closed Sat L & Sun.*

All Bar One £31 ④④④

289-293 Regent St, W1   7467 9901   3–1C
3-4 Hanover St, W1   7518 9931   3–2C
36-38 Dean St, W1   7479 7921   4–2A
5-6 Picton Pl, W1   7487 0161   3–1A
7-9 Paddington St, W1   7487 0071   2–1A
108 New Oxford St, WC1   7307 7980   4–1A
19 Henrietta St, WC2   7557 7941   4–3C
48 Leicester Sq, WC2   7747 9921   4–4A
58 Kingsway, WC2   7269 5171   2–1D
84 Cambridge Circus, WC2   7379 8311   4–2B
311-313 Fulham Rd, SW10   7349 1751   5–3B
587-591 Fulham Rd, SW6   7471 0611   5–4A
152 Gloucester Rd, SW7   7244 5861   5–2B
126-128 Notting Hill Gate, W11   7313 9362   6–2B
74-76 Westbourne Grove, W2   7313 9432   6–1B
197-199 Chiswick High Rd, W4   8987 8211   7–2A
1 Liverpool Rd, N1   7843 0021   8–3D
131 Upper St, N1   7354 9535   8–3D
1-3 Hampstead Ln, N6   8342 7861   8–1B
79-81 Heath St, NW3   7433 0491   8–1A
60 St John's Wood High St, NW8   7483 9931   8–3A
1 Chicheley St, SE1   7921 9471   2–3D
30 London Bridge St, SE1   7940 9981   9–4C
34 Shad Thames, SE1   7940 9771   9–4D
32-38 Northcote Rd, SW11   7801 9951   10–2C
7-9 Battersea Sq, SW11   7326 9831   10–1C
527-529 Old York Rd, SW18   8875 7941   10–2B
42 Mackenzie Walk, E14   7513 0911   11–1C
91-93 Charterhouse St, EC1   7553 9391   9–1B
127 Finsbury Pavement, EC2   7448 9921   9–1C
18-20 Appold St, EC2   7377 9671   9–1D
63 Threadneedle St, EC2   7614 9931   9–2C
16 Byward St, EC3   7553 0301   9–3D
3 Cannon St, EC4   7220 9031   9–3C
44-46 Ludgate Hill, EC4   7653 9901   9–2A
*Its branches are "too cloned" for some tastes, but this "relaxed"
and consistent chain serves "decent" and "appetising" bar food,
and maintains its strong twentysomething following.*
/ www.sixcontinents.com; 10 pm, Fri-Sun 9 pm; Hanover St, Kingsway, City,
WC1, SE1 and E14 branches close all or part of weekend; no booking.

Alloro W1 £41 ❸④❸
20 Dover St   7495 4768   3–3C
*This rather severe, year-old Mayfair Italian "hasn't yet found
a soul"; service which can be "very slow" and "forgetful" doesn't
help, and the cooking, though "beautifully presented", is no
better than one might expect at the prices.* / 10.30 pm; closed Sun.

Alma SW18 £27 ❸❷❷
499 Old York Rd   8870 2537   10–2B
*It gets packed with rugger buggers, but this "traditional"
Wandsworth hostelry is also notable for its "nice, relaxed dining
room", which serves "good and varied pub fare".*
/ www.thealma.co.uk; 10.30 pm.

Alounak   £ 21   ❷❸❸
10 Russell Gdns, W14   7603 1130   7–1D
44 Westbourne Grove, W2   7229 0416   6–1B
"Huge portions" of *"great"* Iranian food, and a jolly atmosphere
make this west London BYO duo well worth knowing about.
/ www.alounak.com; 11.30 pm; no Amex.

Alphabet W1   £ 33   ❸④❸
61-63 Beak St   7439 2190   3–2D
A *"chilled"* twentysomething Soho haunt with competent bar
snacks; service can be *"slow"*, though, and the place gets
"too packed". / www.alphabetbar.com; 10.30 pm; closed Sat L & Sun;
no booking at D.

Amandier W2   £ 45   ❸❷④
26 Sussex Pl   7262 6073   6–1D
*"Surprisingly empty considering the quality of the cooking and
service"* – we suspect it's the *"rather clinical"* setting which
discourages the wider following this Gallic Bayswater venture
deserves. / 10.30 pm; closed Sat L & Sun.

Anarkali W6   £ 24   ❸❸④
303-305 King St   8748 6911   7–2B
"Consistently good" curries have kept this ordinary-looking
Hammersmith Indian in business for over a quarter of
a century. / midnight.

ANDREW EDMUNDS W1   £ 31   ❷❶❶
46 Lexington St   7437 5708   3–2D
It's *"harder than ever to get a table"* at this *"cosy"*, *"Bohemian"*
Soho *"treasure"*; with its *"great value"*, simple food,
its *"attitude-free"* service and its *"excellent, reasonably-priced
wine list"*, it *"just can't be beat"* (especially *"for a date"*).
/ 10.45 pm.

Angel of the North N1   £ 27   ④❷❸
353 Upper St   7704 8323   8–3D
It's a *"cosy"* and *"well-priced"* place, but the cooking at this
small bistro near Islington's Antiques Market is *"nothing
special"*. / 11 pm; no Amex.

The Anglesea Arms W6   £ 27   ❶⑤❸
35 Wingate Rd   8749 1291   7–1B
"The odd celebrity fighting for space" can add lustre to a trip to
this *"top-notch"* boozer, near Ravenscourt Park, which offers
the *"ne plus ultra of gastropub fare"*; *"getting the food is
a challenge"*, though, given the *"mind-numbing waits"* and the
sometimes *"surly"* or *"hostile"* service. / 10.45 pm; no Amex;
no booking.

Anglo Asian Tandoori N16   £ 21   ❸❶❷
60-62 Stoke Newington Church St   7254 9298   1–1C
"I loved the freebie rose" – a typical flourish from the
"extremely friendly" staff of this unusually romantic Stoke
Newington Indian; *"the food's not bad either"*.
/ www.angloasian.co.uk; 11.30 pm, Fri & Sat 11.45 pm; no smoking area; set
weekday L £13(FP).

Antipasto & Pasta SW11 £ 26 ❸❷❸
511 Battersea Park Rd 7223 9765 10–1C
"A good local", this Battersea Italian is "particularly excellent value" on half-price nights (Mon, Thu & Sun). / 11.30 pm.

Aperitivo W1 £ 26 ❸❷❸
41 Beak St 7287 2057 3–2D
It's a shame that the menu errs on the "stodgy" side at this "Italian tapas" bar (on the former site of Leith's Soho, RIP), as its otherwise "fresh" and "interesting" food is "attractively priced" by local standards. / 11 pm; closed Sun.

Aquarium E1 £ 36 ❸❹❸
Ivory Hs, St Katharine-by-the-Tower 7480 6116 11–1A
This "clean-lined" waterside café has a "great location" in a City-fringe marina, and its "innovative" fish cooking can be "scrummy"; it's "expensive", though, and sometimes "poorly trained" staff can "let the place down". / www.theaquarium.co.uk; 11 pm; closed Mon D & Sun.

Aquasia
Conrad International SW10 £ 40 ❸❸❸
Chelsea Harbour 7823 3000 5–4B
"Unfortunately it's in an hotel" – and even fans say it's "expensive" – but the interesting East-meets-West menu and the wonderful terrace make this Chelsea Harbour-view dining room something of a "hidden gem", particularly in summer. / www.hilton.com; 10.30 pm; no smoking area.

Arancia SE16 £ 24 ❶❷❷
52 Southwark Park Rd 7394 1751 11–2A
"Why aren't there more restaurants like this?" – this cosy, "crowded" local in an unlovely Bermondsey location delivers simple, "authentic Italian" grub that shows "class", and it's "keenly priced" too. / 11 pm; closed Mon L & Tue L; no Amex.

Arcadia W8 £ 36 ❹❷❸
Kensington Ct, 35 Kensington High St 7937 4294 5–1A
If you're looking for a "good-value lunch", it's worth remembering this "old-fashioned but pleasant" Kensington restaurant; as a dinner destination, though, its appeal is limited. / 11 pm; closed Sat L.

Archduke Wine Bar SE1 £ 31 ⑤④④
Concert Hall Approach, South Bank 7928 9370 2–3D
This "crowded" South Bank wine bar may be "very convenient pre-theatre, film or concert", but the food it offers "has steadily got worse". / 11 pm; closed Sat L & Sun; no smoking area.

Archipelago W1 £ 56 ❷❷❶
110 Whitfield St 7383 3346 2–1B
"The weirdness factor adds to the fun" at this "eclectic, surreal, and intimate" Fitzrovia establishment, whose "amazing" menu is certainly "refreshingly different" – in many respects the place continues from where its predecessor, The Birdcage (RIP), left off. / 10.30 pm; closed Sat L & Sun; no smoking area; set £36(FP).

The Ark W8 £ 39 ④④❸
122 Palace Gardens Ter 7229 4024 6–2B
A year in, the new régime's "OK but pricey" Italian cooking has yet to win wholehearted support for this "cute" but "cramped" Kensington shack. / 11 pm; closed Mon L & Sun D.

Arkansas Café E1 £ 19 ❷❸❸
107b Commercial St 7377 6999 9–1D
"Bubba needs new anecdotes", say regulars at this "quirky", "no-frills" Spitalfields BBQ, presided over by the man himself; so long as he continues to dish up "simple but tasty grills", however, we guess the punters will just grin and bear it. / L only, closed Sat; no Amex; no smoking.

Aroma II W1 £ 27 ❸④④
118-120 Shaftesbury Ave 7437 0377 4–3A
"What's the fuss?" – this "loud and brash" Theatreland Chinese yearling serves some "creative and interesting" cooking, but reporters can see "nothing to shout about", despite the adulatory press reviews. / www.aromarestaurant.co.uk; 10 pm.

The Artesian Well SW8 £ 30 ④④❸
693 Wandsworth Rd 7627 3353 10–1C
Like Beach Blanket Babylon – with whom it has a wacky designer in common – this extravagantly-converted Wandsworth boozer is often "most notable for the bill", at least if judged on its culinary merits. / 10.30 pm; closed Sun D.

Artigiano NW3 £ 41 ❸❸❸
12a Belsize Ter 7794 4288 8–2A
It's perhaps "rather pricey for a local", but it's "hard to get a booking" nowadays at this emerging Italian, which is "surprisingly original for Belsize Park". / www.etruscagroup.co.uk; 10.30 pm; closed Mon L; set weekday L £27(FP).

L'Artiste Musclé W1 £ 26 ④❸❷
1 Shepherd Mkt 7493 6150 3–4B
You can "pretend you're in France" at this "simple" Shepherd Market corner bistro, which is "best appreciated if you go with someone who speaks the lingo". / 11.30 pm.

Asia de Cuba
St Martin's Lane WC2 £ 62 ❺④❸
45 St Martin's Ln 7300 5500 4–4C
You do get "beautiful people" in the dining room of Ian Schrager's Theatreland design-hotel, but the place "is really let down by its wacky fusion menu" and by "disinterested staff who seem to be paid by the frown". / midnight, Sat 1 am.

Ask! Pizza   £ 23   ④❸❷

160-162 Victoria St, SW1   7630 8228   2–4B
121-125 Park St, W1   7495 7760   2–2A
48 Grafton Way, W1   7388 8108   2–1B
300 King's Rd, SW3   7349 9123   5–3C
345 Fulham Palace Rd, SW6   7371 0392   10–1B
23-24 Gloucester Arc, SW7   7835 0840   5–2B
145 Notting Hill Gate, W11   7792 9942   6–2B
41-43 Spring St, W2   7706 0707   6–1C
Whiteley's, 151 Queensway, W2   7792 1977   6–1C
219-221 Chiswick High Rd, W4   8742 1323   7–2A
222 Kensington High St, W8   7937 5540   5–1A
52 Upper St, N1   7226 8728   8–3D
30 Hawley Cr, NW1   7267 7755   8–2B
216 Haverstock Hill, NW3   7433 3896   8–2A
34 Shad Thames, SE1   7403 4545   9–4D
Station Rd, SW13   8878 9300   10–1A
103 St John St, EC1   7253 0323   9–1A
"Running neck and neck with PizzaExpress" – the pizza may
not be "quite as good" as at its famous rival, but, in terms of
the attractiveness of branches and the friendliness of staff, this
upstart chain now has the advantage. / www.askcentral.co.uk;
11.30 pm; no booking after 7.30 pm.

ASSAGGI W2   £ 44   ❶❶❷

39 Chepstow Pl   7792 5501   6–1B
"It's so tough to get a table here that it feels really special when
you do" – the "stunning" cooking and "great" personal service
at this "basic" room above a Bayswater boozer make it
reporters' "best Italian in town". / 11 pm; closed Sun.

Les Associés N8   £ 29   ❷❶❷

172 Park Rd   8348 8944   1–1C
"France comes to north London" at this "tiny and delightful"
Crouch End "gem", which offers "simple but delicious" cooking
and "excellent" service. / 10 pm; D only, except Sun open L only;
no Amex.

Atlantic Bar & Grill W1   £ 49   ⑤⑤❸

20 Glasshouse St   7734 4888   3–3D
Some still think the "too trendy" scene justifies a trip to this
large Art Deco basement, off Piccadilly Circus; it's "living off the
bar's former reputation", though, and – thanks to "evil" cooking
and "rude" service – many reporters just find a visit here
"deeply depressing". / 11.30 pm, bar food until 2.30 am; D only.

The Atlas SW6   £ 24   ❸④❷

16 Seagrave Rd   7385 9129   5–3A
It's "becoming a victim of its own success", but this revived
boozer, "tucked away" near Earl's Court 2, still has quite
a following for its "delicious and hearty Mediterranean fare".
/ 10.30 pm; no Amex; no booking.

Atrium SW1   £ 35   ⑤⑤④
4 Millbank   7233 0032   2–4C
*"The tables set well apart are good for conversation" – a must,
given the clientèle of politicos and hacks – but otherwise the
restaurant adjacent to Parliament's media centre is "dreadful
and overpriced". / 10 pm; closed Sat & Sun; no smoking area.*

Attica W1   £ 46   ⑤⑤⑤
14-16 Foubert's Pl   7287 6983   3–2C
*"Is it a club, a restaurant or both?"; they've "obviously spent
loads of money" on this trendy new joint near Carnaby Street,
but service is "unskilled" and the pizza-and-more fodder is
"dodgy" in the extreme – "I never thought I'd say this but 'come
back Deals, all is forgiven'". / 11 pm; closed Sun D.*

Auberge   £ 27   ❸④④
6-8 St Christopher's Pl, W1   7486 5557   3–1A
1 Sandell St, SE1   7633 0610   9–4A
35 Tooley St, SE1   7407 5267   9–4C
56 Mark Ln, EC3   7480 6789   9–3D
*These "homely" Gallic bistros sometimes offer surprisingly
"well-presented" cooking, and supporters of their "friendly" and
"unpretentious" charms insist that they are "under-rated".
/ www.giardinogroup.co.uk; 10.30 pm – SE1 11.30 pm; SE1 closed Sun.*

Aubergine SW10   £ 69   ❷❷❸
11 Park Walk   7352 3449   5–3B
*For some, the atmosphere "doesn't quite work", but William
Drabble's "impressive" modern French cooking generally "makes
up for it" at this "discreet" Chelsea establishment; for those
who think it "too expensive", the "great-value lunch" is worth
bearing in mind. / 10.30 pm; closed Sun; jacket required; set weekday L
£43(FP).*

Aurora W1   £ 35   ❷❷❷
49 Lexington St   7494 0514   3–2D
*"It's a shame it's not BYO any more", but this "chilled" and
"sweet" little place still offers "a small but interesting" menu
and "very friendly" service, and its tiny garden "really is
a hidden Soho gem". / 10.30 pm; closed Sun; no Amex; set always
available £19(FP).*

Aurora
Great Eastern Hotel EC2   £ 54   ⑤⑤⑤
40 Liverpool St   7618 7000   9–2D
*"Rubbish food, rubbish service, top-class bill" – even by Conran's
standards, the "sterile" dining room of this design-hotel by
Liverpool Street is a plain and simple "rip-off". / www.conran.com;
10 pm; closed Sat & Sun.*

L'Aventure NW8   £ 40   ❶❷❶
3 Blenheim Ter   7624 6232   8–3A
*"They take pride in their food, their ivy and their fairy lights" at
this "little bit of France" – a "great" St John's Wood
"all-rounder" (and a top "romantic" destination); it's "best in
summer on the patio". / 11 pm; closed Sat L (& Sun in winter); no Switch;
set weekday L £26(FP).*

The Avenue SW1   £ 43   ④④④
7-9 St James's St   7321 2111   3–4D

A "light", "airy" ambience that's "great for biz" wins votes for this sparse St James's bar/restaurant; the cooking, however, is "not up to its presentation", staff can "play hard to get", and the "noisy" setting is "so large it lacks the personal touch". / www.theavenue.co.uk; midnight, Fri & Sat 12.30 am, Sun 10 pm.

Axis WC2   £ 48   ❷❷❸
1 Aldwych   7300 0300   2–2D

"Understated" (almost to a fault) Theatreland basement whose "well-spaced" tables and "efficient" but "not over-formal" service make it "great for a business lunch"; the cooking throws out few fireworks, but is "really consistent". / 11.30 pm; closed Sat L & Sun.

Aykoku-Kaku EC4   £ 45   ❸❷④
9 Walbrook   7248 2548   9–3C

The "super canteen", with its "good set lunches", is the introduction for many City workers to this comfortably worn Japanese "old-timer", behind Mansion House; it also offers a grander dining room and sushi bar. / www.japanweb.co.uk/ak; 10 pm; closed Sat & Sun.

Ayoush W1   £ 36   ⑤④❷
58 James St   7935 9839   3–1A

Some deride "the worst north African food ever" at this clubby Moroccan, near Selfridges, and it's a shame that somewhere which started quite well is now just a "poor imitation of Momo". / www.ayoush.com; 11 pm; set weekday L, Sun L & pre-th. £23(FP).

Azou W6   £ 27   ❸❷❸
375 King St   8563 7266   7–2B

"They want you to enjoy yourself" at this "charming", little Hammersmith Moroccan, which serves "very simple" couscous and tajines at "very fair" prices. / 11 pm; closed Sun; no Amex.

Babe Ruth's E1   £ 31   ⑤⑤⑤
172-176 The Highway   7481 8181   11–1A

It's hardly surprising this American sports bar in Docklands has already lost its north London twin; some reporters do find a visit here a "novelty" – and "kids love the basketball court" – but that doesn't make up for "pricey", "unreliable" cooking and "indifferent" service. / 11 pm, Fri & Sat midnight; no smoking area; no booking.

Babur Brasserie SE23   £ 28   ❷❸❸
119 Brockley Rise   8291 2400   1–4D

"Sophisticated Indian cooking" ensures this "innovative" Brockley subcontinental is "always packed"; the odd comment about it becoming "over-rated and expensive", however, sounds a warning note. / 11.15 pm; closed Fri L; no smoking area.

Babylon
Kensington Roof Gardens W8   £ 60   ⑤❸❷

99 Kensington High St   7368 3993   5–1A

An August '01 visit found good vibes and great views at the Sir Richard Branson's luxurious new bar/restaurant atop Kensington's Roof Gardens; only a tycoon, though, would wish to pay the exorbitant price charged for cooking of such limited ambition. / Rated on Editors' assessment; 11.15 pm; closed Sat L & Sun D; booking essential.

Back to Basics W1   £ 35   ❶❸❸

21a Foley St   7436 2181   2–1B

Is this "the best-value fish restaurant in London"? – its "friendly" Fitzrovia premises may be "cramped" and "plain", but its "creative" dishes are "huge" and "exciting". / www.backtobasics.uk.com; 9.45 pm; closed Sat & Sun.

Bah Humbug SW2   £ 28   ❸❸❶

St Matthew's Church   7738 3184   10–2D

A "spooky" crypt provides the "sexy and special" setting, at this "terminally trendy" Brixton "oasis", whose fish-and-veggie menu "can tempt even an ardent meat eater". / www.bahhumbug.co.uk; 11.30 pm; closed weekday L; no Amex.

Balans   £ 31   ④❸❸

60 Old Compton St, W1   7437 5212   4–3A
239 Brompton Rd, SW3   7584 0070   5–2C
239 Old Brompton Rd, SW5   7244 8838   5–3A
187 Kensington High St, W8   7376 0115   5–1A

"Food seems secondary to cruising" nowadays at this increasingly "complacent" chain of gay-friendly diners; as "great places for weekend brunch", however, they still have many fans. / www.balans.co.uk; 1 am – W1 Mon-Sat 5 am, Sun 1 am; W1 no booking – SW5 Sat & Sun no booking.

Bali Sugar W11   £ 46   ❷❷❸

33a All Saints Rd   7221 4477   6–1B

"Impressive" Pacific Rim cooking keeps the foodie flag flying at this agreeable Notting Hill venture (the original site of the Sugar Club); the setting is "unpretentious", and "on a warm summer's night, the garden is perfect". / 11 pm; closed weekday L; no smoking area; set brunch £29(FP).

Baltic SE1   £ 33   ④❸❶

74 Blackfriars Rd   7928 1111   9–4A

New from the owners of Wòdka, this airy conversion of a 19th-century workshop by Southwark tube station has been executed with cool but welcoming style – on our initial July '01 visit this seemed an attraction rather greater than the Polish cooking. / Rated on Editors' assessment; www.balticrestaurant.co.uk; 11 pm.

Bam-Bou W1   £ 40   ④④❷

1 Percy St   7323 9130   2–1C

"It really looks like Vietnam" at this "characterful" and "very hip" Fitzrovia townhouse; given the "uninspiring" cooking and iffy service, though, some advise "just do cocktails". / www.bam-bou.co.uk; 11.15 pm; closed Sat L & Sun.

The Banana Leaf Canteen SW11   £21   ❸❸❸
75-79 Battersea Rise   7228 2828   10–2C
As the queues attest, "good, quick Asian cuisine" has helped make an instant hit of this "noisy" new Battersea canteen; service can be "off-hand". / 11.15 pm; no smoking area; need 6+ to book.

Bangkok SW7   £32   ❸❸④
9 Bute St   7584 8529   5–2B
It's "gone downhill" a little in recent years, but this "time-honoured" South Kensington canteen – the UK's longest-established Thai – retains a "loyal" clientèle. / 10.45 pm; closed Sun; no Amex or Switch.

Bangkok Brasserie SW1   £31   ④④④
48-49 St James's St   7629 7565   3–3C
Some say the cooking's "mediocre", but "not bad" might be a fairer assessment of this central Thai basement, especially when you bear in mind that the prices are "pretty good for somewhere just off Piccadilly". / 11 pm; set weekday L £18(FP).

BANK WC2   £44   ❸❸❸
1 Kingsway   7379 9797   2–2D
It's "noisy", "impersonal" and "quite expensive", but this huge Theatreland brasserie wins continued popularity – especially for business and for brunch – with its "slick" service and "consistent" cooking. / www.bankrestaurants.com; 11 pm; set weekday L & pre-th. £25(FP).

Bank Westminster
St James Court Hotel SW1   £40   ④❸❸
45 Buckingham Gate   7379 9797   2–4B
"Not great, but nonetheless an oasis" in the thin area around Victoria Street – this "uncluttered" offshoot of the Theatreland brasserie (formerly called Zander) is worth knowing about, even if the cooking is rather "plain". / www.bankrestaurants.com; 11 pm; closed Sat L; pre-th. £25(FP).

Bankside SE1   £25   ❸❷❸
32 Southwark Bridge Rd   7633 0011   9–4B
"A wonderful find, close to Tate Modern"; the operation may be "a bit hit-and-miss", but "long queues for weekend lunch" confirm the "good value" of this new basement brasserie, which offers a "great respite" from culture vulturedom. / www.bankside-ltd.com; 10.30 pm; no smoking area.

Banners N8   £26   ❸❸❶
21 Park Rd   8348 2930   1–1C
The evening cooking can be "a bit hit-and-miss", but "brunch is the deal" at this "laid-back" and perennially popular Crouch End hang-out; non-parents beware – at times, "you can't move for pushchairs". / 11.30 pm, Fri & Sat midnight; no Amex.

Bar Bourse EC4 £ 41 ④❸④
67 Queen St 7248 2200 9–3C
This "lively" bar/restaurant strikes some as quite "a refreshing place for the City", and makes a "decent stop-off" on account of its dependable, "simple" fare. / L only, closed Sat & Sun.

Bar Gansa NW1 £ 20 ❸❸❷
2 Inverness St 7267 8909 8–3B
"Young, bustling, fun and spicy" – this "good-quality", open-till-late Camden Town tapas bar remains as happening as ever. / midnight; no Amex.

Bar Italia W1 £ 7 ❸❸❶
22 Frith St 7437 4520 4–2A
"Exceptional coffee any time of the day or night" fuels the buzz at this phenomenal, cramped Soho "rendezvous". / open 24 hours Mon-Sat, Sun 4 am; no credit cards; no booking.

Bar Japan SW5 £ 24 ❷❸④
251 Old Brompton Rd 7370 2323 5–3A
"Cheap and tasty" sushi – and "cheap but mediocre other options" – are served at this basic Earl's Court café. / 10.45 pm.

Baraonda W1 £ 36 ❸④④
14 Heddon St 7494 2234 3–2D
"Great Italian food" – particularly the generous antipasti buffet – makes this new pizzeria a useful "cheap and cheerful" option, just off Regent Street; boy, is it "loud", though. / midnight; closed Sun; no Amex.

Barcelona Tapas £ 23 ❸❸❷
481 Lordship Ln, SE22 8693 5111 1–4D
1a Bell Ln, E1 7247 7014 9–2D
1 Beaufort Hs, St Botolph St, EC3 7377 5111 9–2D
13 Well Ct, EC4 7329 5111 9–2B
"Very satisfactory" scoff and a "loud", "fun" and "buzzy" atmosphere ensure continued popularity for this small Spanish chain. / 10 pm – SE22 11 pm – EC4 2.30 am; City branches closed Sat & Sun.

Barracuda N16 £ 25 ④❷❷
125 Stoke Newington Church St 7923 7488 1–1C
"A nice jazz cellar" (and, for the summer, a picturesquely overgrown garden) adds to the charm of this scruffy but friendly Stoke Newington spot; the rather miscellaneous menu is incidental. / 11 pm; open Sun L in summer only; no Amex.

Base NW3 £ 31 ❸④❸
71 Hampstead High St 7431 2224 8–2A
"In the Hampstead desert", this "lively" cross between a "pan-Mediterranean" restaurant and an "upmarket coffee shop" makes "a good place for lunch or brunch". / 11 pm; no smoking area.

Basil St Hotel SW3   £ 35   ④❷❷

8 Basil St   7581 3311   5–1D

"Old-style English food" is served by "smiling Italians" in this "comfortable" and unchanging Knightsbridge dining room; it makes an ideal destination for a "wonderful, traditional Sunday lunch" or a solid breakfast; (in the lounge, there's an "excellent value afternoon tea"). / www.absite.com/basil; 9.45 pm; jacket & tie required; no smoking area.

Basilico   £ 27   ❶❸④

690 Fulham Rd, SW6   0800 028 3531   10–1B
175 Lavender Hill, SW11   0800 389 9770   10–2C
178 Upper Richmond Rd, SW15   0800 096 8202   10–2B

"Redefining perceptions of pizza", these "excellent" take-aways (with a few seats in some branches) are unanimously hailed for their "brilliant" cooking. / www.basilico.co.uk; 11pm; no Amex; no booking.

Battersea Rickshaw SW11   £ 24   ❸❷④

15-16 Battersea Sq   7924 2450   5–4C

"Tolerant" staff and "tasty" cooking make this Battersea subcontinental a tried and tested stand-by. / 11.30 pm; D only, Sun also open for brunch; set Sun L £15(FP).

Beach Blanket Babylon W11   £ 38   ⑤⑤❷

45 Ledbury Rd   7229 2907   6–1B

There's still a "fantastic" atmosphere at this brilliantly-designed Baroque destination in Notting Hill, but the food is "lousy" and the service "appalling" – "stick to the bar". / 11.30 pm.

Bedlington Café W4   £ 21   ❸④⑤

24 Fauconberg Rd   8994 1965   7–2A

"The food's now fallen to the same level as the setting", say critics of this once-famous Chiswick "dive" – that's overdoing it, but this "cheap and cheerful" Thai café is certainly no longer the destination it was; (it's finally got a licence, but you can still BYO). / 10 pm; closed Sun L; no credit cards; no smoking.

Beirut Express W2   £ 15   ❶❸④

112-114 Edgware Rd   7724 2700   6–1D

"What a find!", say fans of "the best kebabs", "excellent fruit juices" and other "cheap and plentiful" grub at this "bland"-looking Lebanese, which is open till very late. / www.maroush.com; 1.45 am; no credit cards.

Beiteddine SW1   £ 38   ❸❷④

8 Harriet St   7235 3969   5–1D

"These people try harder" – "attentive" service helps differentiate this long-established Lebanese, off Sloane Street. / midnight.

Belair House SE21   £ 45   ❸❷❶
Gallery Rd, Dulwich Village   8299 9788   1–4C
The "wonderful setting" of this gracious Georgian house by
Dulwich Park still eclipses its cooking, but the latter "has
improved over the past year", and this place may yet realise its
potential to become a major destination. / www.belairhouse.co.uk;
10.30 pm; closed Mon & Sun D.

Belgo   £ 31   ④④④
50 Earlham St, WC2   7813 2233   4–2C
124 Ladbroke Grove, W10   8982 8400   6–1A
72 Chalk Farm Rd, NW1   7267 0718   8–2B
The approach that once seemed so innovative now just seems
"tired" and "formulaic" at these "noisy" and "smoky" Belgian
moules-and-beer halls, where "rushed" but "slow" staff offer
a menu that "promises a lot and delivers very little".
/ www.belgo-restaurants.co.uk; 11.30 pm.

Bellamys SE11   £ 34   ④❸❸
332 Kennington Ln   7582 9569   2–4D
This new little bistro is a "useful addition to the
Vauxhall/Kennington desert", and quite "chic", but its cooking is
rather hit-and-miss. / 10 pm; closed Sat & Sun; no Amex.

Belvedere W8   £ 55   ④❸❶
Holland Park, off Abbotsbury Rd   7602 1238   7–1D
With its "lovely Holland Park location" and its "beautiful" décor,
this "revived" classic has so much going for it; what a shame,
then, that the new régime has delivered "the usual MPW price
inflation, with little improvement over the previous owner's
indifferent standards". / www.whitestarline.org.uk; 11 pm; set Sun L
£35(FP).

Ben's Thai W9   £ 23   ❸❸❸
93 Warrington Cr   7266 3134   8–4A
With its "unique" setting – the upstairs dining room of a huge,
historic Maida Vale pub – this "cheap Thai" makes a "reliable"
destination, if rather a "rushed" and "smoky" one. / 10 pm; D only;
no Amex or Switch.

Bengal Clipper SE1   £ 31   ❷❷❸
Shad Thames   7357 9001   9–4D
"Light" cooking of "reliably good quality" and a "bright and
airy" setting make this "classy" Indian one of the better options
south of Tower Bridge. / www.bengalrestaurants.co.uk; 11.30 pm; set
£19(FP).

Benihana   £ 48   ❸❸④
37 Sackville St, W1   7494 2525   3–3D
77 King's Rd, SW3   7376 7799   5–3D
100 Avenue Rd, NW3   7586 9508   8–2A
"Juggling teppan-yaki chefs provide the entertainment" at this
"consistent" chain of Americo-Japanese restaurants – they're
"great for kids", but the grown-ups may find them "a bit
soulless and expensive". / www.benihana.co.uk; 10.30 pm, Fri & Sat
11 pm.

Bentley's W1   £ 49   ❷❷❸
11-15 Swallow St   7734 4756   3–3D
*Some feel it "needs a facelift", but this charming, "traditional"
seafood specialist is a "peaceful" place – especially when you
consider how near it is to Piccadilly Circus – and its appeal
currently includes some "high-quality" cooking. / 11.30 pm.*

Beotys WC2   £ 40   ❹❷❸
79 St Martin's Ln   7836 8768   4–3B
*"Three generations of my family have known and loved Beotys",
says one member of this Franco-Greek Theatrelander's fan club;
non-initiates, however, may find that the "olde worlde charm
doesn't make up for indifferent realisation of the pricey menu".
/ 11.30 pm; closed Sun; no smoking area.*

Bersagliera SW3   £ 23   ❹❹❸
372 King's Rd   7352 5993   5–3B
*"Dependable" cooking and "comic" service still make this
World's End pizza-and-pasta stop a "fun" and "noisy"
destination, but it's by no means the place it once was.
/ 11.30 pm; closed Mon; no Amex.*

Bertorelli's   £ 35   ❹❹❹
11-13 Frith St, W1   7494 3491   4–2A
19-23 Charlotte St, W1   7636 4174   2–1C
44a Floral St, WC2   7836 3969   4–2D
*Including the premises formerly called Soho Soho (RIP), this
chain of large and "lively" trattorias is now three branches
strong; they're "predictable" places fans find "useful" enough,
but to many they're just plain "disappointing".
/ www.santeonline.com; Charlotte St 11 pm – WC2 11.30 pm – Frith St
midnight; closed Sun (Frith St bar open all day); no smoking area.*

Bibendum SW3   £ 62   ❹❹❸
81 Fulham Rd   7581 5817   5–2C
*Some still feel "spoilt" on a visit to this "assured" establishment
at Brompton Cross, but for too many reporters it's "a real
let-down" nowadays – "haughty" service has always been
a problem, and the modern Gallic cooking now often seems
"bland", as well as "overpriced". / www.bibendum.co.uk; 11.30 pm.*

Bibendum Oyster Bar SW3   £ 36   ❶❸❷
81 Fulham Rd   7589 1480   5–2C
*"Oysters and champagne, what else do you need?" – this
"sleek" bar, in the entrance of the Conran Shop, offers a range
of "first-rate", "simple" seafood in "stylish" surroundings' "why
oh why", though, "can't you make reservations?"
/ www.bibendum.co.uk; 10.30 pm; no booking.*

Bibo Cibo WC2   £ 25   ❸❸❷
59 Endell St   7240 3343   4–1C
*'Future-chintz' is our best shot at describing the wacky décor at
this new bar/restaurant near Covent Garden (on the erstwhile
site of Mars, RIP); the English cooking is plain retro – and none
the worse for that. / Rated on Editors' assessment; 11.30 pm; closed
Sun D.*

Bice W1 £ 46 ④❸④
13 Albemarle St 7409 1011 3–3C
"After Milan and Manhattan, the Mayfair version was
disappointing all round…"; this lacklustre basement offshoot of
a glamorous international Italian chain may be a "safe" choice
– "for business" or "as a lunch spot" – but it's never made any
waves locally. / 10.45 pm; closed Sat L & Sun; set weekday L £30(FP).

Big Easy SW3 £ 36 ④④❸
332-334 King's Rd 7352 4071 5–3C
"Chaos, but fun" – this "noisy and crowded" Chelsea dive,
which offers a diet of seafood and burgers, is "great for
children", but the food is "mediocre", and quite pricey too.
/ 11.20 pm, Fri & Sat 12.20 am; no smoking area; set weekday L £22(FP).

Bistro 1 £ 17 ❸❷❷
75 Beak St, W1 7287 1840 3–2D
33 Southampton St, WC2 7379 7585 4–3D
Who cares if "the formula seems a bit haphazard"? – these
unpretentious budget bistros have "nice" service, and their
"generous" cooking offers "good value and variety", considering.
/ 11.30 pm.

Bistrot 190 SW7 £ 35 ⑤④④
189-190 Queen's Gate 7581 5666 5–1B
"If it weren't convenient, it would be empty" – this once-famous
Mediterranean brasserie near the Albert Hall badly "needs
reviving"; for "a lazy, late breakfast", though, it still has its fans.
/ 11.30 pm.

Black & Blue W8 £ 31 ④❸❸
215-217 Kensington Church St 7727 0004 6–2B
Some report "delicious" steaks and "reliable" burgers at this
year-old diner – others just found them "terrible"; we still think
its spiritual home is a US shopping mall, not Kensington. / 11 pm;
no Amex; no booking.

The Black Truffle NW1 £ 36 ❸❸❸
40 Chalcot Rd 7483 0077 8–3B
"Unexceptional" Italian dishes and sometimes "weak" service
take the edge off this potentially "sophisticated" Primrose Hill
yearling; its interior is "interesting", but also "cramped" and
"noisy". / 10.45 pm; closed Sat L.

Blah! Blah! Blah! W12 £ 23 ❶❷❸
78 Goldhawk Rd 8746 1337 7–1C
"Don't be put off by the outside and the décor" – this
Shepherd's Bush café doles out "fabulous vegetarian food loved
even by committed carnivores"; oddly (especially for a BYO
place), they "won't serve tap water". / 11 pm; closed Sun; no credit
cards.

Blakes NW1 £ 32 ④④❸
31 Jamestown Rd 7482 2959 8–3B
Feedback on the cooking was mixed this year, on this "small
and lively" dining room over a funky Camden Town pub.
/ 10.30 pm; closed Mon D & Sun D; set weekday L £19(FP).

FSA

Blakes Hotel SW7 £ 82 ④❸❶
33 Roland Gdns 7370 6701 5–2B
"You're paying for the seduction" when you visit this *"sensual"* South Kensington boutique-hotel basement; the eclectic cooking is *"very, very expensive"*, especially *"for what it is"*. / 11.30 pm.

Blandford Street W1 £ 45 ❷❸④
5-7 Blandford St 7486 9696 2–1A
A July '01 visit to these stark, rather unexciting Marylebone premises – left vacant by Stephen Bull's departure for the country – found a new establishment rather similar to the old, serving quality cooking. / Rated on Editors' assessment; www.blandford-street.co.uk; 10.30 pm; closed Sat L & Sun; no smoking area.

El Blasõn SW3 £ 44 ❸❷④
8-9 Blacklands Ter 7823 7383 5–2D
"Good tapas" and *"fun service"* win praise for this backstreet Chelsea Spaniard; there's a dining room above, but it's never acquired much of a following. / 11 pm; closed Sun; no smoking.

Bleeding Heart EC1 £ 40 ❷❷❶
Bleeding Heart Yd, Greville St 7242 8238 9–2A
"Hard to find, but worth the effort", this *"tucked-away"* Gallic basement near Holborn is a *"cosy"* and *"inviting"* warren, which offers *"first-class"* food and a *"very good wine list"*; it has *"much more character than most City restaurants"*, and can make a *"romantic"* evening destination. / 10.30 pm; closed Sat & Sun.

BLUE ELEPHANT SW6 £ 42 ❷❷❶
4-6 Fulham Broadway 7385 6595 5–4A
"A total experience"; this vast and *"almost dreamlike"* Fulham Thai – famed for its *"exotic"*, *"jungle"* décor and *"romantic"* atmosphere – defies cynics by consistently delivering cooking that's *"not cheap, but worth it"*. / www.blueelephant.com; midnight; closed Sat L; set weekday L £22(FP).

Blue Jade SW1 £ 27 ❷❷❷
44 Hugh St 7828 0321 2–4B
This is a *"bad district for food"*, so it's a pleasant surprise to come across this backstreet Pimlico Thai, with its *"elegant"* décor and *"honest"*, *"reliable"* cooking. / 11 pm; closed Sat L & Sun.

Blue Lagoon W14 £ 28 ❷❷❸
284 Kensington High St 7603 1231 7–1D
The décor's a tad *"tacky"*, but the cooking is *"well done"* at this *"friendly"* Kensington Thai, near the Odeon. / www.blue-lagoon.co.uk; 11 pm; no smoking area.

Blue Print Café
Design Museum SE1 £ 44 ④④❷
28 Shad Thames, Butler's Whf 7378 7031 9–4D
The *"stunning location"* – a first floor dining room with a *"great view of Tower Bridge"* – is still *"let down by the food"* at this Conran riversider, but its middle-of-the-road survey performance is a notable improvement on the (dire) previous year. / www.conran.com; 10.45 pm; closed Sun D.

The Blue Pumpkin SW15   £ 28   ④❸④
147 Upper Richmond Rd   8780 3553   10–2B
It's "a useful local", say Putney fans of this "small and friendly"
brasserie – perhaps that's another way of saying it's "very
standard". / www.bluepumpkin.co.uk; 10.30 pm, Fri & Sat 11 pm;
no smoking.

Bluebird SW3   £ 44   ⑤⑤⑤
350 King's Rd   7559 1000   5–3C
Some find "compensation in the coolish décor", but Conran's
"mechanical" and "overpriced" Chelsea landmark offers
"luck-of-the-draw" service and "dull" food. / www.conran.com;
11 pm.

Bluebird Café SW3   £ 32   ⑤⑤④
350 King's Rd   7559 1155   5–3C
As a "great place to sit outside and watch the world go by" this
pavement-side café has its advocates; you're "better off just
going for drinks", though, as the food can be "dire", and the
service is too often "rude". / www.conran.com; 10.45 pm; closed Sun D;
no booking.

Blues W1   £ 35   ❸❷❷
42 Dean St   7494 1966   4–2A
"Friendly service" and "good" brasserie fare endear this loud
Soho bar/restaurant to a younger crowd. / www.bluesbistro.com;
11.30 pm, Thu-Sat midnight; closed Sat L & Sun L; pre-th. £19(FP).

Blythe Road Restaurant W14   £ 31   ❸④④
71 Blythe Rd   7371 3635   7–1C
Most locals still praise the "consistent" cooking at this "very
cramped" Olympia spot; as ever, though, some visitors were
made to feel "like a hindrance". / 10.30 pm; closed Sat L & Sun.

Bohème Kitchen & Bar W1   £ 35   ❸❸❷
19 Old Compton St   7734 5656   4–2A
"Wonderful sofas" help make the Café Bohème's "buzzy"
younger sibling "a great place for lounging"; the fare – "solid
burgers", "fab French fries" and the like – is a touch incidental.
/ www.bohemekitchen.co.uk; 11.45 pm.

Boiled Egg & Soldiers SW11   £ 17   ④④❸
63 Northcote Rd   7223 4894   10–2C
"The kids can be overpowering", at this "upmarket greasy
spoon" in Wandsworth's 'Nappy Valley' – you can "barely get in
without tripping over a pram"; the breakfast, though, is "a great
hangover cure". / L & afternoon tea only; only Switch; no booking.

Boisdale SW1   £ 40   ❸❸❷
13-15 Eccleston St   7730 6922   2–4B
Those who say the patron is "wonderful" tend to like this "very
un-PC" Scottish wine bar-cum-restaurant, on the borders of
Belgravia; others find the management "pompous" and the total
experience "far too expensive", but even they admit that the
jazz-fuelled ambience can be "fun". / www.boisdale.uk.com; 10.30 pm;
closed Sat L; set weekday L £26(FP).

The Bollo House W4   £ 24   ❸❷❷

13-15 Bollo Ln   8994 6037   7–2A
A very "welcome addition to the area", this year-old
Chiswick/Acton fringe gastropub offers "good, solid food",
"friendly" staff and a "fun" atmosphere. / 10.30 pm; closed Mon L;
no smoking area; no booking.

Bombay Bicycle Club SW12   £ 32   ❷❷❷

95 Nightingale Ln   8673 6217   10–2C
"Delicious", "fresh" Indian cooking served in a "very European"
environment makes this "old-favourite" Wandsworth
subcontinental a key south London destination; for top value,
however, many tip the take-aways – from Battersea (7720
0500), Putney (8785 1188) or Wimbledon (8540 9997).
/ 11 pm; D only, closed Sun.

Bombay Brasserie SW7   £ 40   ❷❷❷

Courtfield Clo, Gloucester Rd   7370 4040   5–2B
"The best all-rounder, and about as authentic as you can get" –
this large, "tastefully decorated" South Kensington
subcontinental (with an impressive conservatory) makes
a "great but pricey" choice. / www.bombaybrasserielondon.com;
midnight; set always available £26(FP).

Bombay Palace W2   £ 35   ❷❷④

50 Connaught St   7723 8855   6–1D
The attractions of the "authentic" cooking "far exceed those of
the décor" at this "comfortable" and "old-fashioned"
subcontinental, just north of Hyde Park. / www.bombay-palace.co.uk;
11.30 pm; no smoking area; booking essential at D.

Le Bon Choix SW10   £ 32   ❸❷❸

196 Fulham Rd   7352 7757   5–3B
This "teeny", hidden-away Chelsea basement offers "surprisingly
good" simple French cooking, in a quiet and "cosy" setting.
/ 10.30 pm; D only, closed Mon & Sun; no Amex.

Bonjour Vietnam SW6   £ 24   ⑤⑤⑤

593-599 Fulham Rd   7385 7603   5–4A
It's presumably the fact that it's "good for a group" that has
saved this Fulham Chinese from extinction – service "can't be
bothered", and "how can they make food this bad?"
/ www.bonjour-vietnam.co.uk; 11 pm; no Amex.

Il Bordello E1   £ 30   ❷❷❷

75-81 Wapping High St   7481 9950   11–1A
"Huge wagon wheel pizzas" at "affordable prices" win rave
reviews from most reporters for this Wapping Italian, which is
"always full and buzzing"; we're with the minority who find it
"safe, if a little dull". / 11 pm; closed Sat L.

La Bouchée SW7   £ 32   ❸❸❷

56 Old Brompton Rd   7589 1929   5–2B
"The atmosphere is fab and it's always packed" at this "useful",
"romantically French" South Kensington "local hangout", whose
cooking seems to be back on form; "reasonable" prices are key
to its appeal. / 11 pm; no Amex or Switch.

Le Bouchon Bordelais SW11   £ 34   ④❸❸
5-9 Battersea Rise   7738 0307   10–2C
*Even supporters admit the cooking is "rather expensive" – and
critics say it's "mediocre" too – but this "very traditional" Gallic
brasserie in Battersea retains a loyal following nonetheless.*
/ www.thebouchon.co.uk; 11 pm; no smoking area.

Boudin Blanc W1   £ 36   ❸❸❷
5 Trebeck St   7499 3292   3–4B
*This "very atmospheric" bistro is "not what it was", since its
expansion of a year or so ago; that said, it has a "great"
Shepherd Market location – with "nice" outside tables – and
the price/quality balance is still "reasonable, for Mayfair".*
/ 11 pm; set weekday L & pre-th. £19(FP).

Boulevard WC2   £ 26   ❸❸❸
40 Wellington St   7240 2992   4–3D
*This "enjoyable" Covent Garden brasserie may look like a tourist
trap, but it's a "friendly" place, offering "basic" and "reliable"
cooking, at reasonable prices. / www.boulevardbrasserie.com; midnight.*

The Bow Wine Vaults EC4   £ 34   ④❷④
10 Bow Church Yd   7248 1121   9–2C
*In the shadow of St Mary-le-Bow, this "mediocre" City spot is
worth knowing about for its very pleasant outside tables.*
/ www.motcombs.co.uk; L only; closed Sat & Sun.

The Brackenbury W6   £ 33   ❸❸❸
129-131 Brackenbury Rd   8748 0107   7–1C
*This "unfussy" Hammersmith backstreet spot isn't the
gastronomic Mecca it once was, but it remains very popular
locally, given its "lovely food", "reasonable" prices and "jolly
atmosphere"; it's "great outside" in summer too. / 10.45 pm; closed
Sat L & Sun D.*

Bradley's NW3   £ 37   ❷❷❸
25 Winchester Rd   7722 3457   8–2A
*"A gem in a bleak area" – "excellent seafood" is the highlight
at this "friendly" and "attentive" St John's Wood local;
it's a "laid-back" spot, which some find "not hugely
atmospheric". / 11 pm; closed Sat L; set weekday L £21(FP).*

Brady's SW18   £ 20   ❷❸④
513 Old York Rd   8877 9599   10–2B
*Wandsworth's so posh nowadays that it may be fair to describe
Mr Brady's popular "no-frills" seafood bistro as an "upper-class
fish and chip shop" – the grub is certainly superior. / 10.30 pm;
D only, closed Sun; no credit cards; no booking.*

Brahms SW1   £ 22   ❸❷④
147 Lupus St   7233 9828   5–3D
*"Forget the décor" – this "Spartan" Pimlico bistro is
"a treasure", on account of the "extremely affordable" prices of
its "well-cooked, simple fare". / 11.45 pm; no Amex.*

Brass. du Marché aux Puces W10   £ 35   ③③②
349 Portobello Rd   8968 5828   6–1A
This "intimate bistro gem" in North Kensington has long been the kind of "great little local" anyone would value on their doorstep; service can be a touch "variable", though, and "climbing prices" are beginning to dent its appeal. / 11 pm; closed Sun D; set brunch £18(FP).

La Brasserie SW3   £ 36   ⑤⑤④
272 Brompton Rd   7584 1668   5–2C
This long-established Gallic stand-by at Brompton Cross – with its "shoddy" cooking and sometimes "appallingly rude" service – "needs a transformation"; it can, though, still be "a great place for brunch or a ladies' lunch". / www.la-brasserie.co.uk; 11.30 pm; no booking, Sat L & Sun L.

Brasserie Rocque EC2   £ 40   ④④④
37 Broadgate Circle   7638 7919   9–2D
"Good in summer for a quick lunch", but this once-popular business rendezvous by Broadgate's ice rink "has seen better days"; it "wouldn't survive without its captive City audience". / L only (& bar food at D); closed Sat & Sun; no booking at D.

Brasserie St Quentin SW3   £ 35   ④❸④
243 Brompton Rd   7589 8005   5–2C
"Since Chez Gérard took over", this "authentically French", and once very popular, Knightsbridge brasserie "has become increasingly disappointing" – it's "not nearly as busy as it used to be". / www.santeonline.co.uk; 10.45 pm.

La Brasserie Townhouse WC1   £ 34   ❸②❸
24 Coptic St   7636 2731   2–1C
It may take more than fiddling with the name (it was the Townhouse Brasserie) to unlock the potential of this agreeable spot, near the British Museum, but its "interesting" cooking is generally "well prepared". / www.townhousebrasserie.co.uk; 11 pm; closed Sat L & Sun D; no smoking area; set weekday L £20(FP).

Brick Lane Beigel Bake E1   £ 4   ❶②④
159 Brick Ln   7729 0616   1–2D
"The best bagels in London" – "the one filled with salt beef is the best ever" – are "well worth queuing for" at this amazing "no-frills", 24-7 East End institution. / open 24 hours; no credit cards; no smoking; no booking.

Brilliant UB2   £ 26   ❷❸④
72-76 Western Rd   8574 1928   1–3A
It's "not technically in London", but curry pilgrims say it's "well worth the trip" to this large, suburban Southall spot for the "authentic" delights of its subcontinental menu. / www.brilliantrestaurant.com; 11 pm; closed Mon, Sat L & Sun L.

Brinkley's SW10 £ 30 ④④❷
47 Hollywood Rd   7351 1683   5–3B
"Very cheap and yummy wine" fuels the "fun", very Chelsea atmosphere at this "noisy", but attractive bar/restaurant, and provides compensation for food that's "average" at best. / www.brinkleys.com; 11.30 pm; D only.

La Brocca NW6 £ 25 ❸❸❷
273 West End Ln   7433 1989   1–1B
A "round-the-corner Italian" (in West Hampstead) with a "strong local following" for its "good pizza and pasta"; "Sunday lunch is top-notch for the price". / 11 pm; booking: max 8.

Browns £ 32 ④❸❸
47 Maddox St, W1   7491 4565   3–2C
82-84 St Martin's Ln, WC2   7497 5050   4–3B
Islington Grn, N1   7226 2555   8–3D
201 Castelnau, SW13   8748 4486   7–2B
8 Old Jewry, EC2   7606 6677   9–2C
"Reliable for consistent, if uninspired, food" – the "stylish" but "formulaic" outlets of this well-established English brasserie chain are "OK for a visit once in a while"; improved ratings suggest they're bucking themselves up somewhat. / www.browns-restaurants.com; 10 pm – WC2 midnight; no smoking area, WC2 & W1.

Bu San N7 £ 24 ❸❸④
43 Holloway Rd   7607 8264   8–2D
"Really tasty food" helps this faded Korean near Highbury & Islington tube still qualify as a "great local" for most reporters. / 11 pm, Fri & Sat 11.30 pm; closed Sat L & Sun L; no Amex.

Bubb's EC1 £ 46 ❷❷❸
329 Central Mkts, Farringdon St   7236 2435   9–2A
"The temptation to stay is too great", so don't even think of having a quick business lunch at this "quintessentially French" operation, on a corner of Smithfield Market, which offers rich and "traditional" fare. / 9.45 pm; closed Sat & Sun; no smoking area.

Buchan's SW11 £ 37 ❸❷❸
62-64 Battersea Br Rd   7228 0888   5–4C
Local fans laud the "interesting menu", "civilised" décor and "friendly" service at this Battersea wine-bar-cum restaurant; sceptics, though, say the "food's unoriginal, despite the Scottish theme". / www.buchansrestaurant.com; 10.45 pm; set weekday L £24(FP).

The Builder's Arms SW3 £ 29 ❷④❷
13 Britten St   7349 9040   5–2C
Tucked away "in a charming part of Chelsea", this "excellent" boozer offers "good menu variety" and "large portions"; in the best gastropub tradition, however, service can be "grumpy" and "slow". / 9.45 pm; no Amex; no booking.

Buona Sera £ 25 ❸④❷
43 Drury Ln, WC2   7836 8296   4–2D
289a King's Rd, SW3   7352 8827   5–3C
22 Northcote Rd, SW11   7228 9925   10–2C
"Chaotic and loud, but good fun", these popular Italian diners
exert a *"buzzy"*, *"family"* appeal that rarely fails. / midnight;
no Amex.

Burnt Chair TW9 £ 42 ❸❷❸
5 Duke St   8940 9488   1–4A
An *"interesting menu"* and an *"accommodating"* owner – who
dispenses *"very good"* advice on the impressive wine list – win
a disproportionate local following for this small restaurant, off
Richmond Green. / www.burntchair.com; 11 pm; D only, closed Mon & Sun;
no Amex; no smoking before 11 pm.

Busaba Eathai W1 £ 23 ❷❸❶
106-110 Wardour St   7255 8686   3–2D
"Miles better than Wagamama" (with which it shares
a co-founder), this *"enjoyable"* Soho yearling offers *"great-value"*
Thai food in a *"lovely"* and unusually stylish communal setting;
it's hugely popular, so *"get there early to avoid queueing"*.
/ 11 pm, Fri & Sat 11.30 pm; no smoking; no booking.

Busabong Too SW10 £ 33 ❸④❸
1a Langton St   7352 7414   5–3B
Now bereft of its nearby sibling, this long-established World's
End Thai makes a *"safe, but not special"* choice. / 11.15 pm;
closed Sun L; set weekday L £19(FP).

Bush Bar & Grill W14 £ 30 ④⑤❸
45a Goldhawk Rd   8746 2111   7–1C
"Mediocre food, but a fairly fun atmosphere"; this sizeable new
Shepherd's Bush bar/restaurant has strengths and weaknesses
similar to its famous sibling 192 – it's *"already a bit up itself"*,
and service can be *"dreadful"*. / 11 pm; no Amex.

Butlers Wharf Chop-house SE1 £ 50 ④④❷
36e Shad Thames   7403 3403   9–4D
Amongst Conran's complex of eating places by Tower Bridge –
all of which have *"good river views"* – this *"relaxed"* spot, with
its *"lively"* bar, is the best; even here, though, the *"quality"*
British fare is *"expensive for what it is"*. / www.conran.com; 10.45 pm;
closed Sun D; set brunch £28(FP).

Byron's NW3 £ 37 ④❸❷
3a Downshire Hill   7435 3544   8–2A
This *"beautiful"* Hampstead townhouse provides a *"wonderful"*
setting for a meal, but – thanks to its *"uninspired"* cooking –
it's often *"quiet"*. / 11 pm; no smoking area.

Cactus Blue SW3 £ 33 ④④❸
86 Fulham Rd   7823 7858   5–2C
It's ideal for *"great frozen margaritas"*, but *"don't expect much"*
of the southwest American cooking at this *"lively"* and
impressively-designed Chelsea bar/restaurant. / midnight; closed
weekday L.

Café 209 SW6   £ 19   ❸❷❶
209 Munster Rd   7385 3625   10–1B
*"Joy is a joy", say the many fans of the "crazy" patronne at this
"small", "very cheap" and "hysterically funny" Chinese/Thai
BYO café in deepest Fulham. / 10.45 pm; D only, closed Sun; no credit
cards.*

**Café Bagatelle
Wallace Collection W1**   £ 31   ④④❷
Manchester Sq   7563 9505   3–1A
*Potentially it's "a great place", but the Wallace Collection's
impressively glazed atrium café is starting to look like "a wasted
opportunity"; some do praise "interesting" food, but more find it
"pretentious", and service is "poor". / www.wallace-collection.com;
L only; no smoking.*

Café Bohème W1   £ 31   ④❸❶
13 Old Compton St   7734 0623   4–2A
*"Always throbbing, French, smoky and dark" – this
"ever-reliable" Soho linchpin offers anything from a drink to
a full-blown meal, at almost any hour of the day or night.
/ 2.45 am, Thu-Sat open 24 hours, Sun 11.30 pm; booking: max 6, Fri & Sat.*

Café Delancey NW1   £ 29   ④❸❷
3 Delancey St   7387 1985   8–3B
*With its "basic French fare" and "unhurried" service, this large
Camden Town "stand-by" is "usually a safe bet" (if an
unexciting one); it's as a "definitive brunch place", however, that
it's best known. / 11.30 pm; no Amex.*

Café des Amis du Vin WC2   £ 38   ④❸❸
11-14 Hanover Pl   7379 3444   4–2D
*A tolerable Covent Garden "stand-by", in an alley near the Royal
Opera House; the main menu is "fairly unexceptional", but the
"crowded" basement bar – untouched by recent 'improvements'
– is rightly famed for its "Gallic cheeses and wine".
/ www.cafedesamis.co.uk; 11.30 pm; closed Sun; set weekday L & pre-th.
£24(FP).*

Café du Jardin WC2   £ 36   ④❸④
28 Wellington St   7836 8769   4–3D
*"It feels touristy", and the cooking tends to the "uninspired",
but for a "pleasant rather than spectacular" lunch or
pre-theatre dinner, this "trusty" Covent Garden "stand-by" has
quite a wide following. / midnight; set weekday L & pre-th. £21(FP).*

Café du Marché EC1   £ 38   ❷❷❶
22 Charterhouse Sq   7608 1609   9–1B
*"You feel at ease" at this "engaging" "slice of France", on the
fringe of Smithfield – a "bustling" place, which is equally at
home for a "good business lunch" or a "lovely" dinner. / 10 pm;
closed Sat L & Sun; no Amex.*

Café Emm W1   £ 23   ④❸❸

17 Frith St   7437 0723   4–2A
*"Food doesn't come much cheaper" – not in Soho anyway –
than at this "lively" budget bistro, where there's "always
a massive queue".* / www.cafeemm.com; 10.30 pm, Fri & Sat 12.30 am;
closed Sat L & Sun L; no Amex; no booking at D.

Café Fish W1   £ 38   ❸④④

36-40 Rupert St   7287 8989   4–3A
*For "good fish without frills", served in a rather "standard"
atmosphere, this long-established Theatrelander (which moved
a year or so ago) retains quite a following; standards are
slipping, however, and it can seem a "cold" and "unfriendly"
place.* / www.santeonline.co.uk; 11.30 pm, Sun 9 pm; no smoking area.

Café Flo   £ 32   ⑤④④

11 Haymarket, SW1   7976 1313   4–4A
51 St Martin's Ln, WC2   7836 8289   4–4C
25-35 Gloucester Rd, SW7   7589 1383   5–1B
127 Kensington Church St, W8   7727 8142   6–2B
334 Upper St, N1   7226 7916   8–3D
205 Haverstock Hill, NW3   7435 6744   8–2A
38-40 Ludgate Hill, EC4   7329 3900   9–2A
*Even some who find these French-owned brasseries "reliable"
think them "expensive for what they are", and many just
dismiss them as "dreary" – "I expected little and got less".*
/ 11.30 pm.

Café Grove W11   £ 20   ④④❸

253a Portobello Rd   7243 1094   6–1A
*"Great views" make this first-floor Boho café, with its large
terrace overlooking Portobello Market, a prime breakfasting
spot – but only "when the sun is shining".* / www.cafegrove.com;
10 pm, L only in winter; closed Sat D & Sun D in summer; no credit cards;
no booking.

Café Indiya E1   £ 23   ❷❷❸

30 Alie St   7481 8288   9–3D
*It's little-known, but fans of this isolated east-City spot proclaim
the "ridiculously good value" of its "quality" Indian fare.*
/ 11.45 pm; closed Sun; no smoking area.

Café Japan NW11   £ 27   ❶❸④

626 Finchley Rd   8455 6854   1–1B
*"Outstanding sushi" and other "great, inexpensive food" is
winning an ever-wider audience for this "homely" and
"crowded" fixture, near Golders Green BR; it's usually "full of
local Japanese families".* / 10.30 pm; closed Mon & Tue L; no Amex;
no smoking area; set D £13(FP).

Café Laville W2   £ 27   ④④❶

453 Edgware Rd   7706 2620   8–4A
*It's the "great location over the canal" – not the "OK food and
service" – which makes a visit to this intriguingly-situated Maida
Vale café so special.* / www.cafelaville.co.uk; 10 pm; no Amex; no smoking
area.

Café Lazeez £ 37 ❸④④

21 Dean St, W1   7434 9393   4–2A
93-95 Old Brompton Rd, SW7   7581 9993   5–2C
88 St John St, EC1   7253 2224   9–1B

"The food has deteriorated, and prices have gone up"; it's a real shame that this "Anglicised Indian" chain seems to be losing its way – on a good day, it still delivers "interesting" cooking (if in "small portions") in a "stylish" environment. / www.cafelazeez.com; EC1 9 pm – W1 11.45 pm, Fri & Sat 1.30 am – SW7 12.30 am, Sun 10.30 pm; EC1 closed Sun; SW7, no smoking area; set weekday L £23(FP).

Café Med £ 33 ④❸❷

22-25 Dean St, W1   7287 9007   4–2A
184a Kensington Park Rd, W11   7221 1150   6–1B
320 Goldhawk Rd, W6   8741 1994   7–1B
21 Loudon Rd, NW8   7625 1222   8–3A
370 St John's St, EC1   7278 1199   8–3D

"Nothing special, but a good fall-back" – it's the "youthful" and "relaxed" atmosphere which is the strength of this "basic" grills-and-salads chain. / 11.30 pm; set weekday L £21(FP).

Café Mozart N6 £ 21 ❸④❷

17 Swains Ln   8348 1384   8–1B

With its "Continental atmosphere" and pavement tables, this pâtisserie-cum-bistro by Hampstead Heath is "often crowded"; "excellent coffee" and "great all-day breakfasts" are its forte, but there are also "tasty" Eastern European dishes. / 10 pm; no Amex; no smoking; no booking at L.

Café Nikolaj
The Caviar House W1 £ 45 ❸❸④

161 Piccadilly   7409 0445   3–3C

They change the format almost annually at this lofty dining room behind the St James's Caviar House (formerly Cave, RIP), but it never wins much of a following; still, if money is no great object, it's "worth trying if you like the (limited) menu". / www.caviar-house.com; 10 pm; closed Sun.

Café Pacifico WC2 £ 26 ④⑤❸

5 Langley St   7379 7728   4–2C

It's "still the best Mexican in London (sadly)", but "they could do so much better" at this "raucous" Covent Garden cantina, which offers "bland" cooking, and "casual and rude" service. / 11.45 pm; no smoking area; no booking, except Sun-Tue.

Café Pasta £ 24 ⑤④④

15 Greek St, W1   7434 2545   4–2A
184 Shaftesbury Ave, WC2   7379 0198   4–2B
2-4 Garrick St, WC2   7497 2779   4–3C
229-231 Kensington High St, W8   7937 6314   5–1A
373 Kensington High St, W8   7610 5552   7–1D
200 Haverstock Hill, NW3   7431 8531   8–2A
94 Upper Richmond Rd, SW15   8780 2224   10–2B
8 High St, SW19   8944 6893   10–2B
"Bad pasta, worse everything else" -- the mighty PizzaExpress
should sort out, or ditch, this dismal spin-off brand.
/ www.pizzaexpress.co.uk/cpasta.htm; 11 pm-midnight; some branches have
no smoking areas; not all branches take bookings.

Café Portugal SW8 £ 27 ❸❷④

5a-6a Victoria Hs, South Lambeth Rd   7587 1962   10–1D
This "family run", "genuinely Portuguese" Vauxhall fixture is
a "very friendly" and "inexpensive" place; it can get rather
"smoky". / www.outworld.ision.co.uk/cafe; 11 pm.

Café Rouge £ 26 – – –

15 Frith St, W1   7437 4307   4–2A
46-48 James St, W1   7487 4847   3–1A
34 Wellington St, WC2   7836 0998   4–3D
27-31 Basil St, SW3   7584 2345   5–1D
855 Fulham Rd, SW6   7371 7600   10–1B
31 Kensington Park Rd, W11   7221 4449   6–1A
Whiteley's, 151 Queensway, W2   7221 1509   6–1C
227-229 Chiswick High Rd, W4   8742 7447   7–2A
85 Strand on the Green, W4   8995 6575   1–3A
158 Fulham Palace Rd, W6   8741 5037   7–2C
98-100 Shepherd's Bush Rd, W6   7602 7732   7–1C
2 Lancer Sq, Kensington Ch St, W8   7938 4200   5–1A
30 Clifton Rd, W9   7286 2266   8–4A
6 South Grove, N6   8342 9797   8–1B
38-39 High St, NW3   7435 4240   8–1A
120 St John's Wood High St, NW8   7722 8366   8–3A
Hay's Galleria, Tooley St, SE1   7378 0097   9–4D
39-49 Parkgate Rd, SW11   7924 3565   5–4C
200 Putney Br Rd, SW15   8788 4257   10–2B
26 High St, SW19   8944 5131   10–2B
40 Abbeville Rd, SW4   8673 3399   10–2D
10 Cabot Sq, E14   7537 9696   11–1C
140 Fetter Ln, EC4   7242 3469   9–2A
Hillgate Hs, Limeburner Ln, EC4   7329 1234   9–2A
Whitbread finally seems set to put the "pathetic" Café Rouge
formula out of its misery; a July '01 visit to the Frith Street
prototype for the replacement 'Rouge' format found it a vast
improvement, but it's early days... / www.caferouge.co.uk; 11 pm – City,
E14 & W2 earlier; City, E14 & W2 closed some or all of weekend.

Café Spice Namaste £ 32 ❷❷❷

247 Lavender Hill, SW11 7738 1717 10–2C
16 Prescot St, E1 7488 9242 11–1A

"Adventurous combinations" create *"unusual, but vivid tastes"*
at Cyrus Todiwala's large and colourful east-City Indian;
feedback on the Battersea offshoot is limited but positive.
/ 10.30 pm – SW11 Sat 11.30 pm; E1 closed Sat L & Sun – SW11 closed
Mon, Tue-Sat D only, Sun open for L & D; set Sun L £17(FP).

Caffè Nero £ 11 ❸❸❸

2 Charlotte St, W1 7580 7584
225 Regent St, W1 7491 0763
43 Frith St, W1 7434 3887
62 Brewer St, W1 7437 1497
70 Piccadilly, W1 7629 3036
79 Tottenham Court Rd, W1 7580 3885
2 Lancaster Pl, WC2 7836 6346
29 Southampton St, WC2 7240 3433
30 Monmouth St, WC2 7240 8918
32 Cranbourn St, WC2 7836 6772
65-72 Strand, WC2 7930 8483
115 King's Rd, SW3 7352 9008
66 Old Brompton Rd, SW7 7589 1760
168 Portobello Rd, W11 7243 6300
53 Notting Hill Gate, W11 7727 6505
113 Westbourne Grove, W2 7243 5882
184a Edgware Rd, W2 7724 5533
192 Chiswick High Rd, W4 8742 0087
1-5 King St, W6 8741 9939
7 Jamestown Rd, NW1 7482 6969
1 Hampstead High St, NW3 7431 5958
20 St John's Hill, SW11 7978 4750
95 Putney High St, SW15 8785 9762
186 Clapham High St, SW4 7627 8668
22-24 Wormwood St, EC2 7588 4848
Winchester Hs, London Wall, EC2 7588 6001
23 Eastcheap, EC3 7626 3628
88 Leadenhall St, EC3 7621 9883

"The best of the coffee bars", this growing chain numbers
"excellent" lattes, *"brilliant"* espressos and *"good"* paninis
among its market-leading attractions. / 8 pm-11 pm – City branches
earlier – Frith St 2 am, Thu-Sun 4 am; City branches closed Sat & Sun;
no credit cards; no booking.

Caffè Uno £ 26 ④❸④

100 Baker St, W1 7486 8606 2–1A
28 Binney St, W1 7499 9312 3–2A
5 Argyll St, W1 7437 2503 3–1C
64 Tottenham Court Rd, W1 7636 3587 2–1C
24 Charing Cross Rd, WC2 7240 2524 4–3B
37 St Martin's Ln, WC2 7836 5837 4–4C
106 Queensway, W2 7229 8470 6–1C
11 Edgware Rd, W2 7723 4898 6–1D
163-165 Chiswick High Rd, W4 8742 1942 7–2A

Caffè Uno cont'd
9 Kensington High St, W8   7937 8961   5–1A
62 Upper St, N1   7226 7988   8–3D
4 South Grove, N6   8342 8662   8–1B
40-42 Parkway, NW1   7428 9124   8–3B
122 St John's Wood High St, NW8   7722 0400   8–3A
375 Lonsdale Rd, SW13   8876 3414   10–1A
"Bland but dependable" – this *"nice"* Italian chain may be *"uninteresting"*, but it's useful enough for a *"quick, cheerful and reasonably priced"* meal. / www.caffeuno.co.uk; 10 pm-midnight; some branches have no smoking areas.

La Cage Imaginaire NW3   £ 28   ❸❷❸
16 Flask Walk   7794 6674   8–1A
"Blissfully free of the local trendies", this *"traditional little French restaurant"* in a quaint Hampstead lane is *"always welcoming"*, and serves *"tasty and well presented"* fare. / 11 pm, Sat 11.30 pm; closed Mon.

Calabash
Africa Centre WC2   £ 23   ④④④
38 King St   7836 1976   4–3C
The dated basement of Covent Garden's Africa Centre is one of the few in town attempting sub-Saharan cooking; results are generally *"OK"*. / 10.30 pm; closed Sat L & Sun; no Mastercard or Amex.

Caldesi W1   £ 44   ❸❸④
15-17 Marylebone Ln   7935 9226   3–1A
Regulars salute the *"proper seasonal Tuscan food"* at this *"crowded"*, old-style Italian near the Wigmore Hall; service strikes some as *"over-familiar"*. / www.caldesi.com; 11 pm; closed Sat L & Sun; no smoking area.

Calzone   £ 23   ❸❸④
335 Fulham Rd, SW10   7352 9797   5–3B
2a Kensington Park Rd, W11   7243 2003   6–2B
35 Upper St, N1   7359 9191   8–3D
66 Heath St, NW3   7794 6775   8–1A
"Excellent pizza, for a chain" is helping these *"starkly decorated"* spots to make something of a comeback. / 11 pm-midnight – SW10 Fri & Sat 12.30 am.

Cambio de Tercio SW5   £ 37   ❷❶❶
163 Old Brompton Rd   7244 8970   5–2B
"Authentic", *"vibrant"* and *"different"* – this *"buzzy"* Earl's Court venture is emerging as a *"great"* destination, where *"wonderful and efficient"* staff serve *"some of the best Spanish food in London"*. / 11.30 pm.

Camden Brasserie NW1   £ 31   ❸❷❸
216 Camden High St   7482 2114   8–2B
It's *"predictable"*, but that's the joy of this *"dependable"* fixture, which delivers *"great bistro food"* – much of it charcoal-grilled – at *"reasonable prices"*. / 11.30 pm; no Amex.

Cantaloupe EC2   £31   ❸❸❷
35-42 Charlotte Rd   7613 4411   9–1D
It gets a bit "packed with shouty suits" these days, but this "very trendy and informal" Shoreditch bar is still "fun", and still offers a "good selection of tapas"; there's also a (slightly) quieter restaurant at the rear. / www.cantaloupe.co.uk; 11.30 pm; bar menu only Sat L & Sun.

Cantina del Ponte SE1   £38   ④⑤④
36c Shad Thames   7403 5403   9–4D
As ever, it's the "abysmal" service which really grates at Conran's "overpriced" Tower Bridge-side pizzeria; that's a pity, as its perennially poor ratings edged up this year and its alfresco tables have a "wonderful aspect". / www.conran.com; 10.45 pm; set weekday L & D £24(FP).

Cantina Italia N1   £32   ❸❷④
19 Canonbury Ln   7226 9791   8–2D
"Your basic friendly Italian", near the top of Islington's Upper Street, where "very good pizza" is a top attraction; it can get "too loud", and the basement is worth avoiding. / 11 pm; D only; no Amex; no smoking area.

Cantina Vinopolis
Vinopolis SE1   £36   ④④❸
1 Bank End   7940 8333   9–3C
"Forgettable food, but great arches" – the cathedral-like space in which the restaurant of this South Bank œnophiles' theme-park is housed is sadly a greater attraction than its "mediocre" cooking; as you'd expect, there's an "excellent choice of wine". / www.vinopolis.co.uk; 10.15 pm; closed Sun D; no smoking area.

Cantinetta Venegazzú SW11   £33   ❷❷❷
31-32 Battersea Sq   7978 5395   5–4C
"Service and portions can be erratic", but that may be part of the "wonderful authenticity" that charms fans of this "hectic" Battersea Venetian; it's "cramped", but "nice outside in the summer". / 11 pm; set weekday L £16(FP).

Canyon TW10   £38   ⑤④❸
Riverside   8948 2944   1–4A
For an "American-style brunch in a lovely setting near the river", this well-designed Richmond two-year-old still has its advocates; prices are "high" though, especially given the number of reports of "dreadful" food and "disgraceful" service. / www.canyonfood.co.uk; 11 pm; no smoking area.

CAPITAL HOTEL SW3   £72   ❷❷❸
22-24 Basil St   7589 5171   5–1D
Eric Chavot's "classically excellent" cooking makes this small dining room near Harrods "a Gallic heaven" for many reporters; opinions divide, though, on the "formal"-going-on-"sterile" décor. / www.capitalhotel.co.uk; 11 pm; jacket & tie required at D; set weekday L £44(FP).

LE CAPRICE SW1   £ 46   ❷❶❶
Arlington Hs, Arlington St   7629 2239   3–4C
*"Still lovely, even without Corbin and King" – this "slick",
'in'-crowd brasserie near the Ritz seems to have taken its
erstwhile owners' departure in its stride, and praise for the
"always superb" service and the "predictable but enjoyable"
cooking is as strong as ever. / midnight.*

Caraffini SW1   £ 35   ❷❶❷
61-63 Lower Sloane St   7259 0235   5–2D
*Trattorias don't come much more "friendly" and "reliable" than
this "all-time fab" spot, just south of Sloane Square; the chief
drawback with this "energetic" joint is that it's "just too
popular". / www.caraffini.co.uk; 11.30 pm; closed Sun.*

Caravaggio EC3   £ 48   ④④④
107-112 Leadenhall St   7626 6206   9–2D
*"Adequate" cooking and service which come with only
a "modicum of professionalism" make this "expensive" City
Italian a rather "over-rated" experience. / www.etruscagroup.co.uk;
10 pm; closed Sat & Sun.*

Caravan Serai W1   £ 29   ❷❸④
50 Paddington St   7935 1208   2–1A
*Even after the recent revamp, this long-standing Marylebone
fixture can feel a bit "neglected", but the Afghani cooking is
"consistently good" nonetheless. / 11 pm; closed Sun L.*

I Cardi SW10   £ 33   ❸❷④
351 Fulham Rd   7351 2939   5–3B
*Potential abounds at this "good-value" and "very friendly"
Chelsea trattoria; it has yet to arrive at the 'virtuous circle',
however, whereby customers create atmosphere, and vice-versa.
/ 11 pm.*

Carluccio's Caffè   £ 23   ❸❸❸
3-5 Barrett St, W1   7224 1122   3–1A
8 Market Pl, W1   7636 2228   3–1C
*For a "drink, snack or splurge" – "tasty Italian basics, well
executed" are proving a solid foundation for growth at the
Carluccios' mushrooming chain of "bustling" café/delis.
/ www.carluccios.com; 11 pm; no booking weekday L.*

Carnevale EC1   £ 25   ❷❸④
135 Whitecross St   7250 3452   9–1B
*There are "no frills" at this "cramped" spot "near the
Barbican", but its "inventive and substantial" fare makes it
"an exemplary veggie". / www.carnevalerestaurant.co.uk; 10.30 pm;
closed Sat L & Sun; only Switch.*

Casale Franco N1   £ 31   ❸❸❷
rear of 134-137 Upper St   7226 8994   8–3D
*"Still going strong" – and once more on an even keel – this
"traditional but not clichéd" Islington Italian, hidden away down
an alley, is an "all-time favourite" for some locals; "good, large
thin-crust pizzas" win particular praise. / 11 pm, Sun 9 pm; closed
Mon, Tue-Fri D only, Sat & Sun open L & D; no smoking area; no booking.*

Cassia Oriental W1 £ 37 ❷❸❸
12 Berkeley Sq   7629 8886   3–3B
The "broad-ranging" Asian food "is not wildly exciting", but – for
the heart of Mayfair – it's "not expensive" either, at this rather
undiscovered oriental yearling; the opulent setting (which
includes a "great bar") is "impressive" but slightly odd.
/ www.cassiaoriental.com; 11.30 pm; closed Sun.

The Castle SW11 £ 25 ❷❸❸
115 Battersea High St   7228 8181   10–1C
"For a hangover Sunday", this "relaxed" Battersea boozer is
a "good-value" destination, and it benefits from a "nice" garden.
/ www.thecastle.co.uk; 9.45 pm; no Amex; no booking after 1.30 pm, on Sun.

Catch SW5 £ 39 ❸❸④
158 Old Brompton Rd   7370 3300   5–2B
Its corner premises are "poky" and "noisy" and its style can
seem a mite "pretentious", but many proclaim "surprisingly
good" cooking at this fashionable South Kensington fish
specialist. / 11 pm; D only, closed Sun.

Cecconi's W1 £ 49 ❸❸❸
5a Burlington Gdns   7434 1500   3–3C
"The slick, new interior" has probably been the greatest success
of this relaunched grand Mayfair Italian (which was formerly
notorious for its absurd prices); the food is "a lot better" under
the new régime, but some still judge it as "nothing special".
/ 10.45 pm; closed Sun; booking: max 6.

Centuria N1 £ 33 ❸④❸
100 St Paul's Rd   7704 2345   1–1C
It's "always good value for money", say fans of this "noisy"
Islington-fringe gastropub, where Mediterranean fare comes in
"massive" portions; service, though, can be "sloppy". / 10.45 pm;
closed weekday L; no Amex.

Chada £ 35 ❷❸④
16-17 Picton Pl, W1   7935 8212   3–1A
208-210 Battersea Park Rd, SW11   7622 2209   10–1C
The Battersea original of this mini-chain has earned a strong
local name for its "consistently good" Thai cooking, albeit served
in rather "gloomy" surroundings – the new offshoot occupies
"small but charming" premises near Selfridges. / 11 pm, Fri & Sat
11.30 pm; closed Sat L & Sun; no smoking areas.

Chamberlain's EC3 £ 70 ④❷④
23-25 Leadenhall St   7648 8690   9–2D
Even jolly, old-fashioned service isn't enough to raise this new
Leadenhall Market fish and seafood specialist to the level
demanded by its very high prices – that, at least, was our view
from an early-days visit, in July '01. / Rated on Editors' assessment;
www.chamberlains.org; 9.30 pm; closed Sat & Sun; no smoking area.

FSA

Chamomile NW3 £12 ❸❸❸
45 England's Ln 7586 4580 8–2B
"The best-value breakfast in town" is vaunted by fans of this simple Belsize Park café/pâtisserie, whose staff are *"so nice"*. / 6 pm; L only; no Amex; no smoking area; no booking.

Champor-Champor SE1 £28 ❶❶❷
62 Weston St 7403 4600 9–4C
"Odd décor, brilliant food" – it's certainly *"an experience"* to visit this tiny Borough newcomer, where a chef from The Birdcage (the restaurant now known as Archipelago) realises a madly eclectic (mainly Asian) menu surprisingly successfully. / www.champor-champor.com; 10.30 pm; closed Mon L, Sat L & Sun; booking: max 8.

The Chapel NW1 £27 ❸④④
48 Chapel St 7402 9220 6–1D
"It's hard to get a table" at this *"very crowded"* and *"noisy"* gastropub near Edgware Road, not least due to cooking that's *"above-average"* and *"good value"*. / 9.50 pm.

Chapter Two SE3 £32 ❸❸❸
43-45 Montpelier Vale 8333 2666 1–4D
"Still good, given the location"; the '90s décor is *"a bit clichéd"*, and the food may be a touch *"over-rated"*, but this Blackheath venture still wins an impressive volume of praise for its *"consistent"* standards. / 10.30 pm, Fri & Sat 11.30 pm.

Charlotte Street Hotel W1 £48 ⑤❸④
15 Charlotte St 7907 4000 2–1C
"Expensive, but tasteless in every sense" – reporters are mystified about the alleged attractions of this would-be trendy Fitzrovia design-hotel dining room. / www.firmdale.com; 10.30 pm; closed Sun (open to residents only).

Che SW1 £50 ④④④
23 St James's St 7747 9380 3–4D
"Distinctive" but *"corporate"*, this first-floor dining room – which boasts an *"interesting"* wine list and a well-stocked humidor – is fine for a *"St James's business lunch"*; the cooking is *"uninteresting"*, though, making it hard to argue with those who proclaim this just *"another wasted location"*. / 11.30 pm; closed Sat L & Sun; set weekday L £31(FP).

Chelsea Bun Diner £22 ❸❷❸
9a Lamont Rd, SW10 7352 3635 5–3B
70 Battersea Bridge Rd, SW11 7738 9009 5–4C
"From an American gut-buster to a continental" – there's *"no better place for Sunday morning breakfast"* than these *"classy greasy spoons"*; the Chelsea original is the better, and better-known, member of the duo. / SW10 10.45 pm – SW11 L only; no Amex.

FSA

Chelsea Kitchen SW3 £ 12 ④❸④
98 King's Rd   7589 1330   5–2D
"It's very cheap, and you get what you pay for" at this
"zero-sophistication" Chelsea survivor from the '60s. / 11.45 pm;
no credit cards; need 4+ to book.

The Chelsea Ram SW10 £ 30 ❷④❷
32 Burnaby St   7351 4008   5–4B
"A top place for relaxing, reading the newspaper and eating
well", this "comfortable" boozer in a distant Chelsea backstreet
maintains its reputation for "consistently good pub food".
/ www.chelsearam.com; 9.45 pm; no booking, Sun.

CHEZ BRUCE SW17 £ 43 ❶❶❷
2 Bellevue Rd   8672 0114   10–2C
Bruce Poole's "consistently ace" cooking helps guarantee
"a fantastic meal" at this monumentally popular Wandsworth
Common-sider – "friendly" and "knowledgeable" service and
a "great" wine list help make it a "brilliant" "all-rounder".
/ 10.30 pm; closed Sun D; booking: max 6.

Chez Gérard £ 33 ④④④
31 Dover St, W1   7499 8171   3–3C
8 Charlotte St, W1   7636 4975   2–1C
119 Chancery Ln, WC2   7405 0290   2–2D
45 East Ter, Covent Garden, WC2   7379 0666   4–3D
9 Belvedere Rd, SE1   7202 8470   2–3D
84-86 Rosebery Ave, EC1   7833 1515   9–1A
64 Bishopsgate, EC2   7588 1200   9–2D
14 Trinity Sq, EC3   7480 5500   9–3D
As a "good reliable business venue", this popular steak/frites
chain has gathered many supporters over the years;
it's "deteriorating", though, and there are increasing reports of
"patchy" service and "mediocre" cooking. / www.santeonline.com;
10 pm-11.30 pm; Charlotte St closed Sat L – Dover St & SE1 closed
Sat L & Sun L – EC1 closed Sat L & Sun D – EC2, EC3 & Chancery Ln closed
Sat & Sun; no smoking areas.

Chez Liline N4 £ 30 ❶❸⑤
101 Stroud Green Rd   7263 6550   8–1D
Ignore appearances – this "dilapidated" Finsbury Park
institution is "still going strong", and its Mauritian seafood
cooking offers some "amazing" and "fresh" flavours. / 11 pm;
closed Mon L & Sun L.

Chez Lindsay TW10 £ 26 ❷❷❷
11 Hill Rise   8948 7473   1–4A
"Very good crêpes and cider" are highlights of the "authentic"
Breton cuisine on offer at this "informal" and "very friendly"
fixture, near Richmond Bridge. / 11 pm; no Amex.

Chez Moi W11 £ 40 ❷❶❷
1 Addison Ave   7603 8267   6–2A
"Amusing service" enlivens this Holland Park "old favourite",
which has "very romantic" décor and offers "predictable but
good" Gallic food. / www.chezmoi-restaurant.co.uk; 10.30 pm; closed
Mon L, Sat L & Sun; booking: max 8; set weekday L £23(FP).

Chezmax SW10   £ 44   ❶❶❷
168 Ifield Rd   7835 0874   5–3A
"Terrific" French country cooking and a "theatrical" and
"entertaining" maître d' feature largely in reports on this
"intimate" and very "romantic" Earl's Court-fringe basement,
which is widely noted for its "all-round excellence". / 11 pm; closed
Sun.

cheznico
Grosvenor House Hotel W1   £ 87   ❸④⑤
90 Park Ln   7409 1290   3–3A
"Absurd" prices are back – Nico Ladenis's flirtation with
a cheaper populist formula may have generated column inches,
but his Mayfair dining room has quietly returned to being just as
expensive as it ever was; even those who find the cooking
"wonderful" say the place is "dull in many other ways",
and service is well below par. / 10.55 pm; closed Sat L & Sun.

Chiang Mai W1   £ 32   ❶❸④
48 Frith St   7437 7444   4–2A
"Unbeatable for Thai cooking" – this "authentic" Soho "classic"
remains the best in the West End; the ambience is still pretty
dreary but, amazingly, "after all these years, the service is
beginning to improve". / 11 pm; closed Sun L; no smoking area.

Chimes SW1   £ 24   ⑤④❸
26 Churton St   7821 7456   2–4B
Some still like the "good English pies" and "classic fruit wines
and cider" at this Pimlico stalwart, but reporters' overall food
assessment is "average-to-bad". / 10.15 pm.

China City WC2   £ 23   ❸④❸
25a Lisle St   7734 3388   4–3A
"The food tends to be good" (particularly the "great dim sum"),
and service is tolerable at this huge Chinatown establishment,
which is quite smart by the standards of the area. / 11.45 pm;
no smoking area; need 6+ to book & no booking Sun L.

China House W1   £ 30   ④⑤④
160 Piccadilly   7499 6996   3–3C
There aren't many "reasonably priced" places near the Ritz,
so this "glorified noodle bar" – with its "great" Edwardian
interior – was a welcome arrival last year; it's quickly become
"a bit of a machine", though, and one whose performance is
sadly rather "indifferent". / www.chinahouse.co.uk; 11.45 pm; closed Sun;
no smoking area.

Chinon W14   £ 35   ❶❸❸
23 Richmond Way   7602 4082   7–1C
"Outstanding" French food in "huge portions" offers "amazing
value-for-money" at this "remarkably consistent", if somewhat
"eccentric", hide-away, in a Shepherd's Bush backstreet; many
find the "intimate" setting "romantic". / 10.30 pm; D only, closed Sun.

Chiswick Restaurant W4   £ 34   ❸❸④
131-133 Chiswick High Rd   8994 6887   7–2A
*"A refurb has improved the atmosphere", and also, it seems,
the "imaginative" cooking at this "crowded" "neighbourhood"
spot. / 11 pm; closed Sat L & Sun D; no smoking area.*

Chives SW10   £ 38   ❷❸④
204 Fulham Rd   7351 4747   5–3B
*"Haute cuisine at bargain prices" is hardly the Chelsea norm
and it wins high praise for this Red Pepper Group yearling;
the "bare" décor, though, is not an asset – "are they saving up
for the paintings?" / 10.30 pm; D only, closed Sun.*

Chor Bizarre W1   £ 43   ❸❸❸
16 Albemarle St   7629 9802   3–3C
*Stuffed with bric-à-brac, this Mayfair Indian offers "tasty
dishes", but at prices which dim enthusiasm.
/ www.chorbizarrerestaurant.com; 11.30 pm.*

Christian's W4   £ 32   ❸❷❸
1 Station Pde   8995 0382   1–3A
*Regulars applaud this "eccentric and friendly local", opposite
Chiswick BR, where the "temperamental" Gallic cooking "can
be excellent". / 10.30 pm; closed Mon & Sun.*

Christopher's   £ 47   ④④❸
101 Buckingham Palace Rd, SW1   7976 5522   2–4B
18 Wellington St, WC2   7240 4222   4–3D
*Fans love the "guaranteed" ambience and the "reliable" surf 'n'
turf menu at this "attractive" Covent Garden American, saying
it's "great for business" and a "cool" brunch venue; however,
it's also "pricey" and rather "overblown", and some discern an
"attitude problem"; (the Victoria offshoot provoked no
feedback). / www.christophersgrill.com; 11.45 pm; closed Sun D; pre-th.
£30(FP).*

Chuen Cheng Ku W1   £ 25   ❸④④
17 Wardour St   7437 1398   4–3A
*"Still the most exciting dim sum experience", say fans of this
vast and "lively" Chinatown landmark, where there's even the
"odd smile" from the trolley-drivers; the evening fare is
"reasonable" and "quite cheap". / 11.45 pm; no smoking area.*

Chula W6   £ 28   ❸④④
116 King St   8741 5757   7–2C
*It's a bit on the pretentious side but – on the basis of our
August '01 visit – this sparse Indian café offers some tasty
dishes, and certainly helps address the culinary deficit on
Hammersmith's unlovely high street. / Rated on Editors' assessment;
www.chula.co.uk; 11 pm.*

Churchill Arms W8   £ 17   ②④②
119 Kensington Church St   7792 1246   6–2B
"It's hard to get a booking, but worth it" at this *"cheerful"*
annexe to a Kensington boozer, where the *"freshly cooked Thai
dishes for around a fiver"* are a *"bargain"*; service can be
"sloppy". / 9.30 pm; closed Sun D; no Amex; no booking at L.

Chutney Mary SW10   £ 40   ②③③
535 King's Rd   7351 3113   5–4B
"A very different menu and approach" has made this
"consistent" distant-Chelsea *"colonial Indian"* one of the most
popular subcontinentals in town for many years; *"there's a lot
more competition these days"*, however, and ratings slid slightly
this year. / www.realindianfood.com; 11.30 pm; no smoking area; pre-th.
£26(FP).

Chutneys NW1   £ 18   ②④④
124 Drummond St   7388 0604   8–4C
"It's hard to beat the help-yourself buffet for value", say
supporters of this *"Spartan, clean and efficient"* Indian, near
Euston. / 11 pm; no Amex or Switch; no smoking at L.

Cibo W14   £ 40   ②③③
3 Russell Gdns   7371 6271   7–1D
"Wonderful large and colourful plates of great Italian food" and
a *"really stimulating wine list"* still win praise for this *"unusual"*
Olympia fixture; sliding ratings, however, support those who say
it's a *"fading star"*. / www.ciborestaurant.com; 11 pm; closed
Sat L & Sun D.

Cicada EC1   £ 32   ②②②
132-136 St John St   7608 1550   9–1B
"Always fun, and the food is good for such a trendy place" –
this *"friendly"*, *"noisy"* and *"chaotic"* Clerkenwell bar/restaurant
delivers an *"imaginative"* Pacific Rim menu with surprising
consistency. / www.cicada.nu; 10.45 pm; closed Sat L & Sun; no smoking
area.

Cigala WC1   £ 38   ④④④
54 Lamb's Conduit St   7405 1717   2–1D
Press reviews vaunting this *"trendy"* Bloomsbury Spaniard as
a 'new Moro' are only partially reflected by reporters – some do
find *"great food, simply cooked"*, but the more general view is
that this *"cramped"* place is *"disappointing, given all the hype"*.
/ 10.45 pm; closed Sun D; no booking at D.

Cinnamon Cay SW11   £ 27   ②②③
87 Lavender Hill   7801 0932   10–1C
Some say the place *"just misses all round"*, but the *"very tasty
and interesting"* Pacific Rim cooking at this year-old *"local"* has
won it quite a Battersea following. / www.cinnamoncay.co.uk; 11 pm;
closed Mon L & Sun D.

The Cinnamon Club SW1   £ 44   ❶❷❷
Great Smith St   7222 2555   2–4C
*Iqbal Wahhab's new Westminster subcontinental – two years in
preparation – was "worth the wait"; "beautifully presented,
subtly flavoured" Anglo-Indian cuisine is slickly served in
a "gentleman's club setting" which most find "stylish" (but
which some think "lacking in atmosphere").*
/ www.cinnamonclub.com; 11 pm; closed Sat L & Sun D; no smoking area;
booking: max 8; set brunch £21(FP).

Circus W1   £ 44   ④❸❸
1 Upper James St   7534 4000   3–2D
*It's "not cosy" and the cooking is "so-so", but this "slick" and
"noisy" Soho spot has quite a business following of "media
types", and it's good "pre-theatre" too; "the downstairs bar has
great vibes".* / www.circusbar.co.uk; midnight; closed Sat L & Sun; set
weekday L & pre-th. £26(FP).

City Miyama EC4   £ 55   ❶❶④
17 Godliman St   7489 1937   9–3B
*"Very formal" and rather "dull" it may be, but this City
Japanese is "one of the best in town", thanks to its "sensational
sushi" and the "great teppan-yaki bar".* / 9.30 pm; closed
Sat D & Sun; set always available £35(FP).

CITY RHODES EC4   £ 59   ❷❷❸
New Street Sq   7583 1313   9–2A
*Gary Rhodes's "slick", if rather "clinical", operation near Fleet
Street is once again voted reporters' safest bet for a City lunch
– "spot on" service is "efficient without being overbearing",
and the "beautifully-presented" British cooking is often
"excellent".* / 9 pm; closed Sat & Sun.

CLARKE'S W8   £ 55   ❶❶❷
124 Kensington Church St   7221 9225   6–2B
*It's "Sally's choice" – ie none for diners – at Ms Clarke's
long-established Kensington restaurant, but few seem to care, as
her "fresh", deceptively "simple" Californian-style dishes "never
fail", and service is "superb"; the atmosphere strikes most as
"intimate", but it can also seem a touch "dull".*
/ www.sallyclarke.com; 10 pm; closed Sat & Sun; no smoking area at L,
no smoking at D.

CLUB GASCON EC1   £ 40   ❶❷❷
57 West Smithfield   7796 0600   9–2B
*"Wine, foie gras, location, atmosphere..." – this "unique,
and hugely enjoyable" Gascon tapas bar in Smithfield has it all,
and its "superb and creative" cuisine has won a huge following.*
/ 10 pm, Fri & Sat 10.30 pm; closed Sat L & Sun.

Coffee Republic   £ 7   ❸❸❸

1 George St, W1   7935 2191
11 Hanover St, W1   7495 8224
119-121 Baker St, W1   7224 2117
19 Soho Sq, W1   7434 0503
2 South Molton St, W1   7629 4567
23 Rathbone Pl, W1   7436 6046
322 Regent St, W1   7436 8075
38 Berwick St, W1   7437 2328
39 Great Marlborough St, W1   7734 5529
63 Goodge St, W1   7631 5345
99 Tottenham Court Rd, W1   7580 4678
1-3 Villiers St, WC2   7930 0649
105-107 Kingsway, WC2   7405 7329
18 Garrick St, WC2   7240 1323
234 Strand Law Courts, WC2   7583 2456
7 Kingsway, WC2   7240 0078
73-74 Strand, WC2   7379 7084
178 Fulham Rd, SW10   7373 0919
157 King's Rd, SW3   7351 3178
12-14 Fulham Broadway, SW6   7385 2104
72 Old Brompton Rd, SW7   7823 8120
214 Portobello Rd, W11   7229 6259
8 Pembridge Rd, W11   7229 6698
130 Edgware Rd, W2   7724 6643
280 Chiswick High Rd, W4   8995 7772
376 Chiswick High Rd, W4   8742 7854
197 Kensington High St, W8   7938 4261
7 Islington High St, N1   7833 9133
11-13 Parkway, NW1   7485 3444
132 Putney High St, SW15   8789 7808
Unit RS190 Cabot Pl, E14   7519 6381
23 Brushfield St, E1   7247 6163
87 Charterhouse St, EC1   7253 8161
25 Exchange Sq, EC2   7588 5130
47 London Wall, EC2   7588 2220
132 Minories, EC3   7481 2438
25 St Mary Axe, EC3   7623 6564
26 Eastcheap, EC3   7623 0659
59-60 Cornhill, EC3   7623 2926
74 Leadenhall Mkt, EC3   7626 1993
147 Fleet St, EC4   7353 0900
3 Fleet Pl, EC4   7213 9943
30-32 Ludgate Hill, EC4   7329 2522

For a "daily espresso fix that really hits the spot" these
"reliable" coffee shops are often noted as being "cheaper" (not
difficult) and "better" than most of the alternative chains.
/ 6 pm-10 pm – City branches earlier – central branches later; City & Law
Courts branches closed all or part of weekend; no credit cards; no booking.

regular updates at www.hardens.com   63

F S A

The Collection SW3   £ 42   ④⑤❸
264 Brompton Rd   7225 1212   5–2C
*For "great people-watching" (or "a fun night out with the girls"),
this "loud" Brompton Cross bar/restaurant has its place;
the "eclectic" food is "expensive for the quality", however,
and service is "pretty hopeless".* / www.the-collection.co.uk; 11.30 pm;
D only.

Le Colombier SW3   £ 36   ❸❷❷
145 Dovehouse St   7351 1155   5–2C
*"A charming patron and staff" and a "wonderful" terrace help
make this Chelsea fixture quite a local favourite; some find it
rather "stately" though, and the cooking can give the impression
of having "left its imagination at the Channel".* / 11 pm.

The Common Room SW19   £ 40   – – –
18 High St   8944 1909   10–2B
*Formerly called Utah, but still in the same ownership, this
recently-renamed Wimbledon American will have quite a job to
shake off its predecessor's "pretentious" reputation.*
/ www.utahfood.co.uk; 10.45 pm.

Como Lario SW1   £ 36   ④❷❸
22 Holbein Pl   7730 2954   5–2D
*"Great service makes it a joy", say regulars at this "noisy" and
"old-fashioned" trattoria near Sloane Square; the food, though,
is "unreliable".* / 11.30 pm; closed Sun.

CONNAUGHT W1   £ 81   ❸❶❷
Carlos Pl   7499 7070   3–3B
*Will the arrival of the sixth head chef in just over a century
shake this "wonderfully old-fashioned" Mayfair dining room to
the core? – 'new' boy Jerome Ponchelle has already worked here
since 1988, so change at this "country house in the middle of
London" seems a mercifully remote prospect.*
/ www.the-connaught.co.uk; 10.45 pm; Grill closed Sat L; jacket & tie required;
appreciated if guests try to refrain from smoking; set weekday L £49(FP).

Conrad Gallagher W1   £ 62   ❷❷❷
179 Shaftesbury Ave   7836 3111   4–2B
*A groovy basement, on the outskirts of Covent Garden, provides
an odd setting for the new London dining room of a top Irish
chef; on an August '01 visit, we took to the 'vibe', and were
impressed by first-rate cooking; it comes at a pretty price,
though, and whether quality can be maintained on this scale is
a moot point.* / Rated on Editors' assessment; www.conradgallagher.co.uk;
11.30 pm; set weekday L & pre-th. £41(FP).

Conrad Hotel SW10   £ 43   ❸❸❸
Chelsea Harbour   7823 3000   5–4B
*With its "mind-boggling" range of dishes and the "super"
harbour view, this distant-Chelsea hotel offers "a great
champagne buffet brunch" (just on Sundays); "the only minus"?
– "loads of children".* / 10.30 pm; no smoking area.

Il Convivio SW1   £ 39   ❷❷❷

143 Ebury St   7730 4099   2–4A
"Real Italian cooking" that's "reasonably priced" by Belgravia
standards, and staff who are "so professional" are winning
increasing acclaim for this "friendly and stylish" yearling.
/ www.etruscagroup.co.uk; 10.30 pm; closed Sun.

The Cook House SW15   £ 37   – – –

56 Lower Richmond Rd   8785 2300   10–1A
As we were going to press, a new chef took over at this Putney
corner bistro, and the menu has been given a Gallic makeover.
/ www.the-cookhouse.com; 10.30 pm; D only, closed Mon & Sun.

Coopers Arms SW3   £ 25   ❸④❸

87 Flood St   7376 3120   5–3C
"Solid, reliable food" makes this Chelsea backstreet boozer
a handy destination – but not the special place it was a few
years ago. / www.drinkatthecoopers.co.uk; 10 pm; closed Sun D; no booking,
Sun.

Coq d'Argent EC3   £ 50   ⑤④❸

1 Poultry   7395 5000   9–2C
As "a great way to impress", this "slick" and "buzzy" sixth-floor
Conran venue in the heart of the City is hard to beat, and, with
its extensive terraces, it makes a "very attractive" sunny day
destination; the "plain" and "unadventurous" cooking, though, is
"really not worth the prices", and service is "slow".
/ www.conran.com; 10 pm; closed Sat L & Sun D.

Cork & Bottle WC2   £ 29   ④④❷

44-46 Cranbourn St   7734 7807   4–3B
"It's great for Aussie and Kiwi wines", but "don't rush" for the
mundane wine bar fare at this "crowded" cellar of long
standing, next to a sex shop off Leicester Square.
/ www.donhewitsonlondonwinebars.com; 10.15 pm; no smoking at L;
no booking after 6.30 pm.

Corney & Barrow   £ 27   ⑤④④

116 St Martin's Ln, WC2   7655 9800   4–4B
9 Cabot Sq, E14   7512 0397   11–1C
109 Old Broad Street, EC2   7638 9308   9–2C
12 Mason's Ave, EC2   7726 6030   9–2C
19 Broadgate Circle, EC2   7628 1251   9–2D
5 Exchange Sq, EC2   7628 4367   9–2D
1 Leadenhall Pl, EC3   7621 9201   9–2D
16 Royal Exchange, EC3   7929 3131   9–2C
2b Eastcheap, EC3   7929 3220   9–3C
37 Jewry St, EC3   7680 8550   9–2D
3 Fleet Pl, EC4   7329 3141   9–2A
44 Cannon Street, EC4   7248 1700   9–3B
Both at its Trafalgar Square outpost and in its City heartland
branches, these smart wine bars are "reliable" and "buzzing"
stand-bys; fans say the fare is "basic but effective", but it's also
"pricey" and can be "careless". / www.corney-barrow.co.uk; 11 pm –
WC2 midnight, Thu-Sat 2 am – Jewry Thu-Fri midnight; closed Sun.

Coromandel SW11   £ 28   ②❸④
2 Battersea Rise   7738 0038   10–2C
"High-quality" south Indian cooking is not winning this "stark"
Battersea newcomer the following it deserves – if they dimmed
the lights, custom would double overnight. / 11.30 pm; no smoking
area.

Costa's Fish Restaurant W8   £ 16   ②❷❸
18 Hillgate St   7727 4310   6–2B
"Shabby, but still good value" – this ancient chippy, just off
Notting Hill Gate, is a "cheerful" spot, offering "the best fish
and chips in the area". / 10 pm; closed Mon & Sun; no credit cards.

Costa's Grill W8   £ 15   ④④④
12-14 Hillgate St   7229 3794   6–2B
"It's maintained its value for over 40 years", declare devoted
regulars at this "real Greek", near Notting Hill Gate; for the
younger generation, though, it's dropping off the map. / 10.30 pm;
closed Sun (closed Aug); no credit cards; no smoking area.

Cotto W14   £ 37   ❸④④
44 Blythe Rd   7602 9333   7–1D
A year ago, "the critics raved" – us too – about this sparse new
spot behind Olympia; subsequently, some reporters have indeed
praised "quirky and creative" cooking, but rather too many say
it's "average". / 10.30 pm; closed Sat L & Sun.

Cottons NW1   £ 34   ❸④②
55 Chalk Farm Rd   7485 8388   8–2B
This re-launched Camden Town Caribbean was already doing
good business on our early-days (August '01) visit;
it's a characterful place, with pleasant (if fairly slow) service,
serving substantial and enjoyable fare. / Rated on Editors' assessment;
11 pm; Mon-Thu D only, Fri-Sun open L & D; no Amex.

The County Hall Restaurant
London Marriott Hotel SE1   £ 54   ⑤❸④
Queens Walk   7902 8000   2–3D
"Even the location" – opposite Westminster, and with great
views from some tables – "can't save" this "dire" and
"expensive" South Bank dining room. / 11 pm; no smoking at
breakfast.

The Court Restaurant
British Museum WC1   £ 34   ④④❷
Great Russell St   7323 8990   2–1C
The location in the British Museum's wonderful Great Court is
indeed impressive, but no reporter commented on this new
restaurant – perhaps because for the most part it offers
catering rather than cooking. / Rated on Editors' assessment;
britishmuseum@digbytrout.co.uk; 9 pm (5 pm Sun-Wed); L & tea only, except
Thu-Sat when open L & D; no Amex; no smoking.

The Cow W2 £ 39 ❷❸❷
89 Westbourne Park Rd 7221 0021 6–1B
*Thanks to its "great simple food" and "good choice of beers",
the "cosy" bar of Tom Conran's "reliable" Bayswater boozer is
often "crowded"; upstairs, in the dining room, the more
ambitious cooking is of a "high standard" – the setting is "poky
and rickety, but that's half the charm". / 11 pm; D only, closed Sun
(bar open Sun).*

Coyote Café W4 £ 27 ❸❸❸
2 Fauconberg Rd 8742 8545 7–2A
*It's a "brilliant night out" in distant Chiswick, claim local fans of
this "always lively" Tex/Mex café, with its "friendly" service and
"tasty" fare. / 10.30 pm; Mon-Thu D only, Fri-Sun open L & D.*

Cranks £ 12 ④④④
23 Barrett St, W1 7495 1340 3–1B
9-11 Tottenham St, W1 7631 3912 2–1B
17-19 Great Newport St, WC2 7836 5226 4–3B
Unit 11, 8 Adelaide St, WC2 7836 0660 4–4C
Concourse Level, 15 Cabot Pl, E14 7513 0678 11–1C
*"Definitely very pricey for what you get" – London's original
veggie chain may be "OK if you want healthy eating", but has
little else going for it. / 7 pm, Sat & Sun 8.30 pm; some branches closed
part of weekend; no credit cards; no smoking; no booking.*

Creelers SW3 £ 36 ❸❸⑤
3 Bray Pl 7838 0788 5–2D
*A Chelsea backstreet corner site which "tries hard, but lacks
atmosphere" – "good, fresh fish dishes" commend it to some.
/ www.creelers.co.uk; 10.30 pm; closed Sun; no smoking area.*

The Crescent SW3 £ 28 ④❸④
99 Fulham Rd 7225 2244 5–2C
*The "very special wine list" is the key attraction of this
Brompton Cross bar/diner – it's also "good for a quick bite".
/ 10.45 pm; no booking.*

The Criterion W1 £ 50 ④⑤❶
224 Piccadilly Circus 7930 0488 3–3D
*Suffering the perennially "surly" service at this "beautiful"
neo-Byzantine chamber was once a price worth paying for
impressive, 'school-of-MPW' Gallic cuisine; these days, however,
the food at "the most atmospheric dining room in town" is plain
"boring", and the prices are "ridiculous". / 11.30 pm; closed Sun L;
set weekday L & pre-th. £31(FP).*

Crivelli's Garden
National Gallery WC2 £ 30 ④④④
Trafalgar Sq 7747 2439 4–4B
*"Erratic" service contributes to the mixed opinions on this
"rather canteen-like" venue in the Sainsbury Wing – the
cheaper pizza part wins more praise than the grander Gallic
section (though the latter has the fountain-views). / 8.30 pm; L only,
except Wed & Sat open L & D; no smoking.*

Cross Keys SW3   £32   ④④❸

1 Lawrence St   7349 9111   5–3C

This "lively" and "attractive" pub in the backstreets of Chelsea (where food is served in a "bright conservatory") has gone "downhill", and it's now too often noted for "unimaginative" cooking, "slow" service and a generally "pretentious" approach. / www.thexkeys.co.uk; 11 pm.

Cuba Libre N1   £30   ④④❸

72 Upper St   7354 9998   8–3D

"Great cocktails" and "good hearty fun" are the key selling points of this "eclectically-decorated" Cuban, by Islington Green; its Latin American fodder is very much a secondary attraction. / 11 pm, Fri & Sat midnight; no Amex; set weekday L £19(FP).

Cucina NW3   £34   ❸❶❸

45a South End Rd   7435 7814   8–2A

"Why aren't there more good restaurants like this round here?" – "interesting", "good-value" Italian cooking and "excellent" service make this "noisy" local something of a "beacon" in perennially under-provided Hampstead. / 10.30 pm, Fri & Sat 11 pm; closed Sun D; set weekday L £20(FP).

Da Mario SW7   £30   ❸④❸

15 Gloucester Rd   7584 9078   5–1B

This "fun" venue, near the Albert Hall, has held its standards better than the PizzaExpress empire (to which it is historically related); strangely, there's a disco in the basement. / www.damario.co.uk; 11.30 pm; no Switch; set weekday L £20(FP).

Dakota W11   £41   ④④④

127 Ledbury Rd   7792 9191   6–1B

"It's a fun place" that's "still good for brunch in the sun", say fans of this once-hip Notting Hill southwest American; service is often "snotty", though, and cooking standards are distinctly uneven. / www.dakotafood.co.uk; 11 pm.

Dan's SW3   £39   ❸❷❷

119 Sydney St   7352 2718   5–3C

Critics dismiss the cooking as "average British", but it's the "discreet" and "romantic" ambience of this charming Chelsea townhouse (complete with lovely garden) that is its raison d'être. / 10.30 pm; closed Sat L & Sun.

Dan's Bar W11   £27   ④❸❸

105-107 Talbot Rd   7221 8099   6–1B

Formerly called Coin's (and still with the same owners), this Notting Hill side street café is most notable as an "achingly fashionable" brunch spot – "don't forget your copy of the New Yorker". / 10 pm; closed Mon; no Amex; no booking.

Daphne NW1   £21   ❸❷❸

83 Bayham St   7267 7322   8–3C

A "friendly family-run atmosphere" puts fans "in the right mood" to enjoy this "traditional" Camden Town Greek (with a roof terrace in summer); it serves "good, simple food" at "reasonable" prices. / 11.30 pm; closed Sun; no Amex.

Daphne's SW3   £ 50   ④④❸
110-112 Draycott Ave   7589 4257   5–2C
*Last year's 'renaissance' at this once-glamorous Brompton Cross
Italian seems to have been a blip – "mediocre" cooking and
service are once again making it seem like a "disappointing
throwback".* / 11.30 pm.

Daquise SW7   £ 21   ④④❸
20 Thurloe St   7589 6117   5–2C
*The "great, unaltered '50s décor" is the key to the "old-world
charm" of this "scruffy but pleasant" Polish tea room, by South
Kensington tube; the "honest" cooking is at least "warming",
"filling" and "cheap".* / 10.45 pm; no Amex; no smoking area; set
weekday L £10(FP).

De Cecco SW6   £ 33   ❷❷❶
189 New King's Rd   7736 1145   10–1B
*"With this combination, you can never fail", say fans of this
"always buzzing" Italian near Parson's Green – "affordable"
grub and "fabulous" service are re-establishing it as the "local
favourite".* / 11 pm; closed Sun.

Defune W1   £ 55   ❶❸❸
34 George St   7935 8311   2–1A
*"The old place was a dump", but "the new location is vastly
improved" – this long-established, "real Japanese" now has
a "much nicer" Marylebone home (a couple of streets away
from the original) in which to enjoy some of London's "best
sushi at a reasonable price".* / 11 pm; closed Sun L; no smoking; set
weekday L £30(FP).

Del Buongustaio SW15   £ 37   ④④④
283 Putney Br Rd   8780 9361   10–2B
*"Heading south rapidly" – this "cramped" spot long defied its
"unpromising" Putney location and maintained a position as one
of the better Italians in town, but of late there's been an
"amazing slump in standards".* / www.theitalianrestaurant.net; 11 pm;
closed Sun D; set weekday L £23(FP).

Delfina Studio Café SE1   £ 34   ❸❷❷
50 Bermondsey St   7357 0244   9–4D
*"It makes a change from the City" – this "bright and airy"
Bermondsey gallery has "lovely" staff, and the "innovative"
cuisine "can be excellent".* / www.delfina.org.uk; L only, closed Sat & Sun.

La Delizia SW3   £ 18   ❸④④
63-65 Chelsea Manor St   7376 4111   5–3C
*Some still say the pizza is "first-class" (and "very cheap,
especially now that you have to BYO"), but opinions are mixed
on this last relic of what was once a popular small Chelsea
chain.* / midnight; no Amex.

The Depot SW14   £ 29   ④❸❷

Mortlake High St   8878 9462   10–1A
"Poor food, good views" – the formula doesn't vary at this
Barnes riverside fixture; on Sundays, the bad news is that
"if you don't have kids, you'll hate it" – the good news is that,
if you do, there's "no panic if they start running around". / 11 pm;
no smoking area.

Le Deuxième WC2   £ 38   ❷❷❸

65a Long Acre   7379 0033   4–2D
The curtain has fallen for the last time on Magno's Brasserie
(whose proximity to the ROH had long made it a classic
pre-opera venue); an August '01 visit to what is now a sibling to
the nearby Café du Jardin found competent cooking with some
real high points, efficient service, a varied wine list and
a comfortably neutral setting. / Rated on Editors' assessment; midnight.

Dibbens EC1   £ 33   ④❸④

2 Cowcross St   7250 0035   9–1A
"Not bad, but unspectacular" – only the friendly proprietor
injects any character into this "pleasant" but anodyne venture,
near Smithfield Market. / www.dibbens.com; 11 pm; closed Sat & Sun.

Dish Dash W1   £ 31   ④④❷

57-59 Goodge St   7637 7474   2–1B
All agree the "bar is a groovy night out", but as an eatery this
Persian Fitzrovian is quite "expensive", and both food and
service can be iffy. / www.dish-dash.com; 10.30 pm; closed Sat L & Sun D.

Ditto SW18   £ 36   ④❸❸

55-57 East Hill   8877 0110   10–2B
It's been "a hit with local trendies" – as it's located in
Wandsworth, this may explain why this "nice" but "overpriced"
yearling has a slightly limited following. / www.doditto.co.uk; 11 pm;
closed Sat L & Sun D; no Amex; set weekday L £19(FP).

Diverso W1   £ 43   ❸❸④

85 Piccadilly   7491 2222   3–4C
This "stylish"-looking Italian – almost opposite the Ritz –
is tipped as an overlooked "secret" by some, but for too many
it's just "dull" and "expensive". / 11.30 pm; closed Sun L.

Diwana Bhel-Poori House NW1   £ 16   ❷④④

121-123 Drummond St   7387 5556   8–4C
"Cheap and delicious south Indian veggie fare" in a "simple"
setting has long been the stock-in-trade of this '70s survivor,
and its buffet lunch is an institution; BYO.
/ www.diwanarestaurant.com; 11.30 pm; no smoking area; need 5+ to book.

Dixie's Bar & Grill SW11   £ 21   ⑤④❸

25 Battersea Rise   7228 7984   10–2C
Who cares if the food is "dreadful"?, say fans of the "fun",
"redneck" atmosphere at this Battersea American "roadhouse".
/ 11 pm.

DK's EC2   £ 33   ❷❸❸
97-113 Curtain Rd   7729 5051   9–1D
They say it's jumping at weekends, but we dined alone one weekday in June '01 at this large, loud and impressively orange, '60s-lounge-style Shoreditch newcomer; the cooking was surprisingly good. / Rated on Editors' assessment; www.dkclub.co.uk; 10.30 pm; D only Sun-Wed, Thu-Sat open L & D.

Dôme   £ 26   – – –
57-59 Old Compton St, W1   7287 0770   4–3A
32 Long Acre, WC2   7379 8650   4–2C
8 Charing Cross Rd, WC2   7240 5556   4–4B
This well-known café chain – which has consistently underperformed in recent years – moved into new ownership in mid-2001, and the concept is under review by the new owners; we've only listed 'core' branches, as we understand that disposals are mooted. / 10.30 pm-11 pm; some branches have no smoking areas.

The Don EC4   £ 44   ❷❶❷
20 St Swithin's Ln   7626 2606   9–3C
"A wonderful surprise hidden in a City side street"; this charming "new sister to the Bleeding Heart" (similarly offering "a choice of bistro and restaurant") more than lives up to its sibling with its "good-value" Gallic cooking, its "original" wine list and its "excellent" service. / 10.30 pm; closed Sat & Sun.

don Fernando's TW9   £ 21   ❸❷❷
27f The Quadrant   8948 6447   1–4A
It's "a bit crowded", but it can be "good fun" too, at this "lively" and "pretty genuine" Spanish spot, by Richmond BR, where service is "efficient" and the tapas reasonably priced. / www.donfernando.co.uk; 11 pm; no booking.

Don Pepe NW8   £ 28   ❸❸❸
99 Frampton St   7262 3834   8–4A
You get "a real feel of Spain" at this long-established tapas bar/restaurant near Lords, whose small fan club approves of its decent grub and its "lively" atmosphere. / midnight; closed Sun.

Dorchester Grill
Dorchester Hotel W1   £ 65   ❸❷❷
53 Park Ln   7629 8888   3–3A
With its "impressively impressive" Spanish Baronial setting, its "divine" service and its "reliable" British fare (not least "excellent roast beef"), this Mayfair dining room is one of the better options for a grand, traditional meal. / www.dorchesterhotel.com; 11 pm.

Dorchester, Oriental
Dorchester Hotel W1   £ 80   ❷④④
53 Park Ln   7629 8888   3–3A
"Zero atmosphere can ruin the meal" at London's grandest Chinese, whose décor is impressive but "dull"; the "succulent" cooking is of "excellent quality" (but "incredibly expensive"). / www.dorchesterhotel.com; 11 pm; closed Sat L & Sun; no jeans or trainers; booking: max 8; set weekday L £35(FP).

Dover Street W1   £ 42   ⑤⑤④
8-10 Dover St   7629 9813   3–3C
*Even those who find these dine-and-dance Mayfair cellars
"grossly overpriced" admit that they can make "a great place
for a big party"; there is a "cheap and fast" lunch menu that
does offer "good value".* / www.doverst.co.uk; 2 am; closed Sat L & Sun;
no jeans or trainers; set weekday L £26(FP).

Down Mexico Way W1   £ 36   ⑤⑤④
25 Swallow St   7437 9895   3–3D
*"They seem to rely on their clientèle being drunk before the
food arrives", at this "terrible" and "not very Mexican" Mayfair
dive – its magnificent (listed) interior deserves better.*
/ www.downmexway.com; 11.45 pm.

Drones SW1   £ 50   ④❸④
1 Pont St   7235 9555   5–1D
*A "sophisticated" revamp and "good, classic" Gallic cooking win
some plaudits for this relaunched Belgravia veteran; the more
general impression, though, is of a "formulaic" addition to the
MPW empire that "doesn't live up to the hype".*
/ www.whitestarline.org.uk; 11 pm; set weekday L £31(FP).

Duke of Cambridge SW11   £ 27   ❸④❷
228 Battersea Bridge Rd   7223 5662   10–1C
*"Sunday lunch is a special bargain" at this "above-average"
Battersea pub/brasserie.* / 9.30 pm; no Amex; no booking, except at
weekend.

The Duke of Cambridge N1   £ 31   ❸④❷
30 St Peter's St   7359 3066   1–2C
*The organic food is "a touch pricey", but this "impressive"
Islington gastropub makes "a good effort", and the place is
usually "packed" and "full of atmosphere".* / www.singhboulton.co.uk;
10.30 pm; closed Mon L; no smoking.

The Eagle EC1   £ 22   ❷④❷
159 Farringdon Rd   7837 1353   9–1A
*"Excellent, if you like a non-stop environment" – London's
longest-established gastropub is "still the best", and still packs
'em in with its "wonderful", "rustic" Mediterranean fare;
the service "can suffer", though, and some find the smokiness
off-putting.* / 10.30 pm; closed Sun D; only Switch; no booking.

East One EC1   £ 32   ❸❸④
175-179 St John St   7566 0088   9–1A
*For a "fun night out" or a "good place to go after work", many
still recommend this "trendier version of Mongolian BBQ", north
of Smithfield; it's "nothing special", though, and "quite
expensive".* / 11.30 pm; closed Sat L & Sun D.

Eat   £ 9   ❸❸④

3 Duke Of York St, SW1   7930 0960
37 Tothill St, SW1   7222 5855
16a Soho Sq, W1   7287 7702
319 Regent St, W1   7637 9400
9a Vigo St, W1   7734 7429
34-36 High Holborn, WC1   7405 4804
39 Villiers St, WC2   7839 2282
Barge House St, SE1   7928 8179
South Bank Centre, SE1   7928 6848
Unit 1 Canada Pl, E14   7715 9658
62 London Wall, EC2   7374 9555
155 Fenchurch St, EC3   7621 0747
54-55 Cornhill, EC3   7621 1771
Exchequer Ct, 33 St Mary Axe, EC3   7623 4413
123 Cannon St, EC4   7626 0270
170 Fleet St, EC4   7583 2585
"Fabulous homemade soups" outshine the *"imaginative"*
sandwiches at these superior *"snack havens"*; they are *"a bit
pricey"* for some tastes, but they do deliver *"consistent quality"*.
/ www.eatcafe.co.uk; L only – SE1, 10.30pm; City branches & WC1 closed
Sat & Sun – Soho Sq, E14 & SW1 closed Sun; no credit cards; no smoking;
no booking.

Ebury Street Wine Bar SW1   £ 36   ④④❸

139 Ebury St   7730 5447   2–4A
*Opinions divide on this old Belgravia fixture – supporters say it's
a "cheerful" place dispensing "reliably good" fare, whereas for
doubters it's just rather "tired".* / www.eburywinebars.co.uk; 10.30 pm.

Eco   £ 26   ❷④❷

162 Clapham High St, SW4   7978 1108   10–2D
4 Market Row, Brixton Mkt, SW9   7738 3021   10–2D
"Huge and gorgeous" pizzas still pack 'em in at these *"vibrant"*
south London spots, where it's often *"difficult to get a table"*.
/ SW4 11 pm, Sat 11.30 pm – SW9 L only; SW9 closed Wed & Sun; SW9
no booking.

Ed's Easy Diner   £ 23   ④❸❷

12 Moor St, W1   7439 1955   4–2A
Trocadero, W1   7287 1951   3–3D
362 King's Rd, SW3   7352 1956   5–3B
O2 Centre, 255 Finchley Rd, NW3   7431 1958   8–2A
"Children and overgrown teenagers everywhere" still love the
"messy treat" of a trip to these *"spirit-of-the-'50s"* diners, which
serve *"great"* burgers and *"wonderful"* shakes. / midnight – SW3 &
NW3 11 pm – all branches 1 am, Fri & Sat; no booking.

Efes Kebab House   £ 26   ❸❸❸

1) 80 Gt Titchfield St, W1   7636 1953   2–1B
2) 175-177 Gt Portland St, W1   7436 0600   2–1B
*This "unique" Turkish duo of characterful Marylebone venues
serve "huge portions" of "reliable grub"; those with long
memories however, bemoan the fact that "they're not what they
used to be – even the belly-dancers".* / 11.30 pm – Gt Portland St
Fri & Sat 3 am; Gt Titchfield St closed Sun.

1837
Brown's Hotel W1   £ 55   ❸❸❸

Albemarle St   7408 1837   3–3C

Despite a "superb" wine list (and "the ability to buy good wines by the glass"), this "formal but relaxed" Mayfair dining room has never created much of a stir; its "consistent" Gallic cooking won more support this year, however. / www.brownshotel.com; 10.30 pm; closed Sat L & Sun; no smoking area; set always available £36(FP).

Elena's L'Etoile W1   £ 43   ❸❷❷

30 Charlotte St   7636 7189   2–1C

There's a "comfortable", "Continental" ambience at this Fitzrovia old-timer, which octogenarian maîtresse d' Elena Salvoni "runs with unique charm"; the Gallic fare is "reliable". / www.trpplc.com; 10.30 pm; closed Sat L & Sun.

Elephant Royale
Locke's Wharf E14   £ 27   ④❸❸

Westferry Rd   7987 7999   11–2C

Bravely located, on the tip of the Isle of Dogs (near Island Gardens DLR), this large and rather tackily-decorated new Thai benefits from a "stunning" terrace, with river-views; the cooking isn't bad, but we're with those who find it "expensive" for what it is. / 10.30 pm; no smoking area.

Elistano SW3   £ 30   ❷❷❷

25-27 Elystan St   7584 5248   5–2C

A "superb Italian stalwart" – it's the "brilliant, homely style" that makes this "fun and friendly" local hugely popular, despite its rather obscure Chelsea backstreet location. / 10.45 pm.

Emile's SW15   £ 27   ❸❷④

96-98 Felsham Rd   8789 3323   10–2B

A classic "local", this "tucked away" bistro – now shorn of its Fulham twin – offers "lovely" (if unadventurous) British cooking in a "welcoming" (if rather underpowered) environment. / 11 pm; D only, closed Sun; no Amex.

The Engineer NW1   £ 35   ❸④❷

65 Gloucester Ave   7722 0950   8–3B

This "great" Primrose Hill gastropub draws a "glamorous" and "trendy" crowd, thanks to its "easy" and "relaxed" atmosphere and the quality of its "posh pub grub"; "arrive early for a seat in the garden". / www.the-engineer.com; 10.30 pm; no Amex.

English Garden SW3   £ 42   ❸④④

10 Lincoln St   7584 7272   5–2D

The "great" conservatory remains an undoubted plus (especially as a lunch venue), but it's hard to remember that this Chelsea spot was once quite a destination – an "austere" makeover has now robbed it of any character, and some just find it "very dull" nowadays. / 11 pm; closed Mon L; need 6+ to book.

Enoteca Turi SW15 £ 35 ❷❶❷
28 Putney High St 8785 4449 10–2B
"Not your usual Italian", this "excellent" Putney fixture offers "super regional cooking" and an "enormous" wine list, under the all-seeing eyes of owners Mr and Mrs Giuseppe Turi. / 11 pm; closed Sun.

The Enterprise SW3 £ 36 ④❸❷
35 Walton St 7584 3148 5–2C
This "lively" bar/restaurant near Harrods is a "fun" destination for an (unsurprisingly) "well-heeled" crowd; the cooking, though, has proved "variable" of late. / www.sparkjumbo.co.uk; 11 pm; no booking, except weekday L.

Esarn Kheaw W12 £ 26 ❶④④
314 Uxbridge Rd 8743 8930 7–1B
"You get very authentic Thai cooking", and it's "consistently delicious", at this Shepherd's Bush oriental; all other aspects of the place are eminently forgettable. / 11 pm; closed Sat L & Sun L.

L'Escargot W1 £ 40 ❷❷❷
48 Greek St 7437 2679 4–2A
"A quiet oasis in the heart of busy Soho", this "spacious" Gallic "favourite" has lots of "old-style glamour" and is a "simply outstanding" all-round performer that deserves greater recognition; the Picasso (fine dining) Room upstairs is less of an attraction. / www.whitestarline.org; 11.30 pm; closed Sat L & Sun (Picasso Room also closed Mon).

Est Est Est £ 27 ⑤⑤④
147-149 Notting Hill Gate, W11 7221 1110 6–2B
29 Chiswick High Rd, W4 8747 8777 7–2B
57-58 Upper St, N1 7359 9198 8–3D
27-29 Bellevue Rd, SW17 8672 3122 10–2C
"Kids can paint on the tables", at branches of this would-be "trendy" Italian chain; unless you see that as a great attraction, "don't go". / 11 pm.

L'Estaminet WC2 £ 38 ❸❷❸
14 Garrick St 7379 1432 4–3C
The "superb cheeseboard" is a highlight of the "traditional French" style of this "rustic" Covent Garden fixture, where the "excellent pre-theatre menus" are a particular attraction. / 11 pm; closed Sun; set pre-th. £22(FP).

Exhibition SW7 £ 34 ❸❸④
19 Exhibition Rd 7584 8359 5–2C
The change of name (from Tui) has done little to up the profile of this (now rather Europeanised) South Kensington Thai – it still offers "good" cooking, but you'd never guess that this used to be one of the top orientals in town. / 10.45 pm; closed Mon; set weekday L £16(FP).

Eyre Brothers EC2 £ 43 ❷❷❸
70 Leonard St   7613 5346   9–1D
*A very early-days (August '01) visit found promising cooking at
this Shoreditch newcomer – there seemed something of
mismatch, though, between the Iberian/Mediterranean menu
and the smart but rather cold American-retro styling.*

Fairuz W1 £ 27 ❸❸❸
3 Blandford St   7486 8108   2–1A
*"Good-quality Lebanese cooking", "friendly" service and
a "relaxed" atmosphere proves a simple but effective formula at
this small Marylebone spot. / 11.30 pm.*

Fakhreldine W1 £ 42 ❸④⑤
85 Piccadilly   7493 3424   3–4C
*A "great position" overlooking Green Park adds lustre to this
datedly glitzy Mayfair Lebanese – for its small but devoted fan
club, it remains "an old-time favourite". / midnight; no smoking area.*

Il Falconiere SW7 £ 29 ❸❸④
84 Old Brompton Rd   7589 2401   5–2B
*A "dependable" South Kensington "local Italian", whose set
menus, in particular, offer "excellent" value. / 11.45 pm; closed Sun;
set weekday L £19(FP).*

La Famiglia SW10 £ 44 ❸❸❷
7 Langton St   7351 0761   5–3B
*Even fans think it's "expensive for what it is", but that's never
stopped this "very Chelsea" and "very Italian" World's Ender
from being "very busy"; the "wonderful" but "crowded" terrace
is a particular attraction. / 11.45 pm.*

Fat Boy's £ 24 ④❷④
41 Richmond Rd, TW1   8892 7657   1–4A
10a Edensor Rd, W4   8994 8089   10–1A
*"Great food and wonderful value", say fans of this Chiswick
café, which moonlights as a "cheerful" BYO Thai; there is now
also a branch in Richmond. / 11.30 pm.*

Faulkner's E8 £ 21 ❶❷④
424-426 Kingsland Rd   7254 6152   1–2D
*"You slum it, but with great haddock" at this long-established
Dalston stalwart – "the best chippy in London, if not the
Universe!" / 10 pm; no Amex; no smoking area.*

Feng Shang NW1 £ 30 ❷❶❷
Opposite 15 Prince Albert Rd   7485 8137   8–3B
*With its "very high standard of service" and its "attractive
décor", this "posh Chinese" – a barge moored by Regent's Park
– offers a "really special" night out, confounding the cynics with
its very enjoyable food. / 11 pm; closed weekday L.*

Ffiona's W8 £ 30 ❸❶❷
51 Kensington Church St 7937 4152 5–1A
"Ffiona's a good hostess" and *"she makes every visit an
occasion"* for guests at her *"delightful"* and *"homely"*
Kensington bistro. / 11.30 pm; closed Mon, Tue-Sat D only, Sun open
L & D; set D £18(FP).

The Fifth Floor
Harvey Nichols SW1 £ 51 ④④④
Knightsbridge 7235 5250 5–1D
*Fans still vaunt the "minimalist" restaurant atop the
Knightsbridge store as a "see-and-be-seen" destination –
especially for lunch; the wine list is impressive too, but the place
is taking ever more flak for "overpriced" cooking and
a "soulless" ambience. / www.harveynichols.com; 11.30 pm; closed
Sun D; set weekday L £33(FP).*

Fifth Floor (Café)
Harvey Nichols SW1 £ 38 ④④④
Knightsbridge 7823 1839 5–1D
*For a "decent" lunch, fans recommend the simple food at
Harvey Nic's top-floor café; the place can be "a bit of a bun
fight", though, and sceptics say it's "tired and expensive".
/ www.harveynichols.com; 10.30 pm; closed Sun D; no booking at L.*

Film Café
National Film Theatre SE1 £ 20 ④④❸
South Bank 7928 5362 2–3D
*The food (pizza slices, salads, etc) is "not the world's best",
but this lively café is a useful place for a quick, cheap bite on
the South Bank. / 9 pm; no smoking area.*

Fina Estampa SE1 £ 32 ❸❷④
150 Tooley St 7403 1342 9–4D
*It may be "a bit faded", but this "relaxed" Peruvian – not far
from Tower Bridge – does at least offer "something different".
/ 10.30 pm; closed Sat L & Sun.*

La Finca £ 23 ④④❸
96-98 Pentonville Rd, N1 7837 5387 8–3D
185 Kennington Ln, SE11 7735 1061 10–1D
*These large and long-established Spanish bars are "a bit loud,
but always fun"; the "tapas should be better", though.
/ www.thefinca.co.uk; 11.15 pm – N1 Fri & Sat 1.30 am – SE11 Fri & Sat
11.30 pm.*

The Fine Line £ 28 ④⑤④

77 Kingsway, WC2 7405 5004 2–2D
236 Fulham Road, SW10 7376 5827 5–3B
31-37 Northcote Road, SW11 7924 7387 10–2C
182-184 Clapham High St, SW4 7622 4436 10–2D
Fisherman's Wharf, Cabot Sq, E14 7513 0255 11–1C
1 Monument St, EC3 7623 5446 9–3C
124-127 Minories, EC3 7481 8195 9–3D
1 Bow Churchyard, EC4 7248 3262 9–2B
*Ratings for Fullers youthful chain of bright and breezy
bar/restaurants are heading south, on account of "unexciting"
food and "dreadful" service. / 10.45 pm; City branches closed
Sat & Sun.*

The Fire Stables SW19 £ 33 ③④③

27-29 Church Rd 8946 3197 10–2B
*"Wimbledon doesn't have many alternatives", but this "trendy"
new bar/restaurant would be welcome anywhere; that said,
the "good" grub is "pricey" for what it is, and the place can get
"very, very noisy". / 10.30 pm; no smoking area.*

FireBird W1 £ 63 ③③③

23 Conduit St 7493 7000 3–2C
*The "décor's a bit stuffy, but the food is superb", say supporters
of this decadent Mayfair "Russian delight"; compared to the
high-profile NYC original, it's gathered a negligible following,
though, perhaps because it's so "very expensive". / 11 pm; closed
Sun.*

Fish in a Tie SW11 £ 19 ③②②

105 Falcon Rd 7924 1913 10–1C
*"The food's not exceptional, but brilliant for the price", at this
"always busy and bustling" Battersea bistro; it "can get
overcrowded". / 11.45 pm; no Amex or Switch; set weekday L & D £11(FP).*

fish! £ 34 ③③④

92-94 Waterford Rd, SW6 7234 3333 5–4A
3b Belvedere Rd, SE1 7234 3333 2–3D
Cathedral St, SE1 7234 3333 9–4C
296-298 Upper Richmond Rd, SW15 7234 3333 10–2A
41a Queenstown Rd, SW8 7234 3333 10–1C
33 Westferry Circus, E14 7234 3333 11–1B
*"Simplicity is the key" at this "unfussy" ("uncompromising") and
"noisy" canteen chain, whose fish dishes are generally "very
fresh and well prepared"; it's been expanding like mad, so it's
no great surprise that some find the approach
"too commercial" nowadays. / www.fishdiner.co.uk; 11 pm; no smoking
area.*

Fishmarket
Great Eastern Hotel EC2 £ 48 ④④⑤

40 Liverpool St 7618 7200 9–2D
*"Small portions" for "an awful lot of money" contribute to the
impression that this fish and seafood restaurant, by Liverpool
Street station, is just another "cynical Conran machine".
/ www.conran.com; 10.30 pm; closed Sat L & Sun; booking: max 6.*

Flâneur EC1 £ 38 ④❸❷
41 Farringdon Rd 7404 4422 9–1A
*This lofty new Farringdon "food emporium" is a beautiful and
tranquil space in which to dine, but the cooking "falls short of
its pretensions", and we're with those who say it's "way too
expensive".* / 10 pm; closed Sun D; no smoking.

Floriana SW3 £ 55 ❸❸❸
15 Beauchamp Pl 7838 1500 5–1C
*Judged against its initial ambitions, this luxurious Knightsbridge
Italian "just doesn't quite work"; however, with its "soothing"
setting, "charming" service and cooking that's perfectly
acceptable, it makes a "reliable lunch venue".* / 11 pm; set
weekday L £36(FP).

Florians N8 £ 33 ④❷④
4 Topsfield Pde 8348 8348 1–1C
*Perhaps this Hornsey "neighbourhood Italian" of many years
standing has got complacent – some still say you can get
"great" snacks in the "loud" and "smoky" bar, but there's
a feeling that the restaurant cooking is "overrated" and a touch
"overpriced".* / 10.45 pm; no Amex.

Foliage
Mandarin Oriental SW1 £ 60 ❷❸④
66 Knightsbridge 7201 3723 5–1D
*David Nicholls's "interesting" and "beautifully presented"
modern French cooking aside, this dining room overlooking
Hyde Park strikes many as "pretentious" and "tiresome" – last
year's "anonymous" makeover by top American restaurant
designer Adam Tihany seems largely to blame.*
/ www.mandarinoriental.com; 10.30 pm; closed Sat L & Sun; no smoking area;
booking: max 6; set weekday L £39(FP).

La Fontana SW1 £ 40 ④④④
101 Pimlico Rd 7730 6630 5–2D
*"Go for the truffles, but only for the truffles", to this "quaint"
Pimlico Italian – out of season, bills can seem "amazing", given
the standard of cooking.* / 11 pm; no Switch.

Food for Thought WC2 £ 15 ❷④④
31 Neal St 7836 0239 4–2C
*"Very cramped", it may be, but this "crowded" and "rushed"
Covent Garden "veggie delight" remains on cracking culinary
form, and offers "great value"; BYO.* / 8.15 pm; closed Sun D;
no credit cards; no smoking; no booking.

Footstool SW1 £ 32 ⑤⑤❸
St John's, Smith Sq 7222 2779 2–4C
*"A nice setting and a good selection, with buffet and à la carte"
should make a winning formula for this attractive Westminster
church crypt; the cooking is "bad", though – "not very
expensive, but still poor value".* / www.sjss.org.uk; L only (buffet on
concert evenings); closed Sat & Sun (except concert evenings); no smoking
area.

Formula Veneta SW10 £ 35 ④❸④
14 Hollywood Rd   7352 7612   5–3B
"Its heyday has passed" – the food at this once-fashionable
Chelsea-fringe Italian "has deteriorated over the years", and the
place now has no more than "stand-by" status. / 11.15 pm; closed
Sun.

Il Forno W1 £ 32 ❸❸❸
63-64 Frith St   7734 4545   4–2A
The cooking now seems more "average" and the décor less
characterful at this year-old Soho venture; however, for "good
pizza and Italian staples" at "reasonable prices", it remains
a useful West End destination. / www.ilforno-restaurant.co.uk;
10.30 pm, Fri & Sat 11 pm; closed Sat L & Sun L.

Fortnum's Fountain W1 £ 33 ❸❷❸
181 Piccadilly   7734 8040   3–3D
"Crisp linen tablecloths" set the tone in the "tranquil" buttery of
the Queen's grocers; it makes a very versatile central destination
– "with relatives", "on your own", "for breakfast", "as a lunch
venue", "pre-theatre" and, naturally, "for an excellent tea" –
but "queues can be long". / www.fortnumandmason.co.uk; 8 pm; closed
Sun; no booking at L.

Four Regions
County Hall SE1 £ 38 ④④❸
7928 0988   2–3D
You're "paying for the beautiful view" (of Westminster) at this
riverside oriental, where "mediocrity runs riot". / 11.30 pm.

The Fox EC2 £ 27 ❷④④
28 Paul St   7729 5708   9–1C
The first offshoot of the famous Eagle (London's original
gastropub), delivers some good, "homely" Mediterranean fare,
but it's going to take quite some effort to make this small,
unreconstructed Shoreditch boozer a real destination. / 10 pm;
closed Sat & Sun; only Switch.

Fox & Anchor EC1 £ 23 ❸❸❷
115 Charterhouse St   7253 5075   9–1B
"Awesomely big", "cholesterol-packed" early-morning fry-ups
can (thanks to Smithfield Market's licensing laws) be
supplemented by "a great pint of Guinness" at this famous
institution. / breakfast & L only (bar open in evenings); closed Sat & Sun.

The Fox Reformed N16 £ 25 ④❷❸
176 Stoke Newington Church St   7254 5975   1–1C
"Strange on first impression, but the charm gets you in the
end", at this characterful, long-established Stoke Newington
wine bar, which serves a "limited" international menu; it has
a great patio garden. / 10.30 pm; D only, except Sat & Sun open L & D;
no booking.

Foxtrot Oscar £ 29 ④④④
79 Royal Hospital Rd, SW3   7352 7179   5–3D
Riverside Plaza, Chatfield Rd, SW11   7223 0999   10–1C
16 Byward St, EC3   7481 2700   9–3D
Stick to simple fare (like "excellent burgers") at this small chain of wine bar-type diners; the Chelsea original – a favourite toffs' stand-by – remains the most characterful branch. / 11 pm – EC3 8 pm; EC3 closed Sat & Sun.

Franco's SW1 £ 38 ④❸❸
63 Jermyn St   7493 3645   3–3C
It's "slightly overpriced for an averagely good Italian", but this "reliable" old-timer makes a handy refuge for those who find St James's rather too trendy nowadays. / 10.45 pm; closed Sun.

Francofill SW7 £ 29 ④④④
1 Old Brompton Rd   7584 0087   5–2C
A "straightforward" Gallic bar/café, by South Kensington tube, serving "simple", "standard" French fare. / www.francofill.com; 10.45 pm; no smoking area; set always available £19(FP).

Frantoio SW10 £ 35 ④❸❸
397 King's Rd   7352 4146   5–3B
"A good, if limited, menu but lacking Leonardo's touch of class" – this year-old World's End Italian has yet to create the enthusiasm which for many years enveloped its traditional-style predecessor. / 10.30 pm.

Frederick's N1 £ 38 ❷❷❶
106 Camden Pas   7359 2888   8–3D
"Classy, without breaking the bank", this long-established Islington "all-rounder" is currently on top form, with "consistently good" ("but not 'wow'") Gallic cooking and "friendly", "discreet" service; as ever, though, it's the "lovely" conservatory which is the star attraction. / www.fredericks.co.uk; 11.30 pm; closed Sun; no smoking area; set weekday L & pre-th. £24(FP).

Friends SW10 £ 32 ❸④❸
6 Hollywood Rd   7376 3890   5–3B
"A proper attempt at pizza at reasonable prices" helps endear this "bubbly" Chelsea Italian to younger locals, but service is "random" and the setting can seem "smoky" and "loud". / 11.30 pm; closed weekday L; no Amex.

Frocks E9 £ 31 ❸❷❷
95 Lauriston Rd   8986 3161   1–2D
"Fabulous fry-ups" for "slow weekend mornings" are the special forte of this "amazingly friendly" bistro, near Victoria Park; "tasty" cooking also contributes to the place's attractions as a "romantic" evening destination. / 11 pm; closed Mon & Sun D; set weekday L £20(FP).

Front Page SW3   £ 24   ❸❸❷
35 Old Church St   7352 2908   5–3C
*"A Chelsea secret" – this posh backstreet pub (which has no
pretensions to being a restaurant) offers "big portions of
homemade grub" at "good-value" prices.* / www.frontpagepubs.com;
10 pm, Sun 6 pm; closed Sun D.

Fryer's Delight WC1   £ 9   ❷❷④
19 Theobald's Rd   7405 4114   2–1D
*As you might expect for somewhere much "frequented by
cabbies", this "friendly" chippy behind Gray's Inn "cannot be
faulted for its great-value fish and chips"; you can BYO,
but a mug of tea is the usual accompaniment.* / 10 pm; closed Sun;
no credit cards.

Fuego   £ 25   ④❷④
City Circle, 10 Basinghall St, EC2   7600 1633   9–2B
1a Pudding Ln, EC3   7929 3366   9–3C
*"The food can be hit-and-miss", but they must be doing
something right at this lively tapas bar near Monument –
it recently spawned a sibling behind the Guildhall.*
/ www.fuego.co.uk; 9.30 pm; closed Sat & Sun.

Fung Shing WC2   £ 34   ❶④⑤
15 Lisle St   7437 1539   4–3A
*Long hailed as "the best Chinese in Chinatown", this "fine" but
"gloomy" Cantonese is "first-rate for fish and unusual dishes".*
/ www.fungshing.com; 11.15 pm.

Furnace N1   £ 22   ❷④❸
1 Rufus St   7613 0598   9–1D
*For a "cool pizza" in the "happening 'hood", this "buzzy"
parlour "in the heart of Hoxton" has quite a following – "nice to
know there's an alternative to the chains".* / 11 pm; closed
Sat L & Sun; no Amex.

Fusion EC2   £ 11   ❸❸❸
13 Devonshire Row   7375 1202   9–2D
*For a quick lunch in the environs of Liverpool Street, this "funky"
new little sushi bar offers "a refreshing alternative to sarnies".*
/ www.fusionpacific.com; L only, closed Sat & Sun; no Amex; no smoking;
no booking.

Futures EC2   £ 24   ❸④❸
2 Exchange Sq   7638 6341   9–1D
*This veggie bar/restaurant near Broadgate may not be quite as
good as the related take-away, but does offer "inventive" and
"well-prepared" food.* / www.btwebworld.com/futures1; L only, closed
Sat & Sun; no smoking at L.

Futures EC3   £ 9   ❷❸ –
8 Botolph Alley   7623 4529   9–3C
*For a "great vegetarian lunch" in the City, you won't do better
than this take-away near the Monument; be prepared to queue.*
/ www.btwebworld.com/futures1; L only, closed Sat & Sun; no credit cards;
no smoking; no booking.

Gaby's WC2   £ 23   ❷④④
30 Charing Cross Rd   7836 4233   4–3B
The estimable salt beef sandwiches and the "excellent falafel pittas" at this Middle Eastern café/take-away off Leicester Square make "good and different fast food". / www.gabys.net; 11.15 pm; no credit cards.

Galicia W10   £ 25   ❸❷❸
323 Portobello Rd   8969 3539   6–1A
An "authentic" and "cheerful" North Kensington tapas bar, where "bossy but kindly" waiters set the tone. / 11.30 pm; closed Mon; set weekday L £13(FP).

Gallipoli   £ 22   ❸❷❷
102 Upper St, N1   7359 0630   8–3D
120 Upper St, N1   7226 8099   8–3D
"Very basic" but "very friendly" – these "always reliable" Turkish bistros in Islington have a huge following, and they're often "crowded". / 11 pm, Fri & Sat 11.30 pm; no Amex.

Garbo's W1   £ 28   ④❸④
42 Crawford St   7262 6582   2–1A
The "fun smorgasbord lunch" offers "outstanding value" at this "friendly-enough" Scandinavian fixture in Marylebone – otherwise the "interesting-sounding dishes can turn out rather humdrum". / 10.45 pm; closed Sat L & Sun D; no Switch; set weekday L £16(FP).

Gastro SW4   £ 36   ❸④❷
67 Venn St   7627 0222   10–2D
Many find this "Gallic hideaway" ("handily-located opposite Clapham Picture House") an "incredibly atmospheric" destination, and it has built quite a following; "ridiculously haphazard" service lets the place down, though, and the "pricey" cooking (specialising in fish) is tending to "ordinary" nowadays. / midnight; no credit cards; no smoking area; need 15+ to book.

The Gasworks SW6   £ 31   ⑤④❷
87 Waterford Rd   7736 3830   5–4A
As we go to press, this bizarre antique-filled den near Sands End gasworks – consistently one of London's strangest places to eat – is closed; however, the coffin lid has not yet been nailed down, and an October '01 re-opening is promised. / 11 pm; D only, closed Sun-Tue; no credit cards.

Gate W11   £ 32   ❷❸❸
87 Notting Hill Gate   7727 9007   6–2B
"For what seems like a trendy hole in the wall", this "happening" basement on the fringe of Notting Hill offers "surprisingly good" (if not very ambitious) cooking; the scene hots up as the evening progresses, and the noise-level rises accordingly. / www.gaterestaurant.co.uk; 10.45 pm; D only; no smoking area.

The Gate £ 30 ❶❷❷
51 Queen Caroline St, W6   8748 6932   7–2C
72 Belsize Ln, NW3   7435 7733   8–2A
"They do exquisite things with vegetables" at London's best
veggie, *"tucked away in a Hammersmith courtyard"*; it now has
an equally exceptional, more prominently-situated Belsize Park
offshoot, done out in similarly *"plain"* but *"funky"* style.
/ www.gateveg.co.uk; 10.45 pm; W6 closed Sun – NW3 closed Sun D; W6
booking: max 10.

Gaucho £ 27 ❷④④
88 Ifield Rd, SW10   7823 3333   5–3A
Chelsea Farmers' Mkt, Sydney St, SW3   7376 8514   5–3C
"If you like steaks, this is the place" – an Argentinian BYO
shack, just off the King's Road that's best visited on a summer's
day, when you can eat outside; it now has a new
conventionally-housed offshoot on the fringe of Chelsea. / SW3
6 pm – SW10 11.30 pm; SW3 L only – SW10 D only; no credit cards; SW3
no booking in summer.

Gaucho Grill £ 33 ❷❸❸
19-25 Swallow St, W1   7734 4040   3–3D
125-126 Chancery Ln, WC2   7242 7727   2–1D
89 Sloane Ave, SW3   7584 9901   5–2C
64 Heath St, NW3   7431 8222   8–1A
29 Westferry Circus, E14   7987 9494   11–1B
12 Gracechurch St, EC3   7626 5180   9–3C
"Fantastic steaks and crazy décor" make a winning formula for
these *"reliable"* and *"reasonably-priced"* Argentinian grill-rooms
– by far the best mid-range chain restaurants in town.
/ 11 pm-11.45 pm; EC3 closed Sat & Sun.

Gaudi EC1 £ 44 ❸❸④
63 Clerkenwell Rd   7608 3220   9–1A
Yet again, this controversial Clerkenwell Spaniard polarises
debate; the 'ayes' say it serves *"excellent Iberian dishes"* (with
puddings which are *"works of art"*) in *"interesting"* surroundings
– the 'nays' think it offers a *"strange"* experience that's
"over-rated and overpriced". / www.turnmills.com; 10.30 pm; closed
Sat L & Sun.

LE GAVROCHE W1 £ 82 ❶❶❸
43 Upper Brook St   7408 0881   3–2A
"A reminder of how food should be served and cooked"; it can
seem *"starchy"* and *"dated"*, but, for *"old-fashioned quality"*,
Michel Roux Jr's grand Mayfair basement – with its *"brilliant"*
Gallic cooking and service that's *"second to none"* – is *"still the
best"* for many reporters. / www.le-gavroche.co.uk; 11 pm; closed
Sat & Sun; jacket required; set weekday L £43(FP).

Gay Hussar W1 £ 36 ④❷❷
2 Greek St   7437 0973   4–2A
"Old fashioned" but *"always cheerful"*, this Soho *"haunt of Old
Labour types"* exerts a *"timeless"* appeal; the once-splendid
Hungarian grub is *"not what it was"*, however – it's *"very pricey,
but rather everyday"*. / www.trpplc.com; 10.45 pm; closed Sun.

Geale's W8 £ 28 ❸❸⑤
2 Farmer St 7727 7969 6–2B
For some, it's "still a favourite for fish and chips", but ever since the Geale family sold out this once-legendary Notting Hill institution has "lost its buzz". / 10.30 pm; closed Sun L; need 6+ to book.

Geeta NW6 £ 15 ❶❷⑤
59 Willesden Ln 7624 1713 1–1B
"It looks like a greasy spoon, but the food is excellent" – and as "cheap as it gets" – at this "super-friendly", if undeniably "gloomy", Kilburn spot; "terrific south Indian veggie dishes" are the top options. / 10.30 pm, Fri & Sat 11.30 pm; no Switch.

George
Great Eastern Hotel EC2 £ 30 ④⑤④
40 Liverpool St 7618 7000 9–2D
Relatively "reasonable" prices commend Conran's City boozer – with its "very British" cooking – to some; the service is "bad" though. / www.conran.com; 10.30 pm.

George & Vulture EC3 £ 30 ④❸❷
3 Castle Ct 7626 9710 9–3C
"If you like cockney familiarity" and are inured to British fare that's "filling" at best, this Dickensian City "relic" may well be the place for you. / L only, closed Sat & Sun; jacket & tie required.

George II SW11 £ 27 ❷❸④
339 Battersea Park Rd 7622 2112 10–1C
It has something of an identikit 'Battersea gastropub' look to it, but this airy newcomer was offering more-than-usually successful dishes on our July '01 initial visit. / Rated on Editors' assessment; 10 pm; no Amex.

Getti £ 34 ⑤④⑤
16-17 Jermyn St, SW1 7734 7334 3–3D
42 Marylebone High St, W1 7486 3753 2–1A
74 Wardour St, W1 7437 3519 3–2D
This rather "soulless" chain of glitzy Italians is "pricey" for what it is, and its culinary results are "very mediocre". / 11 pm; SW1 & Wardour St closed Sun; no smoking areas; set weekday L £22(FP).

Ghillies £ 32 ④❸❷
271 New King's Rd, SW6 7371 0434 10–1B
94 Point Pleasant, SW18 8877 9267 10–2B
"Fabulous views" are a feature of the new Putney branch of this duo of "friendly" and "relaxed" local restaurants; some reporters find the realisation of the "mostly fish" dishes rather "tired". / SW6 10.30 pm – SW18 10 pm; SW6 closed Sun D.

Gili Gulu WC2 £ 18 ④④❸

50-52 Monmouth St 7379 6888 4–2B
"Surprise yourself with the amount you can eat" at this
sparsely-decorated Theatreland oriental, where – for a fixed
price – you grab whatever you want from the conveyor-belt;
the sushi and other fare are *"decent"* for the money. / 11 pm;
no Amex; no smoking; no booking.

Ginger W2 £ 31 ❷❸❸

115 Westbourne Grove 7908 1990 6–1B
They've put *"a fascinating different twist"* on subcontinental
cooking at this *"clean and modern"* Bayswater newcomer, which
– so they say – is London's first true Bangladeshi.
/ www.gingerrestaurant.co.uk; 10.30 pm, Fri & Sat 11.30 pm; no smoking area.

Giraffe £ 26 ❸❷❷

6-8 Blandford St, W1 7935 2333 2–1A
29-31 Essex Rd, N1 7359 5999 8–3D
46 Rosslyn Hill, NW3 7435 0343 8–2A
"We need more relaxed and child-friendly places" like these
"cute", *"bright"* and *"cheerful"* diners, whose *"interesting"*
menus satisfy *"varied palates"*; breakfasts – *"a ray of sunshine,
even on a grey morning"* – attract special praise. / 11.30 pm – W1
11 pm; no smoking; need 6+ to book.

Gladwins EC3 £ 50 ❸❷❸

Minster Ct, Mark Ln 7444 0004 9–3D
Though some find it *"reminiscent of the '70s"*, this (actually
late-'90s) basement is a *"reliable"* haunt whose *"spacious"*
tables help make it a *"favourite business venue"*; the cooking is
"very good, by City standards". / www.gladwins.co.uk; L only, closed
Sat & Sun.

Glaisters £ 32 ④④❸

4 Hollywood Rd, SW10 7352 0352 5–3B
8-10 Northcote Rd, SW11 7924 6699 10–2C
36-38 White Hart Ln, SW13 8878 2020 10–1A
The bistro cooking may be *"a bit hit-and-miss"*, but for an
"easy-paced" meal, these *"cosy and relaxed"* locals – with
"lovely open air sections" – muster quite a number of younger
fans. / 11.30 pm.

The Glasshouse TW9 £ 38 ❶❶❷

14 Station Pde 8940 6777 1–3A
"Superb food on every visit" and *"enthusiastic"*, *"individual"*
service make it *"worth the trek to Kew"* for this *"bubbly"*
two-year old (sibling to Wandsworth's Chez Bruce) by the
railway station; it's *"noisy"* and *"crowded"*, though. / 10.30 pm.

Globe Restaurant NW3 £ 31 ❸❷❸

100 Avenue Rd 7722 7200 8–2A
"They try very hard" at this poorly-located Swiss Cottage
venture, whose cooking is *"good, if perhaps a bit
over-presented"*; the ambience can be *"cold"*, though – but not
on Thursdays, when *"the cabaret is a real laugh"*.
/ www.globerestaurant.co.uk; 11 pm; closed Mon L & Sat L; no Amex.

Golborne House W10 £ 30 ❸❸❷
36 Golborne Rd 8960 6260 6–1A
At the foot of North Kensington's Trellick Tower, this "casual" and "very trendy" gastropub provides a "reliable" selection of modern staples. / 10 pm; no Amex.

Golden Dragon W1 £ 24 ❷⑤④
28-29 Gerrard St 7734 2763 4–3A
"It's not one for intimate meals" and "you don't go for the service" – it's "like a conveyor belt" – but this "big and loud" establishment can fairly claim to be "the best Chinese on Chinatown's main drag"; "wonderful dim sum" is a highlight. / 11.15 pm, Fri & Sat 11.45 pm.

Good Earth SW3 £ 37 ❷❸④
233 Brompton Rd 7584 3658 5–2C
"Great food, but nul points for atmosphere" – the Knightsbridge branch of this "high-quality" Chinese chain presents a rather dowdy face to the world nowadays. / goodearthgroup.co.uk; 10.45 pm.

Goolies W8 £ 41 ❷❷❸
21 Abingdon Rd 7938 1122 5–1A
"Great for lounging", say regulars at this "upbeat" Kensington bar/restaurant, whose "friendly" service and "interesting" modern menu are consistently approved. / 10.30 pm; set Sun L £21(FP).

Goose EC2 £ 26 ❸❸④
128-130 Curtain Rd 7729 3208 9–1D
This new, "no-frills", organic deli/bistro seems to be becoming a linchpin of the emerging Shoreditch restaurant strip; the food is "good value", but still rather ordinary. / 10.30 pm; Sun-Wed L only, Thu-Sat open L & D.

Gopal's of Soho W1 £ 26 ❷④④
12 Bateman St 7434 1621 4–2A
"It's much better than it looks" – this "somewhat claustrophobic" but "reliably good" Soho curry house is one of the few worth seeking out in the West End. / 11.15 pm.

GORDON RAMSAY SW3 £ 83 ❶❶❷
68-69 Royal Hospital Rd 7352 4441 5–3D
"Really pretty faultless"; Mr Ramsay's other interests – Claridges, Glasgow and Dubai, to name but three – are growing relentlessly, but the "heavenly" modern French food at his "formal, but nicely glamorous" Chelsea dining room just gets better and better; if there is a gripe, it's of sometimes "sycophantic" or "patronising" service. / 11 pm; closed Sat & Sun; booking: max 6; set weekday L £50(FP).

Gordon Ramsay at Claridges
Claridges Hotel W1   £ 83   – – –
55 Brook St   7629 8860   3–2B
*This illustrious Mayfair hotel has long offered a rather lacklustre
culinary experience, but its restaurant has now been put into
the hands of London's leading chef – on its re-opening in
September '01, this wonderful Art Deco chamber could quickly
become one of the capital's top dining rooms.*

Gordon's Wine Bar WC2   £ 22   ④❸❶
47 Villiers St   7930 1408   4–4D
*"Visitors can't believe there is such a place" – the wonderfully
gloomy cellars of this ancient "treasure" of a wine bar by
Embankment tube have a "unique" ambience (and, for the
summer, there are great outside tables); the "plain" fodder is
"expensive" for what it is.* / 9 pm; no Amex; no booking.

Goring Hotel SW1   £ 52   ❸①②
15 Beeston Pl   7396 9000   2–4B
*"Wonderful as ever" – for its (fairly mature) clientèle,
the "well-spaced" tables and "most courteous" service in the
dining room of this family-run Victoria hotel suit it to most
occasions (particularly business); the British cooking may be
"unchallenging", but it is very consistent.* / www.goringhotel.co.uk;
10 pm.

Gourmet Burger Kitchen SW11   £ 17   ❷❸❸
44 Northcote Rd   7228 3309   10–2C
*"Superb, juicy thick ones with all the trimmings" – including
"excellent chips and scrummy dips" – have made an immediate
success of this no-nonsense Battersea diner, which offers the
eponymous dining experience in every flavour you could
imagine.* / gbkinfo.co.uk; 10.45 pm; no smoking; no booking.

Gourmet Pizza Company   £ 26   ❸④④
7-9 Swallow St, W1   7734 5182   3–3D
56 Upper Ground, SE1   7928 3188   9–3A
18 Mackenzie Walk, E14   7345 9192   11–1C
*Thanks to their "weird" – but "not silly" – pizza combinations,
this small chain "really succeeds" in some people's books;
the SE1 branch enjoys a "prime riverside location" (with great
views), but elsewhere the ambience, can be rather a "let-down".*
/ www.gourmetpizzacompany.co.uk; 10.45 pm; W1 & E14, no smoking area;
need 8+ to book.

Gow's EC2   £ 42   ❸❸④
81-82 Old Broad St   7920 9645   9–2C
*"Traditional" and "enduring" fish restaurant, in a basement
near Liverpool Street, which may be a touch on the "pricey"
side, but does what it does with impressive consistency.* / L only,
closed Sat & Sun; no smoking area.

Goya £ 33 ④❸❷

2 Ecclestone Pl, SW1   7730 4299   2–4B
34 Lupus St, SW1   7976 5309   2–4C
"Tapas are average", but *"for a quick snack and bottle of cheap vino"* this *"friendly"* and *"buzzy"* duo make *"cosy"* boltholes; the branch by Victoria Coach Station is well worth knowing about it you're between buses. / 11.30 pm; set weekday L & D £17(FP).

Grand Central EC2 £ 24 ④❸❷

91-93 Great Eastern St   7613 4228   9–1C
There's little beaux-arts about this groovily-decorated addition to the Shoreditch scene; it markets itself as a bar and restaurant, but the latter function seemed incidental to the former on our initial visit in July '01. / *Rated on Editors' assessment;* www.grandcentral.org.uk; 11.30 pm.

Granita N1 £ 35 ❸❸④

127 Upper St   7226 3222   8–3D
Last year's revamp has thrown this iconic Islington establishment off its stride; the décor is *"still stark and hard"*, but the service is now *"unexceptional"* and the food is *"slipping"* – *"it used to be interesting and delicious, and now it's just interesting!"* / 10.30 pm; closed Mon & Tue L; no Amex.

The Grapes E14 £ 38 ❷❸❷

76 Narrow St   7987 4396   11–1B
On sunny days, the riverside tables at this *"atmospheric"* old pub (near the Limehouse Link) offer an *"exceptional"* setting; eat *"tasty fish and chips from the bar"*, or surprisingly good, more ambitious fare in the *"cosy"* and *"tranquil"* upstairs dining room. / 9.15 pm; closed Sat L & Sun D.

Gravy W4 £ 34 ④❺④

142 Chiswick High Rd   8994 6816   7–2B
"Overpriced and decidedly average" cooking, the *"worst service ever"* and *"no atmosphere at all"* – this Chiswick newcomer has certainly made an impression, if not, presumably, in the manner intended. / 10.45 pm.

Great Eastern Dining Room EC2 £ 30 ④④❸

54 Great Eastern St   7613 4545   9–1D
Fans say there's a *"great vibe"* to this *"beautiful people"* haunt on the fringe of Hoxton – it's *"too canteen-like"* for some, however, and the food is *"nice, but nothing special"*. / 10.45 pm; closed Sat L & Sun.

Great Nepalese NW1 £ 22 ❸❷❸

48 Eversholt St   7388 6737   8–3C
"Even the new fascia can't overcome the grotty location" of this *"old favourite"*, by Euston Station; *"cheerful"* staff provide compensation, and – especially if you *"stick to the Nepalese specialities"* – you can eat well here. / 11.30 pm.

The Green Olive W9   £ 36   ❸❸❸
5 Warwick Pl   7289 2469   8–4A
*Reports remain variable, but this "classy" Maida Vale Italian
(part of the Red Pepper group) is generally held to offer "a high
standard of cooking". / 10.45 pm; closed Sat L.*

Green's SW1   £ 46   ❸❸❷
36 Duke St   7930 4566   3–3D
*"An Establishment eatery of the old school", this "discreet"
St James's fixture – with its "good little alcoves for business" –
is "reliable" and "consistently so"; some find it rather "boring".
/ www.greens.org.uk; 11 pm; closed Sun, May-Sep.*

Greenhouse W1   £ 51   – – –
27a Hays Mews   7499 3331   3–3B
*This comfortable and well-established restaurant in Mayfair was
closed at press time for a major relaunch in September '01;
the designer is the ubiquitous David Collins, so the characterful,
if slightly cheesy, interior will presumably be rendered tasteful,
but completely anonymous. / www.capitalgrp.co.uk; 11 pm; closed Sat L.*

Grenadier SW1   £ 35   ④④❷
18 Wilton Row   7235 3074   5–1D
*"Avoid touristy weekends", if you visit this cute and "very
traditional" Belgravia mews boozer; if you're eating, a "sausage
on a stick" in the bar is a "great" experience – meat pies and
so on in the small rear dining room are merely "OK". / 9 pm.*

Grissini
Hyatt Carlton Tower SW1   £ 50   ④❸④
2 Cadogan Pl   7858 7171   5–1D
*With its views over Cadogan Place gardens, this ambitious
Belgravia dining room can make a "lovely" brunch or breakfast
venue; at other times, though it's "too expensive", given its
"average" Italian cooking and the "lack of atmosphere".
/ 10.45 pm; closed Sun D; no smoking area.*

The Grove W6   £ 34   ④❸❸
83 Hammersmith Grove   8748 2966   7–1C
*"Nothing exceptional, but an asset to the neighbourhood" – this
"friendly" Hammersmith gastropub offers an "OK" menu (that
makes something of a feature of organic produce). / 11 pm;
no Amex.*

Grumbles SW1   £ 31   ④❸❷
35 Churton St   7834 0149   2–4B
*Is this "a '60s relic worth keeping"? – the battle lines are clearly
drawn between those who say this Pimlico bistro is "a local
treasure", and the vocal minority for whom it's just a "sad old
friend"; either way, it's "always busy". / 11.45 pm.*

The Guinea W1   £ 60   ❸④④

30 Bruton Pl   7499 1210   3–2B
"Fantastic" steaks and "the best pies in town" have long made
the "cosy" dining room of this "old-fashioned" Mayfair inn a key
carnivores' destination; it's "expensive", though. / 10.45 pm; closed
Sat L & Sun; set weekday L £39(FP).

Gung-Ho NW6   £ 28   ❷❷❷

328-332 West End Ln   7794 1444   1–1B
West Hampstead's "first-class local Chinese" is "difficult to
fault" as an all-round performer, and it "gets very busy".
/ 11.30 pm; no Amex.

Ha! Ha!   £ 25   ❸④❸

43-51 Great Titchfield St, W1   7580 7252   2–1B
6 Villiers St, WC2   7930 1263   4–4C
"A better choice than All Bar One" – these "friendly and busy"
bars serve "a good selection of trendy dishes" and make
"a handy place for a quick bite, drink or coffee".
/ www.hahaonline.co.uk; 11 pm; W1 closed Sat & Sun.

Haandi SW3   £ 32   ❸④④

136 Brompton Rd   7823 7373   5–1C
Refugees from Knightsbridge-chic will rejoice in the arrival of
this new Afro-Indian (which also has a branch in Nairobi);
its tacky charms – based on our July '01 visit – include solid and
unusual cooking, at reasonable prices. / Rated on Editors' assessment;
10.30 pm; no smoking area.

Hakkasan W1   £ 46   ❷❸❶

8 Hanway Pl   7927 7000   4–1A
"Sexy" design and "21st century" Chinese cooking have made
this "expensive" oriental the smash 'beautiful people' hit of the
year – despite its "dodgy" back-alley basement location, off
Tottenham Court Road. / 11 pm; no smoking area.

Halepi   £ 36   ④④④

18 Leinster Ter, W2   7262 1070   6–2C
48-50 Belsize Ln, NW3   7431 5855   8–2A
They have their fans, but "not great, and too expensive" is the
general verdict on this duo of disparate Greeks – both the kitsch
Bayswater original and bright, modern Belsize Park offshoot.
/ W2 12.30 am – NW3 11 pm.

Hanover Square W1   £ 30   ④④④

25 Hanover Sq   7408 0935   3–2C
The "excellent wine list" helps make this basement wine bar in
Mayfair a handy refuge from Oxford Street; the cooking, from
a "small" menu, however, "lets it down".
/ www.donhewitsonlondonwinebars.com; 10.30 pm; closed Sat & Sun;
no smoking area.

Harbour City W1   £ 26   ❸④⑤

46 Gerrard St   7439 7859   4–3B
"One of the best for dim sum" – otherwise this "dreary"
Chinatown spot is distinctly unmemorable. / 11.30 pm.

Hard Rock Café W1 £ 28 ④❷❷
150 Old Park Ln 7629 0382 3–4B
Yes, it's for "tourists and out-of-towners", but this famously "noisy" Mayfair diner – the original of the worldwide chain (now celebrating its 30th birthday) – is still surprisingly "happening", and the faithful insist that it offers "the best burgers anywhere". / www.hardrock.com; midnight, Fri & Sat 1 am; no smoking area; no booking.

Hardy's W1 £ 38 ❸❸❸
53 Dorset St 7935 5929 2–1A
A "very friendly atmosphere" envelops you at this "lovely" Marylebone wine bar; its "small and cosy restaurant" serves "consistent" fare. / 10.30 pm; closed Sat & Sun; no smoking area.

The Havelock Tavern W14 £ 28 ❶④❸
57 Masbro Rd 7603 5374 7–1C
"Get there early", if you want a seat at this "deafening", "no-frills" gastropub, behind Olympia – thanks to the "inspired" and "amazingly tasty" food it gets "ridiculously busy" (and "service suffers as a result"). / 10 pm; no credit cards; no booking.

Heartstone NW1 £ 27 ❷❸❸
106 Parkway 7485 7744 8–3B
"Thankfully the 'right on' food is right on" at this tranquil, New Age Camden Town café, where the "interesting" selection of organic food, wacky juices and rarified teas is pricey but of good quality; "last orders are irritatingly early". / 9 pm; closed Mon; no credit cards; no smoking.

Helter Skelter SW9 £ 34 ❷④❸
50 Atlantic Rd 7274 8600 10–2D
"Innovative cooking" and a "fun" atmosphere again win praise for this quirky Brixton venture; it's a cramped place which strikes some as "a bit pricey", given its recherché location. / 11 pm, Fri & Sat 11.30 pm; D only.

Home EC1 £ 39 ❸❸❶
100-106 Leonard St 7684 8618 9–1D
"Groovy" Shoreditch hang-out, whose "peaceful restaurant is in contrast to the packed downstairs bar"; for such an "image-conscious" place, the surprise is not that the cooking is "uneven", but that it's "quite good". / www.homebar.co.uk; 10 pm; closed Sat L & Sun; no smoking area.

The Honest Cabbage SE1 £ 31 ❸❸❸
99 Bermondsey St 7234 0080 9–4D
"Good wholesome grub at fair prices", "lovely" service and the "intimate" setting win wide-ranging support for this "casual" converted boozer, near Bermondsey antiques market. / 10 pm, Thu-Sat 11 pm; closed Sun D; no Amex.

Hope & Sir Loin EC1 £ 34 ❸❸④
94 Cowcross St 7253 8525 9–1B
For a "nice breakfast" – gargantuan, meaty and served with a pint – this first-floor dining room, overlooking Smithfield Market, is a top choice; the place also does "great steaks" at lunchtime. / L only, closed Sat & Sun.

House E14 £ 31 ④❸④

27 Ropemakers Field, Narrow St 7538 3818 11–1B

It's "not very well known", and reports are mixed, but this simple bar/restaurant near Limehouse Link does win a few votes as a "cheap and cheerful" option in the wastes of Docklands. / 10.30 pm; closed Sun D; no Amex.

The House SW3 £ 41 ❸②❸

3 Milner St 7584 3002 5–2D

"For dinner with your great aunt", you won't do much better than this "quiet" and "cramped" Chelsea townhouse (previously The English House); the limited feedback on the cooking under the current, year-old regime is generally positive. / 11 pm; closed Sat L & Sun D.

House on Rosslyn Hill NW3 £ 29 ⑤⑤④

34 Rosslyn Hill 7435 8037 8–2A

There's still sometimes "a great party atmosphere" at this Hampstead hang-out (which also makes a "relaxing" choice for breakfast); in most respects, though, it's just thoroughly "mediocre" and "overpriced". / 11.30 pm.

Hudson's SW15 £ 27 ❸❸②

113 Lower Richmond Rd 8785 4522 10–1A

It's the "lively" ("chaotic") atmosphere which is the making of this "tightly-packed" Putney bistro, but the "simple", "tasty" grub also gets the thumbs-up. / 10.30 pm.

Hujo's W1 £ 28 ④❸❸

11 Berwick St 7734 5144 3–2D

"What fun, but it's noisy" – "closely-packed tables add to the atmosphere" of this small, inexpensive bistro in a sleazy Soho backstreet. / midnight; closed Sun; pre-th. £17(FP).

Hunan SW1 £ 32 ❶❶❸

51 Pimlico Rd 7730 5712 5–2D

"Excitable but wise service" – "it's best to leave the menu choice to Mr Peng" – delivers "genuinely special" results at this "first-rate" Chinese of long standing, near Pimlico Green. / 11 pm; closed Sun; no smoking area.

Hush W1 £ 45 ④④❸

8 Lancashire Ct 7659 1500 3–2B

Who cares if the food is "distinctly mediocre" and the service "slow"?; this "too-trendy-for-its-own-good" yearling – a bar/brasserie/restaurant, "discreetly" hidden off Bond Street – sails blithely on, oblivious to such banal considerations. / www.hush.co.uk; midnight; closed Sun.

I Thai
The Hempel W2 £ 70 ④④❸
31-35 Craven Hill Gdns   7298 9001   6–2C
"It's almost too cool to talk", say fans awed by the "serene" and almost "surreal" basement dining room of this Bayswater boutique hotel; even they can find the "beautifully presented" fusion cooking "overpriced", though, and critics just say the place is "a real con job". / www.the-hempel.co.uk; 10.45 pm.

Ibla W1 £ 45 ❷❸④
89 Marylebone High St   7224 3799   2–1A
"Serious" Italian cooking that's "different from the norm" has created quite a foodie reputation for this two-room Marylebone spot; "you can't say much about the atmosphere", though. / 10.30 pm; closed Sat L & Sun.

Ichizen Noodle Bar W1 £ 26 ❸❷❷
54 Goodge St   7637 0657   2–1B
"Fun" and "fast" – and funky too – this new oriental snackery in Fitzrovia makes a pleasant cheap 'n' cheerful stand-by; seating upstairs is incredibly tight, though – six-footers should sit downstairs! / 11 pm; closed Sun.

Idaho N6 £ 39 ⑤④④
13 North Hill   8341 6633   1–1C
"Bland" and "overpriced" cooking and often "awful" service create a potent recipe for discontent with this Highgate southwest American – a shame, as its garden is potentially "perfect for a sunny day". / www.neighbourhoodrestaurant.com; 11.30 pm.

The Ifield SW10 £ 31 ❸④❸
59 Ifield Rd   7351 4900   5–3A
This trendified Earl's Court-fringe boozer offers "pleasant pub food", and makes "a good place for an uncomplicated evening". / 11 pm; Mon-Thu D only, Fri-Sun open L & D.

Ikeda W1 £ 60 ④❸⑤
30 Brook St   7629 2730   3–2B
Fans say it's "expensive but good" – for its foes this long-established Mayfair Japanese is just plain "overpriced". / 10.30 pm, Sat 10 pm; closed Sat L & Sun; no Switch; set weekday L £39(FP).

Ikkyu W1 £ 27 ❷④❸
67 Tottenham Court Rd   7636 9280   2–1C
"Almost like being back in Tokyo" – some "unusual dishes", as well as quality sushi, are served at this "cheap" and "characterful" basement, near Goodge Street tube. / 10.30 pm; closed Sat & Sun L; no Switch; no smoking area.

Imperial City EC3 £ 36 ❸❸❸
Royal Exchange, Cornhill   7626 3437   9–2C
This "stylish City Chinese" is "slipping downhill" – it was formerly notable as a good all-rounder, but nowadays it's increasingly delivering "ordinary" food that's "a bit pricey" for what it is. / www.imperial-city.co.uk; 9.30 pm; closed Sat & Sun.

Inaho W2 £ 31 ❶④❸
4 Hereford Rd 7221 8495 6–1B
*"Cheap, but amazing sushi" – perhaps "the best in town" –
and other "exceptional" cooking make it worth truffling out this
"tiny" and "crammed" Japanese café in Bayswater; "shame it's
so slow".* / 11 pm; closed Sat L & Sun; no Amex or Switch; set weekday L
£17(FP).

Incognico WC2 £ 43 ❷❸❸
117 Shaftesbury Ave 7836 8866 4–2B
*Nico Ladenis's "thoroughly slick" and "buzzy" brasserie yearling
has "quickly established itself" as a major Theatreland
destination thanks to its "proper" Gallic cooking and
"reasonable" prices.* / midnight; closed Sun; set weekday L & pre-th.
£25(FP).

L'Incontro SW1 £ 55 ④④④
87 Pimlico Rd 7730 6327 5–2D
*"Unjustified" prices and "snooty" service continue to "mar"
enjoyment of this "airy" Pimlico Italian; it can be "nice for
lunch", though, when it's "less OTT" on the price front.*
/ 11.30 pm; closed Sat L & Sun L; set weekday L £33(FP).

India Club WC2 £ 18 ④④⑤
143 Strand 7836 0650 2–2D
*"The room may not have been decorated in 50 years",
but most reporters love slumming it at this "bizarre",
"time-warp", "colonial"-style subcontinental, in an anonymous
Aldwych hotel; it's "very cheap".* / 11 pm; closed Sun; no credit cards;
need 6+ to book.

Indigo
One Aldwych WC2 £ 51 ❷❷❷
1 Aldwych 7300 0400 2–2D
*With its "amazing friendly service", its "really comfy" and
"spacious" setting and its "good, sensible, tasty food", the "very
urbane and well-placed" mezzanine restaurant of this swish
Covent Garden hotel is something of "a hidden treasure".*
/ www.onealdwych.co.uk; 11.15 pm.

Innecto W1 £ – – – –
66 Baker St 7935 4545 2–1A
*The backer is the man who created the sarf London pizza
phenomenon Eco, but this new modern Italian in Marylebone
(scheduled for a September '01 opening) has much grander
ambitions than that – this could well be one to watch.*
/ www.innecto.uk.com; 11 pm, Fri & Sat midnight.

Ishbilia SW1 £ 34 ❸❷④
9 William St 7235 7788 5–1D
*"A very middle Eastern clientele" adds atmosphere to this
"reliable Lebanese", just off Knightsbridge.* / 11.30 pm; no Switch.

Isola SW1   **£ 45**   – – –

145 Knightsbridge   7838 1044   5–1D

After barely a year, Oliver Peyton has recently had to rejig this brave but unsuccessful two-tier Knightsbridge Italian; the sterile fine dining room is now a trendy bar, while the more atmospheric basement osteria continues broadly as before. / www.isola.co.uk; 11 pm; closed Sun.

Istanbul Iskembecisi N16   **£ 20**   ❸❸❸

9 Stoke Newington Rd   7254 7291   1–1C

The Turkish cooking is "still good, if not as good as it used to be" at this Dalston fixture, which is quite "smart" by local standards. / www.londraturk.com; 5 am; no credit cards.

It's   **£ 22**   ⑤❸❸

197 Baker St, NW1   7486 6027   2–1A

14-16 Quadrant Arcade, Air St, W1   7734 4267   3–3D

60 Wigmore St, W1   7224 3484   3–1B

98 Tottenham Court Rd, W1   7436 5355   2–1C

74 Southampton Row, WC1   7405 2876   2–1D

128 Holland Park Ave, W11   7243 1106   6–2A

17-20 Kendal St, W2   7724 4637   6–1D

404-406 Chiswick High Rd, W4   8995 3636   7–2A

Pity the food at this pizza, pasta and salad-buffet chain is so "bland" – its branches have "more life" than most multiples, and they can be "good value if you're hungry and in a rush". / www.askcentral.co.uk; 11.30 pm; no smoking areas; no booking after 8 pm (12.30 pm at L).

Italian Kitchen WC1   **£ 35**   ❷❷❸

43 New Oxford St   7836 1011   2–1C

"Good", "fresh" and "basic" cooking and an "old-fashioned", "friendly" welcome make it well worth remembering this rather squashed Italian, near the British Museum. / 10.50 pm; set weekday L £22(FP).

Itsu   **£ 28**   ❸❸❷

103 Wardour St, W1   7479 4794   3–2D

118 Draycott Ave, SW3   7584 5522   5–2C

"Like Yo! Sushi, but miles better" – these "conveyor belt experiences" win praise for their "lively, young and trendy" style and their "fun and fresh" oriental-inspired fare. / www.itsu.co.uk; 11 pm; smoking in the bar only; no booking.

THE IVY WC2   **£ 47**   ❷❶❶

1 West St   7836 4751   4–3B

"London's best all-rounder" is still "top for celeb spotting" and – thanks to its "clever, but simple" food, its "spoiling" service and the "perfect" ambience of its Theatreland premises – you "still need to book three months ahead"; those who feared that the departure of Messrs Corbin and King would spell 'The End' may have a while to wait yet. / midnight; set Sat L & Sun L £29(FP).

Iznik N5   £ 21   ❸❷❶
19 Highbury Park   7354 5697   8–2D
*The "jewel in Highbury's small crown" is not shining as brightly
as it did; all reports acknowledge the "delightful" and "intimate"
atmosphere, but whereas some still laud the Turkish cooking as
"excellent and reasonably priced" others find it increasingly
"variable". / 11 pm; no Amex.*

Jade Garden W1   £ 27   ❸④④
15 Wardour St   7437 5065   4–3A
*"Great dim sum" is the highlight at this otherwise merely "OK"
Chinatown spot. / www.londonjadegarden.co.uk; 11.30 pm.*

Jago
The Trafalgar SW1   £ 48   ④④④
2 Spring Gdns   7870 2900   2–3C
*In July '01, we paid our initial visit to this cold and anodyne
basement dining room beneath Hilton's first boutique hotel,
on Trafalgar Square; the influence of the corporate design team
and the heavy hand of portion control were both keenly in
evidence. / Rated on Editors' assessment; www.thetrafalgar.hilton.com;
11 pm; booking: max 6.*

Japanese Canteen   £ 28   ④④④
5 Thayer St, W1   7487 5505   3–1A
19-21 Exmouth Mkt, EC1   7833 3521   9–1A
3 Ludgate Broadway, EC4   7329 3555   9–2A
*"At least it's hot food" – even fans of these "Spartan" outfits
don't claim the cooking as art, but they do praise "cheapish and
reasonable" sushi, tempura and noodle dishes that "make an
escape from sandwiches". / EC1 & EC4 11 pm – W1 9 pm, Sat 6 pm;
EC4 closed Sun – W1 closed Sun D; W1 no credit cards; no smoking area –
W1 no smoking; W1 no booking.*

Jashan HA0   £ 15   ❷❷④
1-2 Coronet Pde, Ealing Rd   8900 9800   1–1A
*"Original" and "delicious" cooking from an encyclopaedic menu,
and "professional staff" make this bright, un-Indian-looking
veggie café a top destination in Wembley's curry quarter.
/ 10.45 pm; no smoking; no booking, Sat & Sun.*

Jason's W9   £ 40   ❷④❷
Opposite 60 Blomfield Rd   7286 6752   8–4A
*"Very good" and "different" fish dishes still make a trip to this
Little Venice café – with its "lovely canal setting" – well
worthwhile; recently, though, "it's gone down a bit", and there's
the odd report of "terrible" service. / www.jasons.co.uk; 10 pm; closed
Sun D.*

Jenny Lo's Tea House SW1   £ 19   ❸❷❸
14 Eccleston St   7259 0399   2–4B
*It's "simple, healthy stuff", say fans of the "good-value noodles"
at this "cheap and cheerful", "reliable and quick" refectory,
near Victoria. / 10 pm; closed Sun; no credit cards; no booking.*

Jim Thompson's £ 29 ❸④❷
617 King's Rd, SW6   7731 0999   5–4A
408 Upper Richmond Rd, SW15   8788 3737   10–1A
"Good food, good atmosphere, good prices" – these *"oriental bazaar"-type joints offer a "great range of dishes"*, usually of surprisingly high quality, and are ideal for parties.
/ www.jimthompsons.com; 11 pm; no smoking areas.

Jimmy's W1 £ 17 ④❷❷
23 Frith St   7437 9521   4–2A
"Hasn't changed since my student days" – this economical basement Greek in the heart of Soho is as *"welcoming"* and *"reliable"* as ever, and *"always fun"*. / 11 pm, Thu-Sat 11.30 pm; closed Sun; no Amex.

Jin Kichi NW3 £ 30 ❶❷❸
73 Heath St   7794 6158   8–1A
"Excellent" yakitori (grills on skewers) is the highlight at this *"cosy"*, *"small"* and *"friendly"* Hampstead Japanese. / 11 pm; closed Mon, Tue-Fri D only, Sat & Sun open L & D.

Joe Allen WC2 £ 35 ④④❷
13 Exeter St   7836 0651   4–3D
For *"good showbizzy fun"* this *"casual"* Covent Garden basement is a celebrated late-night *"old faithful"* (book well ahead); the American cooking is *"ordinary"*, though some claim the burgers (famously *"off-menu"*) as *"the best in town"*.
/ www.joeallen.co.uk; 12.45 am; no smoking area.

Joe's Brasserie SW6 £ 28 – – –
130 Wandsworth Bridge Rd   7731 7835   10–1B
John Brinkley (of the Wine Gallery etc.) has recently taken over this boisterous hang-out, in deepest Fulham; his bargain wines will surely draw the crowds, but don't expect any great shakes on the food front. / 11 pm.

Joe's Café SW3 £ 35 ④④❷
126 Draycott Ave   7225 2217   5–2C
This chic Brompton Cross lunch-and-brunch spot is still praised by some for the *"best people-watching"*, but the cooking is now *"totally ordinary"*, and service can be *"snooty"*. / L only; no booking at weekends.

John Burton-Race
The Landmark NW1 £ 90 ④❸④
222 Marylebone Rd   7723 7800   8–4A
"JB-R can cook, but what a price!" – some reporters are dazzled by his *"refined and rich"* Gallic cooking at this Marylebone 'fine dining' room, but it's the *"astronomical expense"* which stuns most, and the setting is *"terribly dull"*.
/ 10.30 pm; closed Sat L & Sun; set weekday L £47(FP).

F S A

Joy King Lau W1 £ 23 ❸④④
3 Leicester St   7437 1132   4–3A
"Above-average" cooking (with "top dim sum") distinguishes this large, unremarkable-looking Chinese, just off Leicester Square; it's slipping, though, and the "poor" décor and "grumpy" service offer no consolation. / 11.30 pm; no Switch.

Julie's W11 £ 47 ④④❶
135 Portland Rd   7229 8331   6–2A
An "exotic" subterranean Holland Park labyrinth which has long offered one of London's most "seductive" dining experiences; "it's a shame about the food", though, which is very "boring" indeed. / www.juliesrestaurant.com; 11.15 pm; closed Sat L.

Julie's Bar W11 £ 35 ④❸❶
137 Portland Rd   7727 7985   6–2A
This funky bar shares the "great atmosphere" of its parent next door; the cooking is equally humdrum, but seems more "reasonable" at the lower price. / www.juliesrestaurant.com; 10.45 pm.

Julius N1 £ 32 ④❸④
39 Upper St   7226 4380   8–3D
On a good day, the food's "surprisingly tasty" at this Gallic old-timer in Islington; too many "dire" reports, though, make it clear it's a rather up-and-down experience. / www.premierparty.co.uk; 11 pm; closed Sat & Sun.

Just Oriental SW1 £ 31 ④❷❸
19 King St   7930 9292   4–3C
Beneath Just St James's, this new oriental brasserie "is more casual than upstairs"; "for a good-value lunch", it has its uses, but it's difficult to see why one would seek it out otherwise. / www.juststjames.com/joabout.htm; 11 pm; closed Sun.

Just St James SW1 £ 45 ④④④
12 St James's St   7976 2222   3–4D
With its "pretentious" menu, its "disorganised" service and its conversion of a "magnificent" former bank that manages to be both "glitzy" and "dull", Peter Gladwin's large St James's newcomer "misses across the board". / www.juststjames.com; 11 pm, Sat midnight; closed Sun D.

Just The Bridge EC4 £ 38 ④⑤④
1 Paul's Walk   7236 0000   9–3A
The Millennium Bridge (by which it's sited) may have yet to open, but this "cold" bar/restaurant (formerly just 'The Bridge') already seems to be trading on its location, with "clueless" staff serving cooking that's too often "shoddy". / 10 pm; closed Sat & Sun.

K10 EC2 £ 20 ❶❷❷
20 Copthall Ave   7562 8510   9–2C
"The best conveyor-belt sushi in London" and an "interesting" hot selection of Japanese-inspired dishes win rave reviews for this "cool" but "friendly" yearling, near Liverpool Street. / www.k10.net; 10 pm; closed Sat & Sun; no smoking; no booking.

Kai W1 £ 48 ❷❶❷
65 South Audley Street   7493 8507   3–3A
*This "smart" Mayfair Chinese lacks profile, but its "excellent"
(if "very pricey") cooking makes it one of the top orientals in
town. / www.kaimayfair.co.uk; 10.45 pm.*

Kalamaras W2 £ 23 ④❸❸
66 Inverness Mews   7727 5082   6–2C
*Hidden away in a Bayswater mews, this long-established, BYO
taverna is not what it was, but still wins praise as a "friendly,
simple, happy Greek" that can be "great for parties". / 11 pm;
D only.*

Kandoo W2 £ 17 ❸❷❸
458 Edgware Rd   7724 2428   8–4A
*"It's not the best Iranian", but this "friendly" newcomer provides
a "cheap and cheerful" option on the grim stretch of the
Edgware Road north of the Westway; BYO (no corkage).
/ 11.30 pm; no Amex.*

Kaspia W1 £ 60 ❸④④
18-18a Bruton Pl   7493 2612   3–2B
*"Unashamed indulgence – hideously expensive"; that's really all
you need to know about this low-key dining room, behind
a Mayfair mews caviar shop. / www.caviarkaspia.com; 11.30 pm; closed
Sun; no Switch.*

Kastoori SW17 £ 19 ❶❶❸
188 Upper Tooting Rd   8767 7027   10–2C
*"Don't let the exterior put you off" – there's "nothing
run-of-the-mill" about this "faultless" Tooting Indo-African, which
attracts regulars from far and wide with its "friendly" service
and its "outstanding" vegetarian cooking. / 10.30 pm; closed
Mon L & Tue L; no Amex or Switch.*

Kaya Korean W1 £ 43 ④④⑤
42 Albemarle St   7499 0622   3–3C
*Staff are "friendly", but can "lack proper English" at this grand
Korean near the Ritz; its dated décor offers arguably the most
boring restaurant setting in London. / 10.30 pm; closed Sun L; set
weekday L £26(FP).*

Ken Lo's Memories SW1 £ 45 ❶❷❸
67-69 Ebury St   7730 7734   2–4B
*"It keeps standards up year after year", and this "civilised",
"top-class" Chinese near Victoria is 'on a roll' at present,
offering "memorable" cooking that's amongst the best in town;
a major refurbishment was under way at press time. / 10.45 pm;
closed Sun L.*

Kennington Lane SE11 £ 32 ❷❶❷
205-209 Kennington Ln   7793 8313   1–3C
*This understated yearling brings "West End" standards to an
unlovely corner of Kennington; virtues include "consistently
high-quality" cooking, "tirelessly helpful" service and a very
"agreeable" atmosphere (and the terrace is "a gem in
summer"). / 10.30 pm; closed Sat L.*

Kensington Place W8   £ 42   ④④❸
201-205 Kensington Church St   7727 3184   6–2B
*Some claim it's "still a benchmark", but this seminal modern
British brasserie off Notting Hill Gate is pretty "complacent"
nowadays; it still attracts "a good mix of people", though,
and remains a "fun, vibrant and noisy" destination. / 11.45 pm; set
always available £28(FP).*

Kettners W1   £ 29   ⑤④❸
29 Romilly St   7734 6112   4–2A
*"For grandeur", this "splendid" Edwardian remnant of 'Old
Soho' still has its admirers; claims that its pizza-and-burger
menu offers "the best value in the West End" ring very hollow
these days, however, and calls for "updating and refurbishment"
are now urgent. / midnight; no booking.*

Khan's W2   £ 15   ④⑤❸
13-15 Westbourne Grove   7727 5420   6–1C
*A lingering reputation as "Bayswater's finest" maintains the
crush at this "studenty" and "amazingly cheap" subcontinental;
it can still be "fun", but service is often "rude", and the cooking
is not what it used to be; no alcohol. / 11.45 pm; no smoking area.*

Khan's of Kensington SW7   £ 24   ❸❸④
3 Harrington Rd   7581 2900   5–2B
*On a good day you get "lovely, light Indian food" at this South
Kensington subcontinental stand-by; it's always been somewhat
erratic, though. / 11.15 pm, Fri & Sat 11.45 pm; no smoking area; set
weekday L £16(FP).*

Khyber Pass SW7   £ 22   ❸②⑤
21 Bute St   7589 7311   5–2B
*"A dump with style"; "who cares about the terrible décor" of
this South Kensington Indian – the "simple" cooking may not be
as consistent as it was, but it's undeniably cheap and it can be
"very good" on occasions. / 11.15 pm.*

King's Road Café
Habitat SW3   £ 21   ④❸❸
208 King's Rd   7351 6645   5–3C
*"Exceptionally good for an in-store venue"; some reporters tip
this "airy" in-store Italian café as "the best place on the King's
Road" if you're in the market for "coffee and a cake, or a light
lunch". / L only; no Amex; no smoking area.*

Konditor & Cook   £ 21   ❷❷❸
10 Stoney St, SE1   7407 5101   9–4C
66 The Cut, SE1   7620 2700   9–4A
*"Delicious soups", "fantastic espressos", "yummy savouries",
"cakes to die for" – such are the attractions of this simple café
attached to the Young Vic, which now has a tiny Borough
Market sibling. / The Cut 8 pm – Stoney St 6.30pm, Sat 2.30 pm; L & early
evening only; closed Sun; no Amex.*

Krungtap SW10   £ 21   ❸❸④
227 Old Brompton Rd   7259 2314   5–2A
This "café-style" Earl's Court Thai is "completely authentic and good value", but sadly devoid of the buzz it had prior to a fire a couple of years ago. / 10.30 pm.

Kulu Kulu W1   £ 18   ❷④④
76 Brewer St   7734 7316   3–2D
"It's not a very cheerful place", but some of the "best conveyor-sushi" in town – and at "reasonable prices" too – ensures that this small Soho spot is "always packed out". / 10 pm; closed Sun; no Amex; no smoking; no booking.

Kwan Thai SE1   £ 33   ❸④④
The Riverfront, Hay's Galleria   7403 7373   9–4D
It offers "good" Thai cooking, but this large South Bank riverside oriental is curiously "devoid of atmosphere". / www.kwanthairestaurant.co.uk; 10 pm; closed Sat D & Sun; no smoking area.

The Ladbroke Arms W11   £ 31   ❷④❸
54 Ladbroke Rd   7727 6648   6–2B
Some think this "nice" and "relaxed" Notting Hill boozer is "too crowded" nowadays – blame the "reliable and original" cooking, and also the sunny-day attractions of the "good outside seating area". / 9.45 pm; no Amex.

Lahore Kebab House E1   £ 16   ❶⑤④
2 Umberston St   7488 2551   11–1A
It's a "back-to-basics" experience, but – for "stunning" and "authentic" Pakistani fare – "it's worth the journey" to this unpolished East End "gem". / midnight; no credit cards.

The Landmark NW1   £ 45   ④❸❸
222 Marylebone Rd   7631 8000   8–4A
The "amazing winter garden" makes a visit to the soaring atrium of this swanky Marylebone hotel a "special experience"; four meals a day are served – tea is "the only affordable one" – but the food is pretty much "incidental". / www.landmarklondon.co.uk; 12.30 am; closed Sat L & Sun D; no smoking area.

The Lanesborough SW1   £ 56   ④❷❶
Hyde Park Corner   7259 5599   5–1D
"Beautifully-cooked breakfasts" and "very good teas" figure in many reports on the "fantastic", OTT conservatory dining room of this mega-swanky hotel; when it comes to 'proper' food, though, reporters tend to speak in terms of "average" cooking at "extortionate" prices. / www.lanesborough.com; midnight; jacket required at D; set weekday L £28(FP).

Langan's Bistro W1   £ 30   ❸❸❸
26 Devonshire St   7935 4531   2–1A
The tiny and "cosy" Marylebone counterpart to the famed Mayfair brasserie could not really be more different – it offers a classic 'romantic local bistro' experience. / www.langansrestaurants.co.uk; 11 pm; closed Sat L & Sun.

Langan's Brasserie W1   £ 43   ④④❷
Stratton St   7491 8822   3–3C
*If you "love celebrity-spotting" (the B-list kind), this large and
"buzzy" Mayfair stalwart still makes a reliable destination for
"a good night out"; the cooking is "heavy handed", though,
and for those who remember the place's glory-days it now
seems "a pale shadow of its former self".*
/ www.langansrestaurants.co.uk; 11.45 pm; closed Sat L & Sun.

Langan's Coq d'Or SW5   £ 36   ④④❸
254-260 Old Brompton Rd   7259 2599   5–3A
*Some laud this spacious, impressive-looking Gallic brasserie in
Earl's Court as a "good local eatery"; none of the glamour of its
West End parent, however, has ever rubbed off.*
/ www.langansrestaurants.co.uk; 11 pm; closed Mon.

The Langley WC2   £ 28   ④④④
5 Langley St   7836 5005   4–2C
*This "trendily" retro Covent Garden joint has an "interesting"
set-up in a series of large cellars; it's not a bad place for
a snack, but really much more somewhere to hang out rather
than to eat.* / www.latenightlondon.co.uk; 1 am, Sun 10.30 pm.

Lansdowne NW1   £ 29   ❸④❸
90 Gloucester Ave   7483 0409   8–3B
*Thanks to its "very chilled out" atmosphere, this "cool"
Primrose Hill gastropub can get "very crowded"; the cooking is
"inconsistent" however, and service can be "unbelievably
arrogant".* / 10 pm; closed Mon L; no Amex; book only for upstairs.

La Lanterna SE1   £ 30   ❸❷❷
6-8 Mill St   7252 2420   11–2A
*It's "overshadowed by the famous Butler's Wharf complex",
but this notably "friendly" and "well priced" little Italian is
a popular Bermondsey destination.* / 11 pm; closed Sat L.

Latymers W6   £ 22   ❷❸⑤
157 Hammersmith Rd   8741 2507   7–2C
*"Shame about the décor", but the "excellent Thai food at cheap
prices" ensures that the back dining room at this grim-looking
Hammersmith gin palace is "always packed".* / 10 pm; closed Sun;
no booking at L.

Laughing Gravy SE1   £ 33   ④❷❸
154 Blackfriars Rd   7721 7055   9–4A
*A "welcoming" atmosphere is an undoubted plus at this
"relaxed" Southwark bistro, but the cooking, if "imaginative", is
rather up-and-down.* / 10.30 pm; closed Sat L & Sun.

Launceston Place W8   £ 45   ❷❷❶
1a Launceston Pl   7937 6912   5–1B
*"An excellent stand-by for all seasons"; this "exemplary"
Kensington townhouse is "still an English classic", offering
consistently "good" food in a "very civilised" and "romantic"
setting.* / 11.30 pm; closed Sat L & Sun D.

FSA

Laurent NW2   £ 23   ❷❷⑤
428 Finchley Rd   7794 3603   1–1B
"Simple ambitions are all achieved" at this *"basic"* Cricklewood café; you get *"wonderful couscous"* – *"that's it"*. / 11 pm.

Lavender   £ 26   ❸❸❸
112 Vauxhall Walk, SE11   7735 4440   2–4D
171 Lavender Hill, SW11   7978 5242   10–2C
193 Lower Richmond Rd, SW15   8785 6004   10–1A
24 Clapham Rd, SW9   7793 0770   10–1D
Many admire these *"heart-warming"* *and* *"unpretentious"* *south London bistros for their* *"surprisingly good"* *and* *"reasonably-priced"* *fare.* / 10.50 pm.

Lemon Thyme SW13   £ 32   ⑤④⑤
190 Castelnau   8748 3437   7–2C
"Nearly OK" is one of the better reports on this *"deeply disappointing"* Red Pepper Group newcomer, south of Hammersmith Bridge; it's *"such a dull place"*, and the *"average"*, *"Italian-ish"* food is *"too expensive"*. / 10.45 pm; D only, except Sun open L & D.

Lemonia NW1   £ 26   ❸❶❷
89 Regent's Park Rd   7586 7454   8–3B
"Always bustling and fun", this *"ever-friendly"* Primrose Hill taverna *"never fails to please"* its huge following; the *"good, but not exciting"* food is *"not really the point"*. / 11.30 pm; closed Sat L & Sun D; no Amex; set weekday L £17(FP).

Levant W1   £ 34   ④❷❷
Jason Court, 76 Wigmore St   7224 1111   3–1A
Romantics feel *"whisked away on a magic carpet"* by the *"sexy"* ambience of this *"groovy"* basement bar/restaurant near Selfridges; sceptical foodies are unmoved by *"dull"* results from a *"static"* North African menu. / 11.30 pm; closed Sat L & Sun.

The Lexington W1   £ 31   ④④❸
Lexington St   7434 3401   3–2D
Objectively, it's pretty *"average"* *all round (particularly the 'global' cooking), but the* *"friendly"* *staff and nicely hidden-away location of this narrow Soho spot create an ambience some find* *"charming"*. / 11 pm; closed Sat L & Sun.

The Light E1   £ 33   ❸❸❶
233 Shoreditch High St   7247 8989   9–1D
"Light, airy and buzzy", this bar/restaurant/nightclub just north of Liverpool Street *"oozes style"*, and its *"unshowy"* grub is surprisingly *"good value"*. / 11 pm; closed Sat L.

The Light House SW19   £ 39   ❷❸❸
75-77 Ridgway   8944 6338   10–2B
"Wimbledon's finest", cheer fans of the *"interesting fusion cuisine"* and *"trendy, modern setting"* of this year-old venture; doubters say the cooking is *"not as good as they think it is"*, and find the whole set-up *"a bit too bright and shiny"*. / 10.45 pm; no smoking area.

Lime EC2 £ 28 ④❸④
1 Curtain Rd   7247 2225   9–1D
*"Perhaps they should stick to alcohol" at this "so busy" and
"noisy" Shoreditch bar; some say it's "hip", but for others it's
just "poor all round".* / www.limeuk.com; 10 pm; closed Sat & Sun.

Lindsay House W1 £ 63 ❸❸❷
21 Romilly St   7439 0450   4–3A
*This "lovely" Soho townhouse is hailed by some as the "ultimate
romantic destination"; Irish chef Richard Corrigan's "indulgent"
cooking has hit a more consistent beat of late, but it's still "not
as good as it was a couple of years ago".* / www.lindsayhouse.co.uk;
11 pm; closed Sat L & Sun; set weekday L £40(FP).

Lisboa Patisserie W10 £ 6 ❶❷❸
57 Golborne Rd   8968 5242   6–1A
*"Outstanding pasteis de nata" (custard tarts, to the uninitiated)
are the highlight at this "essential" North Kensington
Portuguese café – for many, it's "the best place in town for
a coffee and a bun".* / 8 pm; no credit cards; no booking.

The Little Bay NW6 £ 17 ❸❸❷
228 Belsize Rd   7372 4699   1–2B
*"The food is as cheap as some supermarket ready meals" –
and "very good, considering" – at this "unbeatable-value"
Kilburn bistro; admittedly it "could use a lick of paint",
but "friendly service" helps maintain a "romantic, candle-lit
atmosphere".* / midnight; no credit cards; no smoking area; need 4+ to
book; pre-th. £11(FP).

Little Italy W1 £ 42 ④❸❷
21 Frith St   7734 4737   4–2A
*"Open late in Soho", this "squashed", "lively" and "sometimes
very noisy" joint serves "good and homely", but "overpriced"
Italian fare.* / 4 am, Sun 11.30 pm.

The Little Square W1 £ 34 ④❸④
3 Shepherd Mkt   7355 2101   3–4B
*It "verges on cramped", but this "tiny" bistro makes a "decent"
Shepherd Market stand-by.* / 11 pm.

Livebait £ 41 ❸④④
21 Wellington St, WC2   7836 7161   4–3D
2 Hollywood Rd, SW10   7349 5500   5–3B
175 Westbourne Grove, W8   7727 4321   6–1B
43 The Cut, SE1   7928 7211   9–4A
2 Wandsworth C'n N'side, SW18   7326 8580   10–2C
1 Watling St, EC4   7213 0540   9–3B
*"The zing has gone" from this fish and seafood chain (which
originated at the Waterloo premises which are still its best
outlet); for "unexciting but well-cooked dishes", it does have its
fans, but many feel that the "cafeteria styling is not really
appropriate for the pricey menu".* / www.santeonline.com; 11.30 pm –
W8 11 pm – EC4 10 pm; WC2, SW10 & SE1 closed Sun – EC4 closed
Sat & Sun – SW18 closed Mon L & Tue L; no smoking areas.

LMNT E8 £ 30 ④❸❶
316 Queensbridge Rd 7249 6727 1–2D
*"Amazing opera-set décor" (with "nice little alcoves") has
helped this newly-converted Dalston boozer make quite
a splash; the cooking was "creaking" in the early days, but the
summer '01 arrival of a new chef may pep it up.* / 11 pm;
no Amex.

Lobster Pot SE11 £ 36 ❷❸❸
3 Kennington Ln 7582 5556 1–3C
*"Quaint", "kitsch" and "quirky" – this "bright" bistro rejoices in
a very unlikely Kennington location, but it's as "authentic"
a Froggie as you'll find; "serious" fish and seafood dishes are
"lovingly prepared", but are no great bargain.*
/ www.lobsterpotrestaurant.co.uk; 11 pm; closed Sun & Mon.

Loch Fyne £ 33 ④④❸
676 Fulham Rd, SW6 7610 8020 10–1B
2 Park Rd, N8 8342 7740 1–1C
175 Hampton Rd, TW2 8255 6222 1–4A
*This national chain of mid-priced fish-and-seafood restaurants
has recently reached the capital; some find them
"unpretentious, good value and well organised", but our own
initial experience chimed with a report of "lacklustre" cooking
and "bad" service.* / www.loch-fyne.com; 10 pm – N8 Fri & Sat 11 pm;
no smoking areas.

Lola's N1 £ 36 ❸❸❷
359 Upper St 7359 1932 8–3D
*Even some fans find the food and service "erratic", but this
"atmospheric" and "welcoming" restaurant above Islington's
antiques market remains popular – particularly for "a romantic
dinner", or for "Sunday brunch with jazz and Bloody Marys".*
/ 11 pm; booking: max 8.

Lomo SW10 £ 22 ❸❶❷
222-224 Fulham Rd 7349 8848 5–3B
*"Fab" service and "fun and unusual" culinary combinations
have made quite a name for this "buzzy" tapas bar, and its
Chelsea 'Beach' location makes it "ideal for people-watching".*
/ www.lomo.co.uk; 11.30 pm; closed weekday L; no booking after 7.30 pm.

The Lord Palmerston NW5 £ 23 ❷❸❷
33 Dartmouth Park Hill 7485 1578 8–1B
*"Totally dependable" cooking, a "cosy" setting and "very
friendly staff" make this "relaxed" gastropub, near Archway,
a consistent success.* / 10 pm; no Amex; no booking.

Lots Road SW10 £ 26 ❷❷❷
114 Lots Rd 7352 6645 5–4B
*"Great burgers, chips and salads" are typical of the simple but
"fresh" cooking at this "light", "airy" newcomer; thanks to its
obscure distant-Chelsea location it "never gets overcrowded".*
/ 11 pm.

FSA

Lou Pescadou SW5 £ 38 ❸❸④
241 Old Brompton Rd 7370 1057 5–3A
*"Mad but funny" service adds spice to this "breezily French"
Earl's Court fish veteran, where the cooking "rarely disappoints".*
/ midnight; set Sun L £25(FP).

Luc's Brasserie EC3 £ 36 ❸❸④
17-22 Leadenhall Mkt 7621 0666 9–2D
*Thanks to its "real French atmosphere" and cooking that's
"reasonably priced, for the City", this "tightly-packed" brasserie
is often "overcrowded".* / L only, closed Sat & Sun; no Switch.

Luigi's WC2 £ 46 ④④④
15 Tavistock St 7240 1795 4–3D
*This rather grand Italian in a Covent Garden townhouse is still
a "stand-by" for old fans, but even those who say that
"on a good night, the cooking can still excel" admit that the
place is "getting tired".* / 11.30 pm; closed Sun; pre-th. £25(FP).

Lundum's SW7 £ 37 ❷❶❶
119 Old Brompton Rd 7373 7774 5–2B
*"The owners are in charge, and it shows", at this "formal" but
"comfortable" establishment on the fringe of South Kensington;
its "authentic" and "beautifully-presented" Danish cooking, is
beginning to develop a real following.* / 10.30 pm; closed Sun D.

Ma Goa SW15 £ 29 ❷❷④
244 Upper Richmond Rd 8780 1767 10–2B
*A "different" and "excellent" take on subcontinental cuisine, has
won quite a following for this family-run Goan bistro in Putney;
the place could, perhaps, use "a bit more mood".*
/ www.magoa.co.uk; 11 pm; D only, closed Mon.

Made in Italy SW3 £ 32 ❷④❷
249 King's Rd 7352 1880 5–3C
*Service can still be "slack", but this "loud", "smoky" and "rather
overcrowded" Chelsea Italian has bucked its ideas up of late;
"fantastic bench pizza" is the highlight of a "good-value" menu.*
/ 11.30 pm; closed weekday L; no Amex.

Madhu's Brilliant UB1 £ 24 ❷❸④
39 South Rd 8574 1897 1–3A
*"Indian doesn't get better than this", says a South Kensington
fan justifying his schlep all the way to this Southall "classic"; our
own view would be that it's a good place, but not worth quite
such a journey.* / 11.30 pm; closed Tue, Sat L & Sun L.

Maggie Jones's W8 £ 38 ④❸❶
6 Old Court Pl 7937 6462 5–1A
*"Huge wooden tables", "cosy booths" and other "rustic"
touches create a "great atmosphere" at this immutable
Kensington stalwart; with its "traditional" cooking – "good pies"
and so on – it's "a favourite during the wintry months".* / 11 pm.

Maggiore's WC2 £ 35 ❸❸❸

33 King St 7379 9696 4–3C
*This Covent Garden newcomer (on the site of Plummer's, RIP) is
already "busy" – thanks to its "homely" setting and its Italian
dishes that are "well cooked", and come in "good-size portions".
/ 11.30 pm.*

Maison Bertaux W1 £ 5 ❷❸❷

28 Greek St 7437 6007 4–2A
*Established in 1871, this Bohemian Soho coffee shop is an
institution "to be cherished", and even those who find the coffee
"somewhat ordinary" admit that the cakes are "excellent".
/ 8.30 pm; no credit cards; no smoking area.*

Maison Novelli EC1 £ 45 ❷❸❸

29 Clerkenwell Grn 7251 6606 9–1A
*"He may be no accountant, but he can cook" – J-C Novelli is
back doing what he does best, and many hail the "pleasing
revival" of his ambitious Clerkenwell restaurant; for "a proper
break with the past", some feel the time has come for him to
move on from these rather "tired" premises. / 11 pm; closed
Sat L & Sun; set weekday L & pre-th. £29(FP).*

Malabar W8 £ 26 ❷❷❸

27 Uxbridge St 7727 8800 6–2B
*Newcomers invariably find it a "nice surprise" to visit this
"consistently good" Indian, just off Notting Hill Gate –
a longtime favourite thanks to its "subtly-spiced" cooking and its
(relatively) "serene" setting. / www.malabar-restaurant.co.uk; 11.15 pm;
no Amex.*

Malabar Junction WC1 £ 33 ❷❷❸

107 Gt Russell St 7580 5230 2–1C
*"A real surprise" – it's quite "elegant" inside this
ordinary-looking Bloomsbury south Indian, where "distinctive"
dishes are "properly served" by "helpful" staff. / 11.30 pm;
no smoking area.*

La Mancha SW15 £ 31 ❸❸❷

32 Putney High St 8780 1022 10–2B
*"Great fun and good for big groups" – this large and "reliable",
Putney bar/restaurant serves "cheap, tasty tapas", and is
"always full of people enjoying themselves". / www.lamancha.co.uk;
11 pm, Fri-Sun 11.30 pm; set weekday L £20(FP).*

Mandalay W2 £ 18 ❷❶⑤

444 Edgware Rd 7258 3696 8–4A
*"You need to book, even if it is on Edgware Road" – this "tiny"
Burmese café isn't much to look at, but its service is "very
personable" and its "interesting" cooking offers "great value".
/ 10.30 pm; closed Sun; no smoking; booking essential; set weekday L £11(FP).*

Mandarin Kitchen W2 £ 28 ❶❸④

14-16 Queensway 7727 9012 6–2C
*"Full of happy Chinese eating lobster" – "superb" seafood is the
highlight at this "chaotic" and "boring"-looking Bayswater
oriental. / 11.15 pm; set weekday L £17(FP).*

FSA

Mandola W11 £ 22 ③④②
139 Westbourne Grove 7229 4734 6–1B
The Sudanese grub "is not as good as in yesteryear" at this
Notting Hill café, but the BYO policy helps bolster popularity,
and the place still delivers a "fun", "atmospheric" and
"good-value" night out. / 10.30 pm; no Amex.

Mango Room NW1 £ 29 ②③①
10 Kentish Town Rd 7482 5065 8–3B
A "relaxed, bustling" ambience fills this "funky" Camden Town
Caribbean, but that's not to ignore the "innovative",
"West Indian/fusion food", whose quality comes as a "pleasant
surprise". / 11 pm; closed Mon L; no Amex.

Mango Tree SW1 £ 45 ④②④
46 Grosvenor Pl 7823 1888 2–4B
Pleasant and efficient service is a highlight at this airy new
Belgravia Thai; its well-spaced tables and its rather tame
cooking struck us, on our August '01 visit, as making it better
suited to business than pleasure. / Rated on Editors' assessment;
www.mangotree.org.uk; 10.45 pm; closed Sat L; no smoking area.

Manna NW3 £ 29 ②③③
4 Erskine Rd 7722 8028 8–3B
This "venerable veggie institution" in Primrose Hill is on
"top-class" form at present, serving "ambitious vegetarian fare"
that's "delicious" (and "not too expensive" either) in a "lively"
setting. / www.manna-veg.com; 10.45 pm; closed weekday L; no Amex;
no smoking.

Manor W11 £ 39 ④④②
6-8 All Saints Rd 7243 0969 6–1B
Like its predecessor Mas Café (RIP, same owners), this Notting
Hill newcomer is a cool and laid-back venue – a late-night (and
brunch) kind of place; the food was better than expected on an
early (June '01) visit. / Rated on Editors' assessment; 10 pm; D only.

Manorom WC2 £ 27 ③③④
16 Maiden Ln 7240 4139 4–3D
This "cosy" Covent Garden Thai is a "good-value" place which is
often overlooked – perhaps just as well, as it's so small. / 11 pm;
closed Sat L & Sun; no booking, Thu-Sat.

Manzi's WC2 £ 42 ③③③
1 Leicester St 7734 0224 4–3A
"Still good, if you choose the simple dishes", this "reassuringly
old-fashioned" Theatrelander maintains its "solid" appeal to fish
lovers of a traditional bent; if you go pre-theatre, "insist on
seeing the set menu", which offers particularly good value.
/ www.manzis.co.uk; 11.45 pm (Cabin Room 10.30 pm); closed Sun L; set
weekday L £28(FP).

Mao Tai £ 38 ❷❷❸
96 Draycott Ave, SW3   7225 2500   5–2C
58 New King's Rd, SW6   7731 2520   10–1B
"Imaginative" Chinese cuisine and "sharp" design have long
made the Parson's Green original of this mini-chain a very
popular destination; many reporters find it "a bit overpriced",
though – perhaps it's to help pay for the new branch at
Brompton Cross? / www.maotai.co.uk; 11.30 pm; no smoking area.

Maquis W6 £ 35 – – –
111-115 Hammersmith Grove   no tel   7–1C
Regional French dishes are to be the speciality of this new
Hammersmith deli-restaurant, scheduled to open in
late-September '01 – it's an offshoot of the celebrated Moro,
so the burden of expectation is a high one.

Marché Mövenpick SW1 £ 21 ④⑤⑤
Bressenden Pl   7630 1733   2–4B
Swiss railways may run like clockwork, but their cafeterias,
it seems, don't – such is the evidence at this big basement off
Victoria Street, which offers a wide variety of lacklustre food
which "isn't that cheap", and a "depth of staff ignorance"
which can be "truly incredible". / www.movenpick.ch; 11 pm;
no smoking area.

Marine Ices NW3 £ 23 ❸❸❸
8 Haverstock Hill   7482 9003   8–2B
"The pasta's OK" (and the pizza's fine), "but it's the ice cream
that's so good" at this "old-established" favourite, by Chalk
Farm tube; "nothing bothers them, and children love the place".
/ 10.30 pm; no Amex; no smoking area.

Maroush £ 38 ❷④④
I) 21 Edgware Rd, W2   7723 0773   6–1D
II) 38 Beauchamp Pl, SW3   7581 5434   5–1C
III) 62 Seymour St, W1   7724 5024   2–2A
An "authentic" Lebanese chain which is "generally good,
but can be variable"; top value is to be had at the cafés at I
& II which are "great for a late night shawarma", and serve
"tasty juices" – restaurant prices are quite high. / W1 1 am – W2
2 am – SW3 5 am.

The Marquis W1 £ 37 ❸❶④
121a Mount St   7499 1256   3–3B
"Quiet and discreet", this Mayfair dining room is so
"businesslike" that it's arguably "for business only" – that's
a shame as it's a "reliable" place with "attentive" service,
and it's very reasonably priced for somewhere just opposite the
Connaught. / 10.45 pm; closed Sat & Sun.

Masala Zone W1 £ 19 ❷❷❸
9 Marshall St   7287 9966   3–2D
They're "trying hard" at this "interesting" new concept, just off
Carnaby Street, which serves "good Indian street food" in
a "modern 'designer' hall". / www.realindianfood.com; 11.30 pm;
no Amex; no smoking; no booking.

Mash W1   £ 40   ⑤⑤⑤

19-21 Gt Portland St   7637 5555   3–1C

"The bar's fun" but the restaurant is "awful" at this potentially "cool" venue near Oxford Circus – it combines "terrible" cooking with "poor" service and a "clinical" atmosphere. / www.gruppo.co.uk; 11 pm; closed Sun.

Mash Mayfair W1   £ 38   ⑤⑤⑤

26b Albemarle St   7495 5999   3–3C

"Overpriced" and "truly dreadful" – Oliver Peyton has swapped one failed format (Coast, RIP) for another at this studiously wacky Mayfair newcomer; the food is as "disappointing" as at its sibling north of Oxford Street. / www.gruppo.co.uk; 10.30 pm; closed Sun.

The Mason's Arms SW8   £ 27   ❷④❷

169 Battersea Park Rd   7622 2007   10–1C

"Yummy" pub food is served in a "cool", "noisy" and "crowded" atmosphere at this favourite Battersea boozer; service, though, can be "desultory". / 10 pm.

Matsuri SW1   £ 52   ❷❷④

15 Bury St   7839 1101   3–3D

The "authentic" teppan-yaki makes a "great show" at this "reliable" St James's oriental (which also serves "excellent sushi"); the setting is a touch "sterile", but regulars say "you get used to it". / www.matsuri-restaurant.com; 10.30 pm; closed Sun.

Maxwell's   £ 29   ④④❸

8-9 James St, WC2   7836 0303   4–2D

76 Heath St, NW3   7794 5450   8–1A

Long-established burger chain that isn't bad, but isn't good enough to generate much in the way of survey feedback either. / www.maxwells.co.uk; midnight – NW3 Fri & Sat 1 am; NW3 closed weekday L.

Mediterraneo W11   £ 38   ❷❸❷

37 Kensington Park Rd   7792 3131   6–1A

"Fun, if noisy and squashed" – Notting Hill types are practically unanimous in their praise for this "great local", which offers "terrific pasta" and other "good-value" fare; service, though, can be "too Italian" for some tastes. / 11.30 pm; set weekday L £23(FP).

Mekong SW1   £ 21   ❸❷④

46 Churton St   7630 9568   2–4B

"Reliable", "quick" and "cheap" – this Pimlico Vietnamese is a classic "good old stand-by". / 11.30 pm; no Amex.

Mela WC2   £ 24   ❷④❸

152-156 Shaftesbury Ave   7836 8635   4–2B

"Very good-value" Indian cooking ("with a modern twist") has made this "cramped" café "a nice addition" to the West End; "service has had teething problems", but the staff are "eager to please". / www.melarestaurant.co.uk; midnight; no smoking area.

Melati W1 £ 28 ❷❸⑤
21 Great Windmill St   7437 2745   3–2D
*Though the décor's "not great", this "delicious" and "cheap"
Malaysian canteen near Piccadilly Circus has long been
"a refuge in a seedy part of Soho", and it makes an "ideal"
pre-theatre destination. / 11.30 pm, Fri & Sat 12.30 am.*

Le Mercury N1 £ 22 ④④❷
140a Upper St   7354 4088   8–3D
*"So cheap, and with a great location" – this Bohemian bistro
near Islington's Almeida Theatre may serve "simple French"
food that's far too "hit-and-miss", but it has bags of "cosy,
candle-lit" charm, and at least "you're never surprised by the
bill". / 12.45 am; no Amex; no smoking area; set weekday L £14(FP).*

Mesclun N16 £ 28 ❶❶❷
24 Stoke Newington Church St   7249 5029   1–1C
*"Wow!", "a find" – "'food as good as many West End
restaurants, but at a fraction of the cost" (with "attentive"
service too) is winning an ever-wider north London following for
this "friendly" and "understated" Stoke Newington spot. / 11 pm;
no Amex.*

Meson don Felipe SE1 £ 22 ④❸❶
53 The Cut   7928 3237   9–4A
*"The Spanish guitarist (from Deptford, so they say)" is
a controversial figure at this "vibrant", "cramped" and "noisy"
old favourite, near the Old Vic; "cheap" and "solid" tapas and
"a good selection of Riojas" help make it a "reliable" choice.
/ 11 pm; closed Sun; no Amex; no booking after 8 pm.*

Le Metro SW3 £ 30 ❸❷④
28 Basil St   7589 6286   5–1D
*"Keep it a secret" – the "best, cheap food in the area" is to be
had at this "tiny" basement by Harrods; it also boasts a "very
good wine list". / www.capitalgrp.co.uk; 9.45 pm; closed Sun L & D, but
open for breakfast.*

Metrogusto £ 37 ❷❶❸
13 Theberton St, N1   7226 9400   8–3D
153 Battersea Park Rd, SW8   7720 0204   10–1C
*"Wonderful, personal service" and "accomplished" cooking are
winning quite a name for this duo of Italian locals; the new
branch has already established itself as something of a "leading
light" in Islington. / 10.30 pm – SW8 Fri & Sat 10.45 pm; SW8 closed Sun
– N1 closed Mon; no Amex; no smoking area.*

Mezzanine
Royal National Theatre SE1 £ 32 ④❷❸
South Bank   7452 3600   2–3D
*"Quick service" and fodder that's "not bad, for a theatre
restaurant" prompt applause for this "useful and consistent"
amenity within the RNT. / www.nationaltheatre.org.uk; 11 pm; closed Sun;
no smoking area.*

Mezzo W1   £ 45   ⑤⑤⑤

100 Wardour St   7314 4000   3–2D
*"Conran complacency shines through" at this "noisy" and
"cavernous" Soho tourist-trap; "surly" service and "slapdash"
cooking too often make it "a waste of time and money".*
/ www.conran.com; midnight, Thu-Sat 1 am (bar food until 3 am); closed
Mon L, Tue L & Sat L; set weekday L, Sun L & pre-th.£28(FP).

Mezzonine W1   £ 34   ⑤④④

100 Wardour St   7314 4000   3–2D
*Mezzo's less expensive, but equally poor-value, upstairs section
serves a "pretentious" Asian menu in a huge, "cafeteria"-style
setting.* / www.conran.com; 12.45 am, Fri & Sat 2.45 am; closed Sun.

Mildreds W1   £ 22   ❷❷❷

58 Greek St   7494 1634   4–2A
*"The best veggie food in Soho" – and in "big portions" too –
ensures disproportionate popularity for this "tiny" and
"cramped" café.* / 11 pm; closed Sun D; no credit cards; no smoking;
no booking.

Mimmo d'Ischia SW1   £ 56   ④❸❸

61 Elizabeth St   7730 5406   2–4A
*"Crazy" prices provoke claims that this old-style Belgravia Italian
"trades on its location and its famous friends"; it does not want
for supporters, though, who vaunt the "great" atmosphere and
who say the cooking is "superb".* / 11 pm; closed Sun.

Mims EN4   £ 27   ❸④⑤

63 East Barnet Rd   8449 2974   1–1B
*Fans of this odd Barnet foodie Mecca still find the singular
cooking "quite amazing for the price"; service can be "terrible",
though, and the old hand who says "this place was great in the
early '90s, but the decline continues" probably has it about
right.* / 11 pm; closed Mon; no Amex or Switch; no smoking area; set Sun L
£15(FP).

MIRABELLE W1   £ 52   ❷❷❷

56 Curzon St   7499 4636   3–4B
*"Thirties-style glamour", "good-value" Gallic cooking,
an "impressive" wine list and "slick service" make a smooth
cocktail – one that continues to win huge popularity for MPW's
Mayfair classic.* / www.whitestarline.org.uk; 10.45 pm; no smoking area.

Mitsukoshi SW1   £ 53   ❷❷⑤

14-20 Lower Regent St   7930 0317   3–3D
*The "dated" décor truly is "dreadful", but the sushi counter
offers "beautiful food for introverts" at this "traditional" West
End Japanese; it also makes a serviceable venue for business.*
/ 9.30 pm; closed Sun; set weekday L £20(FP).

regular updates at www.hardens.com   113

Miyabi
Great Eastern Hotel EC2 £ 40 ❸④④

40 Liverpool St 7618 7100 9–2D
"Small, smart and quiet" Japanese Conran café, by Liverpool Street station; service is iffy, but the sushi and other fare are generally well received. / www.conran.com; 10.30 pm; closed Sat & Sun; booking: max 6.

Miyama W1 £ 55 ❸❷⑤

38 Clarges St 7499 2443 3–4B
For a "classic Japanese business lunch", this smart, if soulless, Mayfair fixture has much to recommend it – not least, "excellent sushi and sashimi" and other "very good and authentic fare". / 10.30 pm; closed Sat L & Sun L.

Mju
Millennium Knightsbridge SW1 £ 70 ④❷❸

17 Sloane St 7235 4377 5–1D
Is there enough money – even in Knightsbridge's glitter gulch – to sustain Tetsuya Wakuda's Franco-Japanese fusion newcomer?; we enjoyed our July '01 visit to this comfortable hotel dining room, and service charmed, but prices – even for the beautifully-arranged protein morsels – seemed unjustified. / Rated on Editors' assessment; 10 pm; no smoking; set weekday L £33(FP).

Mohsen W14 £ 17 ❷❸⑤

152 Warwick Rd 7602 9888 7–1D
The location – opposite Kensington's Homebase – couldn't be more "drab", but some of "the best kebabs in town" provide ample compensation at this "great-value" Persian; BYO. / 11.30 pm; no credit cards; no booking.

Momo W1 £ 44 ④❸❶

25 Heddon St 7434 4040 3–2C
"Intriguing" and "exotic" (and "a bit cliquey") – Mourad Mazouz's "low-lit" and "romantic" Mayfair Moroccan still bewitches the faithful, even thought the grub is decidedly "average". / 10.30 pm.

Mon Plaisir WC2 £ 38 ❸❸❶

21 Monmouth St 7836 7243 4–2B
A "traditional French" approach has long made this eminent Covent Garden old-timer – with its "gorgeous nooks and crannies" – a "solid" Theatreland favourite; this year, however, too many reports of "lapses from usual standards" sound a warning note. / www.mon-plaisir.co.uk; 11.15 pm; closed Sat L & Sun; set weekday L £25(FP).

Mona Lisa SW10 £ 15 ❸❶❸

417 King's Rd 7376 5447 5–3B
An "haute cuisine greasy spoon", which offers "basic" but "cheap" Italian fare, in a "jolly" Chelsea caff setting. / 11 pm; closed Sun D; no Amex.

Mongolian Barbecue £ 24 ⑤⑤④
12 Maiden Ln, WC2   7379 7722   4–3D
1-3 Acton Ln, W4   8995 0575   7–2A
It can be "good for groups", but that's the only justification for
this "pretty gross" stir-fry chain; its "DIY slop" is "about as
Mongolian as the Queen". / 11 pm; D only; no Amex.

Monkeys SW3 £ 62 ❷❷❶
1 Cale St   7352 4711   5–2C
"Great" staff help create a "wonderful" atmosphere at this
"discreet" Chelsea fixture, where game is the speciality; for
"an old-fashioned, delicious, traditional meal" – and with
a serious wine list to match – it has few equals. / 10 pm; closed
Sat & Sun; no Amex.

Monsieur Max TW12 £ 50 ❶❷❷
133 High St, Hampton Hill   8979 5546   1–4A
"Sublime" Gallic cooking (and "excellent" service too) have long
succeeded in making Max Renzland's "classy" joint an
improbable destination in suburban Hampton Hill; let's hope it's
not too thrown by the summer '01 loss of chef Morgan
Meunier. / 9.30 pm; closed Mon, Sat L & Sun D.

Montana SW6 £ 41 ④④④
125-131 Dawes Rd   7385 9500   10–1B
This Fulham hang-out may be "the original and the best" of
a small group of southwest American restaurants, but – like its
siblings – this "once-great local" has "lost its edge"; "awesome"
brunch fare, however, still has its fans. / www.montanafood.co.uk;
11 pm, Fri & Sat 11.30 pm; Mon-Thu D only, Fri-Sun open L & D.

Monte's SW1 £ 48 ❸❸④
164 Sloane St   7245 0896   5–1D
Jamie Oliver and this "boring" Knightsbridge club dining room
was an odd marriage, and views on the culinary offspring from
the first year of the union are mixed – from "nondescript" to
"exceptional"; it is clear, however, that "cookbooks everywhere"
do little for the ambience. / www.montes.co.uk; 11.15 pm, Mon
10.45 pm; L only (open for D to members only), closed Sun.

Montpeliano SW7 £ 49 ❸❷❸
13 Montpelier St   7589 0032   5–1C
As usual, regulars say this "noisy" old Knightsbridge trattoria is
simply "the best Italian in London"; equally predictably, there's
a vocal opposition, for whom it's just "ordinary in every way
except the prices". / 11.45 pm; set weekday L £27(FP).

The Montrose NW6 £ 30 ⑤⑤❸
105 Salusbury Rd   7372 8882   1–2B
It's a "nice space", and they seem to try hard at this new
bar/restaurant near Queen's Park (previously The Park, RIP),
but – on our July '01 visit – the cooking was plain poor, and it
came very, very slowly. / Rated on Editors' assessment; 11 pm; D only.

Monza SW3 £39 ❸❶❸
6 Yeoman's Row 7591 0210 5–2C
"Passionate" service and a "secret-hideaway" feel perhaps lead
fans to over-rate the cooking at this "busy" Knightsbridge
trattoria – critics find it a touch "nondescript". / 11.30 pm; closed
Mon L.

MORO EC1 £33 ❶❷❷
34-36 Exmouth Mkt 7833 8336 9–1A
"Thrilling and imaginative" Southern Med/Moorish cooking,
"friendly and helpful" service and a "buzzy" (if "crowded")
ambience are propelling this unpretentious Clerkenwell four-year
old to ever-greater prominence. / 10.30 pm; closed Sat L & Sun.

The Mortimer W1 £25 ❸④④
37-40 Berners St 7436 0451 2–1B
Some find the style too reminiscent of All Bar One, but this large
Fitzrovia gastropub generally pleases with its "delicious" and
"reasonably-priced" fare. / 10 pm; closed Sat & Sun.

Morton's W1 £39 ④❸❸
28 Berkeley Sq 7493 7171 3–3B
The "beautiful" first-floor dining room of this Mayfair club (open
to non-members) undoubtedly has a "good atmosphere",
but the "patchy" cooking "is not what it was a couple of years
ago". / 11.30 pm; closed Sat L & Sun.

Moshi Moshi £23 ❸④❸
2nd Floor, Cabot Place East, E14 7512 9911 11–1C
Unit 24, Liverpool St Station, EC2 7247 3227 9–2D
7-8 Limeburner Ln, EC4 7248 1808 9–2A
"Arrive before noon", if you're "to beat the rush" at these
"handy" conveyor-sushi bars; they were the first such places in
town, and still offer "good sushi and quick service".
/ www.moshimoshi.co.uk; 9 pm; closed Sat & Sun; no Amex; EC2 & E14
no smoking – EC4 no smoking area; EC2 & E14 no booking.

Motcombs SW1 £44 ④❸④
26 Motcomb St 7235 6382 5–1D
This "discreet" Belgravia basement has long been something of
a local institution, certainly for the "older crowd"; the food is no
more than "OK", though, and the atmosphere not what it used
to be. / www.motcombs.co.uk; 11 pm; closed Sun; no smoking area.

MPW Brasserie
Forte Post House NW3 £32 ⑤⑤⑤
215 Haverstock Hill 7435 6080 8–2A
"It tries to trade on the MPW name, and it doesn't work";
perhaps Mr White sees this "pretentious", "incompetent" and
"grossly overpriced" Hampstead brasserie prototype as
a suitable brand 'extension', but a better word would be
'prostitution'. / 10.30 pm, Thu-Sat 11 pm.

Mr Chow SW1 £ 48 ❸❷❷
151 Knightsbridge   7589 7347   5–1D
*Sceptics dismiss the cooking as "almost oriental" – and the
whole experience as "ordinary in most ways" – but this
Knightsbridge "living legend" is highly praised by many for its
"first class, if pricey food", its "keen" (Italian) service and its
"great" atmosphere. / midnight.*

Mr Kong WC2 £ 20 ❷❸④
21 Lisle St   7437 7341   4–3A
*Some of the best dishes are "carefully hidden on the list of
specials" at this "excellent and cheap" Chinatown "fixture";
it's a bit "shabby", and the "awful" basement is best avoided.
/ 2.45 am.*

Mr Wing SW5 £ 40 ❷❷❶
242-244 Old Brompton Rd   7370 4450   5–2A
*"Jungle-o-rama!" – "dazzling tropical fish and plants" set the
scene at this "special" Earl's Court basement; it's long been
seen as a great party or romantic venue, but "don't let the
greenery distract you from the food" – its current form puts it
"among the best Chineses in town". / midnight.*

Murano TW1 £ 35 ④❷④
3 Hill St   8948 8330   1–4A
*"Well organised" service helps make this "lively" – if perhaps
"cheerless" – first-floor Italian a handy refuge from the
chain-hell that is downtown Richmond. / 11 pm; no smoking area.*

Le Muscadet W1 £ 37 ❸④⑤
25 Paddington St   7935 2883   2–1A
*Some long-time fans "still like" this dated Marylebone French
restaurant, but to many it feels a little "run down" nowadays –
an impression which sometimes "poor" service does nothing to
dispel. / 10.45 pm, Sat 10 pm; closed Sat L & Sun; no jeans.*

Mustards Brasserie EC1 £ 28 ④❸④
60 Long Ln   7796 4920   9–1B
*"Uninspiring but convenient", this "reliable" Gallic
bistro/brasserie is a "friendly" Smithfield spot, "good for lunch or
an after-work dinner, near the City". / 11 pm; closed Sat & Sun.*

**Nahm
Halkin Hotel SW1** £ 65 ❷❸④
5 Halkin St   7333 1234   2–3A
*This Belgravia hotel dining room has been given an expensively
understated – or should that be 'underpowered'? – makeover,
and is now home to celebrated Aussie chef David Thompson;
his sock-it-to-'em Thai cooking impressed us on our July '01 visit,
but ill-conceived puds took the gloss off the meal which came at
a hefty price. / Rated on Editors' assessment; 11 pm; closed Sat L & Sun L.*

Naked Turtle SW14   £ 32   ④❷❶
505 Upper Richmond Rd   8878 1995   10–2A
"Entertainment lifts the whole experience" of visiting this
"cheerful" Sheen wine bar, where *"unique singing waitresses"*
and a *"piano player"* make reporters tolerant of the *"eccentric"*
and *"inconsistent"* food. / www.naked-turtle.com; 11 pm;
Mon-Thu D only, Fri-Sun open L & D; no smoking area.

Nam Long SW5   £ 36   ④④❷
159 Old Brompton Rd   7373 1926   5–2B
"The food is overpriced, but you don't go there to eat" – the
"great" (and mega-pricey) cocktails and the *"raffish, even
debauched"* atmosphere are what this South Kensington
Vietnamese is really all about. / 11.30 pm; closed Sat L & Sun.

Nanking W6   £ 29   ❸❸❸
332 King St   8748 7604   7–2B
"Maintaining standards" – this *"reliable and properly priced"*
Hammersmith Chinese is a *"consistently useful stand-by"*.
/ 11.30 pm.

Nautilus NW6   £ 22   ❷❸⑤
27-29 Fortune Green Rd   7435 2532   1–1B
"Ignore the '60s décor", and you can hope to find *"the best fish
and chips in north west London"* at this *"excellent"* West
Hampstead chippie. / 10 pm; closed Sun; no Amex; no booking.

Navajo Joe WC2   £ 32   ④④❸
34 King St   7240 4008   4–3C
Some find the food *"surprisingly good for a bar/restaurant"* –
especially in the heart of Covent Garden – but this *"loud"* venue
is still a better destination for its margaritas than for its
Mexican scoff. / midnight; closed Sun.

Nayaab SW6   £ 22   ❸❸⑤
309 New King's Rd   7731 6993   10–1B
"Not inspired, but totally dependable" – this Parson's Green
Indian offers some quite *"unusual"* dishes, too; the oppressive
décor makes it *"better to take away"*. / midnight.

Neal Street WC2   £ 54   ❸❸④
26 Neal St   7836 8368   4–2C
Antonio Carluccio's *"beautiful"* dishes – with mushrooms the
speciality – can make a trip to this celebrated Covent Garden
Italian worthwhile; the setting is rather *"tired"*, though, and as
ever many find the prices *"greedy"*. / 11 pm; closed Sun.

Neat
Oxo Tower Wharf SE1   £ 66   ❸④❸

Barge House St   7928 4433   9–3A

*Richard Neat has come back from Cannes to establish this
showy restaurant (and brasserie) on the second floor of the
South Bank's Oxo Tower; a June '01 visit found aggressive prices
for cooking that didn't quite deliver, and a setting whose only
real plus was its river views.* / Rated on Editors' assessment; 10 pm
(brasserie 11 pm); closed Sat L & Sun; no smoking area; set always available
£44(FP).

New Culture Revolution   £ 19   ❸❸④

305 King's Rd, SW3   7352 9281   5–3C
157-159 Notting Hill Gate, W11   7313 9688   6–2B
442 Edgware Rd, W2   7402 4841   8–4A
42 Duncan St, N1   7833 9083   8–3D
43 Parkway, NW1   7267 2700   8–3B

*"Wholesome noodles and dumplings" help make these
"efficient", if fairly "uncomfortable", diners a very popular
budget stand-by.* / 11 pm; W2 closed Sun L; need 4+ to book.

New Mayflower W1   £ 29   ❷⑤⑤

68-70 Shaftesbury Ave   7734 9207   4–3A

*It's decidedly "unglamorous", but this long-established fixture is
"the best in Chinatown" for some; it's open till the wee hours.*
/ 3.45 am; D only.

New World W1   £ 25   ❸④❸

1 Gerrard Pl   7734 0677   4–3A

*"Great fun", and "cheap" too; a "massive dim sum selection on
carts" is served at this enormous, "haphazard" Chinatown
fixture; in the evening it makes an OK central stand-by.*
/ 11.45 pm; no smoking area; no booking, Sun L.

Newton's SW4   £ 32   ④④❸

33 Abbeville Rd   8673 0977   10–2D

*This "pleasant neighbourhood bistro" is a "relaxed" Clapham
destination, but its food inspires very mixed reactions.* / 11.30 pm;
set weekday L £17(FP).

Nico Central W1   £ 39   ④④⑤

35 Great Portland St   7436 8846   3–1C

*"Nico should not allow his name to be associated with this" –
too many reporters feel this "rip-off" Gallic brasserie, north of
Oxford Street, is just "not worth the time or money"; (however,
some do value it as a business rendezvous).* / www.trpplc.com;
10.30 pm; closed Sat & Sun.

Nicole's W1   £ 50   ❸❸❸

158 New Bond St   7499 8408   3–3C

*"Ideal for shopping lunches" – with its handy Mayfair location
this "relaxed" spot serves some "good and interesting" food;
it's "expensive", though, "for a store basement".* / 10.45 pm; closed
Sat D & Sun; no smoking area.

Nikita's SW10 £ 37 ⑤④④
65 Ifield Rd 7352 6326 5–3A
"The food is immaterial" at this long-established Russian
basement den on the fringe of Chelsea – *"it's the excellent
flavoured vodkas which are the point"*. / www.nikitasrestaurant.co.uk;
11.30 pm; D only, closed Mon & Sun.

Niksons SW11 £ 37 ❸⑤④
172-174 Northcote Rd 7228 2285 10–2C
The cooking can be *"very good"*, so it's a shame that *"slow"*
and *"incompetent"* service helps too many reporters to the
conclusion that this *"airy"* but *"intimate"* Battersea newcomer is
something of *"a missed opportunity"*. / 10.30 pm; closed Mon L.

911 NW1 £ 27 ④④④
9-11 Jamestown Rd 7482 2770 8–3B
To celebrate its first anniversary, there's been a name change
(from Pie2Mash) at this Camden Town venture; perhaps sorting
out the up-and-down English cooking and the *"casual"* service
might have been a better investment? / 11 pm, Fri & Sat 11.30 pm;
no Amex; no smoking area.

No 6 W1 £ 30 ❷④④
6 George St 7935 1910 2–1A
Handy for visitors to the Wallace Collection, this deli/restaurant
– which we visited in early '01, shortly after it opened, offers
good and simple food, amateurishly. / Rated on Editors' assessment;
L only, closed Sat & Sun; no Amex; no smoking.

No 77 Wine Bar NW6 £ 30 ④❷❷
77 Mill Ln 7435 7787 1–1B
The attractions of *"good wine"* help keep this *"cheerful"* West
Hampstead local *"crowded"*; under the new régime, though,
the food is rather *"ordinary"*. / 10 pm, Wed-Sat 11 pm; no Amex.

Noble Rot W1 £ 52 ❸❸❸
3-5 Mill St 7629 8877 3–2C
"The fantastic bar" (not always open to 'non-members') is the
real selling point at this *"tucked away"* Mayfair spot; opinions
on the ground-floor restaurant divide between those praising the
"interesting" dishes, and those who say the place *"promises,
but does not deliver"*. / 11 pm; closed Sun.

NOBU
METROPOLITAN HOTEL W1 £ 55 ❶❸❷
Old Park Lane 7447 4747 3–4A
"Amazing" Japanese/South American cooking justifies the
"unbelievable expense" – and the *"pain of getting a booking"* –
at this *"very sexy"* Mayfair dining room; as a *"superb venue for
star-spotting"*, it has few equals. / 10.15 pm, Fri & Sat 11 pm; closed
Sat L & Sun L; no smoking area.

Noho £ 25 ⑤④④

32 Charlotte St, W1   7636 4445   2–1C
O2 Centre, 255 Finchley Rd, NW3   7794 5616   8–2A
Some do like these "bright and friendly" noodle parlours, but, the overall view is that they are "unauthentic", and offer "badly cooked" oriental fare. / 11 pm; no smoking areas.

Noodle Noodle SW1 £ 20 ④④④

Vauxhall Bridge Rd   7828 8565   2–4B
This is "not a place to linger", but for "yummy bowls of (guess what) noodles" in the environs of Victoria, you could do worse. / www.noodle-noodle.co.uk; 10.45 pm; no smoking.

Noor Jahan SW5 £ 29 ❷❷❸

2a Bina Gdns   7373 6522   5–2B
This "very reliable" Indian couldn't look more "unfashionable", but its "excellent curries" make it a top South Kensington local. / 11 pm.

The North Pole SE10 £ 33 ❸❸❸

131 Greenwich High Rd   8853 3020   1–3D
There's hardly a plethora of choice around Greenwich, and this "spacious" dining room above a trendy pub is undoubtedly "good for the area"; "singers in the bar below add to the atmosphere". / 10.30 pm; closed Mon L; set D £17(FP).

North Sea Fish WC1 £ 25 ❷❷④

7-8 Leigh St   7387 5892   8–4C
"It should be by the seaside, not in Bloomsbury" – this "down-to-earth" café provides "friendly" service and "marvellously fresh fish", "simply cooked". / 10.30 pm; closed Sun.

Noto £ 23 ❸④④

2-3 Bassishaw Highwalk, EC2   7256 9433   9–2B
7 Bread St, EC4   7329 8056   9–3B
You "fill your face fast" at these "quick and cheap" Japanese "diners", which serve "good standard food", majoring in noodles. / www.noto.co.uk; EC2 9.45 pm – EC4 8.45 pm; closed Sat & Sun; EC2 no Amex – EC4 no credit cards; EC2 no smoking at L; EC2 no booking for L – EC4 no bookings; set weekday L £15(FP).

Notting Hill Brasserie W11 £ 35 ④❸❷

92 Kensington Park Rd   7229 4481   6–2B
"Nice place, shame about the food" – the "understated" and "comfortable" transformation of this large townhouse may seem "amazing" to those who recall Leith's (RIP), but its cooking ranks somewhere between "decent" and "ordinary". / www.firmdale.com; 10 pm.

Noura SW1 £ 39 ❸❷④

16 Hobart Pl   7235 9444   2–4B
In "an interesting Paris/Beirut-style" setting, a few minutes walk from Victoria Station, this "opulent" year-old Lebanese offers some "good-quality" cooking. / www.noura-brasseries.co.uk; 11.30 pm; set weekday L £26(FP).

O'Conor Don W1 £ 31 ④❸❸
88 Marylebone Ln   7935 9311   3–1A
The food "used to be great" at this "warm" and "very homely"
Irish pub near the Wigmore Hall – "now it's just adequate".
/ 10 pm; closed Sat & Sun.

Oak Room Marco Pierre White
Le Meridien W1 £ 61 ❸❸④
21 Piccadilly   7437 0202   3–3D
MPW may have retired from the stoves, but this stately Mayfair
dining room seems essentially unchanged; it "still produces some
classic French food" at prices which (if lower than they used to
be) are "very high for what you get", in a setting some find very
"unrelaxing". / 11.15 pm; closed Sat L & Sun.

L'Odéon W1 £ 48 ④④④
65 Regent St   7287 1400   3–3D
As an "oasis of calm from shoppers", this large Gallic venture
overlooking Regent Street perhaps still has its uses;
it's "too expensive", though, given the "so-so" cooking and
"amateurish" service. / 11.30 pm; closed Sun; no smoking area at L.

Odette's NW1 £ 39 ❷❷❶
130 Regent's Park Rd   7586 5486   8–3B
This "gracious" and "romantic" Primrose Hill fixture is best
known for its "amazing" ("mirrors everywhere") décor; it offers
more than just looks, though – the "traditional-with-a-twist"
cooking is "very well executed", the wine list is excellent,
and service "charms". / 11 pm; closed Sat L & Sun; set weekday L
£22(FP).

Odin's W1 £ 40 ❷❶❶
27 Devonshire St   7935 7296   2–1A
"The sort of place my parents would love", this "civilised"
Marylebone veteran may be, but it's praised by young and old,
business-types and romantics alike for its "very comfortable"
ambience, its "old-fashioned" service and its "high-standard"
(if "not innovative") Anglo/French cuisine.
/ www.langansrestaurants.co.uk; 11 pm; closed Sat & Sun; no smoking area.

Old Parr's Head W14 £ 21 ❸④❸
120 Blythe Rd   7371 4561   7–1C
"Consistently competent, simple, quick Thai food" makes this
Olympia boozer a useful local – especially in summer, when you
can eat in the courtyard out back. / 10 pm; no Amex.

The Old School Thai SW11 £ 24 ❷❶❸
147 Lavender Hill   7228 2345   10–2C
It's a bit "eccentric", but this Battersea Thai has a "nice,
family-run atmosphere"; "excellent" overall value earns it quiet
a following. / 11 pm; D only, closed Sun; no smoking area; no booking at L.

regular updates at www.hardens.com

Ye Olde Cheshire Cheese EC4 £ 27 ④④❷
145 Fleet St 7353 6170 9–2A
*"History for the tasting" – it's the "wonderful ancient
atmosphere" of this "maze of an old pub", off Fleet Street, that
makes it worth a visit, not the "hearty" cooking. / 9.30 pm; closed
Sun D.*

Oliveto SW1 £ 35 ❸④⑤
49 Elizabeth St 7730 0074 2–4A
*"Rotten" acoustics and sometimes "surly" service spoil the
ambience at this Belgravia Italian; it's a shame, as its "crisp and
tasty" pizzas and "above-average" pasta offer "good value" in
a thin area. / 11.30 pm.*

Olivo SW1 £ 38 ❸❸④
21 Eccleston St 7730 2505 2–4B
*The Sardinian cooking can be "excellent" at this well-established
Belgravia-fringe Italian, but some find its premises rather
"unprepossessing". / 11 pm; closed Sat L & Sun L.*

115 at Hodgson's WC2 £ 41 ④❸❸
115 Chancery Ln 7242 2836 2–2D
*"Nice, light and airy", these impressive Victorian premises are
"good for informal business meetings" in 'Legal-land';
the attractions of the cooking, however, never appear to rise
above the incidental. / 10 pm; closed Sat & Sun; no smoking area at L.*

192 W11 £ 38 ⑤⑤④
192 Kensington Park Rd 7229 0482 6–1A
*How sad that a place that was such a destination in its day –
it arguably 'made' Notting Hill – can just seem a "rip-off"
nowadays, and even fans admit that this "favourite old
stand-by" now "trades on its reputation". / 11.30 pm; booking:
max 8.*

1 Lombard Street EC3 £ 48 ❸❸❸
1 Lombard St 7929 6611 9–3C
*It's "one for the expense account", but Herbert Berger's
"efficient business venue", by Bank, is "a solid all-rounder" with
"quality" modern French cooking, "slick" service and
a "bustling" ("loud") setting. / www.1lombardstreet.com; 10 pm; closed
Sat & Sun.*

Opium W1 £ 48 ⑤⑤❷
1a Dean St 7287 9608 3–1D
*It has a "great" setting, and this "stylish" new Vietnamese
basement at the top end of Soho has a lot going for it – as
a cocktail rendezvous; the cooking, though, is "vastly
overpriced", and some say the waiters are "possibly the rudest
around". / 9.30 pm; closed Sat L & Sun.*

Opus 70 W1 £ 43 ④❷④
70 Stratton St 7344 7070 3–3C
*It's little-known, but for a "smooth" business lunch this Mayfair
hotel dining room is a useful-enough option. / 11 pm; closed Sat L;
no smoking area.*

L'Oranger SW1 £ 55 ❷❷❷

5 St James's St   7839 3774   3–4D
*A "first-rate all rounder", this "comfortable" St James's
establishment offers an all-too-rare combination of
"old-fashioned comfort", "excellent French cuisine" and
"impeccable" service. / 11 pm; closed Sat L & Sun.*

Organic Café £ 38 ④④④

51 Prince's Gate, SW7   7596 4006   5–1C
25 Lonsdale Rd, NW6   7372 1232   1–2B
*It's certainly a useful stop-off on the way to the Albert Hall –
ignore the misleading postal address, it's on Exhibition Road –
but this simple, airy new diner is otherwise rather humdrum;
we've never been to the NW6 original – the survey feedback
has always been too depressing to justify the journey.
/ www.organic-cafe.co.uk; 10.30 pm; no smoking areas; set weekday L £24(FP).*

Oriel SW1 £ 32 ⑤④❸

50-51 Sloane Sq   7730 2804   5–2D
*"Go for a coffee" – or for breakfast – to this "Parisian-style"
brasserie, at the centre of the 'known world'; the food is
emphatically "nothing to write home about". / 10.45 pm;
no smoking area; no booking.*

The Orient W1 £ 41 ❷❷❸

157 Piccadilly   7499 6888   3–3C
*An "upmarket", "imaginative" spin on Chinese cooking wins
praise for this luxurious yearling above China House; the place
is relatively little known, however, and its "calm" setting can
sometimes seem rather "soulless". / www.chinahouse.co.uk; 11.30 pm;
closed Sat L & Sun.*

Oriental City Food Court NW9 £ 19 ❷④④

399 Edgware Rd   8200 0009   1–1A
*For "an unrivalled oriental choice" at "take-away prices",
it's worth the schlep to Colindale, and the food court of this
extraordinary Asian shopping centre. / 11 pm; no credit cards;
no smoking area.*

Orrery W1 £ 52 ❷❷❷

55 Marylebone High St   7616 8000   2–1A
*"The only Conran worth bothering with"; this "quiet" dining
room, overlooking a Marylebone churchyard, may be
"expensive", but it's "worth it" for the "meticulously-presented"
modern French cooking and its sometimes "fantastic" service.
/ www.orrery.co.uk; 10.30 pm.*

Orsino W11 £ 40 ④④❷

119 Portland Rd   7221 3299   6–2A
*Its design is "cool and sophisticated", but Orso's country cousin,
in Holland Park perennially offers Italian fare that's "reliable,
rather than exciting". / 11.30 pm; no smoking area; set weekday L, Sun L,
pre & post th. £25(FP).*

Orso WC2   £ 44   ❸❸❸

27 Wellington St   7240 5269   4–3D

*This "former Italian star", handily-located in a basement near
the Royal Opera House, has lost some of its lustre in recent
years; the cooking is still "decent", though, and service has
become more "attentive" of late.* / www.joeallen.co.uk; midnight;
no smoking area; set weekday L & pre-th. £27(FP).

Oslo Court NW8   £ 42   ❷❶❸

Prince Albert Rd   7722 8795   8–3A

*"Harder to get in to than The Ivy" (well, almost), this "amazing"
fixture – at the foot of a Regent's Park apartment block – has
for many years had a (fairly mature) cult following for its
"generous" cooking, its "jolly" atmosphere and its "100%
attentive" service.* / 11 pm; closed Sun.

Osteria Antica Bologna SW11   £ 32   ④④❸

23 Northcote Rd   7978 4771   10–2C

*This "cramped" Battersea Italian had created quite a reputation
for its "rustic" fare and its "fun" style; "sadly, it's gone downhill"
under new ownership, and the cooking is now "solid" at best.*
/ www.osteria.co.uk; 11 pm, Fri & Sat 11.30 pm; set weekday L £20(FP).

Osteria Basilico W11   £ 34   ❷❸❶

29 Kensington Park Rd   7727 9957   6–1A

*A state of "typical Italian mayhem" makes for a "great buzz" at
this "favourite" Notting Hill hang-out, which serves "splendid"
pizzas and "delicious" pasta.* / 11 pm; no booking, Sat L.

Otto W9   £ 35   ⑤⑤❸

215 Sutherland Ave   7266 3131   8–4A

*"The bar is fantastic" at this architecturally striking Maida Vale
newcomer; the "overpriced" restaurant, though, is "really up
itself" – unjustifiably so, given the reports of "tasteless" cooking
and "shocking" service.* / 11 pm; D only; booking: max 8, Sat & Sun.

OXO TOWER
OXO TOWER WHARF SE1   £ 55   ⑤⑤❷

Barge House St   7803 3888   9–3A

*The view is "stunning", but it "can't compensate for the
dreadful, highly-priced food" served on the eighth floor of this
South Bank landmark; the cheaper brasserie is a marginally
better bet than the restaurant.* / www.harveynichols.com; 11.15 pm.

Ozer W1   £ 35   ❸❸❸

4-5 Langham Pl   7323 0505   3–1C

*This innovative Turkish yearling by Broadcasting House still wins
praise for its "sexy décor" and its "excellent value" (particularly
the set menus), but there's a feeling that the "food has declined
since opening", and service likewise.* / midnight; no jeans; set £22(FP).

regular updates at www.hardens.com

Pacific Oriental EC2 £ 42 ④❸④
1 Bishopsgate 7621 9988 9–2C
"Simple oriental lunchbox-type food" is "a great concept", say
fans of this large and "bustling" City bar/restaurant – the overall
verdict, though, is that its more ambitious fusion fare is
"competent" at best. / www.orientalrestaurantgroup.co.uk; 9.30 pm;
closed Sat & Sun.

Il Pagliaccio SW6 £ 22 ④❸❷
184 Wandsworth Bridge Rd 7371 5253 10–1B
It can be "bedlam" at this "crowded" Italian in deepest Fulham,
but the locals applaud its "very friendly" service and its "cheap"
pizza and other fare. / midnight; no Amex.

Le Palais du Jardin WC2 £ 39 ❸④❷
136 Long Acre 7379 5353 4–3C
This vast and "buzzy" Covent Garden brasserie still makes
a "reliable" central rendezvous, particularly "pre-theatre";
"consistently good fish" – notably the "amazing seafood platter"
– is a highlight. / 11.45 pm.

Palatino W4 £ 32 ❸❸④
6 Turnham Green Ter 8994 0086 7–2A
"A local Tuscan" in Turnham Green whose "cooking can be
excellent or merely acceptable, depending on the day";
the patio garden "can be very romantic in summer". / 11 pm;
no smoking area.

Pampa £ 36 ❷④❷
4 Northcote Rd, SW11 7924 1167 10–2C
60 Battersea Rise, SW11 7924 4774 10–2C
The "most amazing" steak and "macho" waiters make a potent
combination at these "loud" Battersea Argentinians – the
original branch now has a sibling just around the corner.
/ 11.30 pm; D only.

Pan-Asian Canteen
Paxton's Head SW1 £ 23 ❷❷❸
153 Knightsbridge 7589 6627 5–1D
Some find the communal tables at this "elegantly" modernised
new dining room of a Knightsbridge pub "a drawback", but the
Thai cooking is "delicious" and "really fresh". / 10.30 pm;
no smoking area.

Paparazzi Café £ 34 ④④❸
9 Hanover St, W1 7355 3337 3–2C
58 Fulham Rd, SW3 7589 0876 5–2C
"Uninteresting food" has always been offset by the fun, brash
style of these "atmospheric" pizzerias; they generated little
feedback this year, however. / SW3 midnight – W1 3 am, Thu-Sat 5 am;
W1 closed Sun & Mon.

The Papaya Tree W8 £ 30 ❷❷④
209 Kensington High St 7937 2260 7–1D
Kensington locals and cinema-goers much approve of the
"authentic" cooking and "very friendly" service at this basement
Thai. / 11 pm; no smoking area; set weekday L £18(FP).

Parade W5 £ 35 ❷❷❷

18-19 The Mall 8810 0202 1–3A

For "excellent value in the suburbs", this large yearling in the "wastelands" of Ealing is hard to beat; like its Barnes sibling, Sonny's, it delivers a good all-round package, including "well-priced" food and a "pleasant", setting. / 11 pm; closed Sun D.

Parisienne Chophouse SW3 £ 36 ④④④

3 Yeoman's Row 7590 9999 5–2C

Some do praise the "decent" Gallic cooking at MPW's newest venture – in a large, rather "dull" basement near Harrods (formerly a Chez Gérard) – but service can be "unbelievably bad", and too many find results on the plate no more than "adequate". / www.whitestarline.org.uk; 11 pm; set weekday L & pre-th. £24(FP).

The Parsee N19 £ 31 ❷❶④

34 Highgate Hill 7272 9091 8–1C

"At last, Highgate has a decent restaurant!"; it's the "fantastic" and "informed" service which is most lavishly fêted at this new Indian, but the menu's "imaginative" ("if mild") flavours are also very well received. / 10.45 pm; D only, closed Mon & Sun; no smoking area.

Pasha SW7 £ 40 ❸❸❶

1 Gloucester Rd 7589 7969 5–1B

"You feel like you're in Morocco" at this "very enticing", "low-lit" Kensington basement; it's quite "expensive for what it is", however, and both the "enjoyable" cooking and the service get a rather mixed press. / 11 pm; closed Sun L.

Pasha N1 £ 27 ❷❶❷

301 Upper St 7226 1454 8–3D

"Great food at easy prices" wins a big north London fan club for this "jolly" Islington Turk; at busy times, "they cram you in", though. / 11.30 pm, Fri & Sat midnight; no Switch.

Passion W9 £ 29 ❷❷⑤

119 Shirland Rd 7289 5667 1–2B

The sometimes "remarkable" cooking can come as "a great surprise" at this "unlikely" Maida Vale newcomer, where a skilled chef is "trying hard" in the face of "terrible interior design and ambience". / 10.45 pm.

Passione W1 £ 41 ❶❶❷

10 Charlotte St 7636 2833 2–1C

Blossoming in its second year of operation, this agreeably "unpretentious" Fitzrovia spot offers "interesting" and "beautifully-cooked" Italian dishes, and "lovely" service. / www.passione.co.uk; 10.15 pm; closed Sat L & Sun.

Patio W12 £ 20 ❸❶❷

5 Goldhawk Rd 8743 5194 7–1C

*"Traditional Polish cooking in a wonderful time-warp '50s
setting, with 3 courses for £11.90 (vodka included)"* is the
"ridiculously good-value" proposition at this
"amusingly-eccentric" Shepherd's Bush outfit. / 11.30 pm; closed
Sat L & Sun L.

Pâtisserie Valerie £ 20 ❸④❷

105 Marylebone High St, W1 7935 6240 2–1A
44 Old Compton St, W1 7437 3466 4–2A
8 Russell St, WC2 7240 0064 4–3D
215 Brompton Rd, SW3 7823 9971 5–2C

"What a great start to the day", say fans of the *"piggy but
delicious"* treats on offer at this Gallic café chain; declining
ratings, however, support those who say they're *"not quite as
good as they were a few years ago"*. / www.patisserie-valerie.co.uk;
7 pm-11 pm, Sun 6 pm (Soho 7 pm); no smoking area; no booking.

Paul WC2 £ 9 ❷❶❷

29-30 Bedford St 7836 3304 4–3C

"A real boulangerie and pâtisserie"; this new Covent Garden
outpost of a major Gallic chain serves *"delicious cakes"*,
"wonderful breads" and *"good coffee"* in a comfortable
tearoom setting that puts most native offerings to shame.
/ 8.30 pm; no smoking.

Paulo's W6 £ 27 ❸❷④

30 Greyhound Rd 7385 9264 7–2C

Not much changes at Paulo and his wife's *"good-value"*,
eat-all-you-can Brazilian buffet, in the shadow of the Charing
Cross Hospital. / 10.30 pm; closed Mon, Sat L & Sun D; no Amex.

The Peasant EC1 £ 28 ④❸❸

240 St John St 7336 7726 8–3D

Once a market-leader, this Clerkenwell gastropub is still
a *"cheerful"* and *"laid back"* place, but its grub generates less
and less excitement nowadays. / 11 pm; closed Sun.

Pellicano SW3 £ 36 ❸④④

19 Elystan St 7589 3718 5–2C

"Just a good Italian, but not as good as it thinks" – we must
admit we didn't especially enjoy our visit to this Chelsea
backstreet newcomer, and reporters divide between those who
say it's *"splendid"* and those who say it's *"dire"*. / 11 pm; set
weekday L & Sun L £24(FP).

The Pen SW6 £ 33 ❸❷❷

51 Parsons Green Ln 7371 8517 10–1B

"Very good food in simple surroundings" makes this *"intimate"*
dining room over a pub, by Parsons Green tube, *"ideal for
groups, or a one-to-one"*. / 11 pm; D only, closed Sun; no Amex.

The People's Palace
South Bank Centre SE1 £41 ④❸❸
7928 9999   2–3D
"The view is sensational", and the Festival Hall's very "spacious"
(if slightly "gloomy") dining room makes a "practical" venue
that's "good pre-theatre/concert" (and also for business);
the cooking, however, "lacks ambition". / www.capitalgrp.co.uk;
11 pm; no smoking area.

The Pepper Tree SW4 £17 ❸②②
19 Clapham Common S'side   7622 1758   10–2D
It's "quick and great", say fans of this "fresh and cheerful"
Clapham Thai "canteen"; it's hugely popular and its communal
tables are "always busy". / 11 pm, Mon & Sun 10.30 pm; no Amex;
no smoking area; no booking at D.

Perc%nto EC4 £39 ④④❸
26 Ludgate Hill   7778 0010   9–2B
It's "handy in the area" – just down the hill from St Paul's – but
this glitzy Italian (a recent addition to the Taberna Etrusca
group) offers a "standard" City experience.
/ www.etruscagroup.co.uk; 10 pm.

Père Michel W2 £30 ❸④④
11 Bathurst St   7723 5431   6–2D
In the "bleak area" near Lancaster Gate, this small restaurant
provides a "cosy" refuge (at least relatively speaking); the menu
is "limited", but the place is "still worth a visit, if not too often".
/ 11 pm; closed Sat L & Sun.

Perla £26 ④❷❸
28 Maiden Ln, WC2   7240 7400   4–4D
803 Fulham Rd, SW6   7471 4895   10–1B
The grub is "really bog-standard", but if you have enough beers
these "very noisy", "friendly" Mexican joints can still provide
a "fun" evening. / WC2 11.45 pm – SW6 11 pm; SW6 D only, except
weekends when L & D.

The Perseverance WC1 £31 ❷④④
63 Lamb's Conduit St   7405 8278   2–1D
The cooking was unusually polished, for a gastropub, on our
July '01 visit to this newly-converted Bloomsbury boozer
(formerly The Sun); its trendy but well-meaning staff can get
distracted. / Rated on Editors' assessment; 9 pm.

Le P'tit Normand SW18 £27 ❸①❸
185 Merton Rd   8871 0233   10–2B
"Old-fashioned French food in an old-fashioned setting" wins
continuing support for this "cosy" and "very friendly" Southfield
stalwart; the "cheeseboard to die for" is a highlight. / 10 pm, Fri &
Sat 11 pm.

PÉTRUS SW1 £ 65 ❶❷❸

33 St James's St 7930 4272 3–4C

The "delicate, subtle and pure flavours" of Marcus Wareing's modern French cooking – and a wine list living up to the place's name – are establishing this "comfortable" but "slightly clinical" St James's dining room as one of the most notable in town; some find service "oppressive". / www.petrus-restaurant.com; 10.45 pm; closed Sat L & Sun; booking: max 6.

Pharmacy W11 £ 49 ⑤⑤④

150 Notting Hill Gate 7221 2442 6–2B

"Keep taking the tablets!" – that's reporters' prescription for the new team trying to resuscitate this contrived Notting Hill landmark; service can be "dire", and "the food-to-wallet ratio is one of the worst ever seen". / www.pharmacylondon.com; 10.45 pm.

Philpotts Mezzaluna NW2 £ 34 ❷❷❸

424 Finchley Rd 7794 0455 1–1B

"It's becoming the premier restaurant around Hampstead", say supporters of this "'70s-looking" but "imaginative" Italian, which has been reinvigorated under the ownership of David Philpott (who used to run Quincy's opposite). / 11 pm; closed Mon & Sat L.

Phoenicia W8 £ 36 ❸❷❸

11-13 Abingdon Rd 7937 0120 5–1A

This "very friendly" Lebanese is a Kensington fixture, whose "attentive" staff deliver food that's "unexceptional but good". / 11.45 pm; no smoking area.

Phoenix Bar & Grill SW15 £ 34 ❷❷❸

Pentlow St 8780 3131 10–1A

"Lovely" food, often "impeccable" service and a "pleasant" atmosphere – reporters find little to criticise at this "very professional" Putney offshoot of Barnes's Sonny's. / 10 pm.

Phoenix Palace NW1 £ 30 ❷④④

3-5 Glentworth St 7486 3515 2–1A

Chinese cooking "of a good standard" and in "generous portions" is the plus-point of this newcomer near Baker Street; neither the setting (formerly the Viceroy, RIP) nor the service offer any special appeal. / 11.30 pm.

Picasso SW3 £ 26 ④❸❸

127 King's Rd 7352 4921 5–3C

A "crowded" café that's "a good place to stop for a quick coffee", and particularly favoured by Chelsea poseurs. / 11.15 pm.

Pied à Terre W1 £ 72 ❷❸④

34 Charlotte St 7636 1178 2–1C

Shane Osborn's "classical but imaginative" Gallic cooking and an "excellent range of interesting wines" make this Fitzrovia fixture one of London's foremost foodie temples; service can be "distant", though, and the setting is "so-so". / www.pied.a.terre.co.uk; 10.45 pm; closed Sat L & Sun; set weekday L £41(FP).

La Piragua N1 £19 ❸④❸
176 Upper St   7354 2843   8–2D
"Amazing-value beef and lamb steaks" are the highlight at this
"very buzzy" South American cantina, near Islington Town Hall;
its "fun" atmosphere is ideal for a group. / midnight; no credit cards.

Pizza Metro SW11 £29 ❶❶❷
64 Battersea Rise   7228 3812   10–2C
"It helps to be Italian when booking", as "it's very hard to get
a table" at this "cramped but fun" Battersea joint; it's known for
"the best pizza outside Napoli" (sold by the metre),
but "incredible antipasti and fish" are also served. / 11 pm; closed
Mon, Tue-Fri D only, Sat & Sun open L & D.

Pizza On The Park SW1 £27 ④❸❷
11 Knightsbridge   7235 5273   5–1D
The décor is "dated" but still attractive at this
PizzaExpress-in-disguise, near Hyde Park Corner, though the
pizza-and-more menu has seen better days; (the basement –
to which there's an entry charge – is a major jazz venue).
/ midnight; no smoking area; no booking.

Pizza Pomodoro £28 ④④❷
51 Beauchamp Pl, SW3   7589 1278   5–1C
7-8 Bishopsgate Churchyard, EC2   7920 9207   9–2D
"Bad music" only adds to the "electric" atmosphere at these
"noisy" pizzerias (of which the seedy original in a Knightsbridge
basement is by far the better known); the pizza is generally
"OK", but can be "awful". / SW3 1 am – EC2 midnight; EC2 closed
Sat & Sun – SW3 D only.

PizzaExpress £22 ④❸❸
154 Victoria St, SW1   7828 1477   2–4C
46 Moreton St, SW1   7592 9488   2–4B
85 Victoria St, SW1   7222 5270   2–4C
10 Dean St, W1   7437 9595   3–1D
13-14 Thayer St, W1   7935 2167   2–1A
133 Baker St, W1   7486 0888   2–1A
20 Greek St, W1   7734 7430   4–2A
21-22 Barrett St, W1   7629 1001   3–1A
23 Bruton Pl, W1   7495 1411   3–2B
29 Wardour St, W1   7437 7215   4–3A
4 Langham Pl, W1   7580 3700   2–1B
6 Upper St James St, W1   7437 4550   3–2D
7-9 Charlotte St, W1   7580 1110   2–1C
30 Coptic St, WC1   7636 3232   2–1C
99 High Holborn, WC1   7831 5305   2–1D
147 Strand, WC2   7836 7716   2–2D
450 The Strand, WC2   7930 8205   2–2C
80-81 St Martins Ln, WC2   7836 8001   4–3B
9-12 Bow St, WC2   7240 3443   4–2D
363 Fulham Rd, SW10   7352 5300   5–3B

PizzaExpress cont'd
150-152 King's Rd, SW3   7351 5031   5–3C
352a King's Rd, SW3   7352 9790   5–3B
6-7 Beauchamp Pl, SW3   7589 2355   5–1C
246 Old Brompton Rd, SW5   7373 4712   5–2A
140 Wandsworth Bridge Rd, SW6   8384 9693   10–1B
895 Fulham Rd, SW6   7731 3117   10–1B
137 Notting Hill Gate, W11   7229 6000   6–2B
7 Rockley Rd, W14   8749 8582   7–1C
26 Porchester Rd, W2   7229 7784   6–1C
252 Chiswick High Rd, W4   8747 0193   7–2A
35 Earls Court Rd, W8   7937 0761   5–1A
335 Upper St, N1   7226 9542   8–3D
30 Highgate High St, N6   8341 3434   8–1B
187 Kentish Town Rd, NW1   7267 0101   8–2B
85-87 Parkway, NW1   7267 2600   8–3B
194 Haverstock Hill, NW3   7794 6777   8–2A
70 Heath St, NW3   7433 1600   8–1A
39-39a Abbey Rd, NW8   7624 5577   8–3A
316 Kennington Rd, SE11   7820 3177   10–1D
4 Borough High St, SE1   7407 2995   9–3C
9 Belvedere Rd, SE1   7928 4091   2–3D
Cardomom Bldg, Shad Thames, SE1   7403 8484   9–4D
230 Lavender Hill, SW11   7223 5677   10–2C
46 Battersea Br Rd, SW11   7924 2774   5–4C
14 Barnes High St, SW13   8878 1184   10–1A
305 Up Richmond Rd W, SW14   8878 6833   10–2A
144 Upper Richmond Rd, SW15   8789 1948   10–2B
539 Old York Rd, SW18   8877 9812   10–2B
43 Abbeville Rd, SW4   8673 8878   10–2D
2nd Flr, Cabot Place East, E14   7513 0513   11–1C
78-80 Wapping Ln, E1   7481 8436   11–1A
26 Cowcross St, EC1   7490 8025   9–1A
59 Exmouth Mkt, EC1   7713 7264   9–1A
125 London Wall, EC2   7600 8880   9–2B
150 London Wall, EC2   7588 7262   9–2D
49-51 Curtain Rd, EC2   7613 5426   9–1D
Leadenhall Market, EC3   7621 0022   9–2D
7-9 St Bride St, EC4   7583 5126   9–2A

"Consistently reasonably good" is, these days, the somewhat ambivalent verdict on this benchmark chain – the proportion of reporters who vote it a "safe bet" is wilting in the face of ever more "complacent" standards. / www.pizzaexpress.co.uk; *11 pm-midnight – Greek St Wed-Sat 1 am – St Bride St 10 pm – London Wall Sat & Sun 8.30 pm; St Bride St & Bruton Pl closed Sat & Sun – Upper St James Street closed Sun D; not all branches take bookings.*

Pizzeria Castello SE1   £20   ❷❶❷
20 Walworth Rd   7703 2556   1–3C
"The garlic hits you straight away", as you enter the Elephant & Castle's leading contribution to the capital's gastronomy; hordes of supporters from far and wide hail "the best pizza in town", "cheerful" staff and the "urban buzz". / www.pizzeria-castello.co.uk; 11 pm, Fri & Sat 11.30 pm; closed Sat L & Sun.

Pizzeria Condotti W1 £27 ❸❷❸

4 Mill St 7499 1308 3–2C

A "sophisticated crowd" adds glamour – particularly at lunch – to this Mayfair PizzaExpress in disguise. / *midnight; closed Sun.*

PJ's SW3 £37 ④④❸

52 Fulham Rd 7581 0025 5–2C

"The Saturday brunch is excellent for people-watching", but otherwise this "where-it's-at" South Kensington diner is on the slide – it attracts far too many complaints nowadays of "lousy" cooking and "awkward" service. / *midnight; no smoking area.*

The Place Below EC2 £20 ❷④❸

St Mary-le-Bow, Cheapside 7329 0789 9–2C

"Flavourful" veggie fare has made quite a name for this "crowded" City church crypt (where there are also charming alfresco dining possibilities on sunny days); some do wonder whether it's not becoming a touch "overpriced".
/ *www.theplacebelow.co.uk; L only, closed Sat & Sun; no Amex; no smoking; no booking.*

Planet Hollywood W1 £33 ⑤④❸

13 Coventry St 7287 1000 4–4A

"Kids like it", but there's "nothing else to be said in favour" of this "tacky" movie-memorabilia Mecca, near Piccadilly Circus.
/ *www.planethollywood.com; midnight; no smoking area.*

The Poet EC3 £34 ④④❸

20 Creechurch Ln 7623 2020 9–2D

As a "quick and easy lunchtime bar" – "with a range of snacks or more substantial dishes" – this cavernous gastropub is a "good-value" option in a thinly-provided part of the City.
/ *www.thepoet.co.uk; L only (bar meals until 9 pm); closed Sat & Sun.*

Poissonnerie de l'Avenue SW3 £51 ❷❷❸

82 Sloane Ave 7589 2457 5–2C

"As good and pricey as ever", this Brompton Cross stalwart continues to please its "older clientèle" with the "excellent seafood" served in its cosy but "cramped" dining room.
/ *11.30 pm; closed Sun.*

The Polish Club SW7 £31 ④❷❶

55 Prince's Gate, Exhibition Rd 7589 4635 5–1C

"One of London's eccentricities" – a "magnificent chandeliered dining room" is the setting for some "stodgy old-world Polish" fodder (and an "impressive vodka selection") at this "curious" émigrés' club near the Science Museum, which is pleased to welcome non-members. / *11 pm; set weekday L & D £16(FP).*

Pollo W1 £14 ⑤④❸

20 Old Compton St 7734 5917 4–2A

"Always fast, always full" – this "shabby" and "studenty" Soho pit stop is famed for its "huge pasta bowls" at low prices; those who say it's just "cheap and extremely bad", however, are ever more voluble. / *midnight; no credit cards.*

Polygon Bar & Grill SW4 £ 30 ③③②
4 The Polygon 7622 1199 10–2D
A *"youthful"* crowd supplies the *"buzz"* at this Clapham
side-street brasserie (whose *"dependable"* fare is particularly
"brilliant for brunch"); bizarrely, the place has *"improved since
its owners focussed on their other project, Smiths of Smithfield"*!
/ 10.45 pm; Mon-Thu D only, Fri-Sun open L & D.

Pomegranates SW1 £ 37 ③②②
94 Grosvenor Rd 7828 6560 2–4C
A *"dark"* Pimlico den – *"stuck in a wonderful time warp"* –
where long-time host Patrick Gwynn-Jones still gives diners his
"personal attention"; his *"inspired"* menu still satisfies the
faithful, but those who say it's *"retro"* are in error – it's always
been like this. / 11.15 pm; closed Sat L & Sun.

Le Pont de la Tour SE1 £ 66 ⑤⑤③
36d Shad Thames 7403 8403 9–4D
It was a star in its day but, ten years on, Conran's original Tower
Bridge-side venture is withering into relative obscurity;
the *"wonderful views"* are still there, but the food just seems
"formulaic" nowadays, and the service is often *"snotty"*.
/ www.conran.com; 11.30 pm; closed Sat L; set weekday L £42(FP).

Le Pont de la Tour Bar & Grill SE1 £ 41 ③③②
36d Shad Thames 7403 8403 9–4D
"The restaurant may lack charisma, but the bar is pleasant" –
steak/frites here is a much cheaper way of enjoying the
"beautiful river views" from Conran's Thames-side gastrodome.
/ www.conran.com; 11.30 pm; no booking.

Poons WC2 £ 22 ③⑤④
4 Leicester St 7437 1528 4–3A
Despite *"iffy"* service and *"squashed"* tables, this generally
"reliable" Cantonese canteen, just off Leicester Square, can still
be a useful stand-by; it used to be so much better, though.
/ 11.30 pm.

Poons, Lisle Street WC2 £ 19 ③④④
27 Lisle St 7437 4549 4–3B
"Choose simple things, and the food is great", at this cheap,
grungy-looking *"old favourite"*, in Chinatown. / 11.30 pm; no Amex;
no smoking area.

Popeseye £ 34 ❶②④
108 Blythe Rd, W14 7610 4578 7–1C
277 Upper Richmond Rd, SW15 8788 7733 10–2A
"If you crave excellent steak, this is the place"; *"top"* meat and
a *"fantastic list of keenly-priced old-world wines"* makes for
a winning formula at this duo of *"friendly"* but basic bistros, in
Olympia and Putney. / 10.30 pm; D only; closed Sun; no credit cards.

Porchetta Pizzeria £18 ❸④❸
141-142 Upper St, N1   7288 2488   8–3D
147 Stroud Green Rd, N4   7281 2892   8–1D
"Fast, frenetic, and cheap" – this lively north London duo are
"not the place for an intimate chat", but they deliver
a wide-ranging Italian menu that's *"amazing value overall"*.
/ midnight; no Amex; booking: need 5+ to book.

La Porte des Indes W1 £43 ❷❷❶
32 Bryanston St   7224 0055   2–2A
Given the *"out-of-this-world"* décor of this lavish Indian, near
Marble Arch, it's no surprise that prices here can seem
"inflated" – the *"exquisite"* cooking, however, is at last living up
to the setting. / www.la-porte-des-indes.com; midnight; closed Sat L; set daily
buffet £29(FP).

Porters WC2 £24 ⑤⑤⑤
17 Henrietta St   7836 6466   4–3D
"Large pies, little else" – the hackneyed English cooking at this
"touristy" and *"uninspired"* Covent Garden spot makes it
a *"truly appalling"* flag-bearer for the native cuisine.
/ www.porters.uk.com; 11.30 pm.

Il Portico W8 £43 ④❷❸
277 Kensington High St   7602 6262   7–1D
"As close as you'll get to Italy in Kensington", this *"warm"* and
"lively", *"'70s-flashback"* trattoria is popular locally for its
"reliable", if uninspired, cooking. / 11.15 pm; closed Sun.

The Portrait
National Portrait Gallery WC2 £37 ④⑤❷
St Martin's Place   7312 2490   4–4B
"A stunning view is not enough" – it's a shame that *"grumpy"*,
"inept" service and *"horrible"* acoustics help to prevent this
potentially *"classy"* venue from achieving its potential. / 8.30 pm;
L only, except Thu & Fri open L & D; smoking in bar only; booking: max 8.

Potemkin EC1 £32 ❸❷❸
144 Clerkenwell Road   7278 6661   9–1A
"A cracking vodka list" and *"very attentive staff"* add sparkle to
this *"grimly cheerful"* Clerkenwell basement, where the Russian
cooking is quite *"good"*, if *"pricey"* for what it is.
/ www.potemkin.co.uk; 10.30 pm; closed Sat L & Sun.

Le Potiron Sauvage SW6 £38 – – –
755 Fulham Rd   7371 0755   10–1B
As we go to press, the Fulham site formerly known as 755 is
being refurbished in preparation for an imminent relaunch as
a French restaurant of some ambition; no further details were
available, and the price is our guesstimate.

LA POULE AU POT SW1 £40 ❷❷❶
231 Ebury St   7730 7763   5–2D
"Still the best for romance" – this old Pimlico charmer is still
sweeping 'em off their feet with its candle-lit, *"dingy-but-good"*
farmhouse décor, its *"hearty French grub"* and its *"authentic"*
(*"nonchalant"*) service. / 11.15 pm; set weekday L £26(FP).

Prego TW9 £ 36 ④④④
106 Kew Rd   8948 8508   1–4A
A loyal few say this once-popular Richmond Italian is "always a pleasure", but too many now slate its extremely "ordinary" Mediterranean cooking. / 11.30 pm; no smoking area.

Pret A Manger £ 9 ❸❷④
Branches throughout London
"Reliable quality, for lunch on the hoof" – thanks in particular to its "consistently good" sandwiches, many "still can't fault" this seminal chain (now partially owned by McDonald's). / www.pret.com; 3.30 pm-11 pm; closed Sun except some more central branches; no credit cards; no smoking areas; no booking.

The Prince Bonaparte W2 £ 26 ❸④❷
80 Chepstow Rd   7313 9491   6–1B
"It's noisy and smoky when busy", but this basic Bayswater boozer still delivers some "delicious and unpretentious British food". / 10 pm; closed Tue L; no Amex; no booking.

Prism EC3 £ 50 ❸❸④
147 Leadenhall St   7256 3888   9–2D
It's "utterly suitable for business", but otherwise reports about Harvey Nichols's City outpost – with its "nothing special" cooking, and its rather "soulless" ex-banking hall setting – are getting more and more ambivalent. / www.harveynichols.com; 10 pm; closed Sat & Sun.

prospectGrill WC2 £ 32 ❸❷❸
4-6 Garrick St   7379 0412   4–3C
This "efficient and friendly" venture – "in the heart of Covent Garden, but without feeling touristy" – offers a "simple" and "reasonably priced" formula, with "organic steak" a top attraction; if you can, "get a booth". / www.prospectgrill.com; midnight; closed Sun; set Sun L £16(FP).

The Providores W1 £ 42 ❷❷❸
109 Marylebone High St   7935 6175   2–1A
Peter Gordon, the original chef at the Sugar Club, launched his new fusion café/restaurant in Marylebone as we were going to press; our first-week impressions, formed on an August '01 visit to the ground-floor Tapa Room, were of a welcoming establishment of serious culinary endeavour – the plainly-decorated first-floor dining room, however, is rather cramped. / Rated on Editors' assessment; www.theprovidores.co.uk; 10.45 pm; no smoking in dining room.

Pucci Pizza SW3 £ 27 ❸④❸
205 King's Rd   7352 2134   5–3C
An "old favourite of the young King's Road set" – this "happy", "cramped" and "very loud" café serves "good thin-crust pizzas" and is still "the place for beautiful youth to be seen". / 12.30 am; closed Sun L; no credit cards.

FSA

Pug W4 £ 29 ④④④
68 Chiswick High Rd 8987 9988 7–2B
This "big" and rather "impersonal" new Chiswick bar/restaurant may be "trying hard to be cool", but it's not living up to its potential; service can be "slapdash" and cooking veers from "overcontrived" to "unexciting". / 10.30 pm.

Purple Sage W1 £ 32 ④④④
90-92 Wigmore St 7486 1912 3–1A
Those who claim that the food is "like Marks & Spencer's 'Italian' range, priced up and served on a plate" are exaggerating, but ratings are sliding fast at this large and once-popular restaurant north of Oxford Street. / 10.30 pm; closed Sat L & Sun L (& Sun D in Aug).

Putney Bridge SW15 £ 64 ❸④❷
Embankment 8780 1811 10–1B
A year on from a major revamp, this "swanky" riverside venture – with its "fantastic outlook" – seems to be losing its way; the modern Gallic food may be "gourmet stuff", but it's "very overpriced", and the service is increasingly lacklustre.
/ www.putneybridgerestaurant.com; 11 pm; closed Mon & Sun D; set Sun L £42(FP).

Quadrato
Four Seasons Hotel E14 £ 42 ❸❷❸
Westferry Circus 7510 1857 11–1C
After a dire start, the smart, if corporate dining room at this year-old Canary Wharf hotel has "turned around" somewhat – with the introduction of some "well-priced" deals and a wider menu, it makes a useful business rendezvous.
/ www.fourseasons.com; 10.30 pm; no smoking area; set (incl glass of sparkling wine) £20(FP).

Quaglino's SW1 £ 44 ⑤⑤④
16 Bury St 7930 6767 3–3D
With its "overpriced but very standard grub", its "sloppy" service and its "impersonal" atmosphere, this Conran brasserie in St James's has now "gone totally downhill". / www.conran.com; midnight, Fri & Sat 1 am; set weekday L, Sun L & pre-th. £26(FP).

The Quality Chop House EC1 £ 36 ❷❷❸
94 Farringdon Rd 7837 5093 9–1A
The benches may be "bloody uncomfortable", but this restored 'working class caterer' in Farringdon is a "homely" place whose "brilliant" staff deliver simple cooking of a "consistently" high standard. / 11.30 pm; closed Sat L; no Amex; no smoking area.

The Queen's NW1 £ 28 ❸❸❸
49 Regents Park Rd 7586 0408 8–3B
It can be "smoky" and "noisy", but this trendified Primrose Hill boozer serves some "good", simple grub, and makes a useful stand-by. / 9.45 pm; no Amex; no booking, except Sun L.

Queen's Head W6 £ 24 ④❸❷
13 Brook Grn   7603 3174   7–1C
The "brilliant garden" – it's huge – is the star feature of this picturesque, if "chintzy", pub on Brook Green; there's a large variety of food, realised to a very variable standard. / 10 pm; no smoking area; no booking.

Quiet Revolution £ 22 ❷❸❷
62 Marylebone High St, W1   7487 5683   2–1B
49 Old St, EC1   7253 5556   9–1B
"Excellent for organics fans"; for "wonderful breakfasts and lunches" this mini-café chain – which specialises in "imaginative and interesting soups, salads and juices" – receives nothing but praise. / www.quietrevolution.co.uk; W1 L only – EC1 11 pm; W1 closed Sat & Sun; no smoking.

Quilon SW1 £ 41 ❸❷④
41 Buckingham Gate   7821 1899   2–4B
The ambience could "do with a bit more zing", but this "good-quality" nouvelle Indian offers "curry with style", and it's useful as a business rendezvous around Victoria Street. / 11 pm; closed Sat L & Sun.

Quincy's NW2 £ 33 ④❷❸
675 Finchley Rd   7794 8499   1–1B
The cooking has "lost quality since the change of ownership" at this "squashed" Gallic fixture, on the way to Golders Green; "friendly" service and the "intimate" atmosphere survive. / 10 pm; D only, closed Sun; no Amex.

Quo Vadis W1 £ 45 ❸❸❸
26-29 Dean St   7437 9585   4–2A
"OK but overhyped" is perhaps the fairest summary on MPW's revamped Soho old-timer, whose Mediterranean fare and "funky"-ish décor continue to attract deeply mixed commentary. / www.whitestarline.org.uk; 11.30 pm; closed Sat L & Sun.

Quod W1 £ 28 ④④④
57 Haymarket   7925 1234   4–4A
Jeremy Mogford – creator of the seminal '70s chain Brown's – is behind this large, new West End Italian; perhaps in 25 years, this barn of a place will be seen as epitomising the spirit of the '00s – on the basis of our early-days (August '01) visit, we hope not. / Rated on Editors' assessment; www.oxford-hotels-restaurants.co.uk; midnight; no smoking area.

Raccolto W11 £ 36 ❸④❷
148 Holland Park Ave   7221 6090   6–2A
With its stylishly-muted décor, this new Holland Park Italian (on the site of Offshore, RIP) offers some decent, moderately-priced fare – "from simple, to more sophisticated dishes"; service "really tries", but "can be slow". / 11 pm.

Ragam W1
£ 23 ❸❷⑤

57 Cleveland St   7636 9098   2–1B
It's a "dreary" place, "but the service is pleasant" and you get some "good south Indian/Keralan vegetarian cooking" at this long-established fixture, in the shadow of the Telecom Tower. / 10.30 pm; set weekday L £13(FP).

Rain W10
£ 34 ❸❸❷

303 Portobello Rd   8968 2001   6–1A
This "cosy" ("cramped") North Kensington joint is an "enchanting and different" destination; even fans of its "yummy" Asian/fusion cooking, however, can emerge "stunned by the cost". / www.rain.uk.com; 10.30 pm; closed Sun; set weekday L £21(FP).

The Rainforest Cafe W1
£ 33 ⑤④❶

20 Shaftesbury Ave   7434 3111   3–3D
It may be "a ghastly place with rotten food", but "kids adore" this huge West End theme diner. / www.rainforestcafe.com; 10.30 pm, Fri & Sat 8 pm; no smoking; set children's meal (incl drink) £21(FP).

Randall & Aubin
£ 40 ❸❸❸

16 Brewer St, W1   7287 4447   3–2D
329-331 Fulham Rd, SW10   7823 3515   5–3B
"Cool" and "fun" joints – both the original bar/rôtisserie in the heart of sleazy Soho, and the less quirky but more comfortable new brasserie in Chelsea – serving grills and seafood. / www.randallandaubin.co.uk; 11.30 pm; no booking.

Rani N3
£ 23 ❷❷❸

7 Long Ln   8349 4386   1–1B
"Good Gujerati food" is on offer at this "inventive" North Finchley veggie, whose "great Sunday buffet" is a feature. / www.rani.com; 10 pm; D only; no smoking area.

Ranoush W2
£ 20 ❶④④

43 Edgware Rd   7723 5929   6–1D
"The best kebabs in town" and "excellent juices" have long made this "slice of Beirut" a popular central destination, particularly late at night; go to the cash machine first, though – it's strictly readies only. / www.maroush.com; 2.45 am; no credit cards.

Ransome's Dock SW11
£ 42 ❷❷❸

35 Parkgate Rd   7223 1611   5–4C
"The best-ever wine list", "helpful staff" and "a great menu" combine to make quite a destination of Martin Lam's "excellent" Battersea local; a few disappointingly "middle-of-the-road" results, however, were reported this year. / www.ransomesdock.co.uk; 11 pm, Sat midnight; closed Sun D.

Raoul's Café W9
£ 24 ❸④❸

13 Clifton Rd   7289 7313   8–4A
Maida Vale's "best local café" is a "trendy" spot best known for its "great" breakfasts; it gets "very crowded at weekends" (when "rich, but unfortunately not famous, people come to show off their kids"). / 10.30 pm; no smoking area; no booking at L.

Rapscallion SW4 £32 ❷❷❷
75 Venn St 7787 6555 10–2D
This "bustling" joint by Clapham Picture House is "great for
a quick yet quality bite", but "the tables are very close together"
and some find the setting just "too loud". / 10.30 pm, Fri & Sat
11.30 pm.

Rasa £30 ❶❶❸
6 Dering St, W1 7629 1346 3–2B
55 Stoke Newington Church St, N16 7249 0344 1–1C
"Everyone would be a veggie if all the food was this good" – the
"sublime" cooking served by this Keralan duo ensures that "they
are certainly not just for the sandals brigade"; service is very
"helpful" too. / www.rasarestaurants.com; 10.30 pm; N16 closed
Mon L-Thu L – W1 closed Sun; no smoking.

Rasa Samudra W1 £39 ❶❷❸
5 Charlotte St 7637 0222 2–1C
"Try not to get stuck in one of the back rooms", if you visit this
"weird sprawl" of a Fitzrovian; wherever you go, however, you
should find some of "the best Indian vegetarian cooking in
London", and "inventive Keralan fish dishes".
/ www.rasarestaurants.com; 10.30 pm; closed Sun L; no smoking area.

Rasa Travancore N16 £25 ❷❷④
56 Stoke Newington Church St 7249 1340 1–1C
There have been rather up-and-down initial reports on the
"carnivorous" addition to this eminent, mostly veggie, Indian
group; our impression was consistent with those who found
"delicious" results at "reasonable" prices. / www.rasarestaurants.com;
10.30 pm; no smoking.

The Real Greek N1 £38 ❷❸❸
15 Hoxton Market 7739 8212 9–1D
"Fantastic Greek food with a twist" and a "brilliant wine list"
have won a heady reputation for this "trendy" Hoxton two-year
old; is it "going downhill", though? – the declining ratings
support those who fear that it is. / www.therealgreek.co.uk; 10.30 pm;
closed Sun; no Amex.

Rebato's SW8 £25 ❸❶❶
169 South Lambeth Rd 7735 6388 10–1D
"No need to go into the West End for a great meal", say
supporters of this Hispanic institution in Vauxhall, which offers
"consistently good food", "brilliant" service and a "fantastic"
and "authentic" ambience (particularly in the tapas bar).
/ www.rebatos.com; 10.45 pm; closed Sat L & Sun; no Switch.

Red Cube WC2 £39 – – –
1 Leicester Pl 7287 0101 4–3B
This clubby Leicester Square newcomer (on the site of Little
Havana, RIP) switched owners just before we went to press;
given its new stablemates (Tiger Tiger, etc), there's no reason to
expect it now to become the great culinary destination it never
was under the original régime. / www.latenightlondon.co.uk; midnight;
closed Mon & Sun.

FSA

Red Fort W1   **£ 40**   – – –
77 Dean St   7437 2525   4–2A
*After a long closure due to fire, this well-known Soho Indian is
scheduled to re-open in September '01; a bold modern new
look is promised; (the price shown is our guesstimate).*
/ 11.30 pm; no smoking area.

The Red Pepper W9   **£ 32**   ❷④❸
8 Formosa St   7266 2708   8–4A
*"Too crowded and with rude service, but still we go back" –
"superb pizza and other good Italian cooking" continue to make
this Maida Vale "local" a popular north London destination.*
/ 10.45 pm; closed weekday L.

Redmond's SW14   **£ 39**   ❷❷④
170 Upper R'mond Rd West   8878 1922   10–1A
*"Welcoming, if dull" Sheen shop-conversion, which "tries hard";
it serves "consistently good modern British cooking" which some
believe is "under-rated", and the wine list is "excellent" for
a local. / 10.30 pm; closed Sat L & Sun D.*

**Restaurant One-O-One
Sheraton Park Tower SW1**   **£ 59**   ❶❶❸
William St, 101 Knightsbridge   7290 7101   5–1D
*Knightsbridge is an odd place to find a 'hidden gem', but the
term fits this "spacious" hotel dining room; it doesn't attract
a vast amount of feedback, but almost all reports confirm the
"excellence" of the Gallic fish cooking, and praise the
"outstanding" service. / 10.30 pm; set weekday L £33(FP).*

Retsina NW1   **£ 19**   ④❷❸
83 Regent's Park Rd   7722 3194   8–3B
*"Cheaper and more welcoming than Lemonia" – this "homely"
family-run Greek is preferred by some over its brasher,
better-known Primrose Hill neighbour. / 11 pm; D only; no Amex.*

Reubens W1   **£ 39**   ❸④⑤
79 Baker St   7486 0035   2–1A
*"Homemade soup" and other "traditional" and "hearty" Jewish
fare generally "hit the spot" at this Marylebone kosher bar/deli;
it generated more interest this year, despite its "ambience-free"
setting. / 10 pm; closed Fri D & Sat; no Amex or Switch.*

Rhodes in the Square SW1   **£ 54**   ❷❷❸
Dolphin Sq, Chichester St   7798 6767   2–4C
*Some feel it "lacks finesse", but most applaud the high-quality
cooking at this "grown up" Pimlico dining room; "generously
spaced" tables and an out-of-the-way location (in a large
apartment complex) make it a discreet venue for business.
/ 10 pm; closed Mon, Sat L & Sun D; set weekday L £35(FP).*

Rib Room & Oyster Bar
Hyatt Carlton Tower Hotel SW1   £ 60   ④❸④
2 Cadogan Pl   7858 7053   5–1D
*Fans vaunt the "best roast beef in town" at this "shockingly
expensive" Knightsbridge grill room, but the "rigid" ambience –
"even after the recent facelift" – is still "too '80s hotel-like".*
/ 10.45 pm.

RIBA Cafe
Royal Assoc of British Architects W1   £   28
④④④
66 Portland Pl   7631 0467   2–1B
*For lunch on a sunny day, there's a top terrace adjoining this
impressive but (literally) institutional Marylebone café;
the simple catering, however, seemed on our August '01 visit to
be up to Milburn's usual forgettable standard. / Rated on Editors'
assessment; L only, closed Sun; no smoking.*

Riccardo's SW3   £ 26   ❸❸❸
126 Fulham Rd   7370 6656   5–3B
*The "yummy" Italian tapas are "great value" at this "totally
relaxed", fun and "very friendly" Chelsea stand-by. / midnight.*

Riso W4   £ 33   ④④⑤
76 South Pde   8742 2121   7–1A
*In the thin area near Acton Green Common, this modern
"neighbourhood Italian" could be a really useful option;
the cooking is "hit-and-miss", though, the décor is "poor", and –
compared with its sibling Tentazioni – the place seems just
"unbelievably disappointing". / 10.30 pm; D only; no Amex.*

Ristorante Italiano W1   £ 33   ⑤❸④
54 Curzon St   7629 2742   3–3B
*"The Italian food of 30 years ago" can still be sampled at this
Mayfair diehard, whose "friendly and accommodating" service
maintains its small, but devoted following. / 11.15 pm; closed
Sat L & Sun; no smoking area.*

The Ritz W1   £ 78   ④❷❶
150 Piccadilly   7493 8181   3–4C
*The cooking is "overpriced" and "not especially memorable",
but – for romantics – the "wonderful" décor of this "grand" and
"beautiful" dining room "just about makes up" for it.*
/ www.theritzlondon.com; 11 pm; jacket & tie required.

Riva SW13   £ 39   ❶❷④
169 Church Rd   8748 0434   10–1A
*"Knocks the River Café into a cocked hat"; Andreas Riva's
"discreet" (but slightly "soulless") Barnes fixture still divides
opinion, but the many vaunting its "amazingly creative and
delicious" Italian cooking were much more to the fore this year.
/ 11 pm, Fri & Sat 11.30 pm; closed Sat L.*

THE RIVER CAFÉ W6 £ 56 ❷❸❸
Thames Whf, Rainville Rd 7386 4200 7–2C
"Buy a ticket to Tuscany instead", say critics – given the "stupid
prices" at this famous Hammersmith Italian, it wouldn't cost
much more; for many reporters, a visit here is still "worth it",
but the ranks of those who think the place "overblown" and
"disappointing" continue to swell. / 9.30 pm; closed Sun D.

Riviera £ 32 ④④❸
56 Upper Ground, SE1 7401 7314 9–3A
Port East Bldg, West India Quay, E14 7515 4245 11–1C
"Nice in summer" – the South Bank original of this Italian duo
has "a great river view"; the cooking is "not up to the scenery",
though, either there or at the Canary Wharf branch.
/ www.gourmetpizzacompany.co.uk; 10.45pm; E14 closed Sun; E14
no smoking area.

Rocket W1 £ 28 ❸❸❷
4-6 Lancashire Ct 7629 2889 3–2B
"Tucked away", just off Bond Street, this "attractive" modern
spot is something of a "find"; its "very good pizzas and salads"
are "reasonably priced, for the area", and the place is equally at
home for "a large party" or "a break from shopping". / 11.30 pm;
closed Sun.

Rodizio Rico W2 £ 26 ❸❸❸
111 Westbourne Grove 7792 4035 6–1B
"You never leave hungry" – and "a rowdy night out" is assured
– at this buffet-style Bayswater Brazilian, where "barbecued
meats are ferried to your table by sabre-carrying waiters".
/ midnight; closed weekday L.

Rosmarino NW8 £ 35 ❸❸❸
1 Blenheim Terrace 7328 5014 8–3A
"Another great local", say fans of this St John's Wood yearling,
whose attractions include "good", if "standard", Italian cooking,
a "nice, busy" atmosphere and "top terrace in summer"; you'd
still never guess, however, that it's from the same stable as the
wonderful Zafferano. / 10.30 pm; no smoking.

The Rôtisserie £ 32 ❷❶❸
56 Uxbridge Rd, W12 8743 3028 7–1C
134 Upper St, N1 7226 0122 8–3D
It's "a spot-on package" that's "very friendly, accomplished and
simple", say fans of these "excellent grill-restaurants" – they
offer "great steak/frites" and "the best roast chicken".
/ www.therotisserie.co.uk; 11 pm; W12 closed Sat L & Sun L – N1 closed
Mon L & Tue L.

Rôtisserie Jules £ 23 ❸❷⑤
6-8 Bute St, SW7 7584 0600 5–2B
133 Notting Hill Gate, W11 7221 3331 6–2B
"As long as you like chicken" – or lamb, if ordered in advance –
these "dependable", no-frills protein-stops are "superb"; even
fans don't find them exciting places, though, and some tip them
"mainly for take-away". / 11 pm.

Roussillon SW1   £ 43   ❶❷❸

16 St Barnabas St   7730 5550   5–2D
*"Brilliant", "nicely idiosyncratic" Gallic cooking is winning
a growing following for this "understated" Pimlico establishment;
as ever, there's a strange gulf between those who say there's
"no ambience" and other who proclaim it "perfect".*
/ www.roussillon.co.uk; 10.45 pm; closed Sat L & Sun; no smoking area; set
weekday L £28(FP).

Rowley's SW1   £ 44   ⑤④⑤

113 Jermyn St   7930 2707   3–3D
*Even supporters concede that this "old-fashioned" St James's
grill is "expensive" for what it is, and for too many reporters the
simple question is "how on Earth can you cock up steak/frites?"*
/ www.rowleys.co.uk; 11.30 pm, Sun 9 pm; set Sun L £27(FP).

Royal Academy W1   £ 15   ④④④

Burlington Hs, Piccadilly   7287 0752   3–3C
*The location makes these basement refreshment rooms "great
for lunch or tea when in Piccadilly", but this venerable
institution's food is no attraction in itself.* / www.royalacademy.org.uk;
8.30 pm; L only, except Fri open L & D; no smoking; no booking, except Fri D.

Royal China SW15   £ 27   ❶❸④

3 Chelverton Rd   8788 0907   10–2B
*"For dim sum, it's as good as the one on Queensway" (now
under separate ownership), say supporters of this "fantastic"
Putney Chinese, where "the slightly faded glamour of the '70s
nightclub décor just adds to the fun".* / 11 pm; only Amex; need 7+ to
book, Sun L.

Royal China   £ 33   ❶❸④

40 Baker St, W1   7487 4688   2–1A
13 Queensway, W2   7221 2535   6–2C
68 Queen's Grove, NW8   7586 4280   8–3A
30 Westferry Circus, E14   7719 0888   11–1B
*The food's "as near to real Chinese as you can get", and the
dim sum are "the best in London", so it's no surprise that you
often have to queue (especially on Sundays) for these
"amusingly kitsch" orientals, done out "like '70s discos".*
/ 10.45 pm, Fri & Sat 11.30 pm.

Royal Court Bar
Royal Court Theatre SW1   £ 28   ④④④

Sloane Sq   7565 5061   5–2D
*The setting can be "crowded" and "noisy" – "brutal" even –
and the simple scoff is humdrum, but this subterranean bar is
"not expensive", given its handy Sloane Square location.*
/ 10.30 pm; closed Sun; no smoking area; set D £19(FP).

Royal Opera House Café WC2   £ 32   ⑤⑤④

Covent Garden   7212 9254   4–3D
*It may have a "lovely view", but otherwise this top-floor
restaurant – with its "institutional" food, "amateurish" service
and "dreary" setting – "could be vastly improved".* / L only, except
for opera-goers; closed Sun; no smoking; set weekday L £20(FP).

RSJ SE1 £ 37 ❸❷④

13a Coin St   7928 4554   9–4A

The "treasure trove" of "wonderful Loire wines at reasonable prices" perennially "outshines the cooking" – and also the low-key setting – at this South Bank fixture. / 11 pm; closed Sat L & Sun.

Ruby in the Dust £ 28 ⑤④❸

53 Fulham Broadway, SW6   7385 9272   5–4A
299 Portobello Rd, W11   8969 4626   6–1A
70 Upper St, N1   7359 1710   8–3D
102 Camden High St, NW1   7485 2744   8–3C

"Not great, but fun" – these "buzzy", "chilled", but rather "hit-and-miss", diners are popular for young-at-heart parties; they're "very well geared-up for kids" too. / 11.30 pm – N1 Fri & Sat 2 am.

Rudland & Stubbs EC1 £ 38 ❸④④

35-37 Greenhill Rents, Cowcross St   7253 0148   9–1A

"Quite good fish" makes this long-established Smithfield parlour – "housed in a setting like an old butchers" – a useful lunch rendezvous; it is "dead in the evenings". / 10.45 pm; closed Sat L & Sun.

La Rueda £ 30 ❸❸❷

102 Wigmore St, W1   7486 1718   3–1A
642 King's Rd, SW6   7384 2684   5–4A
66-68 Clapham High St, SW4   7627 2173   10–2D

If you're timid, "stay away on Fridays", from this traditional tapas bar chain – the original Clapham branch, in particular – which is "good for an all-round fun night out"; the food is "reasonably priced", but "no better than average". / 11.30 pm.

Rules WC2 £ 48 ❸❷❶

35 Maiden Ln   7836 5314   4–3D

"Tradition at its best" – not least the menu of game, grills and solid puds – comes combined with "a surprising degree of modern flair" to make London's oldest restaurant (1798) too good to waste on out-of-towners; the recent ban on cigarette smoking, though, has some patrons up in arms. / www.rules.co.uk; 11.30 pm; no smoking.

Rupee Room EC2 £ 29 ❸❸④

10 Copthall Ave   7628 1555   9–2C

It's never going to set the world on fire, but this basement Indian is "handy" for City folk hungry for a curry. / 11 pm; closed Sat & Sun.

Rusticana W1 £ 28 ❸❸④

27 Frith St   7439 8900   4–3A

Small and relatively unknown, this three-year-old trattoria is a "good, cheap" Soho stand-by, distinguished by "attentive, but unintrusive" service. / 11.30 pm; no Amex.

S&P £ 35 ❷❷❸

181 Fulham Rd, SW3   7351 5692   5–2C
9 Beauchamp Pl, SW3   7581 8820   5–1C
*The seating may be "cramped", but it's "worth it" for the
"authentic" and "tasty" dishes on offer at these Knightsbridge
and Chelsea Thais. / 10.30 pm; no smoking areas; set weekday L £22(FP).*

Sabai Sabai W6 £ 25 ❷❷④

270-272 King St   8748 7363   7–2B
*"Consistently good Thai food" and "efficient service" win a loyal
local fan club for this Hammersmith spot – "if only they'd do
something about the atmosphere". / 11.30 pm; closed Sun L;
no smoking area; set weekday L £16(FP).*

Le Sacré-Coeur N1 £ 25 ④❷❸

18 Theberton St   7354 2618   8–3D
*"The food can be a bit hit-and-miss" at this "cramped" Gallic
bistro, just off Islington's Upper Street, but the staff are
"accommodating", and fans say it's a "good-value" destination
overall. / 11 pm, Sat & Sun 11.30 pm; set weekday L £13(FP).*

Saigon W1 £ 30 ❸❸④

45 Frith St   7437 7109   4–2A
*Service can be "erratic" and the "food can vary", but what is
more surprising is how generally consistent and "enjoyable" this
touristy-looking Soho Vietnamese manages to be. / 11.30 pm;
closed Sun.*

St Moritz W1 £ 34 ④❸❸

161 Wardour St   7734 3324   3–1D
*For a "fun fondue", and a "'70s chalet ambience" this cramped
Soho fixture can be "a good discovery"; there were more gripes
this year, though, of "bland" results. / 11.30 pm; closed Sat L & Sun.*

Saints W11 £ 27 ④❸❸

12 All Saints Rd   7243 2008   6–1B
*Eager-to-please staff make you want to like this Notting Hill
newcomer, occupying the attractive premises vacated by Nosh
Brothers (RIP); on an August '01 visit, the grazing fodder wasn't
bad, but it didn't particularly impress either. / Rated on Editors'
assessment; 11.30 pm; closed weekday L; no Amex.*

Sakonis £ 16 ❶❸④

129 Ealing Rd, HA0   8903 9601   1–1A
180-186 Upper Tooting Rd, SW17   8772 4774   10–2C
*"This is the real thing" – you won't find better value in the
capital than these fabulous Indian veggie cafeterias;
the Wembley original, in particular, gets "very busy", and a new
branch has just opened in Tooting; no alcohol. / www.sakonis.co.uk;
9.30 pm; SW17 closed Tue; no Amex; no smoking.*

Sale e Pepe SW1 £ 41 ❸❷❷

9-15 Pavilion Rd   7235 0098   5–1D
*The noise is "ear-splitting", but this "chaotic" Knightsbridge
Italian of long standing still generally charms the punters with
attractions including "fun" waiters and "the greatest pasta".
/ 11.30 pm; closed Sun.*

regular updates at www.hardens.com 146

The Salisbury Tavern SW6   £ 36   ❸❷❸
21 Sherbrooke Rd   7381 4005   10–1B
*"Unusually good pub food" served in a "super" setting wins high
praise for this large, attractively-converted boozer (the Fulham
cousin of Chelsea's Admiral Codrington). / 10.30 pm; set weekday L
£24(FP).*

Salloos SW1   £ 45   ❶❸④
62-64 Kinnerton St   7235 4444   5–1D
*The décor is "rather dull" and prices are "high", but this
Belgravia mews stalwart has long been a "consistent"
performer, and many still reckon it serves "the best
Indian/Pakistani food in the UK". / 11.15 pm; closed Sun; set
weekday L £27(FP).*

Salon
The House Hotel NW3   £ 38   ❷❸❷
2 Rosslyn Hill   7435 2828   8–2A
*This decadently-furnished dining room lives up to its name,
decoratively speaking, and on an early-days (August '01) visit it
was already delivering some elegant cooking; could this be the
all-round quality restaurant that Hampstead – in recent years at
least – has never managed to sustain? / Rated on Editors' assessment;
11 pm; no smoking area; booking: max 8.*

The Salt House NW8   £ 30   ❸❸❸
63 Abbey Rd   7328 6626   8–3A
*The menu's "limited", but it's "imaginative" too, at this "smart"
former boozer in St John's Wood, which is now a "thoroughly
good neighbourhood restaurant and bar". / 10.30 pm.*

The Salusbury NW6   £ 28   ❷❸❷
50-52 Salusbury Rd   7328 3286   1–2B
*"The best place in the area" (around Queen's Park), this 'Pub
and Dining Room' serves a "proficient" Italianate menu,
and provides a "cosy" and "lively" setting that's ideal "for
a relaxed gathering". / 10.15 pm; closed Mon L; no Amex.*

Sambuca SW1   £ 35   ❸❷④
62-64 Lower Sloane St   7730 6571   5–2D
*"Enjoyably flamboyant service" is the mainstay of this
"old-fashioned" trattoria, which is beginning to recover the
"reliable" form that it misplaced in its move from the other side
of Sloane Square a couple of years ago. / 11.30 pm; closed Sun.*

San Carlo N6   £ 34   ④❷❷
2 Highgate High St   8340 5823   8–1B
*This impressive-looking Highgate Italian "could do so much
better" – staff are "friendly and very professional", but its
"bog-standard" cooking comes at (almost) "West End prices".
/ 11 pm; closed Mon; no jeans; no smoking area.*

San Daniele del Friuli N5   £ 28   ❸❷❸
72 Highbury Park   7226 1609   8–1D
*"A good local atmosphere" and "value-for-money" cooking win
praise for this family-run Highbury Italian. / 10.45 pm; closed Mon L,
Sat L & Sun; no Amex; no smoking area.*

San Frediano SW3 £ 35 ④④⑤

62 Fulham Rd   7589 2232   5–2C

After a series of "poorly executed" relaunches in recent years, this seminal Chelsea trattoria remains a "pale shadow" of its former self; at lunchtime, however, "good-value set meals" offer some consolation. / 11.45 pm; set weekday L £22(FP).

San Lorenzo SW3 £ 50 ⑤⑤❸

22 Beauchamp Pl   7584 1074   5–1C

"Overpriced, overcrowded, over-everything" – this "passé" and "pretentious" Knightsbridge trattoria underperforms on practically all counts. / 11.30 pm; closed Sun; no credit cards.

Sand SW4 £ 35 ❸④❷

156 Clapham Park Rd   7622 3022   10–2D

"A cool place, with a trendy crowd" – the food may not be the main point at this groovy Clapham bar/restaurant, but it's "improved" of late. / www.sandbarrestaurant.co.uk; 1.30 am; D only; no Amex; no booking after 9.30 pm.

Sandrini SW3 £ 39 ❸❷❸

260-262a Brompton Rd   7584 1724   5–2C

This "slick" but "old-fashioned" Brompton Cross Italian hasn't set the world alight in recent years, but it's a "calm and civilised oasis", often hailed as a "safe" choice. / 11.30 pm.

Santa Fe N1 £ 32 ④④④

75 Upper St   7288 2288   8–3D

"Uneven preparation" of the Tex/Mex-type menu continues to afflict this potentially attractive Islington southwest American; it has "really gone downhill" since it first opened. / 10.30 pm; no smoking area.

Santini SW1 £ 56 ❸④⑤

29 Ebury St   7730 4094   2–4B

Even some who deem the cooking "excellent" at this swanky Italian near Victoria find the setting "sterile", and others slam the whole experience as "vastly overpriced". / 11.30 pm; closed Sat L & Sun L; jacket or tie required; set weekday L £31(FP).

Sarastro WC2 £ 30 ⑤❸❶

126 Drury Ln   7836 0101   2–2D

There's "plenty to criticise on the food front", but this "completely bizarre and kitsch" Theatreland Turk is well worth at least one visit for its "magical" and "OTT" décor (which comes complete with "romantic alcoves").
/ www.sarastro-restaurant.com; 11.30 pm; no smoking area; set brunch £17(FP).

Sarkhel's SW18 £ 26 ❶❷❸

199 Replingham Rd   8870 1483   10–2B

Is this "the best Indian in London"?; Udit Sarkhel was formerly head chef at the Bombay Brasserie, and – thanks to his "wonderfully light and inventive cooking" – it's not a ridiculous claim to make for this "delightful" Southfields venture.
/ 10.30 pm, Fri & Sat 11 pm; closed Mon; no smoking area.

Sartoria W1   £ 50   ⑤④④
20 Savile Row   7534 7000   3–2C
*Conran's "expensive" Mayfair Italian is a "dull" place, with
"bland" cooking – it offers "a completely unremarkable
experience".* / www.conran.com; 11.15 pm; closed Sun L.

Satsuma W1   £ 25   ❷④❸
56 Wardour St   7437 8338   3–2D
*"Like Wagamama, but less manic" – "generous portions" of
"better-than-average noodles" served in a "fun", if "crowded",
cafeteria setting make this an "amiable" Soho venture.*
/ www.osatsuma.com; 11 pm, Wed & Thu 11.30 pm, Fri & Sat 1 am;
no smoking; no booking.

Sauce NW1   £ 26   ❸❷④
214 Camden High St   7482 0777   8–2B
*"Plain but good" organic food (including "fabulous" steaks)
makes this "canteen"-like Camden Town basement a useful
destination; the décor, though, "could use some help".* / 11 pm;
closed Sun D; no Amex; no smoking area; need 6+ to book.

Savoy Grill WC2   £ 70   ④❷❸
Strand   7420 2066   4–3D
*It's no longer THE power lunching venue, but this gracious
panelled dining room is still a "great business setting", sustained
by staff who "anticipate and act on every whim"; the "so-so"
traditional fare remains rather beside the point.*
/ www.savoygroup.com; 11.15 pm; closed Sat L & Sun; jacket & tie required;
pre-th. £45(FP).

Savoy River Restaurant WC2   £ 70   ⑤❸❷
Strand   7420 2698   4–3D
*For "dinner overlooking the Thames" (or "a seriously
business-like breakfast"), this "quietly elegant" room "still has
magic"; the staff strike too many reporters as being
"on autopilot", though, and the cooking is far too
"unimaginative" and "very overpriced".* / www.savoygroup.com;
11.30 pm; jacket required at L, jacket & tie at D; no smoking area; set
weekday L, Sun L & pre-th. £44(FP).

Savoy Upstairs WC2   £ 38   ④❸❸
Strand   7836 4343   4–3D
*This small, smart brasserie – with its ringside seat for watching
comings and goings at the hotel's main entrance – can seem
a bit of a "secret"; it offers a "quick and easy" substitute for
a full blown meal in the Grill or River Room, but is similarly
"overpriced".* / www.savoygroup.com; 11.30 pm; closed Sat L & Sun.

Scalini SW3   £ 47   ❸❸❷
1-3 Walton St   7225 2301   5–2C
*"Very lively and European" (read Eurotrash), this "fun" and
"noisy" trattoria behind Harrods is an "old favourite" for many;
it's "overpriced", though, and some feel the food borders on
"so-so".* / midnight.

The Scarsdale W8 £ 26 ④❸❷
23a Edwardes Sq 7937 1811 7–1D
The "great" (but tiny) terrace is the prime spot at this
"charming" and cutely-situated hostelry, near Kensington High
Street; the pub grub staples are "very ordinary". / 9.45 pm.

Scoffers SW11 £ 28 ④❸❷
6 Battersea Rise 7978 5542 10–2C
Still a favourite for many a Battersea twentysomething, but this
"cosy" local's cooking has seemed "less refined and interesting"
of late; for a "gorgeous American breakfast", however,
its attractions are undimmed. / 11 pm.

Scott's W1 £ 56 ❸❸④
20 Mount St 7629 5248 3–3A
This venerable Mayfair establishment – trendily revamped a few
years ago by Groupe Chez Gérard – once again risks "living on
its name"; fans still say it offers "a superb selection" of "the
best seafood", but others complain of "ordinary and overpriced"
food, and "dreadful" service. / 11 pm; no smoking area.

Scuzi £ 32 ❸④④
37 Westferry Circus, E14 7519 6699 11–1C
360 St John St, EC1 7833 4393 9–1B
2 Creechurch Ln, EC3 7623 3444 9–2D
"Interesting pizzas that work" (and "great pasta") have won
instant acclaim for this fledgling chain; the Canary Wharf
branch has "fabulous views". / 11.30 pm; EC1 D only – E14 closed
Sat & Sun; EC3 & E14 no smoking areas.

Seafresh SW1 £ 24 ④④④
80-81 Wilton Rd 7828 0747 2–4B
Portions remain "substantial", but the fare at this "traditional"
Pimlico chippy of long repute can seem rather "ordinary"
nowadays. / 10.30 pm; closed Sun.

Searcy's Brasserie EC2 £ 43 ④④⑤
Level II, Barbican Centre 7588 3008 9–1B
While some remain "pleasantly surprised" by this Gallic venue
within the Barbican, the feeling is growing that it's
a "corridor-like" place that "takes advantage of a captive
clientèle"; for business, however, it has its uses. / 10.30 pm, Sun
6.30 pm; closed Sat L; no smoking area.

Seashell NW1 £ 23 ❷❸④
49 Lisson Grove 7224 9000 8–4A
"Smashing" fish and chips (and "great mushy peas" too)
maintain this "traditional" fixture's name as "the best chippy
around"; "it's on the tourist trail, though", and it's looking pretty
"tired". / 10.30 pm; closed Sun; no smoking area; no booking.

Sedir N1 £ 20 ❸❷❸
4 Theberton St 7226 5489 8–3D
"The delicious, fresh veggie mezze" is a highlight at this
"no-frills" Islington bistro (formerly called Sarcan), but its "basic"
fare also includes plenty for carnivores. / 11.30 pm.

The Sequel SW4　　　　£ 37　④④④
75 Venn St　7622 4222　10–2D
*Both the quality of the cooking and the desirability of the
projection screen divide opinion on this "bustling" outfit, which is
"full of chattering Claphamites"; the majority views, however,
are that the "eclectic" cooking is in need of improvement… and
the screen dies.* / www.sequelonline.com; 11 pm; closed Mon,
Tue-Fri D only, Sat & Sun open L & D.

Serafino W1　　　　£ 35　④❶④
8 Mount St　7629 0544　3–3B
*"Fabulous" staff are the undoubted highlight of this relaunched
Mayfair Italian (originally called La Seppia), whose old-hat style
has been given a thin veneer of modernity; the destruction of
the wonderfully '60s former dining room in the basement is
nothing less than a tragedy.* / 10.45 pm; closed Sat L & Sun.

Shakespeare's Globe SE1　　　　£ 37　④❸❷
New Globe Walk　7928 9444　9–3B
*There are "wonderful views of the Thames" from the
second-floor dining room at this riverside South Bank landmark;
the cooking is very unreliable, though, and while some say it can
be "surprisingly good", others say it's "ghastly".* / 10 pm (or 20 mins
after show).

Shampers W1　　　　£ 31　❸❷❸
4 Kingly St　7437 1692　3–2D
*"Always full of happy people", this "hectic", but very "well-run",
"traditional" wine bar off Regent Street is "a long-standing
favourite" thanks to its "generous" and "honest" Gallic fare and
its "great wine list".* / 11 pm; closed Sun (& Sat in Aug).

Shanghai E8　　　　£ 23　❷❷❷
41 Kingsland High St　7254 2878　1–1C
*Make sure you sit in the front section (which was once an
impressive pie 'n' eel shop) if you visit this "very good
neighbourhood Chinese" in Dalston; "great buffet lunches" are
a particular attraction.* / 11 pm; no Amex.

J SHEEKEY WC2　　　　£ 42　❶❶❷
28-32 St Martin's Ct　7240 2565　4–3B
*"The kingpin of fish cooking at the moment" – this chicly
revitalised Theatreland seafood parlour has become "a real
winner" since the Ivy/Caprice people began to work their magic;
this year, for the first time, it joins its siblings in the 'Top 10'
restaurants reporters talk about the most.* / midnight; set Sun L
£25(FP).

Shepherd's SW1　　　　£ 39　❸❷❸
Marsham Ct, Marsham St　7834 9552　2–4C
*With its "good booths for discussions", this "clubby"
Westminster fixture is a "reliable" spot that's "great for
business"; the traditional British cooking is "nothing outstanding,
but still the best in the area".* / www.langansrestaurants.co.uk; 11 pm;
closed Sat & Sun; no smoking area.

The Ship SW18 £26 ③④❶
41 Jews Row 8870 9667 10–2B
It's "the BBQ, summertime only!" which generates the lofty
ambience rating for this "crowded" Wandsworth boozer – "get
there early" if you want a seat on the river terrace.
/ www.theship.co.uk; 10.30 pm; no booking, Sun L.

Shish NW2 £20 ③④❷
2-6 Station Pde 8208 9292 1–1A
"What is going on in Willesden Green?" – this "funky"
newcomer offers "a great new take on the old-style
shish-kebab", in an impressively "highly designed" environment.
/ midnight; no Amex; no smoking area; no booking.

Shoeless Joe's £30 ④⑤④
1 Abbey Orchard, SW1 7222 4707 2–4C
33 Dover St, W1 7499 2689 3–3C
Temple Pl, WC2 7240 7865 2–2D
555 King's Rd, SW6 7610 9346 5–4B
2 Old Change Ct, EC4 7248 2720 9–3B
Some claim you get "good food in a fun setting" at these
allegedly upscale sports bar/restaurants; overall though,
reporters are minded to wonder "why do they bother?".
/ www.shoelessjoes.co.uk; 9.30 pm – WC2 10 pm; closed Sun – SW1 & EC4
also closed Sat.

Shogun W1 £50 ❷❸④
Adam's Row 7493 1255 3–3A
"Excellent traditional cooking" (including "wonderful sushi")
makes this "very expensive" Mayfair veteran one of the top
Japaneses in town; some think its "dark" cellar setting has
"great atmosphere", but it doesn't do it for everyone. / 11 pm;
D only, closed Mon; no Switch.

Le Shop SW3 £26 ❸❷❷
329 King's Rd 7352 3891 5–3B
"The best galettes" (Breton pancakes) are the simple
proposition which has kept this agreeable Chelsea café in
business for many years now. / www.leshop-chelsea.co.uk; midnight;
no Amex; set weekday L £16(FP).

Signor Sassi SW1 £47 ❸❷❷
14 Knightsbridge Grn 7584 2277 5–1D
"Happy lunacy from the staff" helps keep things nicely ticking
along at this "frantic" Knightsbridge trattoria; the food is
"always good" too. / 11.30 pm; closed Sun; no smoking area.

Silks & Spice £30 ❸❸❸
23 Foley St, W1 7636 2718 2–1B
95 Chiswick High Rd, W4 8995 7991 7–2B
28 Chalk Farm Rd, NW1 7267 5751 8–2B
Temple Ct, 11 Queen Victoria St, EC4 7248 7878 9–2C
"Fairly authentic Malay fare" – "nothing fancy but reliable" –
has won a strong following for this chain of "buzzy" ("cramped"
and "noisy") Thai bistros, though some of them do seem "more
bar than restaurant". / 11 pm – EC4 Thu & Fri 2 am; W1 closed
Sat L & Sun L – EC4 closed Sat & Sun; no smoking areas.

Simply Nico £ 40 ④④④

12 Sloane Sq, SW1 7896 9909 5–2D
48a Rochester Rw, SW1 7630 8061 2–4C
10 London Bridge St, SE1 7407 4536 9–4C
7 Goswell Rd, EC1 7336 7677 9–1B

Except as a business stand-by, there's "nothing to recommend", this "dull" and "formulaic" group of "cramped" and "sterile" bistros, where the Gallic cooking tends to be "bland" and "expensive". / www.trpplc.com; 10.30 pm – SW1 11 pm; EC1 & SE1 closed Sat L & Sun.

Simpson's Tavern EC3 £ 22 ④❷❶

38 1/2 Cornhill 7626 9985 9–2C

If you're looking for a "200-year time-warp", you won't do much better than this "Dickensian" back alley City chop-house, where "endearing waitresses" contribute much to the ambience. / L only, closed Sat & Sun; no booking.

Simpsons-in-the-Strand WC2 £ 49 ④④❸

100 Strand 7836 9112 4–3D

"Dated" standards – reminiscent of the "school canteen" – mean you tend to find a rather "touristy" clientèle nowadays at what was once the most famous of English restaurants; its "luxurious" breakfasts, however, are commended.
/ www.savoygroup.com; 11 pm, Sun 9 pm; closed Sat L; jacket required; set weekday L £32(FP).

Singapore Garden NW6 £ 31 ❷❷④

83-83a Fairfax Rd 7328 5314 8–2A

The food's usually "spicy" – even if the décor isn't – at this well-established Swiss Cottage "local", which serves a mixed bag of Chinese and south east Asian cuisines. / 10.45 pm, Fri & Sat 11.15 pm; set weekday L £18(FP).

Singapura £ 35 ④❸⑤

31 Broadgate Circle, EC2 7256 5045 9–2D
78-79 Leadenhall St, EC3 7929 0089 9–2D
1-2 Limeburner Ln, EC4 7329 1133 9–2A

These "blandly-decorated" City orientals have always rather "lacked atmosphere", but have long made "reliable" options for a business lunch; ratings slumped this year, though, and some now find them "mediocre" across the board. / www.singapuras.co.uk; 10.30 pm; closed Sat & Sun.

Six Degrees W1 £ 36 ⑤⑤⑤

56 Frith St 7734 8300 4–2A

"Truly awful" food and "appalling" service help explain the very limited feedback generated by this large, would-be-trendy Soho venue. / 10.45 pm; closed Sat L & Sun.

606 Club SW10 £ 40 ⑤④❷

90 Lots Rd 7352 5953 5–4B

"Once you get past the ominous entrance" – an anonymous staircase opposite Lots Road power station – there's a "fantastic atmosphere" at this basement jazz club; it serves "mediocre" food, though, and the service is "not much better". / www.606club.co.uk; 1 am, Fri & Sat 1.30 am, Sun 11.30 pm; D only.

regular updates at www.hardens.com 153

Six-13 W1 £ 50 ④④❸

19 Wigmore St 7629 6133 3–1B

"The food's not very Jewish" and *"relatively expensive"*, but – given the dearth of kosher restaurants – this slickly designed newcomer, off Cavendish Square, is undoubtedly a useful addition to the West End, and a popular business venue. / www.six13.com; 10.45 pm; closed Sat L (also Fri D in winter, Sat D in summer); no smoking area; set weekday L & pre-th. £32(FP).

Smiths of Smithfield EC1 £ 48 ❸❸❷

67-77 Charterhouse St 7236 6666 9–1A

"An 'in' place that's almost passed the test of time"; this *"trendy"* Manhattan-inspired complex, in an *"interesting"* building overlooking Smithfield Market, successfully covers a variety of bases – from bar snacks, via brunch in the brasserie (FP £32), to business lunching in the rooftop restaurant (to which the price given relates). / www.smithsofsmithfield.co.uk; 11 pm; closed Sat L (café open all day); set weekday L £30(FP).

Smollensky's £ 39 ⑤④④

105 Strand, WC2 7497 2101 4–3D

255 Finchley Rd, NW3 7431 5007 8–2A

"Children love" these *"busy"* American diners (which offer entertainment at weekends), and some grown-ups proclaim their virtues for *"a fun night out"*; on the culinary front, though, results are somewhere between *"average"* and *"like an Angus Steak House"*. / www.smollenskys.co.uk; WC2 11.30 pm, Fri & Sat midnight – NW3 11 pm; WC2 no smoking areas.

Snows on the Green W6 £ 33 ❸❸④

166 Shepherd's Bush Rd 7603 2142 7–1C

Some still find it a touch *"boring"*, but this long-established Mediterranean on Brook Green has upped its game of late, and there's renewed praise for its *"uncrowded"* setting, its *"friendly"* service and its *"interesting dishes"*. / 11 pm; closed Sat L & Sun.

Sofra £ 27 ④❸④

1 St Christopher's Pl, W1 7224 4080 3–1A

18 Shepherd St, W1 7493 3320 3–4B

36 Tavistock St, WC2 7240 3773 4–3D

They still win some praise as *"healthy"*, *"good-value"* stand-bys, but the *"predictable"* fare at these *"cramped"* Turkish/Middle Eastern restaurants generated notably less enthusiasm this year. / www.sofra.co.uk; midnight; no smoking areas; set weekday L £18(FP).

Soho Spice W1 £ 30 ❷❸❸

124-126 Wardour St 7434 0808 3–1D

The *"interesting modern approach"* of this *"funky"*, *"westernised"* Indian wins it consistent praise, not least for the *"tasty"* and *"affordable"* cooking; late hours make it *"a post-pub favourite"*, particularly for a younger Soho crowd. / www.sohospice.co.uk; 11.30 pm, Fri & Sat 3 am; no smoking area; need 4+ to book at L , 6+ at D.

Solly's Exclusive NW11   £ 24   ❸④❸
148 Golders Green Rd   8455 0004   1–1B
You get "the best shawarma west of Jerusalem", and "great
falafel" too, at this "chaotic" Golders Green Israeli; the kitsch
restaurant upstairs is "less frenetic, and more expensive".
/ 11 pm; closed Fri D & Sat; no smoking area.

Sonny's SW13   £ 38   ❷❷❷
94 Church Rd   8748 0393   10–1A
"Excellent quality" cooking, "sensible" pricing, "thoughtful"
service and a "buzzy" atmosphere – this "well-loved local",
now back on form, is quite an asset in sleepy old Barnes.
/ 11 pm; closed Sun D.

Soshomatch EC2   £ 31   ❸④❸
2a Tabernacle St   7920 0701   9–1C
North of Finsbury Square, this large, trendy new joint (related to
EC1's 'Match') is more bar than restaurant; on the basis of our
July '01 visit, it serves competent staples, slightly incompetently.
/ Rated on Editors' assessment; www.matchbar.com; 11 pm; closed
Sat L & Sun.

Sotheby's Café W1   £ 36   ❸❷❷
34 New Bond St   7293 5077   3–2C
The "buzzy" café off the lobby of the Mayfair auctioneers offers
"nothing overly fancy", but some "delicious", quality bites
enhanced by some "very good wines". / L only, closed Sat & Sun;
no smoking.

Le Soufflé
Inter-Continental Hotel W1   £ 66   ❷❶④
1 Hamilton Pl   7409 3131   3–4A
September '01 sees the departure of Peter Kromberg, who has
been chef at this soulless Mayfair dining room since 1975;
his successor must surely at some point be presented with the
revamp Mr K's cooking has so long deserved. / www.interconti.com;
10.30 pm, Sat 11.15 pm; closed Mon, Sat L & Sun D; no smoking area; set
weekday L £43(FP).

So.uk SW4   £ 27   ❸❸❶
165 Clapham High St   7622 4004   10–2D
It puts "style over substance" – that's the point – but this
"groovy" year-old Clapham Moroccan is a "classy" joint, whose
"fantastic" vibe has made it a "welcome addition to the local
scene". / 11.30 pm; Mon-Thu D only, Fri-Sun open L & D; no booking.

Souk WC2   £ 25   ④❷❶
27 Litchfield St   7240 1796   4–3B
"Great little place, almost next to The Ivy", whose "fabulous",
"fun" atmosphere and affordable prices make it a good bet for
romance, and "excellent for parties"; the Moroccan grub is
"decent enough". / 11.30 pm; no Amex.

Soulard N1 £ 28 ❷❶❷
113 Mortimer Rd 7254 1314 1–1C
"A hidden gem and a real bistro" – this "piece of France" in north Islington charms with its "personal service", "excellent cuisine", and "dim-lit romance". / 10 pm; D only, closed Mon & Sun; no Amex.

Soup Opera £ 9 ❸❸④
2 Hanover St, W1 7629 0174 3–2C
6 Market Pl, W1 7637 7882 3–1C
17 Kingsway, WC2 7379 1333 2–2D
34 Villiers St, WC2 7839 6300 2–3D
Warwick Rd, SW5 7370 8331 5–3A
Concourse Level, Cabot Pl East, E14 7513 0880 11–1C
18 Bloomfield St, EC2 7588 9188 9–2C
56-57 Cornhill, EC3 7621 0065 9–2C
There's a "great selection" of "interesting and appetising soups" at this "efficient" two-year old chain; it's "rather expensive for every day, though". / www.soupopera.co.uk; 4 pm-6 pm; closed Sat & Sun – W1 branches closed Sun; no credit cards; no smoking; no booking.

SOUP Works £ 9 ❸❸④
56 Goodge St, W1 7637 7687 2–1B
9 D'Arblay St, W1 7439 7687 3–1D
29 Monmouth St, WC2 7240 7687 4–2B
"Hearty", "interesting" soups make "a warming alternative to sandwiches" at this ambitious young chain; it's quite "pricey", though, and the branches aren't places to linger. / www.soupworks.co.uk; 5 pm – WC2 6 pm; L only; closed Sun; no credit cards; no smoking; no booking.

Southeast W9 £ 26 ❸❸④
239 Elgin Ave 7328 8883 1–2B
"South east Asian cooking of a generally high standard" makes this "quiet" Maida Vale café a "good" local. / 11 pm; no smoking area.

Soviet Canteen SW10 £ 27 ❸❷❸
430 King's Rd 7795 1556 5–3B
"Fab vodka" helps make this "small and packed" World's End Russian a great "weekend party place"; the food isn't the prime attraction, but it offers reasonable "value for money". / www.sovietcanteen.com; 11 pm; D only, closed Sun.

Spago SW7 £ 25 ❸④❸
6 Glendower Pl 7225 2407 5–2B
"Large and authentic pizzas" top the "Italian café food" menu at this "fun 'n' young, cheap 'n' cheerful" hang-out, near South Kensington tube. / midnight; no credit cards.

Spiga £ 35 ❸❸❸
84-86 Wardour St, W1 7734 3444 3–2D
312-314 King's Rd, SW3 7351 0101 5–3C
"Loud" and fun Soho, and now Chelsea, Italians; the pizza and other dishes are "good, if not exceptional". / 11 pm – W1 Wed-Sat midnight.

La Spighetta W1 £ 32 ❷❷④
43 Blandford St 7486 7340 2–1A
"The basement setting does it no favours", but this "reliable"
Marylebone Italian, which majors in "excellent pizzas", is
"worth knowing about in the area". / 10.30 pm; closed Sun L (&
Sun D in Aug); no smoking area.

Spoon +
The Sanderson W1 £ 75 ⑤⑤⑤
50 Berners St 7300 1444 3–1D
It may offer a "people-watching extravaganza", but the dining
room of Ian Schrager's north-of-Oxford-Street design-hotel is an
extremely "pretentious" place, with a "daft" menu and "crazy"
prices. / 11 pm.

Sporting Page SW10 £ 29 ④❷❷
6 Camera Pl 7349 0455 5–3B
For a light bite, this smart Chelsea boozer – not many pubs
proclaim 'Bollinger' on the awning – makes a pretty reliable
stand-by. / www.frontpagepubs.com; 10 pm; closed Sat D & Sun D.

Springbok Café W4 £ 36 ❷❸❸
42 Devonshire Rd 8742 3149 7–2A
There are those who find the approach "amateur", but the
"esoteric" South African fare on offer at this "cramped"
Chiswick café certainly makes it an "unusual" destination,
and fans say the results are "mind-blowing".
/ www.springbokcafecuisine.com; 10.30 pm; closed Sun;
no Amex; no smoking area.

THE SQUARE W1 £ 71 ❷❸❸
6-10 Bruton St 7495 7100 3–2C
With Philip Howard's "exquisite" modern French cooking,
and a first-rate wine list, this "slick" Mayfair dining room is
simply "the ultimate" for many reporters; it's "best on
expenses", however, and "supercilious" service is a recurrent
complaint. / 10.45 pm; closed Sat L & Sun L; set weekday L £43(FP).

Sree Krishna SW17 £ 20 ❷❸④
192-194 Tooting High St 8672 4250 10–2D
"In ten years I have never had a poor meal" – this "authentic
south Indian" in Tooting still "comes up trumps", thanks to its
"interesting" and "great-value" cooking. / www.sreekrishna.co.uk;
10.45 pm.

Sri Siam W1 £ 33 ❸❸❸
16 Old Compton St 7434 3544 4–2A
There's "something of a conveyor-belt" feel nowadays to this
"buzzing" Soho Thai; it's still "better than many of its local
rivals", just not the 'destination' it once was. / 11.15 pm; closed
Sun L.

Sri Siam City EC2   £ 34   ❸❷④
85 London Wall   7628 5772   9–2C
"Set meals are good value but the à la carte doesn't inspire" at this "crowded" City basement Thai, whose "consistently good" reputation is looking a little under threat. / www.srisiamcity.co.uk; 9.30 pm; closed Sat & Sun; set weekday L £21(FP).

Sri Thai EC4   £ 32   ❸❷④
3 Queen Victoria St   7827 0202   9–3C
A City Thai stalwart, whose "repetitive" cooking is "nice but nothing special", and whose "crowded" premises are a mite "functional". / www.srithai.co.uk; 10 pm; closed Sat & Sun.

St John EC1   £ 40   ❷❷❸
26 St John St   7251 0848   9–1B
"Go with an adventurous foodie" to this "stimulating" and "unusual" former smokehouse in Smithfield – it flies the flag for "gutsy" English dishes, with offal the speciality. / www.stjohnrestaurant.co.uk; 11 pm; closed Sat L & Sun.

Standard Tandoori W2   £ 20   ❷④④
21-23 Westbourne Grove   7229 0600   6–1C
It may "stand in the shadow of Khan's" – its better-known Bayswater neighbour – but cognoscenti know that "everything is superior" at this "tacky" establishment, which precisely lives up to its name. / 11.45 pm; no smoking area.

Stanleys W1   £ 30   ④❸❸
6 Little Portland St   7462 0099   3–1C
It has an appealing concept – "a good selection of sausages" (and beers too) – but the "run-of-the-mill" bangers are a let-down at this "unpretentious" retro café north of Oxford Street. / www.stanleyssausages.com; 11.30 pm; closed Sun; no smoking area.

Star Café W1   £ 19   ❸❷❸
22 Gt Chapel St   7437 8778   3–1D
Fans find a "great" atmosphere at this hidden-away Soho fixture, where cooked breakfasts are "a fab way to start the day"; at other times "big portions" contribute to an overall "good-value" impression. / www.thestarcafesoho.co.uk; 3.30 pm; closed Sat & Sun; no credit cards; no smoking area.

Star of India SW5   £ 39   ❷❸❸
154 Old Brompton Rd   7373 2901   5–2B
It's known as an exercise in "high camp", but there's more to this "long-time favourite Indian" in South Kensington than "poncy" décor, and its "delicious" cooking has been notably consistent of late. / www.starofindia.co.uk; 11.45 pm.

Starbucks   £ 9   ④④④
Branches throughout London
Some find them "formulaic but reliable", but enthusiasm is waning across the board for Uncle Sam's number one coffee chain export. / www.starbucks.com; 6 pm–11 pm; most City branches closed all or part of weekend; no smoking; no booking.

Station Grill SE17   £ 38   ❷❷❸
2 Braganza St   7735 4769   1–3C
"Yes, good food does exist South of the River" – this "fab" but
tiny spot, by Kennington tube, has quite a local reputation for its
"delicious" and "complex" Gallic cooking. / www.stationgrill.co.uk;
9.30 pm; D only, closed Mon & Sun; no smoking area.

The Stepping Stone SW8   £ 35   ❶❶❷
123 Queenstown Rd   7622 0555   10–1C
The epitome of an "excellent local", this "stylish" but "relaxed"
Battersea "all-rounder" is universally hailed for its "imaginative"
and "careful" cooking, and its "attentive" service. / 11 pm, Mon
10.30 pm; closed Sat L & Sun D; no Amex; no smoking area.

Stick & Bowl W8   £ 15   ❷❷⑤
31 Kensington High St   7937 2778   5–1A
"A little piece of Hong Kong in Kensington" – this mega-speedy,
"no-frills caff" is just the place to "eat on the run". / 10.45 pm;
no credit cards; no booking.

Sticky Fingers W8   £ 28   ④❷❸
1a Phillimore Gdns   7938 5338   5–1A
"Stick to the burgers, as other options can disappoint", is one
veteran's advice regarding this "nostalgia rock" Kensington diner
(previously owned by Bill Wyman) – it has long been a popular
destination for those with kids in tow. / 11.30 pm.

Stock Pot   £ 14   ④❸❸
40 Panton St, SW1   7839 5142   4–4A
18 Old Compton St, W1   7287 1066   4–2A
50 James St, W1   7486 9185   3–1A
273 King's Rd, SW3   7823 3175   5–3C
6 Basil St, SW3   7589 8621   5–1D
"For quick, cheap eats", these "cheerful" canteens – largely
unmoved by the culinary fads of the last 30 years – "still have
their place". / 11 pm-midnight; no credit cards; some branches have
no smoking areas; booking restricted at times; set D £8(FP).

Stone Mason's Arms W6   £ 25   ❸④❷
54 Cambridge Grove   8748 1397   7–2C
Staff attitude is "poor" and "inflexible", but "high-quality" food
from a "consistently interesting" menu makes quite a success of
this "buzzy" Hammersmith gastropub. / 9.45 pm.

Strada   £ 30   ❸❸❸
15-16 New Burlington St, W1   7287 5967   3–2C
6 Great Queen St, WC2   7405 6295   4–1D
175 New King's Rd, SW6   7731 6404   10–1B
105 Upper St, N1   7276 9742   8–3D
11-13 Battersea Rise, SW11   7801 0794   10–2C
70 Exmouth Mkt, EC1   7278 0800   9–1A
It's "a little more upmarket than the usual pizza places",
and "great simple dishes" help win consistent applause for the
Belgo group's expanding Italian chain. / www.strada.co.uk; 11 pm.

Stratford's W8 £ 37 **❸❷**④

7 Stratford Rd 7937 6388 5–2A

Some think it "uninspiring", but this Kensington backstreet fish restaurant pleases supporters with its "consistent" cooking, its "homely" atmosphere and its "attentive" service.
/ www.stratfords-restaurant.com; 11 pm; set weekday L & pre-th. £23(FP).

Stream EC1 £ 32 **❸❸❸**

50-52 Long Ln 7796 0070 9–2A

"Nice, fresh seafood" is the culinary highlight of this "attractive" year-old bar/brasserie, overlooking Smithfield Market, whose performance is rather "erratic". / 11 pm; closed Sun; set weekday L & D £20(FP).

Street Hawker £ 25 ④④④

166 Randolph Ave, W9 7286 3869 8–3A

237 West End Ln, NW6 7431 7808 1–1B

Fans vaunt the "great variety" of "delicious" dishes at this oriental duo, but there are also numerous sceptics who say they offer "mundane" food in a "clinical" atmosphere. / 11.15 pm.

THE SUGAR CLUB W1 £ 47 **❶❷❸**

21 Warwick St 7437 7776 3–2D

"Wonderful" Pacific Rim cooking, with "sumptuous" flavours, is making this "minimalist" – some say "stark" – Soho venture an ever-greater success. / www.thesugarclub.co.uk; 11 pm; no smoking area.

Sugar Reef W1 £ 43 – – –

41-44 Great Windmill St 7851 0800 3–2D

"Boring" food and "snotty" staff left many deeply unimpressed by this large and "tacky" bar/club/restaurant on the fringe of Soho; it moved into new ownership (and took on a new chef) in the summer of 2001, so fingers crossed...
/ www.latenightlondon.co.uk; 11 pm; D only, closed Sun; no jeans.

The Sun & Doves SE5 £ 27 **❸❸❷**

61 Coldharbour Ln 7733 1525 1–4C

"If only all pubs could be like this"; this funky boozer – with its "lovely garden" and "good-value" grub – seems all the more appealing in the gastronomic wastes of Camberwell.
/ www.sundoves.com; 10.30 pm; no smoking area.

Suntory SW1 £ 75 **❸**④⑤

72 St James's St 7409 0201 3–4D

This tediously grand St James's veteran is "a favourite for visiting Japanese businessmen", and the cooking "maintains its high standards"; it's "hellishly expensive", though, and the level of service is surprisingly "poor". / 10 pm; closed Sun L; set weekday L £37(FP).

Le Suquet SW3 £ 44 **❷**④**❸**

104 Draycott Ave 7581 1785 5–2C

"Delicious and traditional" cooking – with "huge fruits de mer" a highlight – make this "cramped" Chelsea corner an ever-popular destination; service is in the Gallic style often described as 'inimitable'. / 11.30 pm; set weekday L £26(FP).

Sushi-Say NW2   £ 31   ❷❷❸

33b Walm Ln   8459 7512   1–1A
*This "super, family-run Japanese" makes an excellent find in
distant Willesden Green; the menu highlight is "top-class sushi",
and service is "charming".* / 10.30 pm; closed Mon, Tue-Fri D only,
Sat & Sun open L & D; no smoking area.

Sway WC2   £ 32   ❸④④

61-65 Great Queen St   7404 6114   4–1D
*For chicken 'n' chips (or a selection of tapas-style dishes), this
new brasserie makes an economical Covent Garden choice;
on the basis of our early (July '01) visit, though, we'd steer clear
of anything fancier.* / Rated on Editors' assessment;
www.latenightlondon.co.uk; 10.45 pm, Thu 11.45 pm, Fri & Sat 12.45 am;
closed Sat L & Sun.

Sweetings EC4   £ 36   ❷❷❷

39 Queen Victoria St   7248 3062   9–3B
*For "great fish in a traditional setting", this "splendid" Victorian
"relic" is "a perennial City favourite" (arrive at noon to be sure
of a seat); the head chef became the new proprietor in July '01,
so the policy of "excellence in simplicity" seems unlikely to
change.* / L only, closed Sat & Sun; no credit cards; no booking.

Taberna Etrusca EC4   £ 43   ④④⑤

9 Bow Churchyard   7248 5552   9–2C
*"The terrace is fabulous on a sunny day" (but the interior is
"a bit dingy") at this rather "commercial" City Italian;
the cooking is "reliable" but contains "no surprises".*
/ www.etruscagroup.co.uk; L only, closed Sat & Sun.

Tabla E14   £ 28   ❷④❸

Dockmaster's Hs, Hertsmere Rd   7345 0345   11–1C
*"Interesting" Indian food served in an "interesting"
early-Victorian customs house seems to have provoked
remarkably little, er, interest in this Canary Wharf-fringe
newcomer; "staff who often forget you" may explain why it's
"surprisingly often empty".* / www.tablarestaurant.com; 10.30 pm; closed
Sat L & Sun.

Tajine W1   £ 28   ❸❷❸

7a Dorset St   7935 1545   2–1A
*"A lovely little Moroccan gem in Fitzrovia", this "busy" and
notably "friendly" café serves dishes which are "good, on the
whole" at "reasonable" prices.* / 10.30 pm; closed Sat L & Sun;
no Amex.

Talad Thai SW15   £ 24   ❶❸④

320 Upper Richmond Rd   8789 8084   10–2A
*A "terrific" Putney canteen that's "hard to beat" – "if you don't
mind queuing".* / 10 pm; no credit cards; no smoking; no booking.

Tamarind W1 £ 44 ❶❷❷
20 Queen St   7629 3561   3–3B
"Chic and sophisticated" décor provides a backdrop for some "very refined" cooking at this Mayfair subcontinental, which is among the elite group "taking Indian cuisine to a new level". / 11.15 pm; closed Sat L; set weekday L & Sun L £27(FP).

Tandoori Lane SW6 £ 25 ❸❶❸
131a Munster Rd   7371 0440   10–1B
"Very good service" is the making of this atmospheric deepest Fulham curry house, which fans think "wonderful all round". / 11 pm; no Amex.

Tandoori of Chelsea SW3 £ 45 ❷❷❸
153 Fulham Rd   7589 7749   5–2C
This "upmarket" veteran Indian near Brompton Cross is remarkably little commented on, but local supporters insist its cooking is "under-rated" compared to that of trendier competitors. / midnight; set weekday L £24(FP).

La Tante Claire
Berkeley Hotel SW1 £ 87 ❸❷④
Wilton Pl   7823 2003   5–1D
The setting is still too "hotel-y", but it's pleasing to note some "rekindling" of enthusiasm for Pierre Koffman's once pre-eminent foodie temple (which was disastrously uprooted from Chelsea to Belgravia a couple of years ago); the level of cooking, however, remains "good, but not exceptional". / 11 pm; closed Sat L & Sun; jacket required; set L £47(FP).

Tao EC4 £ 31 ④❷❸
11 Bow Ln   7248 5833   9–2C
"Visit more for the bar than the bites", at this "overcrowded" City spot – the "mix of oriental and European dishes" can be "bland", but "attentive" waitresses and a "lovely outside area" provide much compensation. / www.etruscagroup.co.uk; 10 pm; closed Sat & Sun.

Tartuf N1 £ 26 ❷❶❸
88 Upper St   7288 0954   8–3D
"A wee small place for a fun evening with friends" – "attentive Gallic staff" set the tone at this "cosy" Islington Alsatian, where the 'flammkuchen' (pizza-like dishes) are a "simple" and "tasty" novelty. / midnight; no Amex; set weekday L £16(FP).

Tas £ 20 ❷❷❷
33 The Cut, SE1   7928 2111   9–4A
72 Borough High St, SE1   7403 7200   9–4C
This "tightly-packed" Turkish duo – by the Young Vic, and now near Borough Market – have now got the South Bank covered, and their "excellent-value mezze" make them ideal for "quick and cheerful" meals; despite a complete absence of PR ballyhoo, their top-value charms made them the second most-mentioned new restaurant in this years' survey. / 11.30 pm.

La Tasca   £ 21   ❸❸❷
23-24 Maiden Ln, WC2   7240 9062   4–4C
West India Quay, E14   7531 9990   11–1C
"Spanish, not!" – "the tapas are unauthentic, but it's a good
refuelling stop", say fans of this new cheesily "cheery" Covent
Garden outpost of an expanding national chain.
/ www.latasca.co.uk; 11 pm – E14 10.45 pm; need 10+ at WC2, 8+ at E14
to book.

Tate Britain SW1   £ 42   ④❸❷
Millbank   7887 8877   2–4C
"You just can't beat the choice of wines, and the value it offers"
at this "beautiful" Whistler-muralled dining room; with its
"school-dinner-lady-style" service, it's certainly an experience,
and not one from which the cooking detracts too badly.
/ www.tate.org.uk; L only; no smoking area.

Tate Modern, Level 7 Café SE1   £ 32   ④④❶
Bankside   7401 5020   9–3B
"Sweeping views make up for" the plain food and lacklustre
service at the café atop this South Bank landmark – it really
should be better. / www.tate.org.uk; 5.30 pm, Fri & Sat 9.30 pm; L only,
except Fri & Sat open L & D; no smoking; no booking.

TATSUSO EC2   £ 68   ❶❸④
32 Broadgate Circle   7638 5863   9–2D
"The prices kill your appetite", so "let your broker pay" at this
City Japanese, which is the best in town; on the ground floor
"awesomely fresh meat and fish" are grilled on the teppan-yaki,
while the humbler basement serves "brilliant" sushi and other
"exquisite" delicacies. / 9 pm; closed Sat & Sun.

Tawana W2   £ 26   ❷❸④
3 Westbourne Grove   7229 3785   6–1C
Who cares if it looks "dreadful"? – it's the "consistently
gorgeous" Thai cooking which is the reason to truffle out this
unassuming Bayswater spot. / 11 pm.

Teatro W1   £ 50   ④❸④
93-107 Shaftesbury Ave   7494 3040   4–3A
Celebrity backers ensure this Theatreland club/bar/restaurant
gets more than its fair share of hype; its design makes you feel
you "could be anywhere", though, and the food is "pricey" for
what it is. / 11.45 pm; closed Sat L & Sun; set weekday L & pre-th. £28(FP).

Teca W1   £ 41   ❶❷❸
54 Brooks Mews   7495 4774   3–2B
"If Zafferano is booked, Teca is a good alternative" – "really
top-notch" cooking and staff who "try hard" are elevating this
Mayfair mews Italian (also part of A-Z Restaurants) to the first
rank, even if the setting is "a bit on the bland side"; "there's
a rare selection of fine Italian wines". / 10.30 pm; closed Sun.

regular updates at www.hardens.com   163

10 EC2   **£ 41**   ④④④
10 Cutlers Gardens Arcade   7283 7888   9–2D
*Not a good year for this large and "functional" basement –
its City lunching fare is "overpriced", and reporters now find
"little to recommend it". / L only; closed Sat & Sun.*

Tentazioni SE1   **£ 40**   ❷❷④
2 Mill St   7237 1100   11–2A
*"A surprise, given the location" – this little Italian near Tower
Bridge offers "quality" cooking and "relaxed and attentive"
service; it's "a bit pricey", though, and the setting can seem
"stark", especially when the place is "quiet".
/ www.tentazionirestaurant.co.uk; 11 pm; closed Mon L, Sat L & Sun.*

The Tenth
Royal Garden Hotel W8   **£ 52**   ❷❷❷
Kensington High St   7361 1910   5–1A
*A "well-kept secret"; this 10th-floor dining room not only has
"fabulous views" (over Kensington Gardens) but also offers
"beautifully presented" cooking and "very attentive" service.
/ www.royalgardenhotel.co.uk; 11 pm; closed Sat L & Sun; no smoking area; set
weekday L £34(FP).*

Terminus
Great Eastern Hotel EC2   **£ 39**   ⑤⑤⑤
40 Liverpool St   7618 7400   9–2D
*To be "one of the less impressive Conrans" is no mean feat,
and many are "shocked" by the "beyond unacceptable"
standards of this "nastily loud" City brasserie. / www.conran.com;
11.45 pm.*

The Terrace W8   **£ 42**   ❸❷❷
33c Holland St   7937 3224   5–1A
*A "small but delightful hideaway" in a quiet Kensington street
that serves some "creative" and "well presented" dishes; "the
terrace is great in good weather". / 10.30 pm.*

Terrace
Le Meridien W1   **£ 54**   ④④④
21 Piccadilly   7851 3085   3–3D
*With its good views of Piccadilly, this lofty room is potentially
"stylish", but it just strikes many reporters as "sterile",
"pretentious" and "really very average at the price". / 11 pm;
no smoking area.*

Texas Embassy Cantina SW1   **£ 29**   ⑤④④
1 Cockspur St   7925 0077   2–2C
*"Dire fare for out-of-towners" is the staple at this large and
potentially atmospheric Tex/Mex, off Trafalgar Square, which
too many reporters find "outrageously bad" in every
department. / www.texasembassy.com; 11 pm, Fri & Sat midnight.*

TGI Friday's £ 32 ⑤❸④
25-29 Coventry St, W1 7839 6262 4–4A
6 Bedford St, WC2 7379 0585 4–4C
96-98 Bishops Bridge Rd, W2 7229 8600 6–1C
"It never fails with my ten-year old", but otherwise this "very
American" chain is just many parents' vision of purgatory.
/ www.tgifridays.com; 11.30 pm, Fri & Sat midnight; no smoking area; W1 &
WC2, no booking Fri D & Sat L.

The Thai SW7 £ 30 ④④④
93 Pelham St 7584 4788 5–2C
It may have a fashionable location, near Brompton Cross,
but this new oriental prompts little comment – hardly surprising
as it's a place which badly "needs to get its act together".
/ 11.30 pm; no Amex.

Thai Bistro W4 £ 26 ❸❸④
99 Chiswick High Rd 8995 5774 7–2B
It may be "very cramped", but this "canteen-style" Chiswick
spot is generally still hailed for its "good", "quick", and "fresh"
cuisine. / 11 pm; closed Tue L & Thu L; no Amex; no smoking.

Thai Break W8 £ 27 ❷❸⑤
30 Uxbridge St 7229 4332 6–2B
It's "cramped", boring-looking and not at all well-known,
but fans say this "friendly" oriental, off Notting Hill Gate, serves
some "terrific" food. / 11 pm; closed Sun L; no smoking area.

Thai Corner Café SE22 £ 21 ❷❸④
44 North Cross Rd 8299 4041 1–4D
Denizens of East Dulwich hail the "dependable" cooking at this
"good local stand-by", whose BYO policy helps make it "very
popular". / 10.30 pm; closed Sun; no credit cards.

Thai Garden SW11 £ 25 ❸❷❸
58 Battersea Rise 7738 0380 10–2C
A "good all-round Thai" in Battersea; it's been there for years
without gathering much in the way of commentary – perhaps
its shiny new façade will help draw in the crowds. / 11 pm; D only,
except Sun open L & D; no Amex.

Thai on the River SW10 £ 38 ❸❷❷
15 Lots Rd 7351 1151 5–4B
"Get a table overlooking the river" – it can seem a bit "bleak"
otherwise – at this oriental by Chelsea Harbour; the food is
"beautifully executed", but even some fans find it "expensive"
for what it is. / www.thaiontheriver.co.uk; 11 pm, Fri & Sat 11.30 pm; closed
Mon L & Sat L; set weekday L & Sun L £24(FP).

Thai Pot £ 26 ❸④④

5 Princes St, W1 7499 3333 3–1C
1 Bedfordbury, WC2 7379 4580 4–4C
148 Strand, WC2 7497 0904 2–2D
Neither ambience nor service is a strong point, but these
"reliable" orientals are all "handy for the theatre" and have
quite a following for their "tasty and quick" (if "formulaic")
fodder. / www.thaipot.co.uk; 11.15 pm; closed Sun; no smoking areas, W1 &
Bedfordbury.

Thai Square SW1 £ 33 ❸❷❸

21-24 Cockspur St 7839 4000 2–3C
"Large, open and airy", this Trafalgar Square Thai – with its
"OTT" décor and "good tasty food" – is a useful central
stand-by (and one that's "great for groups"); the music can be
"a bit too loud". / www.thaipot.co.uk; 11 pm; no smoking area.

Thailand SE14 £ 28 ❶❷④

15 Lewisham Way 8691 4040 1–3D
"The best Thai outside Thailand" – well, almost – is found at
this "small", "crowded" oriental, in a "less than pleasant"
corner of Lewisham. / 11 pm; D only, closed Mon; no Amex; no smoking;
set weekday L £15(FP).

The Thatched House W6 £ 28 ❸❷❷

115 Dalling Rd 8748 6174 7–1B
This "welcoming" Hammersmith gastropub is still a boozer at
heart, but it boasts "above-average" grub, "friendly" staff and
a "relaxed", modern-ish setting; at the back, there's
a "good-sized outdoor area" too. / www.establishment.ltd.uk; 10 pm;
no Amex.

Thierry's SW3 £ 38 ⑤④❸

342 King's Rd 7352 3365 5–3C
This cosy Chelsea bistro looks just like the "old-favourite French
restaurant" it still is for some, but it's been drifting for years,
and results can be "terrible". / www.trpplc.com; 10.30 pm; closed
Sun D; no smoking area; set £22(FP).

3 Monkeys SE24 £ 34 ❷❷❸

136-140 Herne Hill 7738 5500 1–4C
This "classy" – some would say "pretentious" – Herne Hill
Indian "favourite" has built an impressive following, thanks to its
"consistently good" cooking and its "airy" modern décor.
/ www.3monkeysrestaurant.com; 11 pm; D only, except Sun open L & D;
no smoking.

Tiger Lil's £ 27 ④❸❸

75 Bishopsbridge Rd, W2 7221 2622 6–1C
270 Upper St, N1 7226 1118 8–2D
15a Clapham Common S'side, SW4 7720 5433 10–2D
Sceptics say it's like "dining in a cheap fat-fryer", but some find
it "lots of fun" to eat at these "entertaining", serve-yourself
"flaming wok" experiences; they are best "for parties".
/ www.tigerlils.com; 11.30 pm – SW4, Fri & Sat midnight; no smoking areas.

Tiger Tiger SW1   **£ 33**   ⑤⑤④
29 Haymarket   7930 1885   4–4A
*The food may be "junk", but fortunately it is utterly "beside the
point" at this huge West End bar/restaurant/club/"pick-up
joint". / www.tigertiger.co.uk; 11.30 pm.*

Titanic
Regent Palace Hotel W1   **£ 42**   ⑤⑤⑤
81 Brewer St   7437 1912   3–3D
*Yes, it's "a disaster!"; with its "sub-standard comfort food",
its "indifferent" service and "zero" atmosphere, MPW's
subterranean brasserie, near Piccadilly Circus, strikes many
reporters as little short of "shocking". / 11 pm; closed Mon & Sun.*

Toast NW3   **£ 39**   ④④❸
50 Hampstead High St   7431 2244   8–1A
*"The West End comes to Hampstead", say fans of this "buzzy"
hang-out – improbably located above the tube station; critics –
citing "patchy" cooking, "huge bills" and "too much smoke" –
say it's "best left to the local trendies". / midnight; closed weekday L;
no smoking area; pre-th. £24(FP).*

Toff's N10   **£ 23**   ④❸④
38 Muswell Hill Broadway   8883 8656   1–1B
*Some still tout this "basic" Muswell Hill chippy as "the best",
but it's producing rather too many "disappointing" experiences
these days. / 10 pm; closed Sun; no smoking area; no booking, Sat; set
weekday L £15(FP).*

Tokyo Diner WC2   **£ 16**   ④❸④
2 Newport Pl   7287 8777   4–3B
*"Shabby, but serves its purpose" – for "solid" and "cheap"
West End sustenance this "great little Chinatown diner" (which
is, of course, Japanese) has many fans. / 11.30 pm; no Amex;
no smoking area; no booking, Fri & Sat.*

Tom's W11   **£ 25**   ❸❸❸
226 Westbourne Grove   7221 8818   6–1B
*"It's worth the inevitable wait for a table" at Tom Conran's
superior deli/café, near Portobello Road, where "pricey,
but excellent" snacks (using "fabulous" ingredients) draw
a trendy crowd; brunch is the highlight. / 10 pm; closed
Sat D & Sun D; no smoking; no booking.*

FSA

Tootsies   £ 25   ④❸④
35 James St, W1   7486 1611   3–1A
177 New King's Rd, SW6   7736 4023   10–1B
107 Old Brompton Rd, SW7   7581 8942   5–2B
120 Holland Park Ave, W11   7229 8567   6–2A
148 Chiswick High Rd, W4   8747 1869   7–2A
198 Haverstock Hill, NW3   7431 3812   8–2A
147 Church Rd, SW13   8748 3630   10–1A
36-38 Abbeville Rd, SW4   8772 6646   10–2D
"Kids love it", and there's "something for everyone" at this
café/diner chain, where "consistently good" burgers and "very
good" shakes are menu mainstays. / 11 pm-11.30 pm, Fri & Sat
midnight; no smoking areas at SW13, W11 & W4; booking at certain
times only.

Topsy-Tasty W4   £ 22   ❸④④
5 Station Pde   8995 3407   1–3A
"Less well known than its sister" (the Bedlington) but "better
furnished", this "good-value" Thai by Chiswick BR is consistently
praised for its "fresh" and "simple" dishes. / 10.30 pm, Sat 11 pm;
D only, closed Sun; no credit cards; no smoking.

Toto's SW1   £ 45   ❷❶❶
Lennox Gardens Mews   7589 0075   5–2D
"Beautiful" and "hidden away", this long-established
Knightsbridge Italian is one of the best all-rounders in town –
"great pasta" is the highlight of the "consistent" menu, service
is "patient and attentive", and there's even a "quiet terrace for
a sunny day". / 11.30 pm.

Touzai EC2   £ 16   ④❷④
147-149 Curtain Rd   7739 4505   9–1D
If you're in Shoreditch, and looking for a "quick" noodle fix, this
new canteen makes a useful-enough destination.
/ www.touzai.co.uk; 11 pm; no Amex; no smoking area.

Trader Vics W1   £ 55   ④❸❶
22 Park Ln   7208 4113   3–4A
"Great cocktails transport you to another world" at the OTT
Polynesian bar in the Hilton's basement; given that the food's
incidental, it's not that bad. / midnight; D only.

The Trafalgar Tavern SE10   £ 28   ④❸❷
Park Row   8858 2437   1–3D
"The splendid riverside view" is the star attraction of this
historic inn by the former Royal Naval College; it serves
"reasonably priced" pub grub. / www.trafalgartavern.co.uk; 9 pm; closed
Mon D & Sun D; no Amex.

Troika NW1   £ 23   ④❷❸
101 Regent's Park Rd   7483 3765   8–2B
"Decent Russian staples" (with some "interesting" vodkas) are
the backbone of the menu at this "charming" and "fun"
Primrose Hill café, which is also a popular breakfast spot;
it's now licensed, but you can still BYO for £3 corkage. / 10.30 pm;
no smoking area; set weekday L £11 (FP).

FSA

Les Trois Garçons E1   £ 42   ❸❷❶
1 Club Row   7613 1924   1–2D
"The most amazing restaurant décor in London" – "OTT" and
"very cool", all at the same time – lends a "marvellous
atmosphere" to this converted East End boozer; the "classic"
French cooking is heftily priced, but surprisingly "good".
/ www.lestroisgarcons.com; 10 pm, Thu-Sat 10.30 pm; closed Sat L & Sun.

La Trompette W4   £ 39   ❶❶❷
5-7 Devonshire Rd   8747 1836   7–2A
"More like Mayfair than Chiswick" – Nigel Platts-Martin (Chez
Bruce etc) has done it again with this stellar newcomer, on the
site of La Dordogne (RIP); "sensational quality and value" and
"first-class service" are among the qualities that make the
whole set-up seem very "glamorous", especially "for an
out-of-town place". / 11 pm; no smoking area; booking: max 8.

Troubadour SW5   £ 24   ❷❷❶
265 Old Brompton Rd   7370 1434   5–3A
This "snug" and "eccentric" Earl's Court coffee shop is a south
west London rarity – a haunt for Bohemians and artistic types;
you don't have to look 'deep' if you stop off for breakfast,
a coffee or a snack... but it helps. / 11 pm; no credit cards;
no booking.

La Trouvaille W1   £ 35   ❷⑤④
12a Newburgh St   7287 8488   3–2C
For hearty and interesting Gallic grub at decent prices, this side
street Soho newcomer (on the site of Barra, RIP) is indeed quite
a find; the décor is unimpressive, though, and service on our
July '01 visit verged on Pythonesque. / Rated on Editors' assessment;
10.30 pm; closed Sun.

Truc Vert W1   £ 29   ❸④⑤
42 North Audley St   7491 9988   3–2A
Fans proclaim this rustic-look, Mayfair deli/café as an "excellent
new venture from the former Villandry owner"; it's "squashed",
though, and while the "simple" delicacies can be "fab and
fresh", they can also be "second-rate". / 9 pm; no smoking.

Tuk Tuk N1   £ 23   ❸④❸
330 Upper St   7226 0837   8–3D
For many years, this bare Islington café has delivered "cheap",
"reliable" and "decent" Thai nosh. / www.tuktuk.co.uk; 11 pm; closed
Sat L & Sun L.

Turner's SW3   £ 51   ④❸④
87-89 Walton St   7584 6711   5–2C
For the faithful, it's still "always a delight to visit" TV-chef Brian
Turner's "friendly", long-established Gallic fixture in
Knightsbridge; ratings are sliding across the board, however,
and the place now risks becoming "a shadow of its former self".
/ 10 pm; closed Sat L & Sun; set weekday L £28(FP).

Tuscan Steak
St Martin's Lane WC2   £ 45   ⑤❸④
45 St Martin's Ln   7300 5500   4–4C
*SaintM (RIP) – the brasserie-style operation at this Covent
Garden design-hotel – soon rightly perished; its "bizarre,
share-a-plate" successor, however, continues some of its key
features – most notably "cardiac arrest on arrival of the bill".
/ 11.30 pm; closed Sun D.*

Twelfth House W11   £ 35   ④❷④
35 Pembridge Rd   7727 9620   6–2B
*We had a very good straightforward lunch on an early visit to
this tiny Notting Hill newcomer, with "charming and attentive"
service; the few early reporters, however, have tended to find
the whole show rather "amateur". / www.twelfth-house.co.uk; 10 pm;
closed Mon.*

Twentyfour
Tower 42 EC2   £ 52   ❸❸❷
Old Broad St   7877 2424   9–2C
*"The City landscape makes a perfect backdrop to a business
meal", at this 24th-floor eyrie in the former NatWest Tower;
the food is "not exceptional", but the "bill matches the
altitude". / 9.30 pm; closed Sat & Sun; no jeans.*

Two Brothers N3   £ 25   ❷❷④
297-303 Regent's Park Rd   8346 0469   1–1B
*"I could smell the sea!" – fans claim this is "the best upmarket
chippie in north London", delivering "good portions" of the
national dish; it's "not so hot on ambience", though. / 10.15 pm;
closed Mon & Sun; no smoking area; no booking at D.*

Ubon E14   £ 55   ❷❸④
34 Westferry Circus   7719 7800   11–1C
*It utterly "lacks the glamour of Nobu", but this new, rather
"corporate" East End cousin of the famed West Ender does at
least bring some "dazzling" Japanese-inspired fare to Canary
Wharf; it's easy to miss the "amazing" view, but it does offer
some compensation for prices, which "make you cry". / 10.15 pm;
closed Sat L & Sun; no smoking area.*

Uli W11   £ 25   ❷❷❸
16 All Saints Rd   7727 7511   6–1B
*It's little-known, but this small Notting Hill café is a "great local
restaurant", with interesting south east Asian cooking,
an "intimate" ambience and a "very amiable owner"; it has
a nice rear courtyard too. / www.uli-oriental.co.uk; 11.15 pm; D only,
closed Sun; no Amex.*

The Union Café W1   £ 34   ❸❸❸
96 Marylebone Ln   7486 4860   3–1A
*John Brinkley's "great-value" wine mark-up policy is paying
dividends at this formerly jaded Marylebone spot; the food's
"improved" under the new régime too, so perhaps these "light"
and "airy" premises will begin again to live up to their potential.
/ 10.30 pm; closed Sun; no smoking area; set Sat brunch £23(FP).*

Uno SW1   £ 34   ❸④④
1 Denbigh St   7834 1001   2–4B
*It looks like quite a chic little place – and there are few enough
of those in Pimlico – but there's quite a feeling that this "lively"
but "pricey" Italian "promises rather more than it delivers".
/ 11.30 pm.*

The Vale W9   £ 28   ❸❷❸
99 Chippenham Rd   7266 0990   1–2B
*Maida Hill at last has a "good local option" – this two-year-old
"hang-out" provides "eclectic and well executed" cooking and
"enthusiastic" service. / 11.30 pm; closed Mon L & Sat L; no Amex;
no smoking area.*

Vama SW10   £ 38   ❶❷❸
438 King's Rd   7351 4118   5–3B
*A "gourmet" Chelsea curry house, near World's End, whose
"very fresh", "perfectly spiced" Indian cooking ranks it amongst
"the best in town". / www.vama.co.uk; 11 pm; set Sun L £25(FP).*

Vasco & Piero's Pavilion W1   £ 39   ❸❶❸
15 Poland St   7437 8774   3–1D
*"The simplest things are best" at this "quirky", "friendly" and
"reliable" old-Soho Italian stalwart, whose "good-value
set-dinner menus" are particularly approved. / 11 pm; closed
Sat L & Sun.*

Veeraswamy W1   £ 37   ❷❸❸
Victory House, 99 Regent St   7734 1401   3–3D
*"Interesting" cooking is winning ever-more praise for London's
oldest Indian (now owned by the Chutney Mary group); a couple
of years ago it took on a "stylish and modern" look, and some
feel it "lost something after the revamp". / www.realindianfood.com;
11.30 pm.*

Vegia Zena NW1   £ 30   ❸❷④
17 Princess Rd   7483 0192   8–3B
*Some still think the cooking "surprisingly good" at this
"cramped" Primrose Hill fixture, but those who remember the
place's glory-days now find it rather "pedestrian". / 11 pm; set
weekday L £15(FP).*

The Verandah SW1   £ 22   ❷❷④
76 Wilton Rd   7630 9951   2–4B
*It looks and feels like a bog-standard Indian, but in the grim
purlieus of Victoria Station, this welcoming spot stands out,
thanks to its unusually broad-ranging and well-prepared menu.
/ Rated on Editors' assessment; midnight; no Amex.*

**Vertigo
Tower 42 EC2**   £ 43   ④❸❷
Old Broad St   7877 7842   9–2C
*"Impress your clients"; there are "excellent views of the City"
from this 42nd-floor eyrie – the top of what used to be called
the NatWest tower; unsurprisingly, the short snack menu,
specialising in seafood, is rather "overpriced". / 9.20 pm; closed
Sat & Sun.*

The Vestry
All Hallows by the Tower EC3   £ 35   ④❸❸
Byward St   7488 4933   9–3D
*If this new building, elegantly designed in 'ecclesiastical' style,
had a view of the nearby Tower it would truly be a great
location; early reports are few and mixed – we're with those
who find the culinary style "pretentious".* / www.the-vestry.com; 9 pm;
closed Sat & Sun; no smoking.

Vic Naylors EC1   £ 34   ④④❷
38 & 42 St John St   7608 2181   9–1B
*Poor service can let down this "lively" Smithfield bar/restaurant;
as a place to eat, it's better at lunch than in the evening.* / 11 pm;
closed Sun.

Il Vicolo SW1   £ 35   ❷❷④
3-4 Crown Passage   7839 3960   3–4D
*"Still great value in the West End" – this St James's trattoria is
"so friendly" and its dependable Italian fare makes it a "good
stand-by" in a pricey area.* / 10 pm; closed Sat & Sun; set party menu
£20(FP).

Viet Hoa E2   £ 21   ❷④④
70-72 Kingsland Rd   7729 8293   9–1D
*"Very basic décor adds to an earthy feel" at this well-known
Vietnamese "canteen" in Shoreditch, whose "totally more-ish"
grub draws a "hip" crowd; service can be "erratic".* / 11.30 pm;
no Amex.

Viet-Anh NW1   £ 17   ❶❶❸
41 Parkway   7284 4082   8–3B
*"Is this the best Vietnamese this side of Paris?" – "lovely" staff
(who "take the trouble to explain things") add lustre to this
small and "basic" Camden Town newcomer, whose cooking is
"genuine" and "good value".* / 11 pm; no smoking area.

Vijay NW6   £ 18   ❶❷④
49 Willesden Ln   7328 1087   1–1B
*Who cares about the "awful" décor? – it's "worth the journey"
to this "simply wonderful" West Hampstead spot for its "fresh"
and "unusual" south Indian cooking, and its "friendly" service.*
/ 10.45 pm, Fri & Sat 11.45 pm; no smoking area.

Villa Bianca NW3   £ 40   ④④❸
1 Perrins Ct   7435 3131   8–2A
*"A great location" in a Hampstead side street allows those with
a vivid imagination to "re-create those Tuscan nights" at this
long-established Italian; it's "pricey", though, and neither food
nor service are as good as you might hope.* / www.villabianca.co.uk;
11.30 pm; set weekday L £26(FP).

Village Bistro N6   £ 34   ❸❸❸
38 Highgate High St   8340 5165   8–1B
*More consistent reports this year on this "tiny" and "quirky"
Highgate cottage, whose moderately adventurous but "reliable"
cooking found general approval.* / 11 pm; closed Sun; no Amex or
Switch; no smoking area.

Villandry W1   £ 39   ③④④
170 Gt Portland St   7631 3131   2–1B
*"Much improved" it may be, but this "extremely noisy"
Marylebone deli-restaurant is still only firing on three cylinders,
with quite a lot of reporters still finding the cooking "expensive"
for what it is.* / 10 pm; closed Sun D; no smoking.

The Vine NW5   £ 32   ③⑤②
86 Highgate Rd   7209 0038   8–1B
*An "enjoyable" Kentish Town boozer whose "marquee area" at
the back is "a good spot in summer" and "a treat in winter
too"; service is seriously "patchy", though, and the cooking is
not as consistent as it was.* / 10.30 pm.

Vingt-Quatre SW10   £ 30   ④③③
325 Fulham Rd   7376 7224   5–3B
*"Great for hunger pangs in the early hours" – this 24-7 Chelsea
diner is "the place to be seen after a night out"; it's popular for
breakfast at more conventional times too.* / open 24 hours;
no booking.

Vong SW1   £ 54   ②③③
Wilton Pl   7235 1010   5–1D
*"The plates are works of art", at this Belgravian outpost of the
famous NYC Thai/French establishment, whose "elegant and
delicious" cooking wins much applause; some find the food
"over-slick and overpriced", however, and the atmosphere can
seem "soulless".* / www.jean-georges.com; 11.30 pm; no smoking area.

Vrisaki N22   £ 26   ②③③
73 Myddleton Rd   8889 8760   1–1C
*"The biggest mezze ever" is the claim to fame of this big, "fun"
Greek, which is "hard to find" in the backwaters of Bounds
Green.* / midnight; closed Sun.

Wagamama   £ 20   ③③③
101a Wigmore St, W1   7409 0111   3–1A
10a Lexington St, W1   7292 0990   3–2D
4a Streatham St, WC1   7323 9223   2–1C
1 Tavistock St, WC2   7836 3330   4–3D
14a Irving St, WC2   7839 2323   4–4B
26 Kensington High St, W8   7376 1717   5–1A
11 Jamestown Rd, NW1   7428 0800   8–3B
*Perhaps "they are a bit like a school canteen", but for
a "cheap", "cheerful", "fast", "healthy" and "reliable" snack,
these stylish oriental noodle-parlours are still a concept "worth
queueing for".* / www.wagamama.com; 11 pm; no smoking; no booking.

Wakaba NW3   £ 41   ②④⑤
122a Finchley Rd   7586 7960   8–2A
*"Is there actually a restaurant behind that cunning façade?" –
much loved by architecture-anoraks, this minimalist Japanese
café (opposite Finchley Road tube station) has an interior that
the uninitiated pronounce simply "awful", but for "very fresh
sushi and sashimi" it has few rivals.* / 11 pm; D only, closed Sun.

The Waldorf Meridien WC2 £ 52 ④❸❷
Aldwych 7759 4091 2–2D
As a dining experience, this Covent Garden hotel passes almost without comment; the Palm Court tea dances are "spectacular" though, and the "huge" breakfasts also have their fans.
/ 9.45 pm; closed Sat L & Sun D; no jeans or trainers; no smoking area.

The Walmer Castle W11 £ 26 ❷❷❷
58 Ledbury Rd 7229 4620 6–1B
"Good and spicy Thai cooking" and a "great buzz" win ringing endorsements for this "charming room above a Notting Hill pub" – a fave rave for "trendy" twentysomethings. / 10.30 pm; closed weekday L.

Wapping Food E1 £ 35 ❸④❶
Wapping Pumping Hs, Wapping Wall 7680 2080 11–1A
Occupying an "outstanding space" – a converted East End machine hall, near the famous Prospect of Whitby – this "exciting" new venture offers a "good", if "rather limited", menu, accompanied by an impressive range of Antipodean wines. / 10.30 pm; closed Sun D.

The Wardroom
The Old Royal Naval College SE10 £ 27 ④❸❸
Greenwich 8269 4747 1–3D
Beneath Greenwich's fabulous Painted Hall, this spacious undercroft (formerly a naval mess, and still dominated by a portrait of Her Majesty) is a good antidote to the brash style of modern times; our May '01 visit found pleasant but unmemorable cooking. / Rated on Editors' assessment; www.greenwichfoundation.org.uk; L only, closed Sat.

The Waterloo Fire Station SE1 £ 31 ④⑤④
150 Waterloo Rd 7401 3267 9–4A
"It's still good", insist fans of this "huge" and "very noisy" bar/restaurant, near the Old Vic; service is as "slow" or "unfriendly" as ever, though, and many now feel that the cooking has "lost its zing". / 11 pm, Sun 9.15 pm.

The Well EC1 £ 30 ④④④
180 St John St 7251 9363 9–1A
Fans say this "laid-back" newcomer on a trendy Clerkenwell corner offers an "interesting menu for what's basically a wine bar"; we're with those who find the setting "cramped", the cooking "average", and a general sense of "mediocrity". / www.downthewell.com; 10 pm.

Weng Wah House NW3 £ 28 ❷❷❸
240 Haverstock Hill 7794 5123 8–2A
"Consistently good" chow, often "excellent" service and a "nice" atmosphere makes this Belsize Park Chinese an "above-average" local in all respects. / 11.30 pm; no Amex.

West Street Restaurant WC2 £ 42 – – –
13-15 West St 7010 8600 4–2B
It's only a few paces from the Ivy, so let's hope that this ambitious new bar/brasserie/restaurant (from the owners of Kensington Place, the Avenue et al) lives up to its aspirations when it.opens in September '01 – if not, there will be unrivalled scope for odious comparisons! / midnight; closed Sun.

The Westbourne W2 £ 27 ④⑤❶
101 Westbourne Park Villas 7221 1332 6–1B
This "posey" Bayswater boozer is still "madly overcrowded" (especially the "great summer terrace"); the "modern pub food" isn't bad, but takes an age and "often runs out". / 10 pm; closed Mon L; need 4+ to book.

White Cross TW9 £ 22 ❸④❷
Water Ln 8940 6844 1–4A
Characterful, large Young's tavern, near Richmond Bridge, whose dependable pub grub and nice riverside garden make it an excellent weekend destination. / www.youngs.co.uk; L only; no Amex; no booking.

White Horse SW6 £ 26 ❸❸❸
1 Parsons Grn 7736 2115 10–1B
"The Sloaney Pony is better than you'd imagine" foodwise and the chief drawback at this "hectic" pub by Parsons Green is "difficulty getting a table" ("especially in summer"). / www.whitehorsesw6.com; 11 pm; no smoking in dining room.

The White House SW4 £ 18 ❸❷❷
65 Clapham Park Rd 7498 3388 10–2D
"Don't expect a feast", but the "tapas-style snacks" are "well done, for bar fare" at this very "buzzy" new Clapham bar/club/restaurant, whose "cosy corners" afford romantic possibilities. / www.thewhitehouselondon.co.uk; 11 pm; D only, except Sun open L & D.

The White Onion N1 £ 37 – – –
297 Upper St 7359 3533 8–3D
Perhaps the April '01 'relaunch', with a French chef and menu, will put this formerly eminent local back to rights; last year's up-and-down performance provided ample justification for the reporter who found this a "typical Islington" production – "all presentation, and no content". / 11 pm; closed Mon L, Tue L & Sun L.

William IV NW10 £ 29 ❸❷❷
786 Harrow Rd 8969 5944 1–2B
"Fab Sunday lunches" are the culinary highlight at "Kensal Green's best gastropub"; it's "cosy in winter, and you can eat outside in summer". / www.william-iv.co.uk; 10.30 pm, Fri & Sat 11 pm.

Willie Gunn SW18   £ 29   ❸❷❷
422 Garratt Ln   8946 7773   10–2B
*"Well loved by all" – well, all living in Earlsfield anyway – this
"unpretentious" and very "friendly" wine bar/restaurant is
a "great local", which serves a "consistently good", if "slightly
dull", menu.* / 11 pm; no Amex.

Wiltons SW1   £ 57   ❸❸❷
55 Jermyn St   7629 9955   3–3C
*"Traditional yes, but simply the best", declare devotees of this
"marvellously stuffy" bastion of old St James's, which – "if you
can afford it" – serves "splendid" fish and seafood,
and "superb" game.* / www.wiltons.co.uk; 10.30 pm; closed Sat; jacket &
tie required; set Sun L £38(FP).

**Windows on the World
Park Lane Hilton Hotel W1**   £ 72   ⑤⑤❷
22 Park Ln   7208 4021   3–4A
*"A breathtaking view is not enough" – this 24th-floor Mayfair
eyrie has "massive" potential, but its current performance is
"completely amateur in all respects".* / 10.30 pm, Fri & Sat 11.30 pm;
closed Sat L & Sun D; jacket & tie required at D; no smoking at breakfast.

Windsor Castle W8   £ 27   ❸④❶
114 Campden Hill Rd   7243 9551   6–2B
*With its "brilliant garden", not to mention an ancient and
atmospheric interior, this Kensington boozer is many
a Londoner's idea of the "perfect" pub, and the "simple"
cooking generally satisfies.* / 9.30 pm; no smoking area at L; no booking.

Wine Factory W11   £ 25   ❸❸❸
294 Westbourne Grove   7229 1877   6–1B
*This Notting Hill Italian is a "functional" but "reliable" place,
where "good pizza" is the speciality; its key attraction, though, is
the "great wine list at stunning prices".* / 11 pm; closed Sun L;
no Amex.

Wine Gallery SW10   £ 26   ⑤❸❷
49 Hollywood Rd   7352 7572   5–3B
*The food is "old hat", but the "impressive and cheap wine list"
keeps the atmosphere "buzzing" at this younger-scene
Chelsea-fringe bistro, which has a "lovely" terrace.* / 11 pm.

The Wine Library EC3   £ 15   ④❷❶
43 Trinity Sq   7481 0415   9–3D
*"Not for food, but for wine"; "a good cheese and pâté
selection" is on hand to help you sink your choice from the
"massive" range of bottles (at merchant's price, plus £3.50
corkage) at these "intimate" and very atmospheric City cellars;
you "need to book".* / L only, closed Sat & Sun.

Wiz W11 £ 30 ④❷❷

123a Clarendon Rd   7229 1500   6–2A
Antony Worrall Thompson's "congenial" Holland Park bar serves "tapas"-style dishes, which can be "great for a group"; it seems to be going the way of all 'Wozza' places, though – the food is "not as interesting as it was" and some feel it's "a complete rip-off". / 11 pm, Fri & Sat midnight; closed Mon L & Sun D.

Wódka W8 £ 35 ❸❸❸

12 St Alban's Grove   7937 6513   5–1B
"Nothing special, but not bad either" – the Polish cooking at this Kensington backstreet fixture helps soak up the "great selection of vodkas" which is key to its appeal as a party and romantic rendezvous. / 11.15 pm; closed Sat L & Sun L; set weekday L £23(FP).

Wok Wok £ 28 ⑤④④

10 Frith St, W1   7437 7080   4–2A
140 Fulham Rd, SW10   7370 5355   5–3B
270 Chiswick High Rd, W4   8995 2100   7–2A
7 Kensington High St, W8   7938 1221   5–1A
67 Upper St, N1   7288 0333   8–3D
51-53 Northcote Rd, SW11   7978 7181   10–2C
"Everything tastes the same and none of it is any good" – many former fans are "never going back" to this increasingly "clueless" oriental chain. / www.wokwok.com; 11 pm – W1 Thu-Sat midnight – SW10 Fri midnight; SW10 Mon-Fri L only; SW10 no bookings at weekends – W1 party bookings (8+) only.

Wolfe's WC2 £ 27 ④④④

30 Gt Queen St   7831 4442   4–1D
Decked out like a '70s American coffee-shop, this Covent Garden fixture still has quite a name for its "consistently good" burgers; otherwise, though, ratings are tailing off across the board. / www.wolfes-grill.com; 11.45 pm, Sun 8.45 pm.

Wong Kei W1 £ 18 ❸⑤⑤

41-43 Wardour St   7437 8408   4–3A
"Being brutalised is part of the fun" at this "vast" Chinatown landmark (recently refurbished), where – despite "infamously rude service" – the food is "very cheap and good". / 11.30 pm; no credit cards.

Woodlands £ 23 ❸❸④

37 Panton St, SW1   7839 7258   4–4A
77 Marylebone Ln, W1   7486 3862   3–1A
They're rather "gloomy", but these "good-value" veggie Indians consistently deliver "acceptable" results overall. / www.woodlandsrestaurant.co.uk; 10.30 pm.

World Food Café WC2 £ 18 ❸④④

First Floor, 14 Neal's Yd   7379 0298   4–2C
For a "deliciously wholesome experience", this simple veggie café – with a view into a characterful Covent Garden yard – remains a useful stand-by. / L only, closed Sun; no Amex; no smoking; no booking.

Yas W14   £ 25   ❷❸❸
7 Hammersmith Rd   7603 9148   7–1D
"Delicious late-night food – what a novelty!"; "interesting"
Persian cooking makes this unprepossessing-looking café,
opposite Olympia, particularly worth seeking out in the early
hours. / www.yasrestaurant.com; 5 am.

Yas on the Park W2   £ 30   ❷④④
31-33 Sussex Pl   7706 2633   6–1D
Naturally it's not on the park at all, but this new Lancaster Gate
offshoot from Olympia's late night café is smarter than the
original, and was already offering deft Persian cooking on an
early-days (July '01) visit. / Rated on Editors' assessment;
www.yasrestaurant.com; 10.45 pm.

Yatra W1   £ 43   ④❷④
34 Dover St   7493 0200   3–3C
This "nouveau" Mayfair Indian yearling – or should that be
"nouvelle"?, both seem appropriate – has innovative cooking
and a fair degree of "potential"; as yet, though, it's sparked very
little interest. / 11 pm; closed Sat L & Sun L.

Yellow River Café   £ 28   ④④④
12 Chiswick High Rd, W4   8987 9791   7–2B
206 Upper St, N1   7354 8833   8–2D
10 Cabot Sq, E14   7715 9515   11–1C
Ratings have marginally improved at this lacklustre, year-old
oriental chain; overall, though, it's still "very disappointing",
"especially given its Ken Hom connection".
/ www.yellowrivercafes.co.uk; N1 & W4 11 pm, Thu-Sat 11.30 pm – E14
9.30 pm; E14 closed Sat & Sun.

Yelo N1   £ 25   ④④❸
8-9 Hoxton Sq   7729 4626   9–1D
It may have an ultra-hip Hoxton Square setting – with a nice
front terrace, to watch the world go by – but what most struck
us on our August '01 visit to this new Thai canteen was how
nondescript it was in every department. / Rated on Editors'
assessment; 11 pm, Fri & Sat 11.30 pm; no booking.

Yima NW1   £ 23   ❸④❷
95 Parkway   7267 1097   8–3B
"Romantic" décor and "simple", "tasty" Moroccan dishes are
beginning to win something of a following for this "charming"
small Camden Town basement; it's "great for lunch or snacks".
/ 10 pm; closed weekday L; no credit cards; no smoking area.

Yo! Sushi   £ 25   ④④④
17 Rupert St, W1   7434 2724   3–3D
52 Poland St, W1   7287 0443   3–1D
11-13 Bayley St, WC1   7636 0076   2–1C
Whiteley's, 151 Queensway, W2   7727 9392   6–1C
255 Finchley Rd, NW3   7431 4499   8–2A
Unit 3b Belvedere Rd, SE1   7928 8871   2–3D
95 Farringdon Rd, EC1   7841 0785   9–1A
"If you've never had sushi before, you might think it's OK" –
and some do find this gimmicky chain *"fun"* – but the *"novelty
experience"* is starting to wear thin with many reporters.
/ www.yosushi.com; 10.30 pm-midnight; no smoking; no booking.

Yoshino W1   £ 33   ❶❷❸
3 Piccadilly Pl   7287 6622   3–3D
"Just like Japan" – this *"smart"* little bar, hidden-away near
Piccadilly Circus, is so *"authentic"* that it only relatively recently
introduced a menu in English; it offers *"the best sashimi in
town"*, and is praised for its *"outstanding value"*, particularly at
lunch. / 9 pm; closed Sun; no smoking area; set weekday L £19(FP).

Yum Yum N16   £ 24   ❷❷❷
30 Stoke Newington Church St   7254 6751   1–1C
Some find the atmosphere a bit *"noisy"* and *"impersonal"*,
but this Stoke Newington favourite consistently delivers *"well
executed"* Thai dishes and *"friendly"* service. / www.yumyum.co.uk;
10.45 pm, Fri & Sat 11.15 pm; set weekday L £14(FP).

Yumi W1   £ 56   ❸❷④
110 George St   7935 8320   2–1A
It's for the *"great lunch value"* that this pleasantly worn-in
Japanese café is most worth knowing about – in the evening,
its *"fabulously fresh"* dishes come at a hefty premium. / 11 pm;
closed Sun L.

ZAFFERANO SW1   £ 48   ❶❶❷
15 Lowndes St   7235 5800   5–1D
"Unchanged, despite the changes" – *"Italian cooking at its
classical best"* matched by *"cracking service"* has survived the
departure of Giorgio Locatelli from this wonderful Belgravian;
it's still *"too difficult to get into"*, and the seating is still rather
"squashed". / 11 pm.

ZAIKA W8   £ 47   – – –
1 Kensington High St   7795 6533   5–1A
It is a brave move for A-Z Restaurants to transfer this inspiring
Indian – London's best – from its *"sophisticated"* Chelsea home
to the cavernous Kensington site vacated by L'Anis (RIP); let's
hope Vineet Bhatia's *"superb and creative"* cooking survives the
transition. / www.zaika-restaurant.co.uk; 10.45 pm; closed Sat L; set
weekday L £29(FP).

F S A

Zaika Bazaar SW3 £ 27 ❶❷④
2a Pond Pl 7584 6655 5–2C
*Zaika's pared-down new basement offshoot (on the site of the
short-lived El Rincon, RIP) may not have huge charm, but the
simple Indian menu is prepared to a standard that – on an
early-days, July '01 visit – offered spectacular value, especially
by Brompton Cross standards. / Rated on Editors' assessment;
10.45 pm; closed Sat L & Sun.*

Zamoyski NW3 £ 23 ⑤❸❷
85 Fleet Rd 7794 4792 8–2A
*"Very good-value" Polish mezze and plenty of "bizarrely
flavoured vodkas" are the culinary highlights at this "cosy and
welcoming" Belsize Park fixture; "the live music can be a bit
much". / 11 pm; D only, closed Mon; no smoking area.*

Zen SW3 £ 37 ❸④④
Chelsea Cloisters, 85 Sloane Ave 7589 1781 5–2C
*This smart Chelsea Chinese was quite a place in its day, but it
currently gets very little (if mainly approving) commentary, along
the lines that it's "not cheap, but very good". / 11.15 pm, Fri & Sat
11.45 pm.*

Zen Central W1 £ 50 ❸❸④
20-22 Queen St 7629 8089 3–3B
*This smart but stark Mayfair oriental can be "a bit empty"
nowadays; its small fan club, though, continues to report
"a good and professional standard". / 11.15 pm.*

ZeNW3 NW3 £ 36 ❸❸❸
83 Hampstead High St 7794 7863 8–2A
*It's "a little expensive" – and they're "a bit arrogant" – at this
still-striking homage to '80s minimalism in Hampstead;
the "top-quality" Chinese fare, however, generally "justifies the
price". / 11.15 pm; no Amex.*

Ziani SW3 £ 35 ❷❷❷
45-47 Radnor Walk 7352 2698 5–3C
*"Great fun, if too crowded" – this small Chelsea backstreet
Italian has long maintained a disproportionately large fan club,
thanks to its "reliable" cooking and its "relaxed" approach.
/ 11.30 pm.*

Zilli W11 £ 37 ④❷④
210 Kensington Park Rd 7792 1066 6–1A
*Service is "keen" – almost "over-enthusiastic" – at this new
Notting Hill outpost of celeb' restaurateur Aldo Zilli; both the
modern Italian grub and the cramped setting are "pretty
boring", though. / www.zillialdo.com; 11.30 pm.*

Zilli Fish W1　　　　£ 44　②③③
36-40 Brewer St　7734 8649　3–2D
*"Fish to die for, and atmosphere too" – for its fans, celeb-chef
Aldo Zilli's "trendy" and "fun" Soho Italian "just hums"; you
"practically sit in your neighbour's lap", though, and other gripes
include "over-seasoned" food and "patchy" service.*
/ www.zillialdo.com; 11.30 pm; closed Sun.

Zilli Fish Too WC2　　　　£ 38　③④④
145 Drury Ln　7240 0011　4–2D
*Some find Signor Zilli's new Covent Garden outlet "more
exhilarating than other fish restaurants"; however, the cooking is
"variable", service can be "appalling" and the setting – if "more
spacious than Soho" – is "noisy" and "smoky". / www.zillialdo.com;
11.30 pm; closed Sun.*

Zinc W1　　　　£ 35　⑤⑤⑤
21 Heddon St　7255 8899　3–2C
*"C**p" food, "arrogant" service and a "bland" atmosphere –
this Conran "cafeteria", just off Regent Street, really is an
"awful" place. / www.conran.com; 11 pm, Thu-Sat 11.30 pm; closed Sun.*

Zizzi　　　　£ 23　④③③
35-38 Paddington St, W1　7224 1450　2–1A
20 Bow St, WC2　7836 6101　4–2D
73-75 Strand, WC2　7240 1717　4–4D
231 Chiswick High Rd, W4　8747 9400　7–2A
87 Allitsen Rd, NW8　7722 7296　8–3A
35-37 Battersea Rise, SW11　7924 7311　10–2C
*This growing group of "fun and fast" eateries is "not bad for
a pizza/pasta chain", and it's quite "child-friendly" too.
/ www.askcentral.co.uk; 11 pm; no smoking areas; no booking.*

Zucca W11　　　　£ 37　④③④
188 Westbourne Grove　7727 0060　6–1B
*The "pizza's great, but the other food misses", at this "rather
sterile" Notting Hill Italian. / 11 pm; no Amex; no booking, Sat L.*

Zuccato　　　　£ 30　④④④
255 Finchley Rd, NW3　7431 1799　8–2A
41 Bow Ln, EC4　7730 6364　9–2C
*A shopping mall location (in Finchley) seemed the natural
habitat for this mediocre-all-round Italian concept – the Taberna
Etrusca group has recently also introduced it to the City. / NW3
11.30 pm – EC4 10.30 pm; EC4 closed Sat & Sun; no smoking areas.*

Zucchina SW11　　　　£ 24　④③③
27 Battersea Rise　7223 0933　10–2C
*In its early days, this "interesting" industrial-style Battersea
Italian has offered a somewhat "average" experience – at least
in comparison to its sibling, Aglio e Olio. / 11.30 pm; closed
weekday L.*

INDEXES & CUISINES

Maison Bertaux *(8.30)*
Marché Mövenpick *(7.30)*
Mash *(7.30, Sat & Sun 11)*
Nicole's *(10)*
No 6 *(8)*
Oriel *(8.30, Sun 9)*
Paparazzi Café: *W1 (3)*
Pâtisserie Valerie: *Old Compton St W1 (7.30, Sun 9); Marylebone High St W1 (8, Sun 9); WC2 (9.30, Sun 9)*
Paul *(7.30)*
Pizza On The Park *(8.15)*
The Portrait *(10)*
Pret A Manger: *Oxford St W1 (10); Tottenham Court Rd W1 (7.15); Victoria St SW1, Marylebone High St W1, Tottenham Court Rd W1, High Holborn WC1 (7.30); Baker St W1 (7.45); Kingsgate Pd, Victoria St SW1, Regent St W1, Oxford St W1, Hanover St W1, Piccadilly W1, Oxford St W1, Piccadilly W1, High Holborn WC1, St Martins Ln WC2, Strand WC2 (8)*
The Providores *(8, Sat & Sun 10)*
Quiet Revolution: *all branches (9)*
Restaurant One-O-One *(7)*
RIBA Cafe *(8)*
The Ritz *(7)*
Royal Academy *(10)*
Royal Opera House Café *(10)*
Savoy River Restaurant *(7, Sun 8)*
Simpsons-in-the-Strand *(7.30 Mon-Fri)*
Sotheby's Café *(9.30)*
Soup Opera: *Market Pl W1 (7); Hanover St W1, both WC2 (7.30)*
Spoon + *(7)*
Star Café *(7)*
Stock Pot: *SW1 (7); James St W1 (8)*
Terrace *(7)*
Tiger Tiger *(8)*
Truc Vert *(7.30)*
Villandry *(8.30)*
The Waldorf Meridien *(7, Sat & Sun 7)*
Windows on the World *(7)*

West

Adams Café *(7.30, Sat 8.30)*
Aix *(7)*
Aquasia *(7)*
Balans: *SW3, SW5 (8)*
Bali Sugar *(11.30 Sat & Sun)*
Basil St Hotel *(7, Sun 7.30)*
Basilico: *all branches (11)*
Bedlington Café *(8)*
Beirut Express *(7.30)*
Bersagliera *(10)*
Bistrot 190 *(7.30)*
Blakes Hotel *(7.30)*
Bluebird Café *(8, Sun 10)*
La Bouchée *(9.30)*
Brass. du Marché *(10, Sun 11)*
La Brasserie *(8, Sun 9)*
Café Flo: *all west branches (9)*
Café Grove *(9.30)*
Café Laville *(10)*

Café Rouge: *SW6, W11, W2, both W4, both W6, W8, W9 (10); SW3 (8.30)*
Caffè Nero: *Notting Hill Gate W11 (7, Sat & Sun 8); SW7, Westbourne Grove W2, W4 (7, Sat & Sun 8); SW3, Edgware Rd W2, W6 (7, Sat 8, Sun 9); Portobello Rd W11 (7, Sun 9)*
Caffè Uno: *W4 (10); Queensway W2 (8); Edgware Rd W2, W8 (9)*
Capital Hotel *(7, Sun 7.30)*
Chelsea Bun Diner: *SW10 (7)*
Chelsea Kitchen *(8)*
Coffee Republic: *SW10, SW3, SW7, W8 (7, Sat & Sun 8); both W4 (7, Sat 8, Sun 9); both W11 (7, Sun 8); SW6 (7.30, Sat & Sun 8); W2 (7.30, Sat 8, Sun 9)*
Conrad Hotel *(7)*
The Crescent *(10, Sun & Mon 11)*
Dan's Bar *(9, Sun 10)*
Ed's Easy Diner: *SW3 (Sat & Sun only, 9)*
The Fine Line: *SW10 (11, Sat & Sun)*
Ghillies: *SW6 (9)*
I Thai *(7)*
Jason's *(9.30)*
Joe's Café *(9.30)*
Julie's Bar *(9)*
Kensington Place *(7.30 Tue-Sat)*
King's Road Café *(10)*
Langan's Coq d'Or *(10.30)*
Lisboa Patisserie *(7.45)*
Maroush: *W2 (10)*
Le Metro *(7.30, Sun 8.30)*
Mona Lisa *(7)*
Pâtisserie Valerie: *SW3 (7.30, Sun 8)*
Picasso *(7.30)*
Pret A Manger: *W8 (7.30); King's Rd SW3, W6 (8)*
Ranoush *(9)*
Raoul's Café *(8.30, Sun 9)*
Ruby in the Dust: *all branches (11)*
Le Shop *(10.30)*
Soup Opera: *SW5 (7.30)*
Stock Pot: *Basil St SW3 (7.30); King's Rd SW3 (8)*
Tom's *(8, Sun 10)*
Tootsies: *SW6, SW7, W4 (10, Sat & Sun); W11 (8, Sat & Sun 9)*
Troubadour *(9)*
Vingt-Quatre *(24 hrs)*

North

Angel of the North *(11, Sat & Sun 10)*
Banners *(9, Sat & Sun 10)*
Bar Gansa *(10)*
Base
Café Delancey *(9)*
Café Flo: *NW3 (10); N1 (9, Sat & Sun 8.30)*
Café Mozart *(9)*
Café Pasta: *NW3 (9)*
Café Rouge: *all north branches (10)*
Caffè Nero: *NW1 (7, Sat 8.30, Sun 9); NW3 (8, Sun 9)*
Caffè Uno: *N1, NW1 (10); N6 (10, Sun 11); NW8 (10)*
Chamomile *(7)*

BRUNCH MENUS

Cranks: *Barrett St W1, Unit 11, 8 Adelaide St WC2*
Dorchester Grill
Eat: *Regent St W1*
1837
Fifth Floor (Café)
Giraffe: *all branches*
Grissini
Hush
The Ivy
Joe Allen
Just St James
The Lanesborough
Mash
Mirabelle
Momo
Oriel
Pâtisserie Valerie: *both W1*
La Perla: *WC2*
Restaurant One-O-One
Scott's
The Sugar Club
Tootsies: *W1*
Villandry
Vong
The Waldorf Meridien
Windows on the World
Zinc

West
The Abingdon
Balans: *SW3, SW5*
Basil St Hotel
Beach
  Blanket Babylon
Bedlington Café
Bistrot 190
Bluebird
Brass. du Marché
La Brasserie
Cactus Blue
Café Grove
Café Laville
Caffè Nero: *SW7, both W11, both W2, W4, W6*
Capital Hotel
Chelsea Bun Diner: *SW10*
Conrad Hotel
The Cow
Coyote Café
Creelers
The Crescent
Cross Keys
Dakota
Dan's Bar
Ed's Easy Diner: *SW3*
The Fine Line: *SW10*
Francofill
Gravy
Joe's Brasserie
Joe's Café
Langan's Coq d'Or
Le Metro
Montana
Pâtisserie Valerie: *SW3*
PJ's

Raoul's Café
Riccardo's
Le Shop
Stone Mason's Arms
Tom's
Tootsies: *all west branches*
The Vale
Vingt-Quatre
White Horse
Wiz

North
Angel of the North
Banners
La Brocca
Café Delancey
Café Mozart
Caffè Nero: *all north branches*
Camden Brasserie
Centuria
The Duke of Cambridge
Ed's Easy Diner: *NW3*
The Engineer
Giraffe: *all branches*
House on Rosslyn Hill
Idaho
Iznik
Lola's
Manna
Santa Fe
Toast
Tootsies: *NW3*
The Vine
The White Onion

South
Alma
Bah Humbug
Battersea Rickshaw
Belair House
Boiled Egg
Le Bouchon Bordelais
Butlers Wharf
  Chop-house
Caffè Nero: *SW11, SW4*
Canyon
Cinnamon Cay
The Common Room
Ditto
Dixie's Bar & Grill
The Fine Line: *all south branches*
Gastro
The Honest Cabbage
Hudson's
Kennington Lane
The North Pole
Ost. Antica Bologna
Phoenix
Polygon Bar & Grill
Le Pont de la Tour
Ransome's Dock
Sand
The Sequel
The Stepping Stone
The Sun & Doves
Tootsies: *SW13*

Cigala *(he)*
Como Lario *(h)*
Corney & Barrow: WC2 *(hp)*
The Court Restaurant *(hp)*
Cranks: all branches *(h)*
The Criterion *(h)*
Diverso *(hp)*
Dorchester Grill *(hm)*
Dorchester, Oriental *(h)*
Down Mexico Way *(h)*
Ebury Street Wine Bar *(p)*
Ed's Easy Diner: Trocadero
    W1 *(hm)*; Moor St W1 *(m)*
Efes Kebab House: Gt Portland St
    W1 *(h)*
1837 *(hp)*
Elena's L'Etoile *(p)*
L'Escargot *(h)*
Fakhreldine *(hp)*
Foliage *(hm)*
La Fontana *(p)*
Food for Thought *(p)*
Footstool *(h)*
Fortnum's Fountain *(m)*
Fung Shing *(h)*
Garbo's *(h)*
Gaucho Grill: all central branches *(h)*
Gay Hussar *(p)*
Giraffe: all branches *(h)*
Goring Hotel *(hm)*
Gourmet Pizza Co.: all
    branches *(hm)*
Goya: all branches *(p)*
Greenhouse *(h)*
Grenadier *(p)*
Grissini *(hm)*
Harbour City *(h)*
Hard Rock Café *(hmo)*
Hardy's *(h)*
Hush *(h)*
Ibla *(hm)*
Incognico *(h)*
Indigo *(hp)*
Ishbilia *(h)*
Isola *(h)*
It's: NW1, Quadrant Arcade, Air St W1,
    Wigmore St W1, WC1 *(hp)*
Italian Kitchen *(m)*
The Ivy *(hp)*
Jade Garden *(h)*
Jago *(h)*
Japanese Canteen: W1 *(hp)*
Joy King Lau *(h)*
Just St James *(m)*
Kettners *(hp)*
The Lanesborough *(hm)*
Langan's Bistro *(p)*
Levant *(m)*
Little Italy *(hm)*
Mango Tree *(h)*
Marché Mövenpick *(hp)*
Maroush: all branches *(p)*
Masala Zone *(p)*
Mash *(hp)*
Mash Mayfair *(h)*
Matsuri *(h)*

Maxwell's: all branches *(m)*
Mezzo *(h)*
Mezzonine *(h)*
Mitsukoshi *(h)*
Mju *(h)*
Momo *(o)*
Monte's *(h)*
The Mortimer *(hmeo)*
New Mayflower *(h)*
New World *(h)*
No 6 *(h)*
Nobu *(h)*
Noura *(p)*
Oak Room MPW *(h)*
L'Odéon *(h)*
Opus 70 *(hm)*
The Orient *(ho)*
Orrery *(h)*
Ozer *(h)*
Passione *(p)*
Paul *(he)*
Pizza On The Park *(he)*
PizzaExpress: Moreton St SW1,
    Victoria St SW1, Baker St W1, Bruton Pl
    W1, Charlotte St W1, Greek St W1,
    Upper St James St W1, Dean St W1,
    Barrett St W1, Wardour St W1, both
    WC1, St Martins Ln WC2, Bow St
    WC2 *(h)*; Langham Pl W1, The Strand
    WC2 *(ho)*; Victoria St SW1 *(o)*
Pizzeria Condotti *(h)*
Planet Hollywood *(hm)*
La Porte des Indes *(h)*
Porters *(hmo)*
prospectGrill *(hp)*
Quaglino's *(hm)*
Quod *(hme)*
The Rainforest Cafe *(hmeo)*
Restaurant One-O-One *(h)*
Reubens *(hp)*
Rib Room *(h)*
RIBA Cafe *(hp)*
The Ritz *(hm)*
Royal Academy *(hp)*
Royal China: W1 *(h)*
Royal Opera House Café *(p)*
La Rueda: all branches *(hp)*
Rules *(h)*
Rusticana *(h)*
Sambuca *(h)*
Sarastro *(p)*
Sartoria *(h)*
Satsuma *(h)*
Savoy Grill *(h)*
Savoy River Restaurant *(h)*
Savoy Upstairs *(h)*
Seafresh *(hp)*
Shampers *(p)*
J Sheekey *(hp)*
Shepherd's *(p)*
Signor Sassi *(h)*
Simpsons-in-the-Strand *(h)*
Six-13 *(h (m Sun))*
Smollensky's: WC2 *(hmo)*
Sofra: all branches *(h)*
Le Soufflé *(hm)*

Souk (h)
Soup Opera: *Hanover St W1* (h)
La Spiga: *W1* (hp)
La Spighetta (hp)
Stanleys (hp)
Star Café (h)
Strada: *all branches* (h)
Sugar Reef (hp)
Tamarind (h)
La Tasca: *WC2* (h)
Tate Britain (hm)
Teatro (h)
Teca (hp)
Terrace (h)
Texas Embassy Cantina (hm)
TGI Friday's: *all branches* (hme)
Tiger Tiger (hp)
Tootsies: *all branches* (hmo)
Trader Vics (h)
La Trouvaille (p)
Truc Vert (hm)
Tuscan Steak (h)
Uno (hm)
Veeraswamy (hm)
Il Vicolo (h)
Villandry (h)
Vong (h)
Wagamama: *both W1, WC1* (h)
The Waldorf Meridien (h)
Windows on the World (h)
Wok Wok: *all branches* (hm)
Wolfe's (hm)
Wong Kei (h)
World Food Café (h)
Yo! Sushi: *all branches* (m)
Zafferano (hp)
Zinc (hp)
Zizzi: *all branches* (hp)

West
The Abingdon (hp)
Admiral Codrington (h)
Aglio e Olio (h)
Aix (h)
Al-Waha (h)
Alastair Little W11 (hp)
Alounak: *W14* (h)
The Anglesea Arms (hp)
Aquasia (hm)
The Ark (h)
Ask! Pizza: *all west branches* (hp)
Assaggi (p)
Aubergine (p)
Babylon *(no children under 12)*
Balans: *SW3* (h); *SW5* (hp)
Basil St Hotel (hm)
Beach
  Blanket Babylon (hm)
Beirut Express (h)
Belgo Zuid: *all branches* (hp)
Belvedere (h)
Ben's Thai (p)
Benihana: *SW3* (hm)
Bersagliera (p)
Bibendum (h)

Bibendum Oyster Bar (h)
Big Easy (hm)
Blakes Hotel (h)
El Blasõn (p)
Blue Elephant (he)
Blue Lagoon (h)
Bluebird (hmo)
Bluebird Café (h)
Blythe Road (h)
The Bollo House (h)
Bombay Brasserie (h)
Bombay Palace (hp)
Bonjour Vietnam (m)
The Brackenbury (h)
Brass. du Marché (hp)
Brilliant (hp)
Café Flo: *all branches* (h)
Café Grove (h)
Café Lazeez: *SW7* (h)
Café Med: *all branches* (hm)
Café Pasta: *Kensington High St W8* (h);
  Kensington High St W8 (hpe)
Café Rouge: *SW3, W11, W2, both
  W4, both W6, W8, W9* (hm);
  SW6 (hmo)
Caffè Uno: *all branches* (hm)
Calzone: *all west branches* (hmo)
Chelsea Bun Diner: *SW10* (p)
Chelsea Kitchen (p)
Chezmax (hp)
Chinon (p)
Chiswick (hp)
Chula (p)
Chutney Mary (hm)
The Collection (h)
Le Colombier (hp)
Conrad Hotel (hm)
Coopers Arms (p)
Costa's Fish (p)
Costa's Grill (p)
Cotto (hp)
Coyote Café (m)
Creelers (p)
Cross Keys (hm)
Da Mario (hmp)
Dakota (hm)
Dan's (p)
Daquise (p)
Ed's Easy Diner: *SW3* (hm)
Elistano (p)
English Garden (h)
Est Est Est: *W11* (hm)
Exhibition (p)
La Famiglia (h)
fish!: *all branches* (hm)
Formula Veneta (p)
Foxtrot Oscar: *SW3* (hp)
Francofill (hpe)
Friends (h)
Galicia (p)
The Gate: *W6* (h)
Gate (p)
Gaucho Grill: *SW3* (h)
Geale's (h)
Ghillies: *SW6* (p)

Glaisters: *all branches (hp)*
Gravy *(hm)*
Haandi *(h)*
Halepi: *W2 (hp)*
The Havelock Tavern *(hp)*
I Thai *(h)*
It's: *all west branches (hp)*
Itsu: *SW3 (p)*
Jason's *(p)*
Jim Thompson's: *all branches (hp)*
Julie's *(ho)*
Julie's Bar *(hm)*
Kalamaras *(hp)*
Khan's *(h)*
Khan's of Kensington *(p)*
King's Road Café *(hp)*
Langan's Coq d'Or *(h)*
Lou Pescadou *(m)*
Lundum's *(p)*
Made in Italy *(h)*
Madhu's Brilliant *(h)*
Maggie Jones's *(h)*
Malabar *(p)*
Mandalay *(hp)*
Mandarin Kitchen *(h)*
Maroush: *all branches (p)*
Mona Lisa *(p)*
Montana *(h)*
Montpeliano *(hp)*
Nayaab *(h)*
Notting Hill Brasserie *(h)*
192 *(m)*
Orsino *(h)*
Il Pagliaccio *(h)*
Palatino *(h)*
Paparazzi Café: *SW3 (hp)*
Parade *(he)*
Passion *(h)*
Paulo's *(m)*
Pellicano *(h)*
La Perla: *SW6 (hm)*
Pharmacy *(h)*
Phoenicia *(h)*
Picasso *(p)*
PizzaExpress: *SW10, Beauchamp Pl SW3, King's Rd SW3, W11, W14, W2, W4, W8 (h); Fulham Rd SW6 (ho)*
PJ's *(hp)*
Poissonnerie de l'Avenue *(p)*
The Polish Club *(p)*
Il Portico *(p)*
Pucci Pizza *(p)*
Pug *(hm)*
Queen's Head *(m)*
Raccolto *(h)*
Ranoush *(m)*
Raoul's Café *(hm)*
Riccardo's *(hmo)*
Riso *(p)*
The River Café *(hp)*
Rodizio Rico *(hp)*
Rôtisserie Jules: *all branches (hm)*
Ruby in the Dust: *all branches (h)*
La Rueda: *all branches (hp)*

Sabai Sabai *(h)*
Saints *(hp)*
The Salisbury Tavern *(h)*
San Frediano *(h)*
San Lorenzo *(h)*
Sandrini *(h)*
Scalini *(h)*
Shoeless Joe's: *SW6 (m)*
Le Shop *(hp)*
Silks & Spice: *W4 (h)*
Soviet Canteen *(p)*
Sticky Fingers *(hme)*
Strada: *all branches (h)*
Street Hawker: *all branches (h)*
The Tenth *(h)*
TGI Friday's: *all branches (hme)*
Thai on the River *(h)*
Tiger Lil's: *all branches (hp)*
Tom's *(h)*
Tootsies: *all branches (hmo)*
La Trompette *(h)*
Troubadour *(h)*
Vama *(hp)*
Wagamama: *W8 (h)*
The Walmer Castle *(h)*
White Horse *(hm)*
Wine Gallery *(p)*
Wiz *(m)*
Wok Wok: *all branches (hm)*
Yas *(h)*
Yas on the Park *(h)*
Yellow River Café: *all branches (hm)*
Yo! Sushi: *all branches (m)*
Zen *(h)*
Zizzi: *all branches (hp)*
Zucca *(h)*

North

Angel of the North *(h)*
Anglo Asian Tandoori *(h)*
Artigiano *(p)*
Ask! Pizza: *all north branches (hp)*
L'Aventure *(h)*
Banners *(hmo)*
Barracuda *(h)*
Base *(h)*
Belgo Noord: *all branches (hp)*
Benihana: *NW3 (hme)*
La Brocca *(p)*
Bu San *(h)*
Byron's *(hp)*
Café Flo: *all branches (h)*
Café Med: *all branches (hm)*
Café Mozart *(p)*
Café Pasta: *NW3 (hpe)*
Café Rouge: *all north branches (hm)*
Caffè Uno: *all branches (hm)*
Calzone: *NW3 (hm); N1 (hmo)*
Camden Brasserie *(hp)*
Casale Franco *(p)*
Centuria *(h)*
Chamomile *(h)*
Cottons *(m)*
Cucina *(hp)*

Daphne (p)
Don Pepe (hp)
The Duke of Cambridge (hp)
Ed's Easy Diner: NW3 (hm)
The Engineer (hm)
La Finca: all branches (he)
Florians (hp)
The Fox Reformed (hp)
Frederick's (hm)
Furnace (p)
Gallipoli: all branches (h)
The Gate: NW3 (hp)
Geeta (h)
Giraffe: all branches (h)
Globe Restaurant (m)
Granita (p)
Great Nepalese (p)
House on Rosslyn Hill (ho)
Idaho (hme)
Istanbul Iskembecisi (hp)
John Burton-Race (h)
Julius (h)
The Landmark (hmo)
Laurent (p)
The Little Bay (p (m on Sun))
Loch Fyne: N8 (h)
Lola's (pe)
The Lord Palmerston (p)
Manna (hp)
Marine Ices (hm)
Maxwell's: all branches (m)
Mesclun (h)
Metrogusto: N1 (h)
Mims (p)
The Montrose (hme)
MPW Brasserie (h)
Nautilus (h)
911 (p)
Organic Café: NW6 (h)
The Parsee (h)
Philpotts Mezzaluna (h)
La Piragua (h)
PizzaExpress: all north branches (h)
La Porchetta Pizzeria: all
    branches (hp)
Rani (hm)
Retsina (m)
Rosmarino (h)
Rôtisserie: N1 (h)
Royal China: NW8 (h)
Ruby in the Dust: all branches (h)
The Salt House (hpe)
The Salusbury (hm)
San Carlo (p)
San Daniele (h)
Santa Fe (hm)
Sauce (hm)
Seashell (hm)
Sedir (h); (hp)
Singapore Garden (h)
Smollensky's: NW3 (hm)
Solly's Exclusive (h)
Soulard (p)
Strada: all branches (h)
Street Hawker: all branches (h)

Tartuf (h)
Tiger Lil's: all branches (hp)
Toast (hm)
Toff's (hm)
Tootsies: all branches (hmo)
Troika (hp)
Two Brothers (m)
Vegia Zena (hp)
Viet-Anh (m)
Vijay (h)
The Vine (m)
Wagamama: NW1 (h)
Weng Wah House (h)
Wok Wok: all branches (hm)
Yellow River Café: all
    branches (hm)
Yima (h)
Yo! Sushi: all branches (m)
Yum Yum (h)
Zamoyski (p)
ZeNW3 (h)
Zizzi: all branches (hp)
Zuccato: NW3 (h)

South

Alma (h)
Antipasto & Pasta (h)
The Artesian Well (h)
Ask! Pizza: all south branches (hp)
Babur Brasserie (h)
Bah Humbug (hp)
The Banana Leaf Canteen (hm)
Bankside (h)
Barcelona Tapas: SE22 (hp)
Battersea Rickshaw (hp)
Belair House (hm)
Bengal Clipper (h)
Blue Print Café (hp)
The Blue Pumpkin (h)
Boiled Egg (hme)
Le Bouchon Bordelais (hm)
Buchan's (h)
Buona Sera: SW11 (h)
Burnt Chair (p)
Butlers Wharf
    Chop-house (h)
Café Portugal (p)
Café Rouge: all south branches (hm)
Café Spice Namaste: all
    branches (hp)
Caffè Uno: all branches (hm)
Cantina del Ponte (hm)
Cantinetta Venegazzú (hp)
Canyon (hmeo)
The Castle (hm)
Champor-Champor (hp)
Chapter Two (hp)
Chez Bruce (h)
Chez Lindsay (h)
Cinnamon Cay (hm)
The Common Room (p)
The Cook House (p)
Coromandel (hm)
The County Hall (hm)
Del Buongustaio (p)
The Depot (h)

Ditto *(hm)*
Dixie's Bar & Grill *(p)*
don Fernando's *(hp)*
Eco: SW4 *(h)*
Enoteca Turi *(hm)*
Fat Boy's: W4 *(hp)*
Film Café *(hp)*
Fina Estampa *(p)*
La Finca: all branches *(he)*
fish!: all branches *(hm)*
Foxtrot Oscar: SW11 *(hm)*
Gastro *(p)*
Ghillies: SW18 *(h)*
Glaisters: all branches *(hp)*
The Glasshouse *(h)*
Gourmet Burger Kitchen *(h)*
Gourmet Pizza Co.: all
   branches *(hm)*
The Honest Cabbage *(hp)*
Jim Thompson's: all branches *(hp)*
Kastoori *(p)*
Kwan Thai *(h)*
La Lanterna *(h)*
Laughing Gravy *(h)*
The Lavender: SW11, SW9 *(p)*;
   SW15 *(phm)*
Lemon Thyme *(hm)*
The Light House *(h)*
Lobster Pot *(p)*
Ma Goa *(hp)*
La Mancha *(h)*
Metrogusto: SW8 *(hp)*
Mezzanine *(h)*
Murano *(hm)*
Naked Turtle *(hm)*
Newton's *(hme)*
Niksons *(h)*
The North Pole *(hmo)*
The Old School Thai *(h)*
Ost. Antica Bologna *(p)*
The People's Palace *(hp)*
The Pepper Tree *(h)*
Le P'tit Normand *(m)*
Phoenix *(h)*
Pizza Metro *(h)*
PizzaExpress: Cardomom Bldg, Shad
   Thames SE1, Lavender Hill SW11,
   SW14, SW15, SW18, SW4 *(h)*;
   Belvedere Rd SE1, Battersea Br Rd
   SW11 *(ho)*
Pizzeria Castello *(h)*
Polygon Bar & Grill *(p)*
Le Pont de la Tour *(h)*
Le Pont de la Tour
   Bar & Grill *(h)*
Prego *(h)*
Ransome's Dock *(hp)*
Rapscallion *(p)*
Redmond's *(m)*
Riva *(hm)*
Riviera: all branches *(hm)*
Royal China *(h)*
La Rueda: all branches *(hp)*
Sarkhel's *(h)*
Scoffers *(hm)*
Shakespeare's Globe *(hp)*

Sonny's *(h)*
The Stepping Stone *(hmo)*
Strada: all branches *(h)*
The Sun & Doves *(hp)*
Tate Modern *(hmo)*
Tentazioni *(hp)*
Thai Corner Café *(p)*
3 Monkeys *(ho)*
Tiger Lil's: all branches *(hp)*
Tootsies: all branches *(hmo)*
The Trafalgar Tavern *(hm)*
The Wardroom *(hp)*
The Waterloo
   Fire Station *(hp)*
Willie Gunn *(hp)*
Wok Wok: all branches *(hm)*
Yo! Sushi: all branches *(m)*
Zizzi: all branches *(hp)*
Zucchina *(h)*

East
Abbaye: EC1 *(h)*
Alba *(hp)*
Aquarium *(h, crèche on weekends)*
Ask! Pizza: EC1 *(h)*
Auberge: EC3 *(hm)*
Aurora *(h)*
Babe Ruth's *(hmeo)*
Bleeding Heart *(p)*
Il Bordello *(h)*
Bubb's *(p)*
Café Flo: all branches *(h)*
Café Med: all branches *(hm)*
Café Rouge: E14 *(hm)*; Fetter Ln
   EC4 *(m)*
Café Spice Namaste: all
   branches *(hp)*
Carnevale *(p)*
Cranks: all branches *(h)*
Faulkner's *(hm)*
fish!: all branches *(hm)*
Fishmarket *(h)*
Frocks *(hp)*
Futures *(hp)*
Gaucho Grill: all east branches *(h)*
Gaudi *(p)*
George *(h)*
Gourmet Pizza Co.: all
   branches *(hm)*
House *(ho)*
Japanese Canteen: EC1 *(hp)*
Miyabi *(h)*
Moro *(hp)*
The Peasant *(hm)*
Perc%nto *(hp)*
PizzaExpress: London Wall EC2,
   EC4 *(h)*; Curtain Rd EC2 *(ho)*; E1,
   Exmouth Mkt EC1 *(o)*
Quadrato *(hme)*
The Quality Chop House *(p)*
Riviera: all branches *(hm)*
Scuzi: EC3 *(hm)*
Searcy's Brasserie *(h)*
Shanghai *(hp)*
Simpson's Tavern *(p)*
Smiths of Smithfield *(h)*
St John *(h)*

Strada: *all branches (h)*
Stream *(p)*
Tabla *(hp)*
Tatsuso *(p)*
10 *(p)*
Terminus *(h)*
Ubon *(hp)*
Viet Hoa *(h)*
Wapping Food *(h)*
The Well *(h)*
Yellow River Café: *all branches (hm)*
Yo! Sushi: *all branches (m)*
Zuccato: *EC4 (hp)*

ENTERTAINMENT
(Check times before you go)

Central
a.k.a.
(DJ, Thu-Sun)
Alphabet
(DJ, Thu & Fri)
Atlantic Bar & Grill
(band & DJ Sun & Mon)
The Avenue
(jazz pianist, nightly; jazz, Sun L)
Ayoush
(African music, Mon; belly dancer Tue, Fri & Sat)
Bank
(jazz, Sat)
Bank Westminster
(DJ, Wed-Sat)
Bohème Kitchen
(band, Tue pm)
Boisdale
(jazz & classical music, Mon-Sat)
La Brasserie Townhouse
(jazz, Fri pm)
Café Bohème
(jazz, Tue-Fri & Sun)
Café du Jardin
(jazz pianist, nightly)
Calabash
(African band, Fri or Sat pm)
Caldesi
(occasional magic by proprietor)
Le Caprice
(pianist, nightly)
Cassia Oriental
(pianist)
Charlotte Street Hotel
(private film screen & club)
The Court Restaurant
(musicians, nightly)
The Criterion
(magician, Wed-Sat)
Dover Street
(band, DJ & dancing, nightly; jazz Mon, salsa Tue)
Down Mexico Way
(DJ & dancing, Mon-Sat; bands, Thu-Sat)
Efes Kebab House: *Gt Portland St W1 (belly dancer, nightly)*
Fakhreldine
(singer, nightly)
FireBird
(pianist & singers, Thu-Sat)
Foliage
(jazz, Mon-Sat in bar)
Goring Hotel
(piano, nightly)

Hakkasan
(DJ, Fri & Sat)
Ishbilia
(music, Thu-Sat)
Jimmy's
(Greek music, Thu-Sat)
Just St James
(pianist, Wed-Sat)
Kai
(harpist, Thu & Sat nights)
Kettners
(pianist, nightly & at L Wed-Sun)
The Lanesborough
(supper dances, Fri & Sat; jazz Sun brunch)
Langan's Brasserie
(jazz, nightly)
The Langley
(DJ, Thu-Sat)
The Lexington
(pianist, Tue & Fri; saxophonist, Mon & Sat)
Little Italy
(DJ, Fri & Sat)
Mash
(DJ Thu-Sat)
Mezzo
(music, nightly)
Mezzonine
(DJ, in lounge bar)
Momo
(live world music, Mon-Wed)
Noble Rot
(DJ, Wed-Sat)
L'Odéon
(jazz, Thu-Sat in winter)
Opium
(DJ, Thu-Sat; cabaret, Tue & Wed)
Opus 70
(guitarist, Sun L)
Paparazzi Café: *all branches (music, nightly)*
Pizza On The Park
(jazz, nightly)
PizzaExpress: *Dean St W1 (jazz, nightly)*
La Porte des Indes
(jazz, Sun brunch)
Quaglino's
(jazz, nightly in bar; pianist at L)
The Rainforest Cafe
(animated wildlife, jungle effects)
Red Cube
(DJ, nightly)
Restaurant One-O-One
(guitarist Fri & Sat)
Rib Room
(pianist, Mon-Sat nights)
The Ritz
(band, Fri & Sat pm (every night in Dec))
Royal Academy
(pianist, Fri pm)
La Rueda: *W1 (Spanish music & dancing, Fri & Sat)*
Sarastro
(opera, Mon & Sun)
Sartoria
(pianist, nightly)
Savoy River Restaurant
(dinner dance, Fri & Sat)
Scott's
(pianist, nightly)
Shoeless Joe's: *SW1 (video screens); WC2 (video screens – DJ, Thu-Sat)*

Six Degrees
(live music, Fri & Sat)
Smollensky's: WC2
(Live Music Thurs-Sun)
Le Soufflé
(string trio, Sun L)
Souk
(belly dancer & DJ, Fri & Sat)
Sugar Reef
(nightclub)
Sway
(DJ, Tue-Sat)
Thai Square
(Thai music & dancing, nightly)
Tiger Tiger
(nightclub)
Titanic
(DJ, Thu-Sat)
Trader Vics
(Latin music, nightly)
The Waldorf Meridien
(jazz, Sun brunch; harpist, Mon-Fri teatime; band Fri)
Windows on the World
(dinner dance, Fri & Sat; jazz, Sun brunch)
Yatra
(DJ)

West

All Bar One: W4
(jazz, Sun night)
Aquasia
(singer & pianist, 4 times a week)
Basil St Hotel
(pianist, nightly)
Beach Blanket Babylon
(DJ, Wed-Sat)
Big Easy
(band, nightly)
Bombay Brasserie
(pianist & singer, nightly; jazz Sat & Sun L)
Cactus Blue
(jazz, Sun, Tue & Wed pm)
Café Laville
(live music, Mon & Tue)
Café Med: W6
(jazz, Sun night)
Chutney Mary
(jazz, Sun L)
The Collection
(DJ, nightly in bar)
Conrad Hotel
(singer & pianist, Tue-Thu)
Da Mario
(disco, nightly except Sun & Mon; magician, Mon)
Gate
(DJ, nightly)
Krungtap
(karaoke)
Maroush: W2
(music & dancing, nightly)
Montana
(jazz, nightly)
Mr Wing
(jazz, Thu-Sat)
Nikita's
(Russian music, weekends)
Organic Café: SW7
(jazz, Sun pm)
Otto
(DJ, Fri & Sat)

Paparazzi Café: all branches
(music, nightly)
Pharmacy
(DJ, Fri & Sat in bar)
Pizza Pomodoro: all branches
(music, nightly)
PizzaExpress: W8
(jazz, Fri & Sat; Beauchamp Pl SW3 (jazz, Sat pm); W14 (jazz, Tue pm)
Shoeless Joe's: SW6
(video screens)
Le Shop
(jazz, Thu)
606 Club
(jazz, nightly)
Spago
(Italian singer Fri & Sat)
Star of India
(singer & jazz pianist, Wed & Thu)
The Tenth
(jazz trio, Sat; dinner dance, once a month)
The Thai
(music, Sat pm)
Vama
(jazz, Sun)
William IV
(DJ, Wed-Sat)
Yas on the Park
(live Persian music, Wed-Sat)

North

Les Associés
(accordion, 1st Fri of month)
Barracuda
(jazz, Fri & Sat)
Benihana: NW3
(children's ents, Sun)
La Brocca
(jazz, Thu in bar)
Café Rouge: NW3
(jazz, Wed)
Caffè Uno: NW1
(music, Wed pm)
Cottons
(band, Fri & Sun)
Cuba Libre
(dancing, nightly)
Don Pepe
(singer & organist, nightly)
La Finca: N1
(salsa, Wed-Fri)
The Fox Reformed
(wine tastings, backgammon tournaments, book club)
Globe Restaurant
(cabaret, Thu pm)
House on Rosslyn Hill
(live music, 3 nights)
The Landmark
(pianist, daily)
Lola's
(pianist, nightly; jazz, Sun L)
MPW Brasserie
(jazz singer, Sun)
Organic Café: NW6
(occasional opera nights)
PizzaExpress: Kentish Town Rd NW1
(jazz, Sat pm)
Ruby in the Dust: N1
(DJ, nightly)
Santa Fe
(live music, Sun)
Smollensky's: NW3
(Live Music Wed-Sun)

LATE
(open till midnight or later as shown; may be earlier Sunday)

Browns: *WC2*
Café Bohème *(2.45 am, Thu-Sat open 24 hours)*
Café du Jardin
Café Emm *(Fri & Sat only, 12.30 am)*
Café Lazeez: *W1 (1.30 am, Fri & Sat only)*
Café Pasta: *W1*
Caffè Nero: *Frith St W1 (2 am, Thu-Sun 4 am)*
Le Caprice
Christopher's: *SW1*
Circus
Corney & Barrow: *WC2 (midnight, Thu-Sat 2 am)*
Dover Street *(2 am)*
Ed's Easy Diner: *all central branches (midnight, Fri & Sat 1 am)*
Efes Kebab House: *Gt Portland St W1 (Fri & Sat only, 3 am)*
Fakhreldine
Gaucho Grill: *W1*
Goya: *all branches (tapas served until midnight)*
Hard Rock Café *(12.30 am, Fri & Sat 1 am)*
Hujo's
Incognico
Ishbilia
The Ivy
Joe Allen *(12.45 am)*
Kettners
The Lanesborough
Little Italy *(4 am)*
Maroush: *W1 (1 am)*
Maxwell's: *all branches*
Melati *(Fri & Sat only, 12.30 am)*
Mezzo *(midnight, Thu-Sat 1 am (crustacea till 3 am))*
Mezzonine *(12.45 am, Fri-Sat 2.45 am)*
Mr Chow
Mr Kong *(2.45 am)*
Navajo Joe
New Mayflower *(3.45 am)*
Orso
Ozer
Paparazzi Café: *W1 (3 am, Thu-Sat 5 am)*
Pizza On The Park
PizzaExpress: *Moreton St SW1, Victoria St SW1, Baker St W1, Bruton Pl W1, Charlotte St W1, Upper St James St W1, Barrett St W1, Wardour St W1, both WC1, St Martins Ln WC2, The Strand WC2, Bow St WC2; Greek St W1, Dean St W1 (midnight, Wed-Sat 1 am)*
Pizzeria Condotti
Planet Hollywood
Pollo
La Porte des Indes
prospectGrill
Quaglino's *(midnight, Fri & Sat 1 am)*
J Sheekey
Shoeless Joe's: *SW1 (Thu & Fri only)*
Smollensky's: *WC2 (Thu-Sat only, 12.15 am)*
Sofra: *all branches*
Soho Spice *(3 am, Fri & Sat only)*
Soup Opera: *Hanover St W1 (Fri only)*

La Spiga: *W1 (Wed-Sat only)*
Texas Embassy Cantina *(Fri & Sat only)*
TGI Friday's: *all branches*
Tiger Tiger *(3 am)*
Tootsies: *all branches (Fri & Sat only)*
Trader Vics
Wok Wok: *W1*
Yo! Sushi: *Poland St W1*

West

Alounak: *all branches*
Anarkali
Balans: *W8 (1 am); SW3, SW5 (1 am)*
Beirut Express *(1.45 am)*
Benihana: *all branches (Fri & Sat only)*
Big Easy *(midnight, Fri & Sat 12.30 am)*
Blue Elephant
Bombay Brasserie
Café Lazeez: *SW7 (12.30 am)*
Calzone: *W11; SW10 (midnight, Fri & Sat 12.30 am)*
La Delizia
Ed's Easy Diner: *SW3 (Fri & Sat only, 1 am)*
Halepi: *W2 (12.30 am)*
Lou Pescadou
Maroush: *W2 (2 am); SW3 (5 am)*
Mr Wing
Nayaab
Il Pagliaccio
Paparazzi Café: *SW3 (1 am)*
Patio
Pizza Pomodoro: *SW3 (1 am)*
PizzaExpress: *SW10, all in SW3, Wandsworth Bridge Rd SW6, W11, W14, W2, W4, W8*
PJ's
Pucci Pizza *(12.30 am)*
Ranoush *(3 am)*
Riccardo's
Rodizio Rico
Scalini
Le Shop
606 Club *(1.30 am, Fri & Sat 2 am)*
Spago
Tandoori of Chelsea
TGI Friday's: *all branches*
Tootsies: *all branches (Fri & Sat only)*
Vingt-Quatre *(24 hours)*
Wiz *(Fri & Sat only)*
Wok Wok: *SW10 (midnight, Fri only)*
Yas *(5 am)*

North

Banners *(Fri & Sat only)*
Bar Gansa
Benihana: *all branches (Fri & Sat only)*
Calzone: *N1*
Cuba Libre *(Fri & Sat only)*
Don Pepe
Ed's Easy Diner: *NW3 (Fri & Sat only, 1 am)*
La Finca: *N1 (1.30 am, Fri & Sat only)*
Istanbul Iskembecisi *(5 am)*
The Little Bay
Maxwell's: *all branches*

Le Mercury (1 am)
Pasha (Fri & Sat only)
La Piragua
PizzaExpress: all north branches
La Porchetta Pizzeria: N4
Rasa: N16 (Fri & Sat only)
Ruby in the Dust: N1 (2 am, Fri & Sat only)
Tartuf
Tiger Lil's: N1 (midnight, Fri & Sat only)
Toast
Tootsies: all branches (Fri & Sat only)
Vrisaki
Zuccato: NW3

South
Buona Sera: SW11
Caffè Uno: SW13 (Fri & Sat only)
La Finca: SE11 (1 am)
The Fine Line: SW4 (midnight, Thu-Sat 1 am)
Gastro
PizzaExpress: Borough High St SE1, Lavender Hill SW11, SW13, SW14, SW15, SW18
Ransome's Dock (Sat only)
Sand (1.30 am)
Tiger Lil's: SW4 (Fri & Sat only)
Tootsies: all branches (Fri & Sat only)

East
Babe Ruth's (midnight, Fri & Sat only)
Barcelona Tapas: EC4 (2.30 am)
Brick Lane Beigel Bake (24 hours)
Corney & Barrow: Jewry St EC3 (Tue-Fri only, 2 am)
Lahore Kebab House
PizzaExpress: E1, Curtain Rd EC2
Shoeless Joe's: EC4 (Thu & Fri only)
Silks & Spice: EC4 (2 am, Thu & Fri only)

NO-SMOKING AREAS
(* completely no smoking)

Central
Abeno
The Admiralty
Archipelago
Atrium
Beotys
Bertorelli's: Charlotte St W1, WC2
La Brasserie Townhouse
Busaba Eathai*
Café Bagatelle*
Café Fish
Café Pacifico
Caldesi
Chez Gérard: all branches
Chiang Mai
China City
China House
Chuen Cheng Ku
The Cinnamon Club
Connaught*
Corney & Barrow: WC2
The Court Restaurant*

Cranks: all central branches*
Crivelli's Garden*
Defune*
1837
Fakhreldine
Foliage
Food for Thought*
Footstool
Getti: Marylebone High St W1*
Gili Gulu*
Gourmet Pizza Co.: W1
Goya: Lupus St SW1
Grissini
Hakkasan
Hanover Square
Hard Rock Café
Hardy's
Hunan
Ikkyu
Joe Allen
Kulu Kulu*
Livebait: WC2
Maison Bertaux
Malabar Junction
Marché Mövenpick
Masala Zone*
Mela
Mildreds*
Mirabelle
Mju*
Motcombs
New World
Nicole's
No 6*
Nobu
Noodle Noodle*
Odin's
Opus 70
Oriel
Orso
Pan-Asian Canteen
Paul*
Pizza On The Park
Planet Hollywood
Poons, Lisle Street
The Portrait*
Pret A Manger: both SW1, Regent St W1, Oxford St W1, Tottenham Court Rd W1, Hanover St W1, Piccadilly W1, Baker St W1, High Holborn WC1, High Holborn WC1, St Martins Ln WC2
The Rainforest Cafe*
Rasa: all branches*
Rasa Samudra
Red Fort
RIBA Cafe*
Ristorante Italiano
Roussillon
Royal Academy*
Royal Court Bar
Royal Opera House Café*
Rules*
Sarastro
Satsuma*
Savoy River Restaurant
Scott's

Shepherd's
Signor Sassi
Silks & Spice: W1
Six-13
Smollensky's: WC2
Soho Spice
Sotheby's Café*
Le Soufflé
La Spighetta
Stanleys
Star Café
The Sugar Club
Tate Britain
Terrace
TGI Friday's: all branches
Thai Pot: Bedfordbury WC2
Thai Square
Tokyo Diner
Truc Vert*
The Union Café
Villandry*
Vong
Wagamama: both W1, WC1*
The Waldorf Meridien
World Food Café*
Yo! Sushi: Poland St W1*
Yoshino

West
Aquasia
Bali Sugar
Basil St Hotel
Bedlington Café*
Big Easy
El Blasón*
Blue Lagoon
The Bollo House
Bombay Palace
Café Laville
Café Lazeez: SW7
Café Pasta: Kensington High St W8
Chiswick
Chutney Mary
Conrad Hotel
Costa's Grill
Creelers
Daquise
Francofill
Gate
Ginger
Itsu: SW3*
Khan's
Khan's of Kensington
King's Road Café
Mandalay*
Mao Tai: SW6
Orsino
Palatino
The Papaya Tree
Phoenicia
PJ's
Pret A Manger: King's Rd SW3, W6, W8
Queen's Head
Raoul's Café

S&P Patara: Beauchamp Pl SW3
Sabai Sabai
Southeast
Springbok Café
Standard Tandoori
Stock Pot: Basil St SW3
The Tenth
TGI Friday's: all branches
Thai Bistro*
Thai Break
Thierry's
Tom's*
Topsy-Tasty*
La Trompette
The White Horse
The Vale

North
Anglo Asian Tandoori
Base
Byron's
Café Japan
Café Mozart*
Café Pasta: NW3
Cantina Italia
Casale Franco
Chamomile
Diwana B-P House
The Duke of Cambridge*
Frederick's
Giraffe: NW3*
Heartstone*
Jashan*
The Landmark
The Little Bay
Loch Fyne: N8
Manna*
Marine Ices
Le Mercury
Mims
911
Organic Café: NW6
Oriental City
The Parsee
Pret A Manger: all north branches
Rani
Rasa: all branches*
Rasa Travancore*
Rosmarino*
San Carlo
San Daniele
Santa Fe
Sauce
Seashell
Shish
Solly's Exclusive
Sushi-Say
Tiger Lil's: N1
Toast
Toff's
Troika
Two Brothers
Viet-Anh
Vijay
Village Bistro

Yima
Zamoyski

South
Archduke Wine Bar
Babur Brasserie
The Banana Leaf Canteen
Bankside
The Blue Pumpkin*
Le Bouchon Bordelais
Burnt Chair*
Cantina Vinopolis
Canyon
Chez Gérard: all branches
Coromandel
The Depot
Film Café
The Fire Stables
fish!: Cathedral St SE1
Gastro
Gourmet Burger Kitchen*
Konditor & Cook: Stoney St SE1*
Kwan Thai
The Light House
Metrogusto: SW8
Mezzanine
Murano
Naked Turtle
Neat
The Old School Thai
The People's Palace
The Pepper Tree
Prego
Sarkhel's
Station Grill
The Stepping Stone
The Sun & Doves
Talad Thai*
Tate Modern*
Thailand*
3 Monkeys*
Tiger Lil's: SW4

East
Abbaye: EC1
Arkansas Café*
Babe Ruth's
Brick Lane Beigel Bake*
Bubb's
Café Indiya
Chez Gérard: all branches
Cicada
Elephant Royale
Faulkner's
Flâneur*
Fusion*
Futures*
Gourmet Pizza Co.: E14
Gow's
Home
K10*
Moshi Moshi: EC2*
The Place Below*
Pret A Manger: EC4*; EC1, Eldon St
EC2, Bishopsgate EC2
Quadrato

The Quality Chop House
Searcy's Brasserie
Touzai
Ubon
The Vestry*
Yo! Sushi: EC1*

OUTSIDE TABLES
(particularly recommended)*

Central
The Admiralty*
Al Hamra*
Al Sultan
Alfred
All Bar One: Leicester Sq WC2*;
Hanover St W1, Regent St W1,
Paddington St W1, Picton Pl W1
Andrew Edmunds
Archipelago
L'Artiste Musclé*
Ask! Pizza: Grafton Way W1
Aurora*
Ayoush
Back to Basics
Balans: W1
Bam-Bou
Bank Westminster
Bar Italia
Baraonda
Bertorelli's: both W1
Bibo Cibo
Blandford Street
Bohème Kitchen
Boisdale
Boudin Blanc*
Boulevard
Brahms*
La Brasserie Townhouse
Café Bohème
Café des Amis du Vin*
Café du Jardin
Café Fish
Café Lazeez: W1
Café Rouge: all central branches
Caffè Nero: Frith St W1, Tottenham
Court Rd W1, Charlotte St W1,
Southampton St WC2, Lancaster Pl WC2,
Cranbourn St WC2
Caffè Uno: Binney St W1, Baker St
W1, Charing Cross Rd WC2
Caldesi
Caraffini
Caravan Serai
Carluccio's Caffè: Barrett St W1*
Chada: W1
Charlotte Street Hotel
Chez Gérard: Dover St W1, East Ter,
Covent Garden WC2*; Charlotte St W1,
Chancery Ln WC2
Chimes
China City
Cigala
Coffee Republic: Villiers St WC2
Il Convivio
Cork & Bottle

Cranks: *both W1, Great Newport St WC2*
Eat: *Soho Sq W1*
Ed's Easy Diner: *Moor St W1*
Elena's L'Etoile
Fairuz
Fifth Floor (Café)
Franco's
Getti: *SW1, Marylebone High St W1*
Giraffe: *W1*
Gordon's Wine Bar*
Goya: *all branches*
Grumbles
Hard Rock Café
Hardy's
Hunan
Hush
Ichizen Noodle Bar
Ishbilia
It's: *Quadrant Arcade, Air St W1, Wigmore St W1*
Italian Kitchen
Jenny Lo's
Langan's Bistro
Little Italy
The Little Square
Maison Bertaux
Mash Mayfair
Maxwell's: *all branches*
Mekong
Mela
Mildreds
Mirabelle*
Momo
Mongolian Barbecue: *WC2*
The Mortimer
Morton's*
Motcombs
Noble Rot
Noho: *all branches*
L'Oranger
Oriel
Orrery
Ozer
Le Palais du Jardin
Passione
Pâtisserie Valerie: *WC2*
Pizza On The Park
PizzaExpress: *Moreton St SW1, Baker St W1, Charlotte St W1, Langham Pl W1, Barrett St W1, both WC1, The Strand WC2*
Porters
La Poule au Pot*
Pret A Manger: *Regent St W1, Tottenham Court Rd W1, Marylebone High St W1, Baker St W1, Tottenham Court Rd W1, High Holborn WC1, High Holborn WC1, St Martins Ln WC2, Strand WC2*
Reubens
RIBA Cafe*
Ristorante Italiano
The Ritz*
Rocket
Royal Academy
Royal Opera House Café*

La Rueda: *all branches*
Sambuca
Santini
Scott's
Shoeless Joe's: *WC2*
Silks & Spice: *W1*
Six Degrees
Sofra: *St Christopher's Pl W1*; Shepherd St W1*
Soup Opera: *both W1, Villiers St WC2*
Soup Works: *Goodge St W1*
La Spighetta
Spoon +*
Star Café
Stock Pot: *both W1*
Strada: *W1*
Tajine
Teca
Terrace
Texas Embassy Cantina
Tootsies: *all branches*
Toto's*
La Trouvaille
Truc Vert
Tuscan Steak*
Uno
Villandry
Wolfe's
Zilli Fish
Zilli Fish Too
Zinc*
Zizzi: *W1, Bow St WC2*

West
Abbaye: *all branches*
The Abingdon*
Admiral Codrington*
Aix*
Al-Waha
Alastair Little W11
All Bar One: *W4*
Amandier
The Anglesea Arms
Aquasia*
Arcadia*
The Ark
Ask! Pizza: *SW6, Spring St W2, W4*
The Atlas*
Babylon*
Balans: *SW3, SW5*
Bali Sugar*
Beach
    Blanket Babylon
Bedlington Café
Belvedere*
Bibendum Oyster Bar
Big Easy
Black & Blue
Blakes Hotel*
Bluebird Café*
Blythe Road
The Bollo House
Bombay Brasserie
Bombay Palace
Le Bon Choix

The Westbourne*
White Horse
William IV*
Windsor Castle*
Wine Factory
Wine Gallery*
Wiz
Wódka
Wok Wok: W4
Yas
Yas on the Park
Zilli
Zizzi: W4
Zucca

North
All Bar One: NW8
Angel of the North
Artigiano*
Ask! Pizza: N1, NW3
Les Associés
L'Aventure*
Bar Gansa
Barracuda*
Base
Benihana: NW3
The Black Truffle
La Brocca
Byron's
Café Delancey
Café Flo: all north branches
Café Med: NW8
Café Mozart*
Café Rouge: all north branches
Caffè Nero: all north branches
Caffè Uno: all north branches
La Cage Imaginaire
Calzone: all branches
Casale Franco*
Centuria
Chamomile
The Chapel
Cottons
Cuba Libre
Daphne's
The Duke of Cambridge
The Engineer*
Florians
The Fox Reformed*
Frederick's*
Gallipoli: all branches
Gaucho Grill: NW3
House on Rosslyn Hill
Idaho*
Julius
Lansdowne
Laurent
Lemonia
The Little Bay
The Lord Palmerston
Mango Room
Manna
Maxwell's: all branches
MPW Brasserie
911

No 77 Wine Bar
Noho: all branches
North Sea Fish
Odette's
Organic Café: NW6
Pasha
Philpotts Mezzaluna
La Piragua
PizzaExpress: Parkway NW1,
    Haverstock Hill NW3, NW8
La Porchetta Pizzeria: N4
The Queen's
The Real Greek
Rosmarino
Rôtisserie: N1
Ruby in the Dust: all branches
Le Sacré-Coeur
Salon*
The Salt House*
The Salusbury
San Carlo*
Santa Fe
Sedir
Silks & Spice: NW1
Singapore Garden
Smollensky's: NW3
Solly's Exclusive
Soulard
Street Hawker: NW6
Tartuf
Tootsies: all branches
Troika
Vegia Zena
Viet-Anh
The Vine*
Wok Wok: N1
Yima

South
All Bar One: Shad Thames SE1
Antipasto & Pasta
Arancia
The Artesian Well
Ask! Pizza: SE1
Auberge: Sandell St SE1
Babur Brasserie
Bah Humbug
Baltic
Barcelona Tapas: SE22
Battersea Rickshaw
Belair House*
The Blue Pumpkin
Boiled Egg*
Le Bouchon Bordelais
Buchan's
Buona Sera: SW11
Butlers Wharf
    Chop-house*
Café Rouge: SW11, SW15, SW4
Café Spice Namaste: SW11
Caffè Nero: SW4
Caffè Uno: SW13*
Cantina del Ponte*
Cantinetta Venegazzú*
Canyon*

PRIVATE ROOMS

(for the most comprehensive
listing of venues for functions –
from palaces to pubs – see
*Harden's Party Guide for
London*, available in all good
bookshops)
* particularly recommended

Central

a.k.a. *(15)*
Alastair Little *(25)*
Alfred *(15-20)*
Alloro *(16)*
Aperitivo *(30)*
Aroma II *(40)*
L'Artiste Musclé *(25)*
Atlantic Bar & Grill *(70)**
Atrium *(24)*
Aurora *(20)*
The Avenue *(20,25)*
Axis *(48)**
Ayoush *(18)*
Back to Basics *(40)*
Bam-Bou *(14)**
Bangkok Brasserie *(40)*
Bank Westminster *(20,20)**
Belgo Centraal: *WC2 (25,30)*
Benihana: *WI (10)*
Bentley's *(16)**
Beotys *(6-60)*
Bertorelli's: *Charlotte St WI (18,40);*
   WC2 (35,50); Frith St WI (50)
Bibo Cibo *(36)*
Bice *(22)*
Bistro 1: *WI (25)*
Blues *(40)*
Boisdale *(20)*
Boudin Blanc *(20)*
Boulevard *(80)*
La Brasserie Townhouse *(40)*
Browns: *WC2 (120,80,50);*
   WI (16,8,8,4)
Café des Amis du Vin *(80)*
Café du Jardin *(60)*
Café Fish *(70)*
Café Flo: *WC2 (20); SWI (70)*
Café Lazeez: *WI (12)*
Caffè Uno: *Baker St WI (60)*
Caldesi *(24)*
Caravan Serai *(14,14)*
Cassia Oriental *(15)*
Charlotte Street Hotel *(30,30)*
Chez Gérard: *Chancery Ln
   WC2 (110); Dover St WI (30)*
cheznico *(20)**
Chiang Mai *(30)*
Chimes *(30)*
China City *(10,20,30,40)*
China House *(10)*
Chor Bizarre *(30)*
Christopher's: *WC2 (50)*
Chuen Cheng Ku *(20-300)*
The Cinnamon Club *(40)*
Circus *(16)*

Como Lario *(14)*
Connaught *(22)**
Conrad Gallagher *(20)*
Il Convivio *(12)*
Cork & Bottle *(40)*
Corney & Barrow: *WC2 (25)*
The Court Restaurant *(30)*
Defune *(8)*
Dorchester, Oriental *(6,10,16)*
Dover Street *(50-70, 100-120)*
Drones *(40)*
1837 *(10)*
Elena's L'Etoile *(8-30)*
L'Escargot *(24,60)**
L'Estaminet *(16)*
The Fine Line: *WC2 (20)*
FireBird *(12)**
Foliage *(22)*
Footstool *(100)*
Franco's *(42)*
Fung Shing *(25,50)*
Garbo's *(40)*
Le Gavroche *(20)**
Gay Hussar *(12,24)**
Getti: *Marylebone High St WI (34)*
Gili Gulu *(40)*
Giraffe: *WI (80)*
Golden Dragon *(40)*
Goring Hotel *(15,10,30)*
Goya: *all branches (80)*
Green's *(34)*
Grissini *(50)*
Grumbles *(12)*
The Guinea *(30)*
Hanover Square *(80)*
Hardy's *(16,80)*
Hush *(120)*
Ibla *(25)*
Ichizen Noodle Bar *(50)*
Ikeda *(8-12)*
Ikkyu *(10)*
L'Incontro *(34)*
Indigo *(48)*
Ishbilia *(6)*
The Ivy *(25-60)**
Jago *(40)*
Jenny Lo's *(20)*
Joy King Lau *(60)*
Just St James *(110)*
Kai *(6,12)*
Kaspia *(12)*
Kaya Korean *(8,12)*
Ken Lo's Memories *(20-25)*
Kettners *(12-80)*
The Lanesborough *(100)*
The Langley *(45,20,20,20)*
Levant *(8-10)*
The Lexington *(18)**
Lindsay House *(8,18)*
Luigi's *(14,20,35)*
Malabar Junction *(70)*
Manzi's *(40)*
Marché Mövenpick *(20)*
Maroush: *WI (85)*

Spago *(40)*
Standard Tandoori *(55)*
Star of India *(12,14)*
Stick & Bowl *(20)*
Stratford's *(32)*
Le Suquet *(16)*
Tawana *(40)*
The Thai *(50)*
Thai on the River *(90 (+90 outside))*
The Thatched House *(40)*
Thierry's *(30)*
Twelfth House *(24)*
The Vale *(14,30,40)*
Vama *(30)*
White Horse *(45)*
William IV *(35)*
Wine Factory *(50)*
Wine Gallery *(18,20,45)*
Wiz *(50)*
Wódka *(30)*
Yas *(34)*
Yas on the Park *(30)*
Yellow River Café: *W4 (100)*
Zaika *(16)*
Zen *(20)*
Zucca *(40)*

North

Afghan Kitchen *(25)*
Angel of the North *(50)*
Anglo Asian Tandoori *(30-40)*
Barracuda *(35)*
Base *(18)*
The Black Truffle *(8)*
Byron's *(30)*
Café Delancey *(55)*
Café Med: *NW8 (30)*
Café Rouge: *NW8 (20)*
Caffè Uno: *NW1 (22); N1 (25)*
Casale Franco *(60)*
The Chapel *(30)*
Chutneys *(60,35)*
Cottons *(50)*
Daphne *(50)*
Diwana B-P House *(35)*
The Duke of Cambridge *(40)*
The Engineer *(32)*
La Finca: *N1 (150)*
Florians *(23,50)*
Frederick's *(18,32)*
Geeta *(10-35)*
Giraffe: *NW3 (45); N1 (70)*
Globe Restaurant *(25)*
Great Nepalese *(32)*
Idaho *(60,55)*
Julius *(45)*
Lemonia *(40)*
The Little Bay *(80)*
The Lord Palmerston *(30)*
Mango Room *(30)*
Maxwell's: *NW3 (100)*
The Montrose *(16)*
MPW Brasserie *(22)*
No 77 Wine Bar *(12)*

North Sea Fish *(40)*
Odette's *(8,30)**
The Parsee *(18)*
Phoenix Palace *(30)*
PizzaExpress: *Kentish Town Rd NW1 (25); Heath St NW3 (30); Haverstock Hill NW3 (40); NW8 (55); N1 (70)*
The Real Greek *(8)*
Royal China: *NW8 (15,20)*
Ruby in the Dust: *N1 (50); NW1 (60)*
The Salt House *(25)*
Santa Fe *(25,40)*
Sedir *(40); (42)*
Singapore Garden *(6)*
Solly's Exclusive *(85)*
Soulard *(18)*
Sushi-Say *(6)*
Tartuf *(40)*
Vegia Zena *(20)*
Villa Bianca *(40)*
Village Bistro *(20,30)*
The Vine *(30)*
Vrisaki *(14)*
Weng Wah House *(80)*
The White Onion *(28)*
Wok Wok: *N1 (18)*
Yellow River Café: *N1 (100)*
Yum Yum *(30)*
Zamoyski *(42)*
ZeNW3 *(24)*

South

Alma *(70)*
Antipasto & Pasta *(30)*
The Artesian Well *(30)**
Auberge: *Sandell St SE1 (180)*
Baltic *(35)*
Bankside *(70)*
Barcelona Tapas: *SE22 (15)*
Belair House *(14)*
The Blue Pumpkin *(35)*
Bombay Bicycle Club *(24)*
Le Bouchon Bordelais *(35)*
Buchan's *(50-60)*
Caffè Uno: *SW13 (25)*
Cantina Vinopolis *(100)*
The Castle *(30)*
Chada: *SW11 (40)*
Chez Bruce *(18)*
Chez Gérard: *SE1 (60)*
Chez Lindsay *(36)*
Coromandel *(30)*
The County Hall *(60)*
Del Buongustaio *(50)*
Delfina Studio Café *(5-300)*
Ditto *(20)*
Duke of Cambridge *(20)*
Emile's *(45,35)*
Enoteca Turi *(30)*
La Finca: *SE11 (75)*
The Fine Line: *SW11 (15); SW4 (50)*
Fish in a Tie *(40)*
Four Regions *(180)*
Foxtrot Oscar: *SW11 (60)*

ROMANTIC

An asterisk (*) after an entry indicates exceptional or very good cooking

ALSATIAN

North
Tartuf (N1)*

BELGIAN

Central
Belgo Centraal (WC2)

West
Abbaye (SW7)
Belgo Zuid (W10)

North
Belgo Noord (NW1)

East
Abbaye (EC1)

BRITISH, MODERN

Central
a.k.a. (WC1)
Alastair Little (W1)*
Alfred (WC2)
All Bar One (W1, WC1, WC2)
Andrew Edmunds (W1)*
Atlantic Bar & Grill (W1)
Atrium (SW1)
Attica (W1)
Aurora (W1)*
The Avenue (SW1)
Axis (WC2)*
Bank (WC2)
Bank Westminster (SW1)
Bibo Cibo (WC2)
Blandford Street (W1)*
Blues (W1)
Café du Jardin (WC2)
Café Fish (W1)
Café Med (W1)
Le Caprice (SW1)*
Charlotte Street Hotel (W1)
Che (SW1)
Circus (W1)
Conrad Gallagher (W1)*
Cork & Bottle (WC2)
Corney & Barrow (WC2)
The Court Restaurant (WC1)
Le Deuxième (WC2)*
Ebury Street Wine Bar (SW1)
The Fifth Floor (SW1)
Fortnum's Fountain (W1)
Giraffe (W1)
Greenhouse (W1)
Ha! Ha! (W1, WC2)
Hush (W1)

Indigo (WC2)*
The Ivy (WC2)*
Jago (SW1)
The Lanesborough (SW1)
Langan's Brasserie (W1)
The Lexington (W1)
Lindsay House (W1)
The Little Square (W1)
The Marquis (W1)
Mash (W1)
Mash Mayfair (W1)
Mezzo (W1)
The Mortimer (W1)
Morton's (W1)
Motcombs (SW1)
Nicole's (W1)
No 6 (W1)*
Noble Rot (W1)
115 at Hodgson's (WC2)
Opus 70 (W1)
The Perseverance (WC1)*
The Portrait (WC2)
Quaglino's (SW1)
Red Cube (WC2)
Rhodes in the Square (SW1)*
RIBA Cafe (W1)
Rowley's (SW1)
Royal Opera House Café (WC2)
Scott's (W1)
Six Degrees (W1)
Six-13 (W1)
Sotheby's Café (W1)
The Sugar Club (W1)*
Sugar Reef (W1)
Sway (W1)
Tate Britain (SW1)
Teatro (W1)
The Union Café (W1)
Villandry (W1)
The Waldorf Meridien (WC2)
West Street Restaurant (WC2)
Zinc (W1)

West
The Abingdon (W8)
Admiral Codrington (SW3)
Alastair Little W11 (W11)*
All Bar One (SW10, SW6, SW7, W11, W2, W4)
The Anglesea Arms (W6)*
Arcadia (W8)
Babylon (W8)
Beach Blanket Babylon (W11)
Belvedere (W8)
Bistrot 190 (SW7)
Bluebird (SW3)
Blythe Road (W14)
The Bollo House (W4)
The Brackenbury (W6)

Brinkley's (SW10)
The Builder's Arms (SW3)*
Bush Bar & Grill (W14)
Café Med (W11, W6)
Catch (SW5)
The Chelsea Ram (SW10)*
Chinon (W14)*
Chiswick (W4)
Clarke's (W8)*
The Collection (SW3)
Coopers Arms (SW3)
Cotto (W14)
The Cow (W2)*
Creelers (SW3)
The Crescent (SW3)
Dan's (SW3)
English Garden (SW3)
Gate (W11)*
Golborne House (W10)
Goolies (W8)*
Gravy (W4)
The Grove (W6)
The Havelock Tavern (W14)*
The House (SW3)
The Ifield (SW10)
Joe's Brasserie (SW6)
Joe's Café (SW3)
Julie's (W11)
Julie's Bar (W11)
Kensington Place (W8)
The Ladbroke Arms (W11)*
Launceston Place (W8)*
Lots Road (SW10)*
Manor (W11)
Le Metro (SW3)
Notting Hill Brasserie (W11)
192 (W11)
Otto (W9)
Parade (W5)*
Passion (W9)*
The Pen (SW6)
Pharmacy (W11)
The Prince Bonaparte (W2)
Pug (W4)
Raoul's Café (W9)
The Salisbury Tavern (SW6)
Snows on the Green (W6)
Stone Mason's Arms (W6)
The Tenth (W8)*
The Terrace (W8)
The Thatched House (W6)
Twelfth House (W11)
The Vale (W9)
Vingt-Quatre (SW10)
The Westbourne (W2)
White Horse (SW6)
William IV (NW10)

North

All Bar One (N1, N6, NW3, NW8)
Blakes (NW1)

Bradley's (NW3)*
Byron's (NW3)
Café Med (NW8)
The Chapel (NW1)
Cucina (NW3)
The Duke of Cambridge (N1)
The Engineer (NW1)
Frederick's (N1)*
Giraffe (N1, NW3)
Globe Restaurant (NW3)
Granita (N1)
Lansdowne (NW1)
Lola's (N1)
The Lord Palmerston (NW5)*
Mango Room (NW1)*
Mesclun (N16)*
Mims (EN4)
The Montrose (NW6)
No 77 Wine Bar (NW6)
North Sea Fish (WC1)*
Odette's (NW1)*
The Queen's (NW1)
Quincy's (NW2)
Salon (NW3)*
The Salt House (NW8)
The Vine (NW5)

South

All Bar One (SE1, SW11, SW18)
Archduke Wine Bar (SE1)
The Artesian Well (SW8)
Bah Humbug (SW2)
Bankside (SE1)
Belair House (SE21)
Bellamys (SE11)
Blue Print Café (SE1)
The Blue Pumpkin (SW15)
Burnt Chair (TW9)
Cantina Vinopolis (SE1)
The Castle (SW11)*
Chapter Two (SE3)
Chez Bruce (SW17)*
The County Hall (SE1)
The Depot (SW14)
Ditto (SW18)
The Fire Stables (SW19)
George II (SW11)*
Glaisters (SW11)
The Glasshouse (TW9)*
Helter Skelter (SW9)*
The Honest Cabbage (SE1)
Hudson's (SW15)
Kennington Lane (SE11)*
Konditor & Cook (SE1)*
Laughing Gravy (SE1)
The Lavender (SE11, SW11, SW15, SW9)
The Light House (SW19)*
The Mason's Arms (SW8)*
Mezzanine (SE1)

Newton's (SW4)
Niksons (SW11)
The North Pole (SE10)
Oxo Tower (SE1)
The People's Palace (SE1)
Phoenix (SW15)*
Le Pont de la Tour (SE1)
Ransome's Dock (SW11)*
Rapscallion (SW4)*
Redmond's (SW14)*
RSJ (SE1)
Sand (SW4)
Scoffers (SW11)
Shakespeare's Globe (SE1)
Sonny's (SW13)*
Station Grill (SE17)*
The Stepping Stone (SW8)*
The Sun & Doves (SE5)
The Waterloo
  Fire Station (SE1)
Willie Gunn (SW18)

East

All Bar One (E14, EC1, EC2, EC3, EC4)
Bar Bourse (EC4)
Café Med (EC1)
Cantaloupe (EC2)
City Rhodes (EC4)*
Corney & Barrow (E14, EC2, EC3, EC4)
Dibbens (EC1)
The Don (EC4)*
Flâneur (EC1)
The Fox (EC2)
Frocks (E9)
Gladwins (EC3)
Goose (EC2)
Grand Central (EC2)
Home (EC1)
House (E14)
The Light (E1)
Lime (EC2)
LMNT (E8)
1 Lombard Street (EC3)
The Poet (EC3)
Prism (EC3)
Quadrato (E14)
The Quality Chop
  House (EC1)*
Searcy's Brasserie (EC2)
Soshomatch (EC2)
St John (EC1)*
10 (EC2)
Terminus (EC2)
The Vestry (EC3)
Vic Naylors (EC1)
The Well (EC1)

BRITISH, TRADITIONAL

Central

Chimes (SW1)
Connaught (W1)
Dorchester Grill (W1)
Fryer's Delight (WC1)*
Goring Hotel (SW1)
Green's (SW1)
Grenadier (SW1)
The Guinea (W1)
The Langley (WC2)
Odin's (W1)*
Porters (WC2)
Rib Room (SW1)
The Ritz (W1)
Rules (WC2)
Savoy Grill (WC2)
Seafresh (SW1)
Shepherd's (SW1)
Simpsons-in-the-Strand (WC2)
Stanleys (W1)
Wiltons (SW1)

West

Basil St Hotel (SW3)
Costa's Fish (W8)*
Ffiona's (W8)
Geale's (W8)
Gravy (W4)
Maggie Jones's (W8)
Monkeys (SW3)*
Queen's Head (W6)
Windsor Castle (W8)

North

Nautilus (NW6)*
911 (NW1)
Seashell (NW1)*
Toff's (N10)
Two Brothers (N3)*

South

Brady's (SW18)*
Butlers Wharf
  Chop-house (SE1)
The Trafalgar Tavern (SE10)
The Wardroom (SE10)

East

The Bow Wine Vaults (EC4)
Fox & Anchor (EC1)
George (EC2)
George & Vulture (EC3)
Hope & Sir Loin (EC1)
Ye Olde Cheshire
  Cheese (EC4)
The Quality Chop
  House (EC1)*
Simpson's Tavern (EC3)
The Wine Library (EC3)

DANISH

West
Lundum's (SW7)*

EAST & CENTRAL EUROPEAN

Central
Gay Hussar (W1)
St Moritz (W1)

North
Café Mozart (N6)
Troika (NW1)

FRENCH

Central
The Admiralty (WC2)
L'Artiste Musclé (W1)
Auberge (W1)
Beotys (WC2)
Boudin Blanc (W1)
La Brasserie
   Townhouse (WC1)
Café Bagatelle (W1)
Café Bohème (W1)
Café des Amis du Vin (WC2)
Café Flo (SW1, WC2)
Café Nikolaj (W1)
Café Rouge (W1, WC2)
Chez Gérard (W1, WC2)
cheznico (W1)
Connaught (W1)
The Criterion (W1)
Drones (SW1)
1837 (W1)
Elena's L'Etoile (W1)
L'Escargot (W1)*
L'Estaminet (WC2)
Foliage (SW1)*
Le Gavroche (W1)*
Incognico (WC2)*
Langan's Bistro (W1)
Maggiore's (WC2)
Mirabelle (W1)*
Mju (SW1)
Mon Plaisir (WC2)
Le Muscadet (W1)
Nico Central (W1)
Oak Room MPW (W1)
L'Odéon (W1)
L'Oranger (SW1)*
Orrery (W1)*
Le Palais du Jardin (WC2)
Pétrus (SW1)*
Pied à Terre (W1)*
La Poule au Pot (SW1)*
Quo Vadis (W1)
Randall & Aubin (W1)

Restaurant One-O-
   One (SW1)*
The Ritz (W1)
Roussillon (SW1)*
Simply Nico (SW1)
Le Soufflé (W1)*
The Square (W1)*
La Tante Claire (SW1)
Terrace (W1)
La Trouvaille (W1)*
Villandry (W1)
Windows on the World (W1)

West
Aix (W11)
Amandier (W2)
Aubergine (SW10)*
Belvedere (W8)
Bibendum (SW3)
Bibendum Oyster Bar (SW3)*
Le Bon Choix (SW10)
La Bouchée (SW7)
Brass. du Marché (W10)
La Brasserie (SW3)
Brasserie St Quentin (SW3)
Café Flo (SW7, W8)
Café Rouge (SW3, SW6, W11, W2,
   W4, W6, W8, W9)
Capital Hotel (SW3)*
Chez Moi (W11)*
Chezmax (SW10)*
Chinon (W14)*
Christian's (W4)*
Le Colombier (SW3)
Francofill (SW7)
Gordon Ramsay (SW3)*
Langan's Coq d'Or (SW5)
Lou Pescadou (SW5)
Monkeys (SW3)*
Parisienne Chophouse (SW3)
Père Michel (W2)
Poissonnerie
   de l'Avenue (SW3)*
Le Potiron Sauvage (SW6)
Randall & Aubin (SW10)
Stratford's (W8)
Le Suquet (SW3)*
Thierry's (SW3)
La Trompette (W4)*
Turner's (SW3)

North
Les Associés (N8)*
L'Aventure (NW8)*
Base (NW3)
Café Delancey (NW1)
Café Flo (N1, NW3)
Café Rouge (N6, NW3, NW8)
La Cage Imaginaire (NW3)
Camden Brasserie (NW1)
John Burton-Race (NW1)

Julius (N1)
The Landmark (NW1)
Le Mercury (N1)
MPW Brasserie (NW3)
Oslo Court (NW8)*
Le Sacré-Coeur (N1)
Soulard (N1)*
Village Bistro (N6)
The White Onion (N1)

South
Auberge (SE1)
Le Bouchon Bordelais (SW11)
Café Rouge (SE1, SW11, SW15, SW19, SW4)
Chez Gérard (SE1)
Chez Lindsay (TW10)*
The Cook House (SW15)
Emile's (SW15)
Gastro (SW4)
Lobster Pot (SE11)*
Monsieur Max (TW12)*
Neat (SE1)
Le P'tit Normand (SW18)
Putney Bridge (SW15)
Simply Nico (SE1)

East
Auberge (EC3)
Aurora (EC2)
Bleeding Heart (EC1)*
Bubb's (EC1)*
Café du Marché (EC1)*
Café Flo (EC4)
Café Rouge (E14, EC4)
Chez Gérard (EC1, EC2, EC3)
Club Gascon (EC1)*
Coq d'Argent (EC3)
Luc's Brasserie (EC3)
Maison Novelli (EC1)*
Simply Nico (EC1)
Les Trois Garçons (E1)

GAME

Central
Dorchester Grill (W1)
The Marquis (W1)
Rules (WC2)
Wiltons (SW1)

West
Monkeys (SW3)*

GREEK

Central
Beotys (WC2)
Jimmy's (W1)

West
Costa's Grill (W8)
Halepi (W2)
Kalamaras (W2)

North
Daphne (NW1)
Halepi (NW3)
Lemonia (NW1)
The Real Greek (N1)*
Retsina (NW1)
Vrisaki (N22)*

HUNGARIAN

Central
Gay Hussar (W1)

North
Café Mozart (N6)

IRISH

Central
O'Conor Don (W1)

ITALIAN

Central
Al Duca (SW1)*
Alloro (W1)
Aperitivo (W1)
Baraonda (W1)
Bertorelli's (W1, WC2)
Bice (W1)
Buona Sera (WC2)
Café Pasta (W1, WC2)
Caffè Uno (W1, WC2)
Caldesi (W1)
Caraffini (SW1)*
Carluccio's Caffè (W1)
Cecconi's (W1)
Como Lario (SW1)
Il Convivio (SW1)*
Crivelli's Garden (WC2)
Diverso (W1)
La Fontana (SW1)
Il Forno (W1)
Franco's (SW1)
Getti (SW1, W1)
Grissini (SW1)
Ibla (W1)*
L'Incontro (SW1)
Innecto (W1)
Isola (SW1)
Italian Kitchen (WC1)*
Little Italy (W1)
Luigi's (WC2)
Maggiore's (WC2)
Mimmo d'Ischia (SW1)
Neal Street (WC2)
Oliveto (SW1)
Olivo (SW1)
Orso (WC2)
Paparazzi Café (W1)
Passione (W1)*
Pizza On The Park (SW1)

Pollo *(W1)*
Purple Sage *(W1)*
Quod *(W1)*
Ristorante Italiano *(W1)*
Rusticana *(W1)*
Sale e Pepe *(SW1)*
Sambuca *(SW1)*
Santini *(SW1)*
Sartoria *(W1)*
Serafino *(W1)*
Signor Sassi *(SW1)*
La Spiga *(W1)*
La Spighetta *(W1)*
Strada *(W1, WC2)*
Teca *(W1)**
Toto's *(SW1)**
Tuscan Steak *(WC2)*
Uno *(SW1)*
Vasco & Piero's Pavilion *(W1)*
Il Vicolo *(SW1)**
Zafferano *(SW1)**
Zilli Fish *(W1)**
Zilli Fish Too *(WC2)*
Zizzi *(W1, WC2)*

West
L'Accento Italiano *(W2)*
Aglio e Olio *(SW10)**
Al San Vincenzo *(W2)**
The Ark *(W8)*
Assaggi *(W2)**
Bersagliera *(SW3)*
Buona Sera *(SW3)*
Café Pasta *(W8)*
Caffè Uno *(W2, W4, W8)*
Calzone *(SW10, W11)*
I Cardi *(SW10)*
Cibo *(W14)**
Da Mario *(SW7)*
Daphne's *(SW3)*
De Cecco *(SW6)**
La Delizia *(SW3)*
Elistano *(SW3)**
Est Est Est *(W11, W4)*
Il Falconiere *(SW7)*
La Famiglia *(SW10)*
Floriana *(SW3)*
Formula Veneta *(SW10)*
Frantoio *(SW10)*
Friends *(SW10)*
The Green Olive *(W9)*
King's Road Café *(SW3)*
Made in Italy *(SW3)**
Mona Lisa *(SW10)*
Montpeliano *(SW7)*
Monza *(SW3)*
Orsino *(W11)*
Osteria Basilico *(W11)**
Il Pagliaccio *(SW6)*
Palatino *(W4)*
Paparazzi Café *(SW3)*

Pellicano *(SW3)*
Picasso *(SW3)*
Il Portico *(W8)*
Raccolto *(W11)*
The Red Pepper *(W9)**
Riccardo's *(SW3)*
Riso *(W4)*
The River Café *(W6)**
San Frediano *(SW3)*
San Lorenzo *(SW3)*
Sandrini *(SW3)*
Scalini *(SW3)*
Spago *(SW7)*
Spiga *(SW3)*
Strada *(SW6)*
Wine Factory *(W11)*
Ziani *(SW3)**
Zilli *(W11)*
Zizzi *(W4)*
Zucca *(W11)*

North
Artigiano *(NW3)*
The Black Truffle *(NW1)*
La Brocca *(NW6)*
Café Pasta *(NW3)*
Caffè Uno *(N1, N6, NW1, NW8)*
Calzone *(N1, NW3)*
Cantina Italia *(N1)*
Casale Franco *(N1)*
Est Est Est *(N1)*
Florians *(N8)*
Marine Ices *(NW3)*
Metrogusto *(N1)**
Philpotts Mezzaluna *(NW2)**
La Porchetta Pizzeria *(N1, N4)*
Rosmarino *(NW8)*
The Salusbury *(NW6)**
San Carlo *(N6)*
San Daniele *(N5)*
Strada *(N1)*
Vegia Zena *(NW1)*
Villa Bianca *(NW3)*
Zizzi *(NW8)*
Zuccato *(NW3)*

South
Antipasto & Pasta *(SW11)*
Arancia *(SE16)**
Buona Sera *(SW11)*
Café Pasta *(SW15, SW19)*
Caffè Uno *(SW13)*
Cantina del Ponte *(SE1)*
Cantinetta Venegazzú *(SW11)**
Del Buongustaio *(SW15)*
Eco *(SW4)**
Eco Brixton *(SW9)**
Enoteca Turi *(SW15)**
Est Est Est *(SW17)*
La Lanterna *(SE1)*
Lemon Thyme *(SW13)*

Metrogusto *(SW8)**
Murano *(TW1)*
Osteria Antica
   Bologna *(SW11)*
Pizzeria Castello *(SE1)**
Prego *(TW9)*
Riva *(SW13)**
Strada *(SW11)*
Tentazioni *(SE1)**
Zizzi *(SW11)*
Zucchina *(SW11)*

East
Alba *(EC1)**
Il Bordello *(E1)**
Caravaggio *(EC3)*
Gt Eastern Dining Rm *(EC2)*
The Peasant *(EC1)*
Perc%nto *(EC4)*
Scuzi *(E14, EC1, EC3)*
Strada *(EC1)*
Taberna Etrusca *(EC4)*
Zuccato *(EC4)*

MEDITERRANEAN

Central
Atrium *(SW1)*
Bistro 1 *(W1, WC2)*
Fifth Floor (Café) *(SW1)*
Hujo's *(W1)*
Monte's *(SW1)*
Rocket *(W1)*
Truc Vert *(W1)*

West
Aquasia *(SW10)*
The Atlas *(SW6)**
Chives *(SW10)**
Cross Keys *(SW3)*
Made in Italy *(SW3)**
Mediterraneo *(W11)**
Snows on the Green *(W6)*
Tom's *(W11)*

North
Centuria *(N1)*
The Little Bay *(NW6)*
The Vine *(NW5)*

South
Fish in a Tie *(SW11)*
Riviera *(SE1)*

East
The Eagle *(EC1)**
The Peasant *(EC1)*
Riviera *(E14)*

POLISH

West
Daquise *(SW7)*
Patio *(W12)*

The Polish Club *(SW7)*
Wódka *(W8)*

North
Café Mozart *(N6)*
Zamoyski *(NW3)*

South
Baltic *(SE1)*

PORTUGUESE

South
Café Portugal *(SW8)*

RUSSIAN

Central
FireBird *(W1)*
Kaspia *(W1)*

West
Nikita's *(SW10)*
Soviet Canteen *(SW10)*

North
Troika *(NW1)*

East
Potemkin *(EC1)*

SCANDINAVIAN

Central
Garbo's *(W1)*

SCOTTISH

Central
Boisdale *(SW1)*

West
Loch Fyne *(SW6)*

North
Loch Fyne *(N8)*

South
Buchan's *(SW11)*
Loch Fyne *(TW2)*

SPANISH

Central
Cigala *(WC1)*
Goya *(SW1)*
La Rueda *(W1)*
La Tasca *(WC2)*

West
El Blasõn *(SW3)*
Cambio de Tercio *(SW5)**
Galicia *(W10)*
Lomo *(SW10)*
La Rueda *(SW6)*

North
Bar Gansa *(NW1)*

Don Pepe (NW8)
La Finca (N1)

South
Barcelona Tapas (SE22)
don Fernando's (TW9)
La Finca (SE11)
La Mancha (SW15)
Meson don Felipe (SE1)
Rebato's (SW8)
La Rueda (SW4)

East
Barcelona Tapas
   (E1, EC3, EC4)
Fuego (EC2, EC3)
Gaudi (EC1)
Moro (EC1)*
La Tasca (E14)

SWISS

Central
Marché Mövenpick (SW1)
St Moritz (W1)

INTERNATIONAL

Central
Alphabet (W1)
Balans (W1)
Bohème Kitchen (W1)
Boulevard (WC2)
Brahms (SW1)
Browns (W1, WC2)
Café Emm (W1)
Dôme (W1, WC2)
Dover Street (W1)
The Fine Line (WC2)
Footstool (SW1)
Gordon's Wine Bar (WC2)
Grumbles (SW1)
Hanover Square (W1)
Hardy's (W1)
Just St James (SW1)
Marché Mövenpick (SW1)
Oriel (SW1)
Pomegranates (SW1)
Royal Court Bar (SW1)
Sarastro (WC2)
Savoy River Restaurant (WC2)
Savoy Upstairs (WC2)
Shampers (SW1)
Spoon + (W1)
Star Café (W1)
Stock Pot (SW1, W1)
Tiger Tiger (SW1)
Titanic (W1)
The Waldorf Meridien (WC2)

West
Balans (SW3, SW5, W8)
Blakes Hotel (SW7)

Café Grove (W11)
Café Laville (W2)
Chelsea Bun Diner (SW10)
Chelsea Kitchen (SW3)
Conrad Hotel (SW10)
Coopers Arms (SW3)
The Enterprise (SW3)
The Fine Line (SW10)
Foxtrot Oscar (SW3)
Front Page (SW3)
The Gasworks (SW6)
Glaisters (SW10)
Queen's Head (W6)
Ruby in the Dust (SW6, W11)
Saints (W11)
The Scarsdale (W8)
606 Club (SW10)
Sporting Page (SW10)
Stock Pot (SW3)
Windsor Castle (W8)
Wine Gallery (SW10)
Wiz (W11)

North
Angel of the North (N1)
Banners (N8)
Barracuda (N16)
Browns (N1)
The Fox Reformed (N16)
The Gate (NW3)*
Heartstone (NW1)*
House on Rosslyn Hill (NW3)
Ruby in the Dust (N1, NW1)
Sauce (NW1)
Shish (NW2)
Toast (NW3)

South
Alma (SW18)
Browns (SW13)
Chelsea Bun Diner (SW11)
Delfina Studio Café (SE1)
Duke of Cambridge (SW11)
Film Café (SE1)
The Fine Line (SW11, SW4)
Foxtrot Oscar (SW11)
Glaisters (SW13)
Naked Turtle (SW14)
The Sequel (SW4)
The Ship (SW18)
So.uk (SW4)
Tate Modern (SE1)
White Cross (TW9)
The White House (SW4)

East
Al's (EC1)
Brasserie Rocque (EC2)
Browns (EC2)
DK's (EC2)*
The Fine Line (E14, EC3, EC4)
Foxtrot Oscar (EC3)

Mustards Brasserie *(EC1)*
Twentyfour *(EC2)*
Wapping Food *(E1)*

EAST/WEST

Central
Archipelago *(W1)**
Asia de Cuba *(WC2)*
Bam-Bou *(W1)*
Mju *(SW1)*
Nobu *(W1)**
The Providores *(W1)**
The Sugar Club *(W1)**
Vong *(SW1)**

West
Bali Sugar *(W11)**
I Thai *(W2)*
Rain *(W10)*

South
Champor-Champor *(SE1)**
Cinnamon Cay *(SW11)**

East
Just The Bridge *(EC4)*
Tao *(EC4)*
Ubon *(E14)**

FISH & SEAFOOD

Central
Back to Basics *(W1)**
Bank *(WC2)*
Belgo Centraal *(WC2)*
Bentley's *(W1)**
Café Fish *(W1)*
Fung Shing *(WC2)**
Green's *(SW1)*
Kaspia *(W1)*
Livebait *(WC2)*
Manzi's *(WC2)*
Motcombs *(SW1)*
Le Palais du Jardin *(WC2)*
Quaglino's *(SW1)*
Rasa Samudra *(W1)**
Restaurant One-O-
One *(SW1)**
Rib Room *(SW1)*
Savoy Upstairs *(WC2)*
Scott's *(W1)*
J Sheekey *(WC2)**
Wiltons *(SW1)*
Zilli Fish *(W1)**
Zilli Fish Too *(WC2)*

West
Belgo Zuid *(W10)*
Bibendum Oyster Bar *(SW3)**
Big Easy *(SW3)*
Catch *(SW5)*
Costa's Fish *(W8)**

Creelers *(SW3)*
fish! *(SW6)*
Ghillies *(SW6)*
Jason's *(W9)**
Livebait *(SW10, W8)*
Loch Fyne *(SW6)*
Lou Pescadou *(SW5)*
Mandarin Kitchen *(W2)**
Poissonnerie
  de l'Avenue *(SW3)**
Stratford's *(W8)*
Le Suquet *(SW3)**
Zilli *(W11)*

North
Belgo Noord *(NW1)*
Bradley's *(NW3)**
Chez Liline *(N4)**
Loch Fyne *(N8)*

South
Bah Humbug *(SW2)*
fish! *(SE1, SW15, SW8)*
Gastro *(SW4)*
Ghillies *(SW18)*
Livebait *(SE1, SW18)*
Lobster Pot *(SE11)**
Loch Fyne *(TW2)*
Polygon Bar & Grill *(SW4)*
Le Pont de la Tour
  Bar & Grill *(SE1)*

East
Aquarium *(E1)*
Chamberlain's *(EC3)*
fish! *(E14)*
Fishmarket *(EC2)*
Gow's *(EC2)*
The Grapes *(E14)**
Home *(EC1)*
Livebait *(EC4)*
Moro *(EC1)**
Rudland & Stubbs *(EC1)*
Stream *(EC1)*
Sweetings *(EC4)**
Vertigo *(EC2)*
The Vestry *(EC3)*
The Well *(EC1)*

STEAKS & GRILLS

Central
Chez Gérard *(W1, WC2)*
Christopher's *(SW1, WC2)*
Gaucho Grill *(W1, WC2)**
The Guinea *(W1)*
prospectGrill *(WC2)*
Quaglino's *(SW1)*
Rib Room *(SW1)*
Smollensky's *(WC2)*
Tuscan Steak *(WC2)*
Wolfe's *(WC2)*

West
Black & Blue *(W8)*
El Gaucho *(SW10, SW3)**
Gaucho Grill *(SW3)**
Popeseye *(W14)**
Rodizio Rico *(W2)*
Rôtisserie *(W12)**
Rôtisserie Jules *(SW7, W11)*

North
Camden Brasserie *(NW1)*
Gaucho Grill *(NW3)**
Rôtisserie *(N1)**

South
Chez Gérard *(SE1)*
La Pampa *(SW11)**
Polygon Bar & Grill *(SW4)*
Le Pont de la Tour
  Bar & Grill *(SE1)*
Popeseye *(SW15)**

East
Arkansas Café *(E1)**
Chez Gérard *(EC1, EC2, EC3)*
Fox & Anchor *(EC1)*
Gaucho Grill *(E14, EC3)**
Hope & Sir Loin *(EC1)*
Simpson's Tavern *(EC3)*
Smiths of Smithfield *(EC1)*

ORGANIC (CERTIFIED)

Central
Quiet Revolution *(W1)**

West
Organic Café *(SW7)*

North
The Duke of Cambridge *(N1)*
Heartstone *(NW1)**
Organic Café *(NW6)*
Sauce *(NW1)*

East
Quiet Revolution *(EC1)**

VEGETARIAN

Central
Chiang Mai *(W1)**
Cranks *(W1, WC2)*
Dorchester Grill *(W1)*
Food for Thought *(WC2)**
India Club *(WC2)*
The Lanesborough *(SW1)*
Malabar Junction *(WC1)**
Masala Zone *(W1)**
Mildreds *(W1)**
La Porte des Indes *(W1)**
Ragam *(W1)*
Rasa *(W1)**
Rasa Samudra *(W1)**
Woodlands *(SW1, W1)*

World Food Café *(WC2)*

West
Blah! Blah! Blah! *(W12)**
Blue Elephant *(SW6)**
Blue Lagoon *(W14)**
Café Grove *(W11)*
The Gate *(W6)**

North
Bu San *(N7)*
Chutneys *(NW1)**
Diwana Bhel-Poori
  House *(NW1)*
The Gate *(NW3)**
Geeta *(NW6)**
Iznik *(N5)*
Jashan *(HA0)**
Manna *(NW3)**
Rani *(N3)**
Rasa *(N16)**
Sedir *(N1)*
Vijay *(NW6)**
Yum Yum *(N16)**

South
Bah Humbug *(SW2)*
Battersea Rickshaw *(SW11)*
The Honest Cabbage *(SE1)*
Kastoori *(SW17)**
Le Pont de la Tour *(SE1)*
Sree Krishna *(SW17)**

East
Carnevale *(EC1)**
Cranks *(E14)*
Futures *(EC2)*
Futures *(EC3)**
The Place Below *(EC2)**
Sri Siam City *(EC2)*

AMERICAN

Central
Christopher's *(SW1, WC2)*
Joe Allen *(WC2)*
Maxwell's *(WC2)*
Navajo Joe *(WC2)*
Planet Hollywood *(W1)*
Shoeless Joe's *(SW1, W1, WC2)*
Smollensky's *(WC2)*
TGI Friday's *(W1, WC2)*

West
Big Easy *(SW3)*
Dakota *(W11)*
Montana *(SW6)*
PJ's *(SW3)*
Shoeless Joe's *(SW6)*
TGI Friday's *(W2)*

North
Idaho *(N6)*
Maxwell's *(NW3)*

Santa Fe *(N1)*
Smollensky's *(NW3)*

South
Canyon *(TW10)*
The Common Room *(SW19)*

East
Arkansas Café *(E1)**
Babe Ruth's *(E1)*
Shoeless Joe's *(EC4)*

ARGENTINIAN

Central
Gaucho Grill *(W1, WC2)**

West
Gaucho Grill *(SW3)**

North
Gaucho Grill *(NW3)**

South
La Pampa *(SW11)**

East
Gaucho Grill *(E14, EC3)**

BRAZILIAN

West
Paulo's *(W6)*
Rodizio Rico *(W2)*

CUBAN

North
Cuba Libre *(N1)*

MEXICAN/TEXMEX

Central
Café Pacifico *(WC2)*
Down Mexico Way *(W1)*
La Perla *(WC2)*
Texas Embassy Cantina *(SW1)*

West
Coyote Café *(W4)*
La Perla *(SW6)*

South
Dixie's Bar & Grill *(SW11)*

East
Al's *(EC1)*

SOUTH AMERICAN

West
Cactus Blue *(SW3)*
El Gaucho *(SW10, SW3)**

North
La Piragua *(N1)*

South
Fina Estampa *(SE1)*

AFTERNOON TEA

Central
Aurora *(W1)**
Fifth Floor (Café) *(SW1)*
The Lanesborough *(SW1)*
Pâtisserie Valerie *(W1, WC2)*
Royal Academy *(W1)*
Villandry *(W1)*
The Waldorf Meridien *(WC2)*

West
Basil St Hotel *(SW3)*
Daquise *(SW7)*
Julie's Bar *(W11)*
Pâtisserie Valerie *(SW3)*

BURGERS, ETC

Central
Ed's Easy Diner *(W1)*
Hard Rock Café *(W1)*
Joe Allen *(WC2)*
Kettners *(W1)*
Maxwell's *(WC2)*
Planet Hollywood *(W1)*
prospectGrill *(WC2)*
The Rainforest Cafe *(W1)*
Smollensky's *(WC2)*
Tootsies *(W1)*
Wolfe's *(WC2)*

West
Big Easy *(SW3)*
Black & Blue *(W8)*
Ed's Easy Diner *(SW3)*
Foxtrot Oscar *(SW3)*
PJ's *(SW3)*
Ruby in the Dust *(SW6, W11)*
Sticky Fingers *(W8)*
Tootsies *(SW6, SW7, W11, W4)*

North
Ed's Easy Diner *(NW3)*
Maxwell's *(NW3)*
Ruby in the Dust *(N1, NW1)*
Sauce *(NW1)*
Tootsies *(NW3)*

South
Foxtrot Oscar *(SW11)*
Gourmet Burger
   Kitchen *(SW11)**
Tootsies *(SW13, SW4)*

East
Arkansas Café *(E1)**
Babe Ruth's *(E1)*
Foxtrot Oscar *(EC3)*
Smiths of Smithfield *(EC1)*

CRÊPES

West
Bluebird Café (SW3)
Le Shop (SW3)

South
Chez Lindsay (TW10)*

FISH & CHIPS

Central
Fryer's Delight (WC1)*
Seafresh (SW1)

West
Costa's Fish (W8)*
Geale's (W8)

North
Nautilus (NW6)*
North Sea Fish (WC1)*
Seashell (NW1)*
Toff's (N10)
Two Brothers (N3)*

South
Brady's (SW18)*

East
Faulkner's (E8)*

ICE CREAM

North
Marine Ices (NW3)

PIZZA

Central
Ask! Pizza (SW1, W1)
Caffè Uno (W1, WC2)
Crivelli's Garden (WC2)
Gourmet Pizza
  Company (W1)
Innecto (W1)
It's (NW1, W1, WC1)
Kettners (W1)
Mash (W1)
Oliveto (SW1)
Paparazzi Café (W1)
Pizza On The Park (SW1)
PizzaExpress (SW1, W1, WC1,
  WC2)
Pizzeria Condotti (W1)
Purple Sage (W1)
Rocket (W1)
La Spiga (W1)
La Spighetta (W1)
Strada (W1, WC2)
Zizzi (W1, WC2)

West
Ask! Pizza (SW3, SW6, SW7, W11,
  W2, W4, W8)
Basilico (SW6)*

Bersagliera (SW3)
Buona Sera (SW3)
Caffè Uno (W2, W4, W8)
Calzone (SW10, W11)
Da Mario (SW7)
La Delizia (SW3)
Friends (SW10)
It's (W11, W2, W4)
Made in Italy (SW3)*
Osteria Basilico (W11)*
Paparazzi Café (SW3)
Pizza Pomodoro (SW3)
PizzaExpress (SW10, SW3, SW6,
  W11, W14, W2, W4, W8)
Pucci Pizza (SW3)
The Red Pepper (W9)*
Spago (SW7)
Spiga (SW3)
Strada (SW6)
Wine Factory (W11)
Zizzi (W4)
Zucca (W11)

North
Ask! Pizza (N1, NW1, NW3)
La Brocca (NW6)
Caffè Uno (N1, N6, NW1, NW8)
Calzone (N1, NW3)
Cantina Italia (N1)
Casale Franco (N1)
Furnace (N1)*
Marine Ices (NW3)
PizzaExpress (N1, N6, NW1, NW3,
  NW8)
La Porchetta Pizzeria (N1, N4)
Strada (N1)
Zizzi (NW8)

South
Ask! Pizza (SE1, SW13)
Basilico (SW11, SW15)*
Buona Sera (SW11)
Caffè Uno (SW13)
Eco (SW4)*
Eco Brixton (SW9)*
Gourmet Pizza Co. (SE1)
La Lanterna (SE1)
Pizza Metro (SW11)*
PizzaExpress (SE1, SE11, SW11,
  SW13, SW14, SW15, SW18, SW4)
Pizzeria Castello (SE1)*
Strada (SW11)
Zizzi (SW11)

East
Ask! Pizza (EC1)
Il Bordello (E1)*
Gourmet Pizza Co. (E14)
Pizza Pomodoro (EC2)
PizzaExpress (E1, E14, EC1, EC2,
  EC3, EC4)
Scuzi (E14, EC1, EC3)
Strada (EC1)

SANDWICHES, CAKES, ETC

Central
Bar Italia (W1)
Caffè Nero (W1, WC2)
Coffee Republic (W1, WC2)
Eat (SW1, W1, WC1, WC2)
Maison Bertaux (W1)*
Pâtisserie Valerie (W1, WC2)
Paul (WC2)*
Pret A Manger (SW1, W1, WC1, WC2)
Royal Academy (W1)
Starbucks (SW1, W1, WC2)

West
Bluebird Café (SW3)
Café Grove (W11)
Caffè Nero (SW3, SW7, W11, W2, W4, W6)
Coffee Republic (SW10, SW3, SW6, SW7, W11, W2, W4, W8)
Dan's Bar (W11)
King's Road Café (SW3)
Lisboa Patisserie (W10)*
Pâtisserie Valerie (SW3)
Pret A Manger (SW3, W6, W8)
Starbucks (SW3, SW5, SW6, SW7, W11, W2, W8)
Tom's (W11)
Troubadour (SW5)*

North
Caffè Nero (NW1, NW3)
Chamomile (NW3)
Coffee Republic (N1, NW1)
Pret A Manger (N1, NW1)
Starbucks (NW8)

South
Boiled Egg (SW11)
Caffè Nero (SW11, SW15, SW4)
Coffee Republic (SW15)
Eat (SE1)
Konditor & Cook (SE1)*
Starbucks (SW11, SW4)

East
Brick Lane Beigel Bake (E1)*
Caffè Nero (EC2, EC3)
Coffee Republic (E1, E14, EC1, EC2, EC3, EC4)
Eat (E14, EC2, EC3, EC4)
Pret A Manger (EC1, EC2, EC4)
Starbucks (EC1, EC2, EC3, EC4)

SOUP

Central
Eat (SW1, W1, WC1, WC2)
Soup Opera (W1, WC2)
Soup Works (W1, WC2)

West
Soup Opera (SW5)

South
Eat (SE1)

East
Eat (E14, EC2, EC3, EC4)
Soup Opera (E14, EC2, EC3)

AFRO-CARIBBEAN

Central
Calabash (WC2)

North
Banners (N8)
Cottons (NW1)
Mango Room (NW1)*

MOROCCAN

Central
Momo (W1)
Tajine (W1)

West
Adams Café (W12)
Pasha (SW7)

North
Yima (NW1)

East
Moro (EC1)*

NORTH AFRICAN

Central
Ayoush (W1)
Souk (WC2)

West
Azou (W6)

North
Laurent (NW2)*

South
So.uk (SW4)

SOUTH AFRICAN

West
Springbok Café (W4)*

SUDANESE

West
Mandola (W11)

TUNISIAN

West
Adams Café (W12)

North
Laurent (NW2)*

ISRAELI

North
Solly's Exclusive (NW11)

KOSHER

Central
Reubens (W1)
Six-13 (W1)

North
Nautilus (NW6)*
Solly's Exclusive (NW11)

LEBANESE

Central
Al Hamra (W1)
Al Sultan (W1)*
Beiteddine (SW1)
Fairuz (W1)
Fakhreldine (W1)
Ishbilia (SW1)
Maroush (W1)*
Noura (SW1)

West
Beirut Express (W2)*
Maroush (SW3, W2)*
Phoenicia (W8)
Ranoush (W2)*

MIDDLE EASTERN

Central
Gaby's (WC2)*
Levant (W1)

North
Shish (NW2)
Solly's Exclusive (NW11)

PERSIAN

Central
Dish Dash (W1)

West
Alounak (W14, W2)*
Kandoo (W2)
Mohsen (W14)*
Yas (W14)*
Yas on the Park (W2)*

TURKISH

Central
Efes Kebab House (W1)
Ozer (W1)
Sofra (W1, WC2)

North
Gallipoli (N1)
Istanbul Iskembecisi (N16)

Iznik (N5)
Pasha (N1)*
Sedir (N1)

South
Tas (SE1)*

AFGHANI

Central
Caravan Serai (W1)*

North
Afghan Kitchen (N1)*

BURMESE

West
Mandalay (W2)*

CHINESE

Central
Aroma II (W1)
China City (WC2)
China House (W1)
Chuen Cheng Ku (W1)
Dorchester, Oriental (W1)*
Fung Shing (WC2)*
Golden Dragon (W1)*
Hakkasan (W1)*
Harbour City (W1)
Hunan (SW1)*
Jade Garden (W1)
Jenny Lo's (SW1)
Joy King Lau (W1)
Kai (W1)*
Ken Lo's Memories (SW1)*
Mekong (SW1)
Mr Chow (SW1)
Mr Kong (WC2)*
New Mayflower (W1)*
New World (W1)
The Orient (W1)*
Poons (WC2)
Poons, Lisle Street (WC2)
Royal China (W1)*
Wong Kei (W1)
Zen Central (W1)

West
Good Earth (SW3)*
Mandarin Kitchen (W2)*
Mao Tai (SW3, SW6)*
Mr Wing (SW5)*
Nanking (W6)
New Culture Rev'n (SW3, W11, W2)
Royal China (W2)*
Stick & Bowl (W8)
Zen (SW3)

North
Feng Shang (NW1)*

Gung-Ho *(NW6)**
New Culture Rev'n *(NI, NWI)*
Phoenix Palace *(NWI)**
Royal China *(NW8)**
Singapore Garden *(NW6)**
Weng Wah House *(NW3)**
ZeNW3 *(NW3)*

South
Four Regions *(SEI)*
Royal China *(SWI5)**

East
Imperial City *(EC3)*
Royal China *(EI4)**
Shanghai *(E8)**

CHINESE, DIM SUM

Central
Chuen Cheng Ku *(WI)*
Dorchester, Oriental *(WI)**
Golden Dragon *(WI)**
Harbour City *(WI)*
Jade Garden *(WI)*
Joy King Lau *(WI)*
New World *(WI)*
Royal China *(WI)**

West
Royal China *(W2)**
Zen *(SW3)*

North
Royal China *(NW8)**

South
Royal China *(SWI5)**

East
Royal China *(EI4)**
Shanghai *(E8)**

FRENCH-VIETNAMESE

Central
Bam-Bou *(WI)*

INDIAN

Central
Café Lazeez *(WI)*
Chor Bizarre *(WI)*
The Cinnamon Club *(SWI)**
Gopal's of Soho *(WI)**
India Club *(WC2)*
Malabar Junction *(WCI)**
Masala Zone *(WI)**
Mela *(WC2)**
La Porte des Indes *(WI)**
Quilon *(SWI)*
Ragam *(WI)*
Rasa *(WI)**
Rasa Samudra *(WI)**
Red Fort *(WI)*

Salloos *(SWI)**
Soho Spice *(WI)**
Tamarind *(WI)**
Veeraswamy *(WI)**
The Verandah *(SWI)**
Woodlands *(SWI, WI)*

West
Al-Waha *(W2)**
Anarkali *(W6)*
Bombay Brasserie *(SW7)**
Bombay Palace *(W2)**
Brilliant *(UB2)**
Café Lazeez *(SW7)*
Chula *(W6)*
Chutney Mary *(SWI0)**
Ginger *(W2)**
Haandi *(SW3)*
Khan's *(W2)*
Khan's of Kensington *(SW7)*
Khyber Pass *(SW7)*
Madhu's Brilliant *(UBI)**
Malabar *(W8)**
Nayaab *(SW6)*
Noor Jahan *(SW5)**
Standard Tandoori *(W2)**
Star of India *(SW5)**
Tandoori Lane *(SW6)*
Tandoori of Chelsea *(SW3)**
Vama *(SWI0)**
Zaika *(W8)*
Zaika Bazaar *(SW3)**

North
Anglo Asian Tandoori *(N16)*
Chutneys *(NWI)**
Diwana B-P House *(NWI)**
Geeta *(NW6)**
Great Nepalese *(NWI)*
Jashan *(HA0)**
The Parsee *(N19)**
Rani *(N3)**
Rasa *(N16)**
Sakonis *(HA0)**
Vijay *(NW6)**

South
Babur Brasserie *(SE23)**
Battersea Rickshaw *(SWII)*
Bengal Clipper *(SEI)**
Bombay Bicycle Club *(SWI2)**
Café Spice Namaste *(SWII)**
Kastoori *(SWI7)**
Ma Goa *(SWI5)**
Sakonis *(SWI7)**
Sarkhel's *(SWI8)**
Sree Krishna *(SWI7)**
3 Monkeys *(SE24)**

East
Café City Lazeez *(ECI)*
Café Indiya *(EI)**
Café Spice Namaste *(EI)**

Lahore Kebab House *(E1)**
Rupee Room *(EC2)*
Tabla *(E14)**

INDIAN, SOUTHERN

Central
India Club *(WC2)*
Malabar Junction *(WC1)**
Ragam *(W1)*
Rasa *(W1)**
Woodlands *(SW1, W1)*

North
Chutneys *(NW1)**
Geeta *(NW6)**
Rani *(N3)**
Rasa *(N16)**
Rasa Travancore *(N16)**
Vijay *(NW6)**

South
Coromandel *(SW11)**
Kastoori *(SW17)**
Sree Krishna *(SW17)**

INDONESIAN

Central
Melati *(W1)**
Trader Vics *(W1)*

JAPANESE

Central
Abeno *(WC1)**
Benihana *(W1)*
Defune *(W1)**
Gili Gulu *(WC2)*
Ichizen Noodle Bar *(W1)*
Ikeda *(W1)*
Ikkyu *(W1)**
Itsu *(W1)*
Japanese Canteen *(W1)*
Kulu Kulu *(W1)**
Matsuri *(SW1)**
Mitsukoshi *(SW1)**
Miyama *(W1)*
Mju *(SW1)*
Nobu *(W1)**
Satsuma *(W1)**
Shogun *(W1)**
Suntory *(SW1)*
Tokyo Diner *(WC2)*
Wagamama *(W1, WC1, WC2)*
Yo! Sushi *(W1, WC1)*
Yoshino *(W1)**
Yumi *(W1)*

West
Bar Japan *(SW5)**
Benihana *(SW3)*
Inaho *(W2)**

Itsu *(SW3)*
Wagamama *(W8)*
Yo! Sushi *(W2)*

North
Benihana *(NW3)*
Bu San *(N7)*
Café Japan *(NW11)**
Jin Kichi *(NW3)**
Sushi-Say *(NW2)**
Wagamama *(NW1)*
Wakaba *(NW3)**
Yo! Sushi *(NW3)*

South
Yo! Sushi *(SE1)*

East
Aykoku-Kaku *(EC4)*
City Miyama *(EC4)**
Japanese Canteen *(EC1, EC4)*
K10 *(EC2)**
Miyabi *(EC2)*
Moshi Moshi *(E14, EC2, EC4)*
Noto *(EC2, EC4)*
Tatsuso *(EC2)**
Ubon *(E14)**
Yo! Sushi *(EC1)*

KOREAN

Central
Kaya Korean *(W1)*

North
Bu San *(N7)*

MALAYSIAN

Central
Melati *(W1)**

West
Street Hawker *(W9)*

North
Singapore Garden *(NW6)**
Street Hawker *(NW6)*

East
Singapura *(EC2, EC3, EC4)*

PAKISTANI

Central
Salloos *(SW1)**

West
Nayaab *(SW6)*

East
Lahore Kebab House *(E1)**

PAN-ASIAN

Central
Cassia Oriental *(W1)**

Ichizen Noodle Bar *(W1)*
Just Oriental *(SW1)*
Mezzonine *(W1)*
Mongolian Barbecue *(WC2)*
Noodle Noodle *(SW1)*
Pan-Asian Canteen *(SW1)**
Wok Wok *(W1)*
Yatra *(W1)*

West
Aquasia *(SW10)*
Bonjour Vietnam *(SW6)*
Jim Thompson's *(SW6)*
Mongolian Barbecue *(W4)*
Southeast *(W9)*
Tiger Lil's *(W2)*
Uli *(W11)**
Wok Wok *(SW10, W4, W8)*
Yellow River Café *(W4)*

North
Oriental City *(NW9)**
Tiger Lil's *(N1)*
Wok Wok *(N1)*
Yellow River Café *(N1)*

South
The Banana Leaf
  Canteen *(SW11)*
Jim Thompson's *(SW15)*
Tiger Lil's *(SW4)*
Wok Wok *(SW11)*

East
Cicada *(EC1)**
East One *(EC1)*
Fusion *(EC2)*
Pacific Oriental *(EC2)*
Tao *(EC4)*
Touzai *(EC2)*
Yellow River Café *(E14)*

THAI

Central
Bangkok Brasserie *(SW1)*
Blue Jade *(SW1)**
Busaba Eathai *(W1)**
Chada *(W1)**
Chiang Mai *(W1)**
Mango Tree *(SW1)*
Manorom *(WC2)*
Nahm *(SW1)**
Noho *(W1)*
Silks & Spice *(W1)*
Sri Siam *(W1)*
Thai Pot *(W1, WC2)*
Thai Square *(SW1)*

West
Bangkok *(SW7)*
Bedlington Café *(W4)*
Ben's Thai *(W9)*
Blue Elephant *(SW6)**

Blue Lagoon *(W14)**
Busabong Too *(SW10)*
Café 209 *(SW6)*
Churchill Arms *(W8)**
Esarn Kheaw *(W12)**
Exhibition *(SW7)*
Krungtap *(SW10)*
Latymers *(W6)**
Old Parr's Head *(W14)*
The Papaya Tree *(W8)**
S&P Patara *(SW3)**
Sabai Sabai *(W6)**
Silks & Spice *(W4)*
Street Hawker *(W9)*
Tawana *(W2)**
The Thai *(SW7)*
Thai Bistro *(W4)*
Thai Break *(W8)**
Thai on the River *(SW10)*
Topsy-Tasty *(W4)*
The Walmer Castle *(W11)**

North
Noho *(NW3)*
Silks & Spice *(NW1)*
Street Hawker *(NW6)*
Tuk Tuk *(N1)*
Yelo *(N1)*
Yum Yum *(N16)**

South
Chada *(SW11)**
Fat Boy's *(TW1, W4)*
Kwan Thai *(SE1)*
The Old School Thai *(SW11)**
The Pepper Tree *(SW4)*
Talad Thai *(SW15)**
Thai Corner Café *(SE22)**
Thai Garden *(SW11)*
Thailand *(SE14)**

East
Elephant Royale *(E14)*
Silks & Spice *(EC4)*
Sri Siam City *(EC2)*
Sri Thai *(EC4)*

VIETNAMESE

Central
Mekong *(SW1)*
Opium *(W1)*
Saigon *(W1)*

West
Nam Long *(SW5)*

North
Viet-Anh *(NW1)**

East
Viet Hoa *(E2)**

AREA OVERVIEWS

CENTRAL

Soho, Covent Garden & Bloomsbury
(Parts of W1, all WC2 and WC1)

Price	Name	Cuisine	Ratings
£70+	Savoy Grill	*British, Traditional*	④❷❸
	Savoy River Restaurant	*International*	⑤❸❷
£60+	Conrad Gallagher	*British, Modern*	❷❷❷
	Lindsay House	"	❸❸❷
	Asia de Cuba	*East/West*	⑤④❸
£50+	Indigo	*British, Modern*	❷❷❷
	Teatro	"	④❸④
	The Admiralty	*French*	④④④
	The Criterion	"	④⑤❶
	Neal Street	*Italian*	❸❸④
	The Waldorf Meridien	*Afternoon tea*	④❸❷
£40+	Alastair Little	*British, Modern*	❷❷④
	Atlantic Bar & Grill	"	⑤⑤❸
	Attica	"	⑤⑤⑤
	Axis	"	❷❷❸
	Bank	"	❸❸❸
	Circus	"	④❸❸
	The Ivy	"	❷❶❶
	Mezzo	"	⑤⑤⑤
	115 at Hodgson's	"	④❸❸
	Sugar Reef	"	– – –
	West Street Restaurant	"	– – –
	Rules	*British, Traditional*	❸❷❶
	Simpsons-in-the-Strand	"	④④❸
	Beotys	*French*	④❷❸
	L'Escargot	"	❷❷❷
	Incognico	"	❷❸❸
	Quo Vadis	"	❸❸❸
	Randall & Aubin	"	❸❸❸
	Little Italy	*Italian*	④❸❷
	Luigi's	"	④④④
	Orso	"	❸❸❸
	The Sugar Club	*East/West*	❶❷❸
	Livebait	*Fish & seafood*	❸④④
	Manzi's	"	❸❸❸
	J Sheekey	"	❶❶❷
	Zilli Fish	"	❷❸❸
	Tuscan Steak	*Steaks & grills*	⑤❸④
	Christopher's	*American*	④④❸
	Red Fort	*Indian*	– – –
	Opium	*Vietnamese*	⑤⑤❷
£35+	a.k.a.	*British, Modern*	④④❸
	Alfred	"	❸❸④
	Aurora	"	❷❷❷

Blues	"	③②②
Café du Jardin	"	④③④
Le Deuxième	"	②②③
The Portrait	"	④⑤②
Red Cube	"	– – –
Six Degrees	"	⑤⑤⑤
Café des Amis du Vin	French	④③③
L'Estaminet	"	③②③
Maggiore's	"	③③③
Mon Plaisir	"	③③①
Le Palais du Jardin	"	③④②
La Trouvaille	"	②⑤④
Gay Hussar	Hungarian	④②②
Bertorelli's	Italian	④④④
Italian Kitchen	"	②②③
Vasco & Piero's Pavilion	"	③①③
Zilli Fish Too	"	③④④
Cigala	Spanish	④④④
Bohème Kitchen	International	③③②
Savoy Upstairs	"	④③③
Joe Allen	American	④④②
Smollensky's	"	⑤④④
La Spiga	Pizza	③③③
Café Lazeez	Indian	③④④

£30+	Belgo Centraal	Belgian	④④④
	All Bar One	British, Modern	④④④
	Andrew Edmunds	"	②①①
	Café Med	"	④③②
	The Court Restaurant	"	④④②
	The Lexington	"	④④③
	The Perseverance	"	②④④
	Royal Opera House Café	"	⑤⑤④
	Sway	"	③④④
	La Brasserie Townhouse	French	③②③
	Café Bohème	"	④③①
	Café Flo	"	⑤④④
	Chez Gérard	"	④④④
	Crivelli's Garden	Italian	④④④
	Il Forno	"	③③③
	Getti	"	⑤④⑤
	Strada	"	③③③
	St Moritz	Swiss	④③③
	Alphabet	International	③④③
	Balans	"	④③③
	Browns	"	④③③
	Sarastro	"	⑤③①
	Shampers	"	③②③
	Gaucho Grill	Steaks & grills	②③③
	prospectGrill	"	③②③
	Navajo Joe	American	④④③
	Shoeless Joe's	"	④⑤④
	TGI Friday's	"	⑤③④

			Rating
	Planet Hollywood	Burgers, etc	⑤④❸
	The Rainforest Cafe	"	⑤④❶
	Fung Shing	Chinese	❶④⑤
	Malabar Junction	Indian	❷❷❸
	Soho Spice	"	❷❸❸
	Mezzonine	Pan-Asian	⑤④④
	Chiang Mai	Thai	❶❸④
	Sri Siam	"	❸❸❸
	Saigon	Vietnamese	❸❸④
£25+	Bibo Cibo	British, Modern	❸❸❷
	Cork & Bottle	"	④④❷
	Corney & Barrow	"	⑤④④
	Ha! Ha!	"	❸④❸
	The Langley	British, Traditional	④④④
	Café Rouge	French	– – –
	Aperitivo	Italian	❸❷❸
	Buona Sera	"	❸④❷
	Caffè Uno	"	④❸④
	Rusticana	"	❸❸④
	Hujo's	Mediterranean	④❸❸
	Boulevard	International	❸❸❸
	Dôme	"	– – –
	The Fine Line	"	④⑤④
	Maxwell's	American	④④❸
	Café Pacifico	Mexican/TexMex	④⑤❸
	La Perla	"	④❷❸
	Wolfe's	Burgers, etc	④④④
	North Sea Fish	Fish & chips	❷❷④
	Kettners	Pizza	⑤④❸
	Souk	North African	④❷❶
	Sofra	Turkish	④❸④
	Aroma II	Chinese	❸④④
	Chuen Cheng Ku	"	❸④④
	Harbour City	"	❸④⑤
	Jade Garden	"	❸④④
	New Mayflower	"	❷⑤⑤
	New World	"	❸④❸
	Gopal's of Soho	Indian	❷④④
	Abeno	Japanese	❷❶❸
	Itsu	"	❸❸❷
	Satsuma	"	❷④❸
	Yo! Sushi	"	④④④
	Melati	Malaysian	❷❸⑤
	Wok Wok	Pan-Asian	⑤④④
	Manorom	Thai	❸❸④
	Thai Pot	"	❸④④
£20+	Porters	British, Traditional	⑤⑤⑤
	Café Pasta	Italian	⑤④④
	Zizzi	"	④❸❸
	La Tasca	Spanish	❸❸❷
	Café Emm	International	④❸❸

	Gordon's Wine Bar	"	④❸❶
	Mildreds	Vegetarian	❷❷❷
	Ed's Easy Diner	Burgers, etc	④❸❷
	It's	Pizza	⑤❸❸
	PizzaExpress	"	④❸❸
	Pâtisserie Valerie	Sandwiches, cakes, etc	❸④❷
	Calabash	Afro-Caribbean	④④④
	Gaby's	Middle Eastern	❷④④
	China City	Chinese	❸④❸
	Golden Dragon	"	❷⑤④
	Joy King Lau	"	❸④④
	Mr Kong	"	❷❸④
	Poons	"	❸⑤④
	Mela	Indian	❷④❸
	Wagamama	Japanese	❸❸❸
	Mongolian Barbecue	Pan-Asian	⑤⑤④
	Busaba Eathai	Thai	❷❸❶
£15+	Jimmy's	Greek	④❷❷
	Bistro 1	Mediterranean	❸❷❷
	Star Café	International	❸❷❸
	Food for Thought	Vegetarian	❷④④
	World Food Café	"	❸④④
	Poons, Lisle Street	Chinese	❸④④
	Wong Kei	"	❸⑤⑤
	India Club	Indian	④④⑤
	Masala Zone	"	❷❷❸
	Gili Gulu	Japanese	④④❸
	Kulu Kulu	"	❷④④
	Tokyo Diner	"	④❸④
£10+	Pollo	Italian	⑤④❸
	Stock Pot	International	④❸❸
	Cranks	Vegetarian	④④④
	Caffè Nero	Sandwiches, cakes, etc	❸❸❸
£5+	Fryer's Delight	Fish & chips	❷❷④
	Bar Italia	Sandwiches, cakes, etc	❸❸❶
	Coffee Republic	"	❸❸❸
	Eat	"	❸❸④
	Maison Bertaux	"	❷❸❷
	Paul	"	❷❶❷
	Pret A Manger	"	❸❷④
	Starbucks	"	④④④
	Soup Opera	Soup	❸❸④
	Soup Works	"	❸❸④

Mayfair & St James's (Parts of W1 and SW1)

Price	Name	Cuisine	Ratings
£80+	Connaught	British, Traditional	3 1 2
	cheznico	French	3 4 5
	Le Gavroche	"	1 1 3
	G Ramsay at Claridges	"	– – –
	Dorchester, Oriental	Chinese	2 4 4
£70+	The Ritz	French	4 2 1
	The Square	"	2 3 3
	Windows on the World	"	5 5 2
	Suntory	Japanese	3 4 5
£60+	Dorchester Grill	British, Traditional	3 2 2
	Oak Room MPW	French	3 3 4
	Pétrus	"	1 2 3
	Le Soufflé	"	2 1 4
	FireBird	Russian	3 3 3
	Kaspia	"	3 4 4
	The Guinea	Steaks & grills	3 4 4
	Ikeda	Japanese	4 3 5
£50+	Che	British, Modern	4 4 4
	Greenhouse	"	– – –
	Nicole's	"	3 3 3
	Noble Rot	"	3 3 3
	Rhodes in the Square	"	2 2 3
	Scott's	"	3 3 4
	Six-13	"	4 4 3
	Wiltons	British, Traditional	3 3 2
	1837	French	3 3 3
	Mirabelle	"	2 2 2
	L'Oranger	"	2 2 2
	Terrace	"	4 4 4
	Sartoria	Italian	5 4 4
	Nobu	East/West	1 3 2
	Zen Central	Chinese	3 3 4
	Trader Vics	Indonesian	4 3 1
	Matsuri	Japanese	2 2 4
	Mitsukoshi	"	2 2 5
	Miyama	"	3 2 5
	Shogun	"	2 3 4
£40+	The Avenue	British, Modern	4 4 4
	Bank Westminster	"	4 3 3
	Le Caprice	"	2 1 1
	Hush	"	4 4 3
	Jago	"	4 4 4
	Langan's Brasserie	"	4 4 2
	Opus 70	"	4 2 4
	Quaglino's	"	5 5 4
	Rowley's	"	5 4 5

	Green's	British, Traditional	❸❸❷
	Café Nikolaj	French	❸❸④
	L'Odéon	"	④④④
	Alloro	Italian	❸④❸
	Bice	"	④❸④
	Cecconi's	"	❸❸❸
	Diverso	"	❸❸④
	Teca	"	❶❷❸
	Dover Street	International	⑤⑤④
	Titanic	"	⑤⑤⑤
	Bentley's	Fish & seafood	❷❷❸
	Momo	Moroccan	④❸❶
	Fakhreldine	Lebanese	❸④⑤
	Hakkasan	Chinese	❷❸❶
	Kai	"	❷❶❷
	The Orient	"	❷❷❸
	Chor Bizarre	Indian	❸❸❸
	Quilon	"	❸❷④
	Tamarind	"	❶❷❷
	Benihana	Japanese	❸❸④
	Kaya Korean	Korean	④④⑤
	Yatra	Pan-Asian	④❷④
£35+	The Marquis	British, Modern	❸❶④
	Mash Mayfair	"	⑤⑤⑤
	Morton's	"	④❸❸
	Sotheby's Café	"	❸❷❷
	Zinc	"	⑤⑤⑤
	Boudin Blanc	French	❸❸❷
	Baraonda	Italian	❸④④
	Franco's	"	④❸❸
	Serafino	"	④❶④
	Il Vicolo	"	❷❷④
	Café Fish	Fish & seafood	❸④④
	Down Mexico Way	Mexican/TexMex	⑤⑤④
	Al Hamra	Lebanese	❸④④
	Al Sultan	"	❷❷④
	Veeraswamy	Indian	❷❸❸
	Cassia Oriental	Pan-Asian	❷❸❸
£30+	All Bar One	British, Modern	④④④
	Fortnum's Fountain	"	❸❷❸
	The Little Square	"	④❸④
	Café Flo	French	⑤④④
	Chez Gérard	"	④④④
	Al Duca	Italian	❷❷❸
	Getti	"	⑤④⑤
	Ristorante Italiano	"	⑤❸④
	Strada	"	❸❸❸
	Browns	International	④❸❸
	Hanover Square	"	④④④
	Tiger Tiger	"	⑤⑤④

	Gaucho Grill	Steaks & grills	❷❸❸
	Shoeless Joe's	American	④⑤④
	Paparazzi Café	Pizza	④④❸
	Levant	Middle Eastern	④❷❷
	China House	Chinese	④⑤④
	Rasa	Indian	❶❶❸
	Yoshino	Japanese	❶❷❸
	Bangkok Brasserie	Thai	④④④
	Thai Square	"	❸❷❸
£25+	L'Artiste Musclé	French	④❸❷
	Caffè Uno	Italian	④❸④
	Quod	"	④④④
	Rocket	Mediterranean	❸❸❷
	Truc Vert	"	❸④⑤
	Hard Rock Café	Burgers, etc	④❷❷
	Gourmet Pizza Co.	Pizza	❸④④
	Pizzeria Condotti	"	❸❷❸
	Sofra	Turkish	④❸④
	Thai Pot	Thai	❸④④
£20+	Ask! Pizza	Pizza	④❸❷
	It's	"	⑤❸❸
	PizzaExpress	"	④❸❸
	Woodlands	Indian	❸❸④
	Noodle Noodle	Pan-Asian	④④④
£15+	Royal Academy	Sandwiches, cakes, etc	④④④
£10+	Stock Pot	International	④❸❸
	Caffè Nero	Sandwiches, cakes, etc	❸❸❸
£5+	Coffee Republic	Sandwiches, cakes, etc	❸❸❸
	Eat	"	❸❸④
	Pret A Manger	"	❸❷④
	Starbucks	"	④④④
	Soup Opera	Soup	❸❸④

Fitzrovia & Marylebone (Part of W1)

£70+	Pied à Terre	French	❷❸④
	Spoon +	International	⑤⑤⑤
£50+	Orrery	French	❷❷❷
	Archipelago	East/West	❷❷❶
	Defune	Japanese	❶❸❸
	Yumi	"	❸❷④
£40+	Blandford Street	British, Modern	❷❸④
	Charlotte Street Hotel	"	⑤❸④
	Mash	"	⑤⑤⑤
	Odin's	British, Traditional	❷❶❶
	Elena's L'Etoile	French	❸❷❷

	Caldesi	*Italian*	③	③	④
	Ibla	"	②	③	④
	Passione	"	①	①	②
	The Providores	*East/West*	②	②	③
	Bam-Bou	*French-Vietnamese*	④	④	②
	La Porte des Indes	*Indian*	②	②	①
£35+	Le Muscadet	*French*	③	④	⑤
	Nico Central	"	④	④	⑤
	Villandry	"	③	④	④
	Bertorelli's	*Italian*	④	④	④
	Hardy's	*International*	③	③	③
	Back to Basics	*Fish & seafood*	①	③	③
	Ayoush	*North African*	⑤	④	②
	Reubens	*Kosher*	③	④	⑤
	Maroush	*Lebanese*	②	④	④
	Ozer	*Turkish*	③	③	③
	Rasa Samudra	*Indian*	①	②	③
	Chada	*Thai*	②	③	④
£30+	All Bar One	*British, Modern*	④	④	④
	No 6	"	②	④	④
	The Union Café	"	③	③	③
	Stanleys	*British, Traditional*	④	③	③
	Café Bagatelle	*French*	④	④	②
	Langan's Bistro	"	③	③	③
	O'Conor Don	*Irish*	④	③	③
	Getti	*Italian*	⑤	④	⑤
	Purple Sage	"	④	④	④
	La Spighetta	"	③	②	④
	La Rueda	*Spanish*	③	③	②
	Dish Dash	*Persian*	④	④	②
	Royal China	*Chinese*	①	③	④
	Silks & Spice	*Thai*	③	③	③
£25+	Giraffe	*British, Modern*	③	②	②
	Ha! Ha!	"	③	④	③
	The Mortimer	"	③	④	④
	RIBA Cafe	"	④	④	④
	Auberge	*French*	③	④	④
	Café Rouge	"	–	–	–
	Caffè Uno	*Italian*	④	③	④
	Garbo's	*Scandinavian*	④	③	④
	Tootsies	*Burgers, etc*	④	③	④
	Tajine	*Moroccan*	③	②	③
	Fairuz	*Lebanese*	③	③	③
	Efes Kebab House	*Turkish*	③	③	③
	Sofra	"	④	③	④
	Caravan Serai	*Afghan*	②	③	④
	Ichizen Noodle Bar	*Japanese*	③	②	②
	Ikkyu	"	②	④	③
	Japanese Canteen	"	④	④	④

			Rating
	Noho	Thai	⑤④④
£20+	Carluccio's Caffè	Italian	❸❸❸
	Zizzi	"	④❸❸
	Quiet Revolution	Organic	❷❸❷
	Ask! Pizza	Pizza	④❸❷
	It's	"	⑤❸❸
	PizzaExpress	"	④❸❸
	Pâtisserie Valerie	Sandwiches, cakes, etc	❸④❷
	Ragam	Indian	❸❷⑤
	Woodlands	"	❸❸④
	Wagamama	Japanese	❸❸❸
£10+	Stock Pot	International	④❸❸
	Cranks	Vegetarian	④④④
	Caffè Nero	Sandwiches, cakes, etc	❸❸❸
£5+	Coffee Republic	Sandwiches, cakes, etc	❸❸❸
	Pret A Manger	"	❸❷④
	Starbucks	"	④④④
	Soup Works	Soup	❸❸④

Belgravia, Pimlico, Victoria & Westminster (SW1, except St James's)

			Rating
£80+	La Tante Claire	French	❸❷④
£70+	Mju	East/West	④❷❸
£60+	Foliage	French	❷❸④
	Rib Room	Steaks & grills	④❸④
	Nahm	Thai	❷❸④
£50+	The Fifth Floor	British, Modern	④④④
	The Lanesborough	"	④❷❶
	Goring Hotel	British, Traditional	❸❶❷
	Drones	French	④❸④
	Restaurant One-O-One	"	❶❶❸
	Grissini	Italian	④❸④
	L'Incontro	"	④④④
	Mimmo d'Ischia	"	④❸❸
	Santini	"	❸④⑤
	Vong	East/West	❷❸❸
£40+	Motcombs	British, Modern	④❸④
	Tate Britain	"	④❸❷
	La Poule au Pot	French	❷❷❶
	Roussillon	"	❶❷❸
	Simply Nico	"	④④④
	La Fontana	Italian	④④④
	Isola	"	– – –
	Sale e Pepe	"	❸❷❷
	Signor Sassi	"	❸❷❷
	Toto's	"	❷❶❶

	Zafferano	"	❶❶❷
	Monte's	Mediterranean	❸❸❹
	Boisdale	Scottish	❸❸❷
	Just St James	International	❹❹❹
	Christopher's	American	❹❹❸
	Ken Lo's Memories	Chinese	❶❷❸
	Mr Chow	"	❸❷❷
	The Cinnamon Club	Indian	❶❷❷
	Salloos	"	❶❸❹
	Mango Tree	Thai	❹❷❹
£35+	Atrium	British, Modern	❺❺❹
	Ebury Street Wine Bar	"	❹❹❸
	Grenadier	British, Traditional	❹❹❷
	Shepherd's	"	❸❸❸
	Caraffini	Italian	❷❶❷
	Como Lario	"	❹❷❸
	Il Convivio	"	❷❷❷
	Olivo	"	❸❸❹
	Sambuca	"	❸❷❹
	Fifth Floor (Café)	Mediterranean	❹❹❹
	Pomegranates	International	❸❷❷
	Oliveto	Pizza	❸❹❺
	Beiteddine	Lebanese	❸❷❹
	Noura	"	❸❷❹
£30+	Uno	Italian	❸❹❹
	Goya	Spanish	❹❸❷
	Footstool	International	❺❺❸
	Grumbles	"	❹❸❷
	Oriel	"	❺❹❸
	Ishbilia	Lebanese	❸❷❹
	Hunan	Chinese	❶❶❸
	Just Oriental	Pan-Asian	❹❷❸
£25+	Pizza On The Park	Italian	❹❸❷
	Royal Court Bar	International	❹❹❹
	Texas Embassy Cantina	Mexican/TexMex	❺❹❹
	Blue Jade	Thai	❷❷❷
£20+	Chimes	British, Traditional	❺❹❸
	Marché Mövenpick	Swiss	❹❺❺
	Brahms	International	❸❷❹
	Seafresh	Fish & chips	❹❹❹
	Ask! Pizza	Pizza	❹❸❷
	PizzaExpress	"	❹❸❸
	The Verandah	Indian	❷❷❹
	Pan-Asian Canteen	Pan-Asian	❷❷❸
	Mekong	Vietnamese	❸❷❹
£15+	Jenny Lo's	Chinese	❸❷❸
£5+	Pret A Manger	Sandwiches, cakes, etc	❸❷❹
	Starbucks	"	❹❹❹

WEST

Chelsea, South Kensington, Kensington, Earl's Court & Fulham (SW3, SW5, SW6, SW7, SW10 & W8)

£80+	Gordon Ramsay	French	❶❶❷
	Blakes Hotel	International	④❸❶
£70+	Capital Hotel	French	❷❷❸
£60+	Babylon	British, Modern	⑤❸❷
	Aubergine	French	❷❷❸
	Bibendum	"	④④❸
	Monkeys	"	❷❷❶
£50+	Clarke's	British, Modern	❶❶❷
	The Tenth	"	❷❷❷
	Belvedere	French	④❸❶
	Turner's	"	④❸④
	Daphne's	Italian	④④❸
	Floriana	"	❸❸❸
	San Lorenzo	"	⑤⑤❸
	Poissonnerie de l'Avenue	Fish & seafood	❷❷❸
£40+	Bluebird	British, Modern	⑤⑤⑤
	The Collection	"	④⑤❸
	English Garden	"	❸④④
	Goolies	"	❷❷❸
	The House	"	❸❷❸
	Kensington Place	"	④④❸
	Launceston Place	"	❷❷❶
	The Terrace	"	❸❷❷
	Chezmax	French	❶❶❷
	Randall & Aubin	"	❸❸❸
	Le Suquet	"	❷④❸
	La Famiglia	Italian	❸❸❷
	Montpeliano	"	❸❷❸
	Il Portico	"	④❷❸
	Scalini	"	❸❸❷
	El Blasón	Spanish	❸❷④
	Conrad Hotel	International	❸❸❸
	606 Club	"	⑤④❷
	Livebait	Fish & seafood	❸④④
	Montana	American	④④④
	Pasha	Moroccan	❸❸❶
	Mr Wing	Chinese	❷❷❶
	Bombay Brasserie	Indian	❷❷❷
	Chutney Mary	"	❷❸❸
	Tandoori of Chelsea	"	❷❷❸
	Zaika	"	– – –
	Benihana	Japanese	❸❸④
	Aquasia	Pan-Asian	❸❸❸

	Blue Elephant	*Thai*	②②❶
£35+	The Abingdon	*British, Modern*	❸❸❸
	Admiral Codrington	"	❸❸❸
	Arcadia	"	④②❸
	Bistrot 190	"	⑤④④
	Catch	"	❸❸④
	Creelers	"	❸❸⑤
	Dan's	"	❸②②
	Joe's Café	"	④④②
	The Salisbury Tavern	"	❸②❸
	Basil St Hotel	*British, Traditional*	④②②
	Maggie Jones's	"	④❸❶
	Lundum's	*Danish*	②❶❶
	La Brasserie	*French*	⑤⑤④
	Brasserie St Quentin	"	④❸④
	Le Colombier	"	❸②②
	Langan's Coq d'Or	"	④④❸
	Lou Pescadou	"	❸❸④
	Parisienne Chophouse	"	④④④
	Le Potiron Sauvage	"	– – –
	Thierry's	"	⑤④❸
	The Ark	*Italian*	④④❸
	Formula Veneta	"	④❸④
	Frantoio	"	④❸❸
	Monza	"	❸❶❸
	Pellicano	"	❸④④
	San Frediano	"	④④⑤
	Sandrini	"	❸❸❸
	Ziani	"	②②②
	Chives	*Mediterranean*	②❸④
	Wódka	*Polish*	❸❸❸
	Nikita's	*Russian*	⑤④④
	Cambio de Tercio	*Spanish*	②❶❶
	The Enterprise	*International*	④❸②
	Bibendum Oyster Bar	*Fish & seafood*	❶❸②
	Stratford's	"	❸②④
	Organic Café	*Organic*	④④④
	Big Easy	*American*	④④❸
	PJ's	"	④④❸
	Spiga	*Pizza*	❸❸❸
	Maroush	*Lebanese*	②④④
	Phoenicia	"	❸②❸
	Good Earth	*Chinese*	②❸④
	Mao Tai	"	②②❸
	Zen	"	❸④④
	Café Lazeez	*Indian*	❸④④
	Star of India	"	②❸❸
	Vama	"	❶②❸
	S&P	*Thai*	②②❸
	Thai on the River	"	❸②②
	Nam Long	*Vietnamese*	④④②

£30+	Abbaye	*Belgian*	④⑤④
	All Bar One	*British, Modern*	④④④
	Brinkley's	*"*	④④❷
	The Chelsea Ram	*"*	❷④❷
	The Ifield	*"*	❸④❸
	Le Metro	*"*	❸❷④
	The Pen	*"*	❸❷❷
	Vingt-Quatre	*"*	④❸❸
	Ffiona's	*British, Traditional*	❸①❷
	Le Bon Choix	*French*	❸❷❸
	La Bouchée	*"*	❸❸❷
	Café Flo	*"*	⑤④④
	I Cardi	*Italian*	❸❷④
	Da Mario	*"*	❸④❸
	De Cecco	*"*	❷❷①
	Elistano	*"*	❷❷❷
	Made in Italy	*"*	❷④❷
	Strada	*"*	❸❸❸
	Cross Keys	*Mediterranean*	④④❸
	The Polish Club	*Polish*	④❷①
	La Rueda	*Spanish*	❸❸❷
	Balans	*International*	④❸❸
	The Gasworks	*"*	⑤④❷
	Glaisters	*"*	④④❸
	fish!	*Fish & seafood*	❸❸④
	Ghillies	*"*	④❸❷
	Loch Fyne	*"*	④④❸
	Black & Blue	*Steaks & grills*	④❸❸
	Gaucho Grill	*"*	❷❸❸
	Shoeless Joe's	*American*	④⑤④
	Cactus Blue	*South American*	④④❸
	Friends	*Pizza*	❸④❸
	Paparazzi Café	*"*	④④❸
	Bluebird Café	*Sandwiches, cakes, etc*	⑤⑤④
	Haandi	*Indian*	❸④④
	Bangkok	*Thai*	❸❸④
	Busabong Too	*"*	❸④❸
	Exhibition	*"*	❸❸④
	The Papaya Tree	*"*	❷❷④
	The Thai	*"*	④④④
£25+	The Builder's Arms	*British, Modern*	❷④❷
	The Crescent	*"*	④❸④
	Joe's Brasserie	*"*	– – –
	Lots Road	*"*	❷❷❷
	White Horse	*"*	❸❸❸
	Café Rouge	*French*	– – –
	Francofill	*"*	④④④
	Aglio e Olio	*Italian*	❷❸❸
	Buona Sera	*"*	❸④❷
	Caffè Uno	*"*	④❸④
	Il Falconiere	*"*	❸❸④

	Picasso	"	4 3 3
	Riccardo's	"	3 3 3
	Spago	"	3 4 3
	Soviet Canteen	Russian	3 2 3
	Coopers Arms	International	3 4 3
	The Fine Line	"	4 5 4
	Foxtrot Oscar	"	4 4 4
	Ruby in the Dust	"	5 4 3
	The Scarsdale	"	4 3 2
	Sporting Page	"	4 2 2
	Windsor Castle	"	3 4 1
	Wine Gallery	"	5 3 2
	La Perla	Mexican/TexMex	4 2 3
	El Gaucho	South American	2 4 4
	Sticky Fingers	Burgers, etc	4 2 3
	Tootsies	"	4 3 4
	Le Shop	Crêpes	3 2 2
	Geale's	Fish & chips	3 3 5
	Basilico	Pizza	1 3 4
	Pizza Pomodoro	"	4 4 2
	Pucci Pizza	"	3 4 3
	Malabar	Indian	2 2 3
	Noor Jahan	"	2 2 3
	Tandoori Lane	"	3 1 3
	Zaika Bazaar	"	1 2 4
	Itsu	Japanese	3 3 2
	Jim Thompson's	Pan-Asian	3 4 2
	Wok Wok	"	5 4 4
	Thai Break	Thai	2 3 5
£20+	Bersagliera	Italian	4 4 3
	Café Pasta	"	5 4 4
	King's Road Café	"	4 3 3
	Il Pagliaccio	"	4 3 2
	The Atlas	Mediterranean	2 4 2
	Daquise	Polish	4 4 3
	Lomo	Spanish	3 1 2
	Chelsea Bun Diner	International	3 2 3
	Front Page	"	3 3 2
	Rôtisserie Jules	Steaks & grills	3 2 5
	Ed's Easy Diner	Burgers, etc	4 3 2
	Ask! Pizza	Pizza	4 3 2
	Calzone	"	3 3 4
	PizzaExpress	"	4 3 3
	Pâtisserie Valerie	Sandwiches, cakes, etc	3 4 2
	Troubadour	"	2 2 1
	Khan's of Kensington	Indian	3 3 4
	Khyber Pass	"	3 2 5
	Nayaab	"	3 3 5
	Bar Japan	Japanese	2 3 4
	Wagamama	"	3 3 3
	Bonjour Vietnam	Pan-Asian	5 5 5

	Krungtap	Thai	❸❸④
£15+	Costa's Grill	Greek	④④④
	Mona Lisa	Italian	❸❶❸
	Costa's Fish	Fish & chips	❷❷❸
	La Delizia	Pizza	❸④④
	New Culture Rev'n	Chinese	❸❸④
	Stick & Bowl	"	❸❷⑤
	Café 209	Thai	❸❷❶
	Churchill Arms	"	❷④❷
£10+	Chelsea Kitchen	International	④❸④
	Stock Pot	"	④❸❸
	Caffè Nero	Sandwiches, cakes, etc	❸❸❸
£5+	Coffee Republic	Sandwiches, cakes, etc	❸❸❸
	Pret A Manger	"	❸❷④
	Starbucks	"	④④④
	Soup Opera	Soup	❸❸④

Notting Hill, Holland Park, Bayswater, North Kensington & Maida Vale (W2, W9, W10, W11)

£70+	I Thai	East/West	④④❸
£40+	Julie's	British, Modern	④④❶
	Pharmacy	"	⑤⑤④
	Aix	French	❸❷❸
	Amandier	"	❸❷④
	Chez Moi	"	❷❶❷
	Al San Vincenzo	Italian	❷❷❸
	Assaggi	"	❶❶❷
	Orsino	"	④④❷
	Bali Sugar	East/West	❷❷❸
	Jason's	Fish & seafood	❷④❷
	Dakota	American	④④④
£35+	Alastair Little	British, Modern	❷❷④
	Beach Blanket Babylon	"	⑤⑤❷
	The Cow	"	❷❸❷
	Julie's Bar	"	④❸❶
	Manor	"	④④❷
	Notting Hill Brasserie	"	④❸❷
	192	"	⑤⑤④
	Otto	"	⑤⑤❸
	Twelfth House	"	④❷④
	Brass. du Marché	French	❸❸❷
	Halepi	Greek	④④④
	The Green Olive	Italian	❸❸❸
	Raccolto	"	❸④❷
	Zilli	"	④❷④
	Zucca	"	④❸④

	Mediterraneo	*Mediterranean*	② ③ ②
	Maroush	*Lebanese*	② ④ ④
	Bombay Palace	*Indian*	② ② ④
£30+	Belgo Zuid	*Belgian*	④ ④ ④
	All Bar One	*British, Modern*	④ ④ ④
	Café Med	"	④ ③ ②
	Gate	"	② ③ ③
	Golborne House	"	③ ③ ②
	The Ladbroke Arms	"	② ④ ③
	Père Michel	*French*	③ ④ ④
	L'Accento Italiano	*Italian*	③ ④ ④
	Osteria Basilico	"	② ③ ①
	The Red Pepper	"	② ④ ③
	Wiz	*International*	④ ③ ②
	Rain	*East/West*	③ ③ ②
	TGI Friday's	*American*	⑤ ③ ④
	Yas on the Park	*Persian*	② ④ ④
	Royal China	*Chinese*	① ③ ④
	Ginger	*Indian*	② ③ ②
	Inaho	*Japanese*	① ④ ③
£25+	Passion	*British, Modern*	② ② ⑤
	The Prince Bonaparte	"	③ ④ ②
	The Vale	"	③ ③ ③
	The Westbourne	"	④ ⑤ ①
	Café Rouge	*French*	– – –
	Caffè Uno	*Italian*	④ ③ ④
	Est Est Est	"	⑤ ⑤ ④
	Wine Factory	"	③ ③ ③
	Galicia	*Spanish*	③ ② ③
	Café Laville	*International*	④ ④ ①
	Ruby in the Dust	"	⑤ ④ ③
	Saints	"	④ ③ ③
	Rodizio Rico	*Brazilian*	③ ③ ③
	Tootsies	*Burgers, etc*	④ ③ ④
	Dan's Bar	*Sandwiches, cakes, etc*	④ ③ ③
	Tom's	"	③ ③ ③
	Mandarin Kitchen	*Chinese*	① ③ ④
	Al-Waha	*Indian*	② ② ④
	Yo! Sushi	*Japanese*	④ ④ ④
	Southeast	*Pan-Asian*	③ ③ ④
	Tiger Lil's	"	④ ③ ③
	Uli	"	② ② ③
	Street Hawker	*Thai*	④ ④ ④
	Tawana	"	② ③ ④
	The Walmer Castle	"	② ② ②
£20+	Raoul's Café	*British, Modern*	③ ④ ③
	Kalamaras	*Greek*	④ ③ ③
	Café Grove	*International*	④ ④ ③
	Rôtisserie Jules	*Steaks & grills*	③ ② ⑤

			Rating
	Ask! Pizza	Pizza	④❸❷
	Calzone	"	❸❸④
	It's	"	⑤❸❸
	PizzaExpress	"	④❸❸
	Mandola	Sudanese	❸④❷
	Ranoush	Lebanese	❶④④
	Alounak	Persian	❷❸❸
	Standard Tandoori	Indian	❷④④
	Ben's Thai	Thai	❸❸❸
£15+	Beirut Express	Lebanese	❶❸④
	Kandoo	Persian	❸❷❸
	Mandalay	Burmese	❷❶⑤
	New Culture Rev'n	Chinese	❸❸④
	Khan's	Indian	④⑤❸
£10+	Caffè Nero	Sandwiches, cakes, etc	❸❸❸
£5+	Coffee Republic	Sandwiches, cakes, etc	❸❸❸
	Lisboa Patisserie	"	❶❷❸
	Starbucks	"	④④④

Hammersmith, Shepherd's Bush, Olympia, Chiswick & Ealing (W4, W5, W6, W12, W14)

			Rating
£50+	The River Café	Italian	❷❸❸
£40+	Cibo	Italian	❷❸❸
£35+	Cotto	British, Modern	❸④④
	Parade	"	❷❷❷
	Chinon	French	❶❸❸
	Maquis	"	– – –
	La Trompette	"	❶❶❷
	Springbok Café	South African	❷❸❸
£30+	All Bar One	British, Modern	④④④
	Blythe Road	"	❸④④
	The Brackenbury	"	❸❸❸
	Bush Bar & Grill	"	④⑤❸
	Café Med	"	④❸❷
	Chiswick	"	❸❸④
	Gravy	"	④⑤④
	The Grove	"	④❸❸
	Snows on the Green	"	❸❸④
	Christian's	French	❸❷❸
	Palatino	Italian	❸❸④
	Riso	"	④④⑤
	Popeseye	Steaks & grills	❶❷④
	Rôtisserie	"	❷❶❸
	The Gate	Vegetarian	❶❷❷
	Silks & Spice	Thai	❸❸❸

			Ratings
£25+	The Anglesea Arms	*British, Modern*	①⑤③
	The Havelock Tavern	"	①④③
	Pug	"	④④④
	Stone Mason's Arms	"	③④②
	The Thatched House	"	③②②
	Café Rouge	*French*	– – –
	Caffè Uno	*Italian*	④③④
	Est Est Est	"	⑤⑤④
	Paulo's	*Brazilian*	③②④
	Coyote Café	*Mexican/TexMex*	③③③
	Tootsies	*Burgers, etc*	④③④
	Azou	*North African*	③②③
	Yas	*Persian*	②③③
	Nanking	*Chinese*	③③③
	Brilliant	*Indian*	②③④
	Chula	"	③④④
	Wok Wok	*Pan-Asian*	⑤④④
	Yellow River Café	"	④④④
	Blue Lagoon	*Thai*	②②③
	Esarn Kheaw	"	①④④
	Sabai Sabai	"	③②④
	Thai Bistro	"	③③④
£20+	The Bollo House	*British, Modern*	③②②
	Queen's Head	*British, Traditional*	④③②
	Zizzi	*Italian*	④③③
	Patio	*Polish*	③①②
	Blah! Blah! Blah!	*Vegetarian*	①②③
	Ask! Pizza	*Pizza*	④③②
	It's	"	⑤③③
	PizzaExpress	"	④③③
	Adams Café	*Moroccan*	③②③
	Alounak	*Persian*	②③③
	Anarkali	*Indian*	③③④
	Madhu's Brilliant	"	②③④
	Mongolian Barbecue	*Pan-Asian*	⑤⑤④
	Bedlington Café	*Thai*	③④⑤
	Latymers	"	②③⑤
	Old Parr's Head	"	③④③
	Topsy-Tasty	"	③④④
£15+	Mohsen	*Persian*	②③⑤
£10+	Caffè Nero	*Sandwiches, cakes, etc*	③③③
£5+	Coffee Republic	*Sandwiches, cakes, etc*	③③③
	Pret A Manger	"	③②④

NORTH

Hampstead, West Hampstead, St John's Wood, Regent's Park, Kilburn & Camden (NW postcodes)

£90+	John Burton-Race	*French*	④❸④
£40+	L'Aventure	*French*	❶❷❶
	The Landmark	"	④❸❸
	Oslo Court	"	❷❶❸
	Artigiano	*Italian*	❸❸❸
	Villa Bianca	"	④④❸
	Benihana	*Japanese*	❸❸④
	Wakaba	"	❷④⑤
£35+	Bradley's	*British, Modern*	❷❷❸
	Byron's	"	④❸❷
	The Engineer	"	❸④❷
	Odette's	"	❷❷❶
	Salon	"	❷❸❷
	Halepi	*Greek*	④④④
	The Black Truffle	*Italian*	❸❸❸
	Rosmarino	"	❸❸❸
	Toast	*International*	④④❸
	Organic Café	*Organic*	④④④
	Smollensky's	*American*	⑤④④
	ZeNW3	*Chinese*	❸❸❸
£30+	Belgo Noord	*Belgian*	④④④
	All Bar One	*British, Modern*	④④④
	Blakes	"	④④❸
	Café Med	"	④❸❷
	Cucina	"	❸❶❸
	Globe Restaurant	"	❸❷❸
	The Montrose	"	⑤⑤❸
	No 77 Wine Bar	"	④❸❷
	Quincy's	"	④❷❸
	The Salt House	"	❸❸❸
	The Vine	"	❸⑤❷
	Base	*French*	❸④❸
	Café Flo	"	⑤④④
	Camden Brasserie	"	❸❷❸
	MPW Brasserie	"	⑤⑤⑤
	Philpotts Mezzaluna	*Italian*	❷❷❸
	Vegia Zena	"	❸❷④
	Zuccato	"	④④④
	Gaucho Grill	*Steaks & grills*	❷❸❸
	The Gate	*Vegetarian*	❶❷❷
	Cottons	*Afro-Caribbean*	❸④❷
	Feng Shang	*Chinese*	❷❶❷
	Phoenix Palace	"	❷④④
	Royal China	"	❶❸④

	Jin Kichi	Japanese	❶❷❸
	Sushi-Say	"	❷❷❸
	Singapore Garden	Malaysian	❷❷④
	Silks & Spice	Thai	❸❸❸
£25+	The Chapel	British, Modern	❸④④
	Giraffe	"	❸❷❷
	Lansdowne	"	❸④❸
	Mims	"	❸④⑤
	The Queen's	"	❸❸❸
	William IV	"	❸❷❷
	911	British, Traditional	④④④
	Café Delancey	French	④❸❷
	Café Rouge	"	– – –
	La Cage Imaginaire	"	❸❷❸
	Lemonia	Greek	❸❶❷
	La Brocca	Italian	❸❸❷
	Caffè Uno	"	④❸④
	The Salusbury	"	❷❸❷
	Don Pepe	Spanish	❸❸❸
	House on Rosslyn Hill	International	⑤⑤④
	Ruby in the Dust	"	⑤④❸
	Heartstone	Organic	❷❸❸
	Sauce	"	❸❷④
	Manna	Vegetarian	❷❸❸
	Maxwell's	American	④④❸
	Tootsies	Burgers, etc	④❸④
	Mango Room	Afro-Caribbean	❷❸❶
	Gung-Ho	Chinese	❷❷❷
	Weng Wah House	"	❷❷❸
	Café Japan	Japanese	❶❸④
	Yo! Sushi	"	④④④
	Noho	Thai	⑤④④
	Street Hawker	"	④④④
£20+	The Lord Palmerston	British, Modern	❷❸❷
	Daphne	Greek	❸❷❸
	Café Pasta	Italian	⑤④④
	Marine Ices	"	❸❸❸
	Zizzi	"	④❸❸
	Zamoyski	Polish	⑤❷④
	Troika	Russian	④❷❸
	Bar Gansa	Spanish	❸❸❷
	Ed's Easy Diner	Burgers, etc	④❸❷
	Nautilus	Fish & chips	❷❸⑤
	Seashell	"	❷❸④
	Ask! Pizza	Pizza	④❸❷
	Calzone	"	❸❸④
	It's	"	⑤❸❸
	PizzaExpress	"	④❸❸
	Yima	Moroccan	❸④❷
	Laurent	Tunisian	❷❷⑤

	Solly's Exclusive	*Israeli*	③④③
	Shish	*Middle Eastern*	③④②
	Great Nepalese	*Indian*	③③③
	Wagamama	*Japanese*	③③③
£15+	Retsina	*Greek*	④②③
	The Little Bay	*Mediterranean*	③③②
	New Culture Revolution	*Chinese*	③③④
	Chutneys	*Indian*	②④④
	Diwana B-P House	*"*	②④④
	Geeta	*"*	①②⑤
	Jashan	*"*	②②④
	Sakonis	*"*	①③④
	Vijay	*"*	①②④
	Oriental City	*Pan-Asian*	②④④
	Viet-Anh	*Vietnamese*	①①③
£10+	Caffè Nero	*Sandwiches, cakes, etc*	③③③
	Chamomile	*"*	③③③
£5+	Coffee Republic	*Sandwiches, cakes, etc*	③③③
	Pret A Manger	*"*	③②④
	Starbucks	*"*	④④④

Hoxton, Islington, Highgate, Crouch End, Stoke Newington, Finsbury Park & Finchley (N postcodes)

£35+	Frederick's	*British, Modern*	②②①
	Granita	*"*	③③④
	Lola's	*"*	③③②
	The White Onion	*French*	– – –
	The Real Greek	*Greek*	②②③
	Metrogusto	*Italian*	②①③
	Idaho	*American*	⑤④④
£30+	All Bar One	*British, Modern*	④④④
	The Duke of Cambridge	*"*	③④②
	Café Flo	*French*	⑤④④
	Julius	*"*	④③④
	Village Bistro	*"*	③③③
	Cantina Italia	*Italian*	③②④
	Casale Franco	*"*	③③②
	Florians	*"*	④②④
	San Carlo	*"*	④②②
	Strada	*"*	③③③
	Centuria	*Mediterranean*	③④③
	Browns	*International*	④③③
	Chez Liline	*Fish & seafood*	①③⑤
	Loch Fyne	*"*	④④③
	Rôtisserie	*Steaks & grills*	②①③
	Santa Fe	*American*	④④④
	Cuba Libre	*Cuban*	④④③

	The Parsee	Indian	❷❶④
	Rasa	"	❶❶❸
£25+	Tartuf	Alsatian	❷❶❸
	Giraffe	British, Modern	❸❷❷
	Mesclun	"	❶❶❷
	Les Associés	French	❷❶❷
	Café Rouge	"	– – –
	Le Sacré-Coeur	"	④❷❸
	Soulard	"	❷❶❷
	Vrisaki	Greek	❷❸❸
	Caffè Uno	Italian	④❸④
	Est Est Est	"	⑤⑤④
	San Daniele	"	❸❷❸
	Angel of the North	International	④❷❸
	Banners	"	❸❸❶
	Barracuda	"	④❷❷
	The Fox Reformed	"	④❷❸
	Ruby in the Dust	"	⑤④❸
	Two Brothers	Fish & chips	❷❷④
	Pasha	Turkish	❷❶❷
	Rasa Travancore	Indian, Southern	❷❷④
	Tiger Lil's	Pan-Asian	④❸❸
	Wok Wok	"	⑤④④
	Yellow River Café	"	④④④
	Yelo	Thai	④④❸
£20+	Le Mercury	French	④④❷
	Café Mozart	Hungarian	❸④❷
	La Finca	Spanish	④④❸
	Toff's	Fish & chips	④❸④
	Ask! Pizza	Pizza	④❷❷
	Calzone	"	❸❸④
	Furnace	"	❷④❸
	PizzaExpress	"	④❸❸
	Gallipoli	Turkish	❸❷❷
	Istanbul Iskembecisi	"	❸❸❸
	Iznik	"	❸❷❶
	Sedir	"	❸❷❸
	Anglo Asian Tandoori	Indian	❸❶❷
	Rani	"	❷❷❸
	Bu San	Korean	❸❸④
	Tuk Tuk	Thai	❸④❸
	Yum Yum	"	❷❷❷
£15+	La Porchetta Pizzeria	Italian	❸④❸
	La Piragua	South American	❸④❸
	Afghan Kitchen	Afghani	❷④④
	New Culture Rev'n	Chinese	❸❸④
£5+	Coffee Republic	Sandwiches, cakes, etc	❸❸❸
	Pret A Manger	"	❸❷④

SOUTH

South Bank (SE1)

£60+	Le Pont de la Tour	British, Modern	⑤⑤❸
	Neat	French	❸④❸
£50+	The County Hall	British, Modern	⑤❸④
	Oxo Tower	"	⑤⑤❷
	Butlers Wharf Chop-house	British, Traditional	④④❷
£40+	Blue Print Café	British, Modern	④④❷
	The People's Palace	"	④❸❸
	Simply Nico	French	④④④
	Tentazioni	Italian	❷❷④
	Livebait	Fish & seafood	❸④④
	Le Pont de la Tour Bar & Grill	Steaks & grills	❸❸❷
£35+	Cantina Vinopolis	British, Modern	④④❸
	RSJ	"	❸❷④
	Shakespeare's Globe	"	④❸❷
	Cantina del Ponte	Italian	④⑤④
	Four Regions	Chinese	④④❸
£30+	All Bar One	British, Modern	④④④
	Archduke Wine Bar	"	⑤④④
	The Honest Cabbage	"	❸❸❸
	Laughing Gravy	"	④❷❸
	Mezzanine	"	④❷❸
	Waterloo Fire Station	"	④⑤④
	Chez Gérard	French	④④④
	La Lanterna	Italian	❸❷❷
	Riviera	Mediterranean	④④❸
	Baltic	Polish	④❸❶
	Delfina Studio Café	International	❸❷❷
	Tate Modern	"	④④❶
	fish!	Fish & seafood	❸❸④
	Fina Estampa	South American	❸❷④
	Bengal Clipper	Indian	❷❷❸
	Kwan Thai	Thai	❸④④
£25+	Bankside	British, Modern	❸❷❸
	Auberge	French	❸④④
	Café Rouge	"	– – –
	Champor-Champor	East/West	❶❶❷
	Gourmet Pizza Co.	Pizza	❸④④
	Yo! Sushi	Japanese	④④④
£20+	Konditor & Cook	British, Modern	❷❷❸
	Meson don Felipe	Spanish	④❸❶
	Film Café	International	④④❸

	Ask! Pizza	*Pizza*	④❸❷
	PizzaExpress	"	④❸❸
	Pizzeria Castello	"	❷❶❷
	Konditor & Cook	*Sandwiches, cakes, etc*	❷❷❸
	Tas	*Turkish*	❷❷❷
£5+	Eat	*Sandwiches, cakes, etc*	❸❸④

Battersea, Clapham, Wandsworth, Barnes, Putney, Wimbledon, Brixton & Lewisham (All postcodes south of the river except SE1)

£60+	Putney Bridge	*French*	❸④❷
£50+	Monsieur Max	*French*	❶❷❷
£40+	Belair House	*British, Modern*	❸❷❶
	Burnt Chair	"	❸❷❸
	Chez Bruce	"	❶❶❷
	Ransome's Dock	"	❷❷❸
	Livebait	*Fish & seafood*	❸④④
	The Common Room	*American*	– – –
£35+	Ditto	*British, Modern*	④❸❸
	The Glasshouse	"	❶❶❷
	The Light House	"	❷❸❸
	Niksons	"	❸⑤④
	Redmond's	"	❷❷④
	Sand	"	❸④❷
	Sonny's	"	❷❷❷
	Station Grill	"	❷❷❸
	The Stepping Stone	"	❶❶❷
	The Cook House	*French*	– – –
	Gastro	"	❸④❷
	Del Buongustaio	*Italian*	④④④
	Enoteca Turi	"	❷❶❷
	Metrogusto	"	❷❶❸
	Murano	"	④❷④
	Prego	"	④④④
	Riva	"	❶❷④
	Buchan's	*Scottish*	❸❷❸
	The Sequel	*International*	④④④
	Lobster Pot	*Fish & seafood*	❷❸❸
	Canyon	*American*	⑤④❸
	La Pampa	*Argentinian*	❷④❷
	Chada	*Thai*	❷❸④
£30+	All Bar One	*British, Modern*	④④④
	The Artesian Well	"	④④❸
	Bellamys	"	④❸❸
	Chapter Two	"	❸❷❸
	The Fire Stables	"	❸④❸

Glaisters	"	④④❸
Helter Skelter	"	❷④❸
Kennington Lane	"	❷①❷
Newton's	"	④④❸
The North Pole	"	❸❸❸
Phoenix	"	❷❷❸
Rapscallion	"	❷❷❷
Le Bouchon Bordelais	French	④❸❸
Cantinetta Venegazzú	Italian	❷❷❷
Lemon Thyme	"	⑤④⑤
Ost. Antica Bologna	"	④④❸
Strada	"	❸❸❸
La Mancha	Spanish	❸❸❷
La Rueda	"	❸❸❷
Browns	International	④❸❸
Glaisters	"	④④❸
Naked Turtle	"	④❷①
fish!	Fish & seafood	❸❸④
Ghillies	"	④❸❷
Loch Fyne	"	④④❸
Polygon Bar & Grill	Steaks & grills	❸❸❷
Popeseye	"	①❷④
Bombay Bicycle Club	Indian	❷❷❷
Café Spice Namaste	"	❷❷❷
3 Monkeys	"	❷❷❸

£25+	Bah Humbug	British, Modern	❸❸①
	The Blue Pumpkin	"	④❸④
	The Castle	"	❷❸❸
	The Depot	"	④❸❷
	George II	"	❷❸④
	Hudson's	"	❸❸❷
	The Lavender	"	❸❸❸
	The Mason's Arms	"	❷④❷
	Scoffers	"	④❸❷
	The Sun & Doves	"	❸❸❷
	Willie Gunn	"	❸❷❷
	The Trafalgar Tavern	British, Traditional	④❸❷
	The Wardroom	"	④❸❸
	Café Rouge	French	– – –
	Chez Lindsay	"	❷❷❷
	Emile's	"	❸❷④
	Le P'tit Normand	"	❸①❸
	Antipasto & Pasta	Italian	❸❷❸
	Buona Sera	"	❸④❷
	Caffè Uno	"	④❸④
	Est Est Est	"	⑤⑤④
	Café Portugal	Portuguese	❸❷④
	Rebato's	Spanish	❸①①
	Alma	International	❸❷❷
	Duke of Cambridge	"	❸④❷
	The Fine Line	"	④⑤④

			Ratings
	Foxtrot Oscar	"	4 4 4
	The Ship	"	3 4 1
	Cinnamon Cay	East/West	2 2 3
	Tootsies	Burgers, etc	4 3 4
	Basilico	Pizza	1 3 4
	Eco	"	2 4 2
	Pizza Metro	"	1 1 2
	So.uk	North African	3 3 1
	Royal China	Chinese	1 3 4
	Babur Brasserie	Indian	2 3 3
	Ma Goa	"	2 2 4
	Sarkhel's	"	1 2 3
	Coromandel	Indian, Southern	2 3 4
	Jim Thompson's	Pan-Asian	3 4 2
	Tiger Lil's	"	4 3 3
	Wok Wok	"	5 4 4
	Thai Garden	Thai	3 2 3
	Thailand	"	1 2 4
£20+	Arancia	Italian	1 2 2
	Café Pasta	"	5 4 4
	Zizzi	"	4 3 3
	Zucchina	"	4 3 3
	Barcelona Tapas	Spanish	3 3 2
	don Fernando's	"	3 2 2
	La Finca	"	4 4 3
	Chelsea Bun Diner	International	3 2 3
	White Cross	"	3 4 2
	Dixie's Bar & Grill	Mexican/TexMex	5 4 3
	Brady's	Fish & chips	2 3 4
	Ask! Pizza	Pizza	4 3 2
	PizzaExpress	"	4 3 3
	Battersea Rickshaw	Indian	3 2 4
	Sree Krishna	"	2 3 4
	The Banana Leaf Canteen	Pan-Asian	3 3 3
	Fat Boy's	Thai	4 2 4
	The Old School Thai	"	2 1 3
	Talad Thai	"	1 3 4
	Thai Corner Café	"	2 3 4
£15+	Fish in a Tie	Mediterranean	3 2 2
	The White House	International	3 2 2
	Gourmet Burger Kitchen	Burgers, etc	2 3 3
	Boiled Egg & Soldiers	Sandwiches, cakes, etc	4 4 3
	Kastoori	Indian	1 1 3
	Sakonis	"	1 3 4
	The Pepper Tree	Thai	3 2 2
£10+	Caffè Nero	Sandwiches, cakes, etc	3 3 3
£5+	Coffee Republic	Sandwiches, cakes, etc	3 3 3
	Starbucks	"	4 4 4

EAST

Smithfield & Farringdon (EC1)

£40+			
St John	British, Modern		② ② ③
Bleeding Heart	French		② ② ①
Bubb's	"		② ② ③
Club Gascon	"		① ② ②
Maison Novelli	"		② ③ ③
Simply Nico	"		④ ④ ④
Gaudi	Spanish		③ ③ ④
Smiths of Smithfield	Steaks & grills		③ ③ ②

£35+			
Flâneur	British, Modern		④ ③ ②
Home	"		③ ③ ①
The Quality Chop House	"		② ② ③
Café du Marché	French		② ② ①
Alba	Italian		② ③ ④
Rudland & Stubbs	Fish & seafood		③ ④ ④
Café City Lazeez	Indian		③ ④ ④

£30+			
Abbaye	Belgian		④ ⑤ ④
All Bar One	British, Modern		④ ④ ④
Café Med	"		④ ③ ②
Dibbens	"		④ ③ ④
Vic Naylors	"		④ ④ ②
The Well	"		④ ④ ④
Chez Gérard	French		④ ④ ④
Strada	Italian		③ ③ ③
Potemkin	Russian		③ ② ③
Stream	Fish & seafood		③ ③ ③
Hope & Sir Loin	Steaks & grills		③ ③ ④
Scuzi	Pizza		③ ④ ④
Moro	Moroccan		① ② ②
Cicada	Pan-Asian		② ② ②
East One	"		③ ③ ④

£25+			
The Peasant	Italian		④ ③ ③
Al's	International		④ ④ ③
Mustards Brasserie	"		④ ③ ④
Carnevale	Vegetarian		② ③ ④
Japanese Canteen	Japanese		④ ④ ④
Yo! Sushi	"		④ ④ ④

£20+			
Fox & Anchor	British, Traditional		③ ③ ②
The Eagle	Mediterranean		② ④ ②
Quiet Revolution	Organic		② ③ ②
Ask! Pizza	Pizza		④ ③ ②
PizzaExpress	"		④ ③ ③

£5+			
Coffee Republic	Sandwiches, cakes, etc		③ ③ ③
Pret A Manger	"		③ ② ④
Starbucks	"		④ ④ ④

The City (EC2, EC3 & EC4)

£70+	Chamberlain's	*Fish & seafood*	④②④
£60+	Tatsuso	*Japanese*	①③④
£50+	City Rhodes	*British, Modern*	②②③
	Gladwins	"	③②③
	Prism	"	③③④
	Aurora	*French*	⑤⑤⑤
	Coq d'Argent	"	⑤④③
	Twentyfour	*International*	③③②
	City Miyama	*Japanese*	①②④
£40+	Bar Bourse	*British, Modern*	④③④
	The Don	"	②①②
	Eyre Brothers	"	②②③
	I Lombard Street	"	③③③
	Searcy's Brasserie	"	④④⑤
	10	"	④④④
	Caravaggio	*Italian*	④④④
	Taberna Etrusca	"	④④⑤
	Brasserie Rocque	*International*	④④④
	Fishmarket	*Fish & seafood*	④④⑤
	Gow's	"	③③④
	Livebait	"	③④④
	Vertigo	"	④③②
	Aykoku-Kaku	*Japanese*	③②④
	Miyabi	"	③④④
	Pacific Oriental	*Pan-Asian*	④③④
£35+	Terminus	*British, Modern*	⑤⑤⑤
	The Vestry	"	④③③
	Luc's Brasserie	*French*	③③④
	Perc%nto	*Italian*	④④③
	Just The Bridge	*East/West*	④⑤④
	Sweetings	*Fish & seafood*	②②②
	Imperial City	*Chinese*	③③③
	Singapura	*Malaysian*	④③⑤
£30+	All Bar One	*British, Modern*	④④④
	Cantaloupe	"	③③②
	The Poet	"	④④③
	Soshomatch	"	③④③
	The Bow Wine Vaults	*British, Traditional*	④②④
	George	"	④⑤④
	George & Vulture	"	④③②
	Café Flo	*French*	⑤④④
	Chez Gérard	"	④④④
	Gt Eastern Dining Room	*Italian*	④④③
	Zuccato	"	④④④
	Browns	*International*	④③③
	DK's	"	②③③

	Gaucho Grill	*Steaks & grills*	②②③
	Shoeless Joe's	*American*	④⑤④
	Scuzi	*Pizza*	③④④
	Tao	*Pan-Asian*	④②③
	Silks & Spice	*Thai*	③③③
	Sri Siam City	*"*	③②④
	Sri Thai	*"*	③②④
£25+	Corney & Barrow	*British, Modern*	⑤④④
	The Fox	*"*	③④④
	Goose	*"*	③③④
	Lime	*"*	④③④
	Ye Olde Cheshire Cheese	*British, Traditional*	④④②
	Auberge	*French*	③④④
	Café Rouge	*"*	– – –
	Fuego	*Spanish*	④②④
	The Fine Line	*International*	④⑤④
	Foxtrot Oscar	*"*	④④④
	Pizza Pomodoro	*Pizza*	④④②
	Rupee Room	*Indian*	③③④
	Japanese Canteen	*Japanese*	④④④
£20+	Grand Central	*British, Modern*	④③②
	Simpson's Tavern	*British, Traditional*	④②①
	Barcelona Tapas	*Spanish*	③③②
	Futures	*Vegetarian*	③④③
	The Place Below	*"*	②④③
	PizzaExpress	*Pizza*	④③③
	K10	*Japanese*	①②②
	Moshi Moshi	*"*	③④③
	Noto	*"*	③④④
£15+	The Wine Library	*British, Traditional*	④②①
	Touzai	*Pan-Asian*	④②④
£10+	Caffè Nero	*Sandwiches, cakes, etc*	③③③
	Fusion	*Pan-Asian*	③②③
£5+	Futures	*Vegetarian*	②③ –
	Coffee Republic	*Sandwiches, cakes, etc*	③③③
	Eat	*"*	③③④
	Pret A Manger	*"*	③②④
	Starbucks	*"*	④④④
	Soup Opera	*Soup*	③③④

**East End & Docklands
(All E postcodes)**

Price	Name	Cuisine	Rating
£50+	Ubon	East/West	2 3 4
£40+	Quadrato	British, Modern	3 2 3
	Les Trois Garçons	French	3 2 1
£35+	Wapping Food	International	3 4 1
	Aquarium	Fish & seafood	3 4 3
	The Grapes	"	2 3 2
£30+	All Bar One	British, Modern	4 4 4
	Frocks	"	3 2 2
	House	"	4 3 4
	The Light	"	3 3 1
	LMNT	"	4 3 1
	Il Bordello	Italian	2 2 2
	Riviera	Mediterranean	4 4 3
	fish!	Fish & seafood	3 3 4
	Gaucho Grill	Steaks & grills	2 3 3
	Babe Ruth's	American	5 5 5
	Scuzi	Pizza	3 4 4
	Royal China	Chinese	1 3 4
	Café Spice Namaste	Indian	2 2 2
£25+	Corney & Barrow	British, Modern	5 4 4
	Café Rouge	French	– – –
	The Fine Line	International	4 5 4
	Gourmet Pizza Co.	Pizza	3 4 4
	Tabla	Indian	2 4 3
	Yellow River Café	Pan-Asian	4 4 4
	Elephant Royale	Thai	4 3 3
£20+	Barcelona Tapas	Spanish	3 3 2
	La Tasca	"	3 3 2
	Faulkner's	Fish & chips	1 2 4
	PizzaExpress	Pizza	4 3 3
	Shanghai	Chinese	2 2 2
	Café Indiya	Indian	2 2 3
	Moshi Moshi	Japanese	3 4 3
	Viet Hoa	Vietnamese	2 4 4
£15+	Arkansas Café	Steaks & grills	2 3 3
	Lahore Kebab House	Indian	1 5 4
£10+	Cranks	Vegetarian	4 4 4
£5+	Coffee Republic	Sandwiches, cakes, etc	3 3 3
	Eat	"	3 3 4
	Soup Opera	Soup	3 3 4
£1+	Brick Lane Beigel Bake	Sandwiches, cakes, etc	1 2 4

MAPS

MAP I – LONDON OVERVIEW

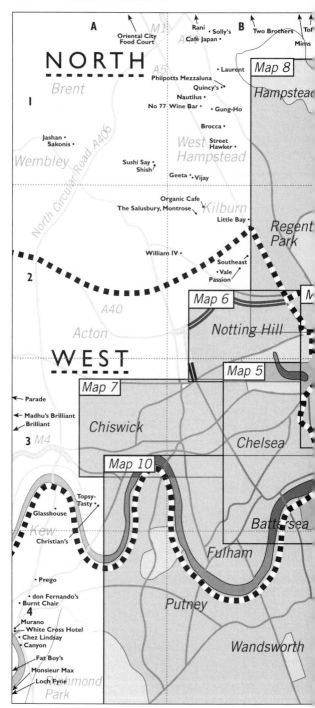

A

B

Oriental City Food Court

Rani •   • Solly's

Café Japan •

Two Brothers •   Tof

Mims •

NORTH

Brent

Map 8

Hampstead

Philpotts Mezzaluna •

Quincy's •

Nautilus •

No 77 Wine Bar •   • Gung-Ho

• Laurent

I

Jashan •

Sakonis •

Wembley

Sushi Say •

Shish •

Geeta • • Vijay

Brocca •

West Hampstead

Street Hawker •

Organic Cafe •

The Salusbury, Montrose →

Little Bay •

Kilburn

Regent Park

William IV •

Southeast •

• Vale Passion

2

A40

Acton

Map 6

Notting Hill

M

WEST

Map 5

← Parade

← Madhu's Brilliant

← Brilliant

Map 7

Chiswick

Chelsea

3   *M4*

Map 10

Topsy-Tasty •

Glasshouse •

Christian's •

Kew

Battersea

Fulham

• Prego

• don Fernando's

• Burnt Chair

4

Murano •

— White Cross Hotel

• Chez Lindsay

• Canyon

Putney

Wandsworth

• Fat Boy's

Monsieur Max •

Loch Fyne •

Park

MAP I – LONDON OVERVIEW

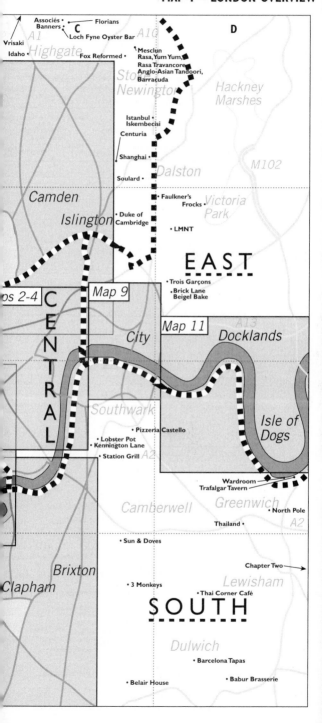

Vrisaki •

Idaho •

Associés •
Banners •

Florians

Loch Fyne Oyster Bar

C

Fox Reformed •

A1

Highgate

D

A10

Mesclun
Rasa, Yum Yum,
Rasa Travancore
Anglo-Asian Tandoori,
Barracuda

*Stoke
Newington*

*Hackney
Marshes*

Istanbul •
Iskembecisi

Centuria •

Shanghai •

Soulard •

Dalston

M102

Faulkner's
Frocks •

*Victoria
Park*

• Duke of
Cambridge

• LMNT

EAST

Camden

Islington

Map 9

• Trois Garçons

• Brick Lane
Beigel Bake

os 2-4

**C
E
N
T
R
A
L**

City

Map 11

A13

Docklands

Southwark

• Pizzeria Castello

• Lobster Pot
Kennington Lane

• Station Grill

A2

*Isle of
Dogs*

Wardroom
Trafalgar Tavern

Camberwell

Greenwich

• North Pole

A2

Thailand •

• Sun & Doves

Brixton

Chapter Two →

Lewisham

Clapham

• 3 Monkeys

• Thai Corner Café

SOUTH

Dulwich

• Barcelona Tapas

• Belair House

• Babur Brasserie

MAP 2 – WEST END OVERVIEW

MAP 2 – WEST END OVERVIEW

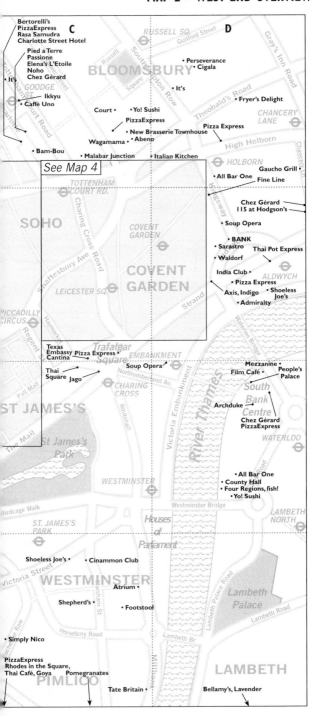

Bertorelli's
PizzaExpress
Rasa Samudra
Charlotte Street Hotel

C

RUSSELL SQ.

Guilford Street

D

Gray's Inn Road

Pied a Terre
Passione
Elena's L'Etoile
Noho
Chez Gérard

GOODGE

• Perseverance
• Cigala

BLOOMSBURY

• It's

• Ikkyu

• Caffè Uno

• It's

Theobald's Road

• Fryer's Delight

*CHANCERY
LANE*

Court •

• Yo! Sushi

PizzaExpress

Pizza Express

Wagamama

• New Brasserie Townhouse
• Abeno

High Holborn

• Bam-Bou

• Malabar Junction   • Italian Kitchen

HOLBORN

| See Map 4 |

*TOTTENHAM
COURT RD.*

Gaucho Grill •
• All Bar One   Fine Line

Kingsway

SOHO

Charing Cross Road

*COVENT
GARDEN*

Chez Gérard
115 at Hodgson's

• Soup Opera

**COVENT
GARDEN**

• BANK
• Sarastro   Thai Pot Express
• Waldorf

Shaftesbury Ave Road

LEICESTER SQ.

India Club •

ALDWYCH

• Pizza Express
Axis, Indigo •   • Shoeless
Joe's
• Admiralty

Strand

*PICCADILLY
CIRCUS*

Haymarket

Regent

Texas
Embassy Pizza Express •
Cantina

*Trafalgar
Square*   EMBANKMENT
• Soup Opera •

Thai Square   Jago

Northumberland Av.

*CHARING
CROSS*

Waterloo Bridge

Mezzanine •
Film Café •   • People's
Palace

River Thames

*South
Bank
Centre*

Archduke •

Chez Gérard
PizzaExpress

WATERLOO

ST JAMES'S

Pall Mall

Whitehall

Victoria Embankment

*St James's
Park*

The Mall

WESTMINSTER

• All Bar One
• County Hall
• Four Regions, fish!
• Yo! Sushi

Westminster Bridge

*LAMBETH
NORTH*

Birdcage Walk

*ST. JAMES'S
PARK*

*Houses
of
Parliament*

Shoeless Joe's •   • Cinammon Club

Victoria Street

WESTMINSTER

Atrium •

Shepherd's •   • Footstool

Marsham St.

Lambeth Palace Road

*Lambeth
Palace*

Lambeth Road

• Simply Nico

Horseferry Road

Lambeth Br.

Millbank

PizzaExpress
Rhodes in the Square,
Thai Café, Goya   Pomegranates

PIMLICO

Tate Britain •

LAMBETH

Bellamy's, Lavender

MAP 3 – MAYFAIR, ST JAMES'S & WEST SOHO

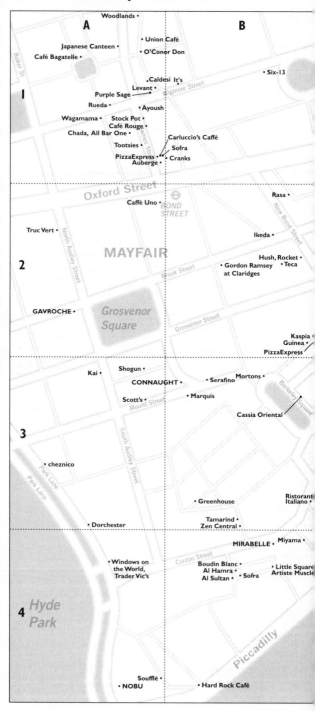

A

B

Woodlands •

Japanese Canteen •
• Union Café
Café Bagatelle •
• O'Conor Don

• Six-13

• Caldesi It's
Levant •
Purple Sage •
Rueda •
• Ayoush
Wagamama •   Stock Pot •
Café Rouge •
Chada, All Bar One •
• Carluccio's Caffè
Tootsies •
• Sofra
PizzaExpress •
• Cranks
Auberge •

Oxford Street

Rasa •

Caffè Uno • BOND STREET

Truc Vert •

Ikeda •

MAYFAIR

Hush, Rocket •
• Gordon Ramsey • Teca
at Claridges

GAVROCHE •

Grosvenor
Square

Grosvenor Street

Kaspia •
Guinea •
PizzaExpress •

Kai •   Shogun •

CONNAUGHT •   • Serafino   Mortons •

Scott's •   • Marquis

Cassia Oriental

Mount Street

• cheznico

• Greenhouse

Ristorant
Italiano •

• Dorchester

Tamarind •
Zen Central •

MIRABELLE •   Miyama •

Curzon Street

Boudin Blanc •
• Windows on
the World,
Trader Vic's

Al Hamra •
Al Sultan •   • Sofra

• Little Square
Artiste Muscle

Hyde
Park

Piccadilly

Soufflé •
• NOBU
• Hard Rock Café

MAP 3 – MAYFAIR, ST JAMES'S & WEST SOHO

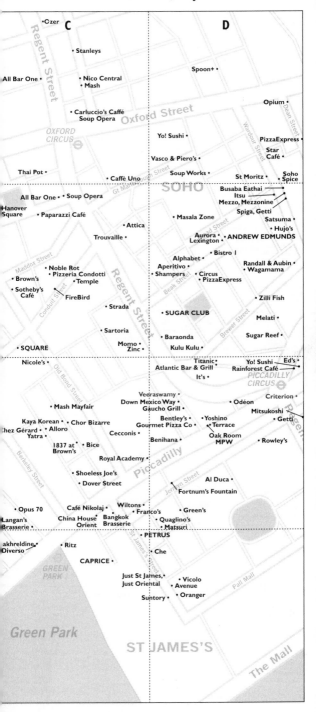

MAP 4 – EAST SOHO, CHINATOWN & COVENT GARDEN

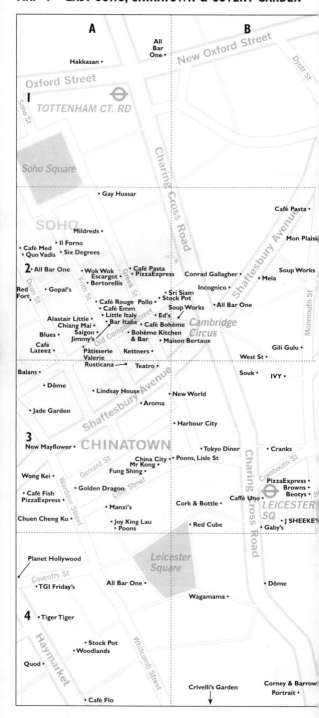

MAP 4 – EAST SOHO, CHINATOWN & COVENT GARDEN

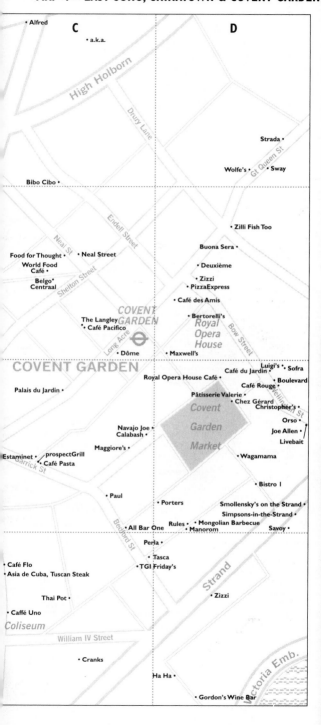

• Alfred

C

D

• a.k.a.

High Holborn

Drury Lane

Strada •

Wolfe's • • Sway

Gt Queen St

Bibo Cibo •

Endell Street

• Zilli Fish Too

Neal St

Buona Sera •

Food for Thought • • Neal Street

World Food
Café •

• Deuxième

Belgo •
Centraal

• Zizzi
• PizzaExpress

Shelton Street

• Café des Amis

COVENT
GARDEN

• Bertorelli's

The Langley •

*Royal
Opera
House*

• • Café Pacifico

Long Acre

Bow Street

• Dôme

• Maxwell's

COVENT GARDEN

Luigi's • • Sofra

Café du Jardin •

Royal Opera House Café •

• Boulevard

Café Rouge •

Palais du Jardin •

Pâtisserie Valerie •

• Chez Gérard

Christopher's •

Orso •

Navajo Joe •
Calabash

Joe Allen •

Maggiore's •

Livebait

Estaminet •   / prospectGrill

• Wagamama

• Café Pasta

Garrick St

• Bistro 1

• Paul

• Porters

Smollensky's on the Strand •

Simpsons-in-the-Strand •

Bedford St

• All Bar One

Rules • • Mongolian Barbecue

Savoy •

• Manorom

Perla •

• Café Flo

• Tasca

• Asia de Cuba, Tuscan Steak

• TGI Friday's

Strand

Thai Pot •

• Zizzi

• Caffé Uno

Coliseum

William IV Street

• Cranks

Ha Ha •

Victoria Emb.

• Gordon's Wine Bar

MAP 5 – KNIGHTSBRIDGE, CHELSEA & SOUTH KENSINGTON

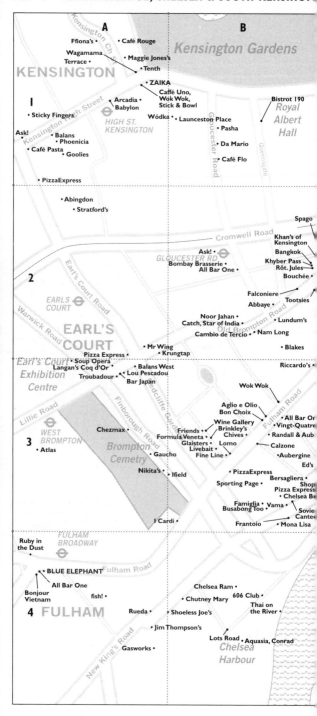

Kensington Ch.

A

B

Kensington Gardens

Ffiona's •
• Café Rouge

Wagamama
Terrace •
• Maggie Jones's

KENSINGTON
• Tenth

• ZAIKA

Bistrot 190

Caffè Uno,
Wok Wok,
Stick & Bowl

Royal
Albert
Hall

I

Kensington High Street

• Sticky Fingers

Arcadia •
Babylon •

*HIGH ST.
KENSINGTON*

Wódka •

• Launceston Place

Ask! •

• Balans

• Phoenicia
• Café Pasta
• Goolies

• Pasha

Queensgate

• Da Mario

• Café Flo

• PizzaExpress

• Abingdon

• Stratford's

Spago

Cromwell Road

Khan's of
Kensington

GLOUCESTER RD

Ask! •

Bangkok

Bombay Brasserie •
All Bar One •

Khyber Pass •
Rôt. Jules •

2

Earl's Court Road

Bouchée •

Falconiere •
Tootsies

**EARLS
COURT**

Abbaye •

Warwick Road

**EARL'S
COURT**

Noor Jahan •
Catch, Star of India •
Cambio de Tercio •

Old Brompton Road

• Lundum's

• Nam Long

• Mr Wing

• Krungtap

• Blakes

Pizza Express •

Earl's Court
Exhibition
Centre

• Soup Opera
Langan's Coq d'Or •

• Balans West

• Riccardo's

Troubadour •

• Lou Pescadou
Bar Japan •

Finborough Road

Wok Wok •

Aglio e Olio •
Bon Choix •

Redcliffe Gardens

Fulham Road

• All Bar On

Lillie Road

Chezmax •

Wine Gallery •
Brinkley's •
Chives •

• Vingt-Quatre

**WEST
BROMPTON**

Brompton
Cemetery

Formula Veneta •
Glaisters •

Friends •

• Randall & Aub

• Atlas

Lomo

Calzone •

3

• Gaucho

Livebait •
Fine Line •

• Aubergine

Ed's

Nikita's •

• Ifield

• PizzaExpress

Bersagliera •
Shop
Pizza Express

Sporting Page •

• Chelsea Be

I Cardi •

Famiglia •
Busabong Too •

• Vama •

Sove
Cante

Frantoio •

• Mona Lisa

*FULHAM
BROADWAY*

Ruby in
the Dust

• BLUE ELEPHANT

Fulham Road

Chelsea Ram •

All Bar One

606 Club •

Bonjour
Vietnam •

fish! •

• Chutney Mary

Thai on
the River •

4 FULHAM

Rueda •

• Shoeless Joe's

• Jim Thompson's

Gasworks •

New King's Road

Lots Road

• Aquasia, Conrad

*Chelsea
Harbour*

MAP 5 – KNIGHTSBRIDGE, CHELSEA & SOUTH KENSINGTON

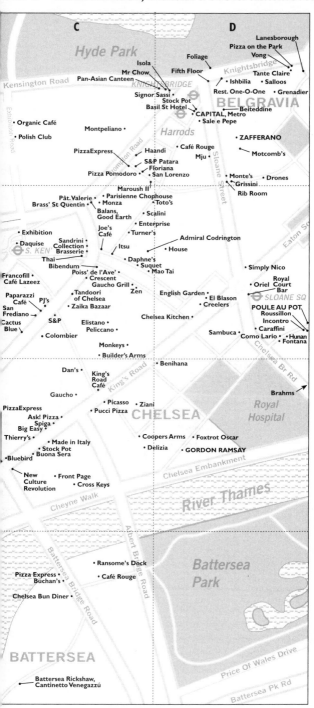

C

D

Hyde Park

Lanesborough
Pizza on the Park
Vong
Foliage
Isola
Tante Claire
Fifth Floor
Mr Chow
Knightsbridge
Pan-Asian Canteen
Ishibilia • Salloos
KNIGHTSBRIDGE
Signor Sassi
Rest. One-O-One • Grenadier
Stock Pot
Basil St Hotel
Beiteddine
BELGRAVIA
CAPITAL, Metro
Sale e Pepe

Kensington Road

• Organic Café
• Polish Club

Montpeliano •
Harrods
• ZAFFERANO
• Café Rouge
PizzaExpress
Mju •
Motcomb's
• Haandi
S&P Patara
Floriana
Pizza Pomodoro
• San Lorenzo
• Monte's • Drones
Grissini
Maroush II •
Rib Room

Exhibition Road
Brompton Road
Sloane Street
Eaton Gate

Pât.Valerie • Parisienne Chophouse
Brass' St Quentin • • Monza
• Toto's
Balans,
Good Earth
• Scalini
• Exhibition
• Enterprise
• Daquise
Sandrini •
Joe's
Collection •
Café
• Turner's
S. KEN'
Brasserie •
• Admiral Codrington
Thai
Itsu
• House
Bibendum
• Daphne's
Poiss' de l'Ave' •
• Suquet
• Crescent
• Mao Tai
• Simply Nico
Francofill •
Gaucho Grill •
Royal
Café Lazeez
Zen
• Oriel Court
• Tandoori
English Garden •
• El Blason
Bar
Paparazzi
of Chelsea
• Creelers
SLOANE SQ
Café
PJ's
• Zaika Bazaar
POULE AU POT
San
Roussillon
Frediano →
Chelsea Kitchen •
Incontro
Cactus
S&P
• Caraffini
Blue \
Elistano •
Como Lario • • Hunan
• Colombier
Peliccano •
Sambuca •
• Fontana

Monkeys •
• Builder's Arms

King's Road
• Benihana
Dan's •
King's
• Brahms
Road
Café
Gaucho •
Royal
• Picasso
• Ziani
Hospital
PizzaExpress
• Pucci Pizza
Ask! Pizza •
CHELSEA
Spiga •
Big Easy •
Thierry's •
• Coopers Arms • Foxtrot Oscar
• Made in Italy
• Stock Pot
• Delizia • GORDON RAMSAY
• Bluebird
Buona Sera •
New
Chelsea Embankment
• Front Page
Culture
• Cross Keys
Revolution
Cheyne Walk
River Thames

Albert Bridge Road
Chelsea Br Rd

• Ransome's Dock
Battersea
Park
• Café Rouge
Pizza Express •
Buchan's •

Battersea Bridge Road
Chelsea Bun Diner •

BATTERSEA
Price Of Wales Drive

← Battersea Rickshaw,
Cantinetto Venegazzú
Battersea Pk Rd

MAP 6 – NOTTING HILL & BAYSWATER

MAP 7 – HAMMERSMITH & CHISWICK

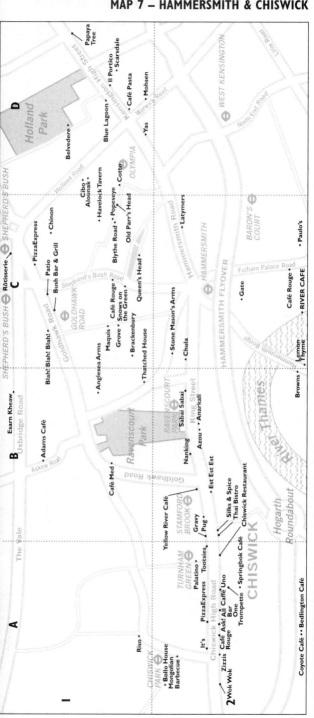

MAP 8 – HAMPSTEAD, CAMDEN TOWN & ISLINGTON

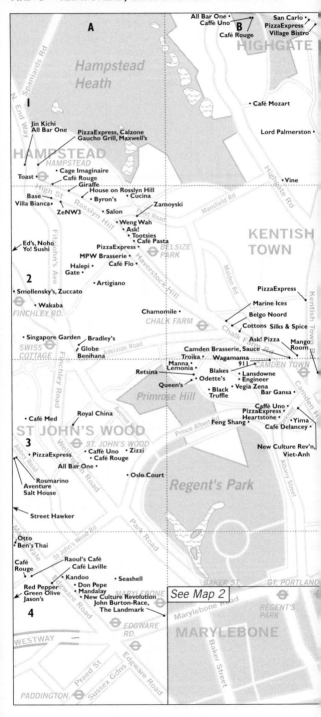

A

Hampstead Heath

All Bar One •
Caffè Uno • **B**
Café Rouge •

San Carlo •
PizzaExpress •
Village Bistro •

HIGHGATE

• Café Mozart

Lord Palmerston •

Jin Kichi •
All Bar One •
PizzaExpress, Calzone •
Gaucho Grill, Maxwell's •

1

HAMPSTEAD
HAMPSTEAD

Toast •
• Cage Imaginaire
• Café Rouge
Giraffe •
• House on Rosslyn Hill
• Byron's • Cucina
Base •
Villa Bianca •
ZeNW3 •
• Salon
• Zamoyski
• Weng Wah
• Ask!
• Tootsies
• Café Pasta
PizzaExpress •
Ed's, Noho •
Yo! Sushi •
MPW Brasserie •
• Café Flo
Halepi •
Gate •
• Artigiano
• Smollensky's, Zuccato
• Wakaba

2

FINCHLEY RD.

Chamomile •
CHALK FARM

KENTISH TOWN

PizzaExpress •

Marine Ices
Belgo Noord
Cottons Silks & Spice
Ask! Pizza
Mango Room

• Singapore Garden • Bradley's
• Globe
Benihana
Camden Brasserie, Sauce
Troika • Wagamama
Manna •
Lemonia •
Retsina •
Queen's •
• Odette's
Camden Brasserie, Sauce
911
Blakes
• Lansdowne
• Engineer
Vegia Zena •
Bar Gansa •
• Black Truffle

SWISS COTTAGE
FINCHLEY ROAD

• Café Med
Royal China •

CAMDEN TOWN

ST JOHN'S WOOD
ST. JOHN'S WOOD

3

• PizzaExpress
• Caffè Uno • Zizzi
• Café Rouge
All Bar One •
• Oslo Court

Caffè Uno •
PizzaExpress •
Heartstone •
Feng Shang •
• Yima
Café Delancey •

New Culture Rev'n,
Viet-Anh

Rosmarino
Aventure
Salt House

← Street Hawker

Primrose Hill

Regent's Park

Otto
Ben's Thai
Café Rouge
Raoul's Café
Café Laville
Kandoo
• Don Pepe • Seashell
Red Pepper •
Green Olive •
Jason's •
• Mandalay
• New Culture Revolution
John Burton-Race,
The Landmark

4

WESTWAY

See Map 2

BAKER ST.

GT. PORTLAND

REGENT'S PARK

Marylebone Road

EDGWARE RD.

MARYLEBONE

PADDINGTON

Praed St.

Sussex Gdns

Edgware Road

Baker Street

MAP 8 – HAMPSTEAD, CAMDEN TOWN & ISLINGTON

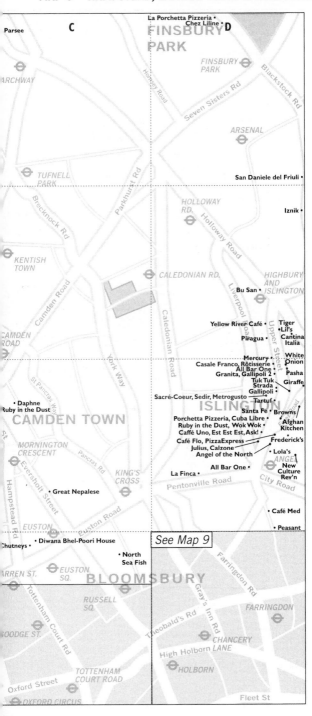

Parsee

C

La Porchetta Pizzeria •
Chez Liline • D

FINSBURY PARK

FINSBURY PARK

ARCHWAY

Homsey Road

Seven Sisters Rd

Blackstock Rd

ARSENAL

TUFNELL PARK

San Daniele del Friuli •

Brecknock Rd

Parkhurst Rd

HOLLOWAY RD.

Holloway Road

Iznik •

KENTISH TOWN

Camden Road

CALEDONIAN RD.

HIGHBURY AND ISLINGTON

Liverpool Road

Bu San •

CAMDEN ROAD

York Way

Caledonian Road

Yellow River Café •

Piragua •

Tiger
• Lil's
Cantina Italia

White Onion

St Pancras Rd

Mercury •
Casale Franco, Rôtisserie •
All Bar One •
Granita, Gallipoli 2 •

Upper Street

Pasha

• Daphne
Ruby in the Dust

CAMDEN TOWN

Tuk Tuk
Strada
Gallipoli •

Giraffe

Sacré-Coeur, Sedir, Metrogusto —

Tartuf •

Santa Fe • Browns

Pancras Rd

MORNINGTON CRESCENT

Porchetta Pizzeria, Cuba Libre •
Ruby in the Dust, Wok Wok •
Caffè Uno, Est Est Est, Ask! •
Café Flo, PizzaExpress •
Julius, Calzone
Angel of the North

• Afghan Kitchen

• Frederick's

• Lola's

Eversholt Street

KING'S CROSS

All Bar One •

ANGEL
New Culture Rev'n

Hampstead Rd

Great Nepalese

La Finca •

Pentonville Road

City Road

• Café Med

EUSTON

Euston Road

• Diwana Bhel-Poori House

See Map 9

Farringdon Rd

• Peasant

Chutneys •

WARREN ST.

EUSTON SQ.

• North Sea Fish

BLOOMSBURY

Gray's Inn Rd

Tottenham Court Rd

GOODGE ST.

RUSSELL SQ.

Theobald's Rd

FARRINGDON

High Holborn

CHANCERY LANE

HOLBORN

TOTTENHAM COURT ROAD

Oxford Street

OXFORD CIRCUS

Fleet St

MAP 9 – THE CITY

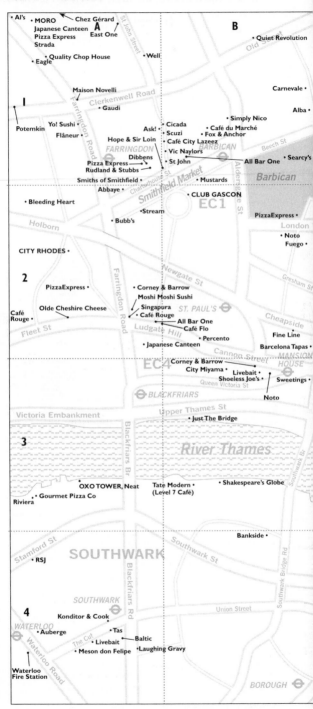

• Al's
• MORO   • Chez Gérard
Japanese Canteen   **A**
Pizza Express   East One
Strada

• Quality Chop House
• Eagle   • Well

St John Street

B

• Quiet Revolution

Old Street

Maison Novelli
Clerkenwell Road   Carnevale •

I   • Gaudi   Alba •

Farringdon Road

Potemkin   Yo! Sushi •   • Simply Nico
Flâneur •   • Cicada   • Café du Marché
Ask! •   Scuzi   • Fox & Anchor
Hope & Sir Loin   • Café City Lazeez
Dibbens   • Vic Naylors   BARBICAN
Pizza Express   • St John   Aldersgate St   All Bar One   • Searcy's
Rudland & Stubbs   Beech St
Smiths of Smithfield   Smithfield Market   **Barbican**
Abbaye •   • Mustards

FARRINGDON

• Bleeding Heart   • **CLUB GASCON**
      EC1
Holborn   PizzaExpress •
      London
• Bubb's   • Stream   • Noto
      Fuego •
CITY RHODES •

2   Newgate St   Gresham St
PizzaExpress •   • Corney & Barrow
      Moshi Moshi Sushi
Olde Cheshire Cheese   Singapura   **ST. PAUL'S**
Café   • Café Rouge   Cheapside
Rouge •   • All Bar One
Fleet St   Ludgate Hill   • Café Flo
      • Percento   Fine Line •
      • Japanese Canteen   Barcelona Tapas •
      Cannon Street   **MANSION**
EC4   • Corney & Barrow   **HOUSE**
      City Miyama •   Livebait •
      Shoeless Joe's •   Sweetings •
      Queen Victoria St
⊖ **BLACKFRIARS**   Noto •

Victoria Embankment   Upper Thames St
      • Just The Bridge
Blackfriars Br

3   **River Thames**

      OXO TOWER, Neat   Tate Modern •   • Shakespeare's Globe
• Gourmet Pizza Co   (Level 7 Café)   Southwark Br
Riviera •

      Bankside •

Stamford St   **SOUTHWARK**   Southwark St
• RSJ   Blackfriars Rd
      SOUTHWARK   Union Street   Southwark Bridge Rd

4
Konditor & Cook •
WATERLOO
• Auberge   • Tas
⊖   • Livebait   Baltic
Waterloo Road   The Cut
      • Meson don Felipe   • Laughing Gravy
Waterloo
Fire Station   **BOROUGH** ⊖

MAP 9 – THE CITY

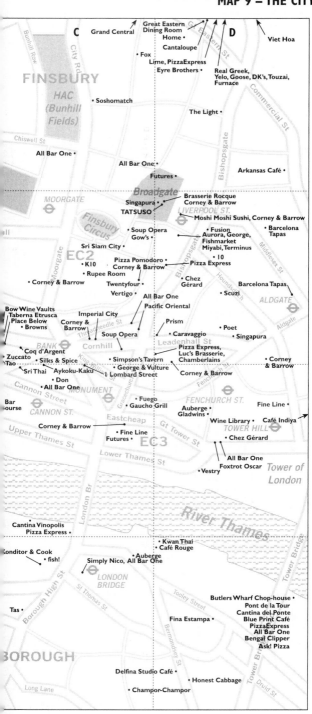

C Grand Central · Great Eastern Dining Room, Home · Cantaloupe · **D** Viet Hoa
· Fox
Lime, PizzaExpress · Eyre Brothers ·
Real Greek, Yelo, Goose, DK's, Touzai, Furnace

FINSBURY
HAC (Bunhill Fields)
· Soshomatch
The Light ·
· All Bar One
· All Bar One ·
Arkansas Café ·
· Futures ·
Broadgate
Brasserie Rocque, Corney & Barrow
Singapura · LIVERPOOL ST.
TATSUSO ·
Moshi Moshi Sushi, Corney & Barrow
Finsbury Circus
· Soup Opera · Fusion, Aurora, George, Fishmarket, Miyabi, Terminus
Gow's ·
· Barcelona Tapas
Sri Siam City ·
EC2
· K10
· Rupee Room
Pizza Pomodoro ·
Corney & Barrow
· 10
Pizza Express
· Corney & Barrow
Twentyfour ·
Vertigo ·
· Chez Gérard
Barcelona Tapas ·
All Bar One
· Scuzi
Pacific Oriental
ALDGATE
Bow Wine Vaults, Taberna Etrusca, Place Below · Browns
Imperial City
Corney & Barrow
Prism
· Poet
· Singapura
BANK
Soup Opera
Caravaggio ·
Pizza Express, Luc's Brasserie, Chamberlains
Cornhill
Coq d'Argent
· Zuccato
·Tao
· Silks & Spice
Sri Thai
Aykoku-Kaku
· Simpson's Tavern
· George & Vulture
I Lombard Street
· Corney & Barrow
· Corney & Barrow
· Don
· All Bar One
MONUMENT
Cannon Street
Bar ·ourse
CANNON ST.
· Fuego
· Gaucho Grill
FENCHURCH ST.
Auberge · Gladwins ·
· Fine Line
Eastcheap
Corney & Barrow
Wine Library · Café Indiya
Upper Thames St
· Fine Line
Futures · EC3
Gt Tower St
TOWER HILL
· Chez Gérard
Lower Thames St
· All Bar One
Foxtrot Oscar
·Vestry
Tower of London
River Thames
Cantina Vinopolis
Pizza Express ·
·onditor & Cook
· fish!
· Kwan Thai
· Café Rouge
· Auberge
Simply Nico, All Bar One
LONDON BRIDGE
Butlers Wharf Chop-house ·
Pont de la Tour ·
Cantina del Ponte
Blue Print Café
PizzaExpress
All Bar One
Bengal Clipper
Ask! Pizza
Tas ·
Fina Estampa ·
·OROUGH
Long Lane
Delfina Studio Café ·
· Honest Cabbage
· Champor-Champor

MAP 10 – SOUTH LONDON (& FULHAM)

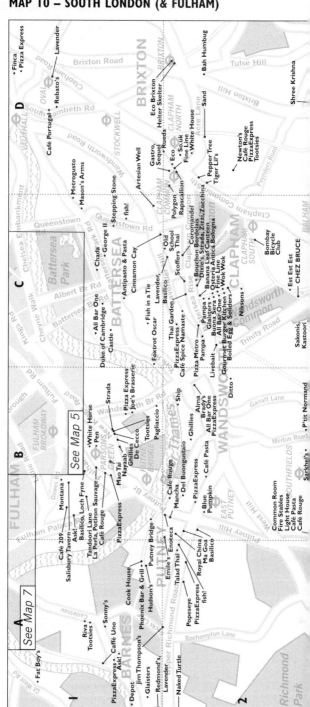

MAP 11 – EAST END & DOCKLANDS

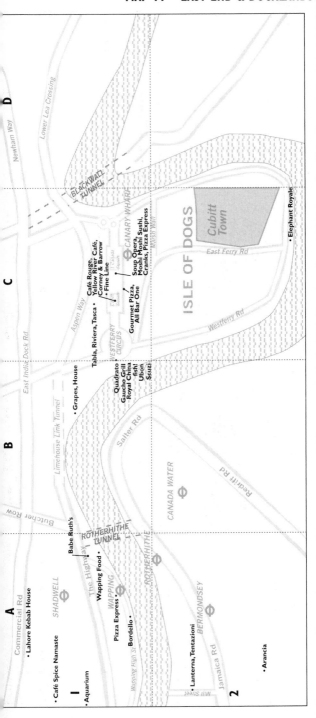

D

Newham Way

Lower Lea Crossing

BLACKWALL TUNNEL

CANARY WHARF

ISLE OF DOGS

Cubitt Town

East Ferry Rd

• Elephant Royale

C

Aspen Way

East India Dock Rd

• Café Rouge,
Yellow River Café,
Corney & Barrow
• Fine Line

Soup Opera,
Moshi Moshi, Sushi,
Cranks, Pizza Express

Tabla, Riviera, Tasca •

Gourmet Pizza,
All Bar One

WESTFERRY
CIRCUS

Westferry Rd

• Grapes, House

Quadrato •
Gaucho Grill •
Royal China •
fish! •
Ubon •
Scu zi •

B

Limehouse Link Tunnel

Salter Rd

CANADA WATER

Redriff Rd

Butcher Row

Babe Ruth's •

The Highway

ROTHERHITHE
TUNNEL

Wapping Food •

WAPPING

Pizza Express •

Bordello •

ROTHERHITHE

Wapping High St

A

Commercial Rd

• Lahore Kebab House

SHADWELL

• Café Spice Namaste

• Aquarium

BERMONDSEY

Jamaica Rd

Mill Street

• Lanterna, Tentazioni

• Arancia

1

2

MAP 11 – EAST END & DOCKLANDS